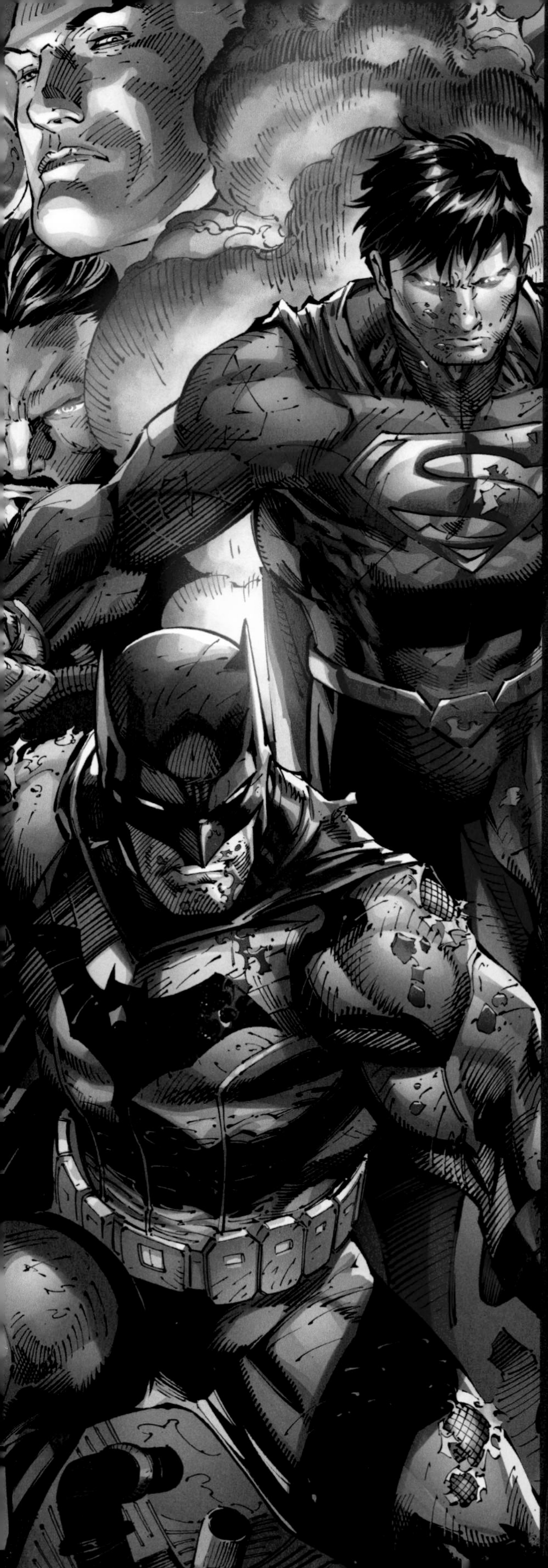

VOLUME 4
SIEGE

BATMAN/SUPERMAN

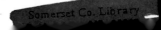

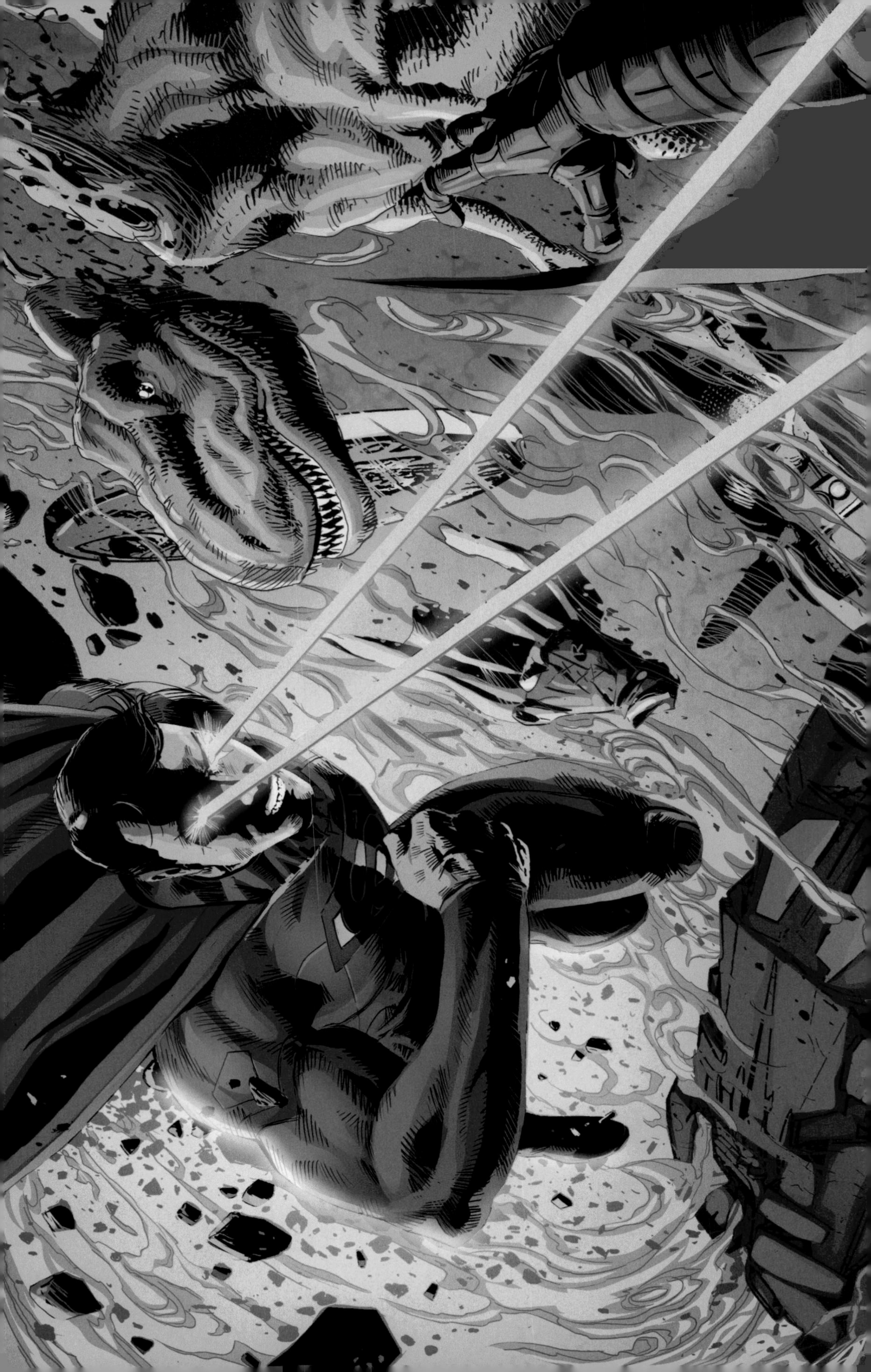

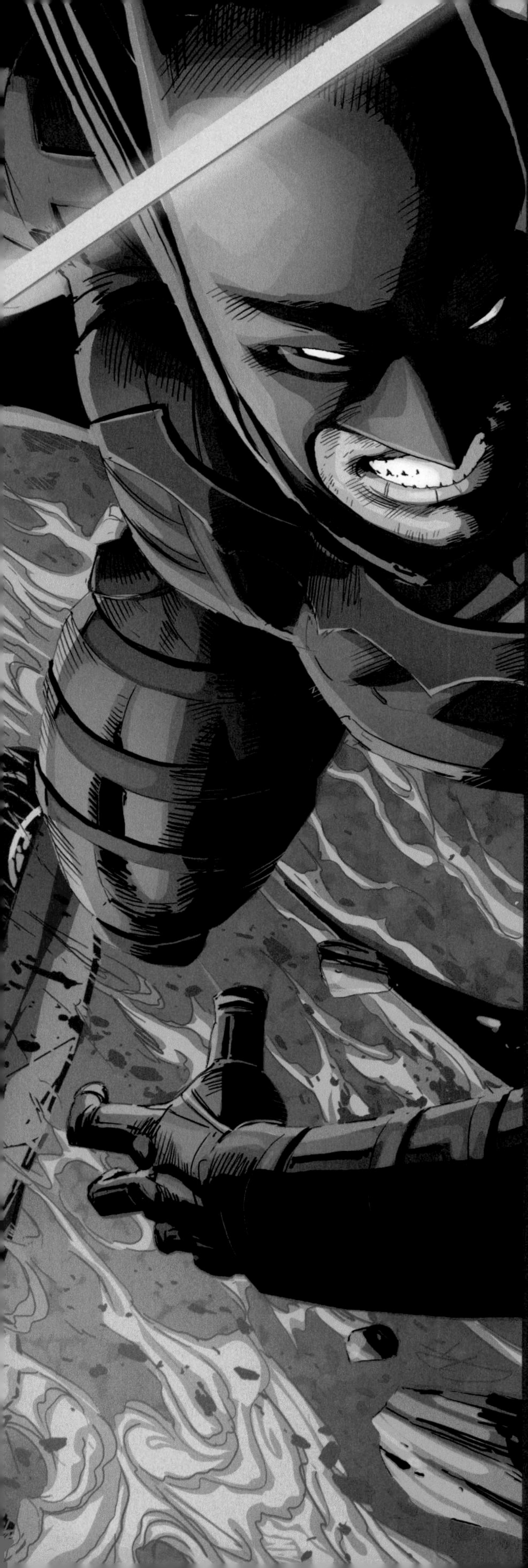

BATMAN/SUPERMAN

VOLUME 4
SIEGE

WRITTEN BY
GREG PAK

PENCILS BY
ARDIAN SYAF
TOM DERENICK
TYLER KIRKHAM
IAN CHURCHILL
EMANUELA LUPACCHINO
CLIFF RICHARDS
JACK HERBERT

INKS BY
SANDRA HOPE ARCHER
JONATHAN GLAPION
JAIME MENDOZA
MARK MORALES
DON HO
VICENTE CIFUENTES
DAVID MEIKIS
RAY MCCARTHY
TYLER KIRKHAM
CLIFF RICHARDS

COLOR BY
ULISES ARREOLA
ARIF PRIANTO
FAHRIZA KAMAPUTRA
JESSICA KHOLINNE
GLORIA CAELI
HI-FI

LETTERS BY
ROB LEIGH

COLLECTION COVER BY
ARDIAN SYAF, DANNY MIKI
AND **WIL QUINTANA**

BATMAN CREATED BY
BOB KANE

SUPERMAN CREATED BY
JERRY SIEGEL & JOE SHUSTER
BY SPECIAL ARRANGEMENT WITH
THE JERRY SIEGEL FAMILY

EDDIE BERGANZA Editor - Original Series
RICKEY PURDIN Associate Editor - Original Series
JEREMY BENT Assistant Editor - Original Series
JEB WOODARD Group Editor - Collected Editions
LIZ ERICKSON Editor - Collected Edition
DAMIAN RYLAND Publication Design

BOB HARRAS Senior VP - Editor-in-Chief, DC Comics

DIANE NELSON President
DAN DIDIO AND JIM LEE Co-Publishers
GEOFF JOHNS Chief Creative Officer
AMIT DESAI Senior VP - Marketing & Global Franchise Management
NAIRI GARDINER Senior VP - Finance
SAM ADES VP - Digital Marketing
BOBBIE CHASE VP - Talent Development
MARK CHIARELLO Senior VP - Art, Design & Collected Editions
JOHN CUNNINGHAM VP - Content Strategy
ANNE DEPIES VP - Strategy Planning & Reporting
DON FALLETTI VP - Manufacturing Operations
LAWRENCE GANEM VP - Editorial Administration & Talent Relations
ALISON GILL Senior VP - Manufacturing & Operations
HANK KANALZ Senior VP - Editorial Strategy & Administration
JAY KOGAN VP - Legal Affairs
DEREK MADDALENA Senior VP - Sales & Business Development
JACK MAHAN VP - Business Affairs
DAN MIRON VP - Sales Planning & Trade Development
NICK NAPOLITANO VP - Manufacturing Administration
CAROL ROEDER VP - Marketing
EDDIE SCANNELL VP - Mass Account & Digital Sales
COURTNEY SIMMONS Senior VP - Publicity & Communications
JIM (SKI) SOKOLOWSKI VP - Comic Book Specialty & Newsstand Stales
SANDY YI Senior VP - Global Franchise Management

BATMAN/SUPERMAN VOLUME 4: SIEGE

DC Comics, 2900 West Alameda Avenue, Burbank, CA 91505
Printed by RR Donnelley, Salem, VA, USA. 11/13/15. First Printing.
ISBN: 978-1-4012-5755-2

Pak, Greg.
Batman/Superman. Volume 4 / Greg Pak, writer ; Ardian Syaf, artist.
pages cm.
ISBN 978-1-4012-5755-2 (hardback)
1. Graphic novels. I. Syaf, Ardian, illustrator. II. Title.
PN6728.B36P345 2015
741.5'973--dc23
2015031181

PEFC Certified
Printed on paper from sustainably managed forests and controlled sources
PEFC/29-31-75
www.pefc.org

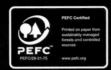

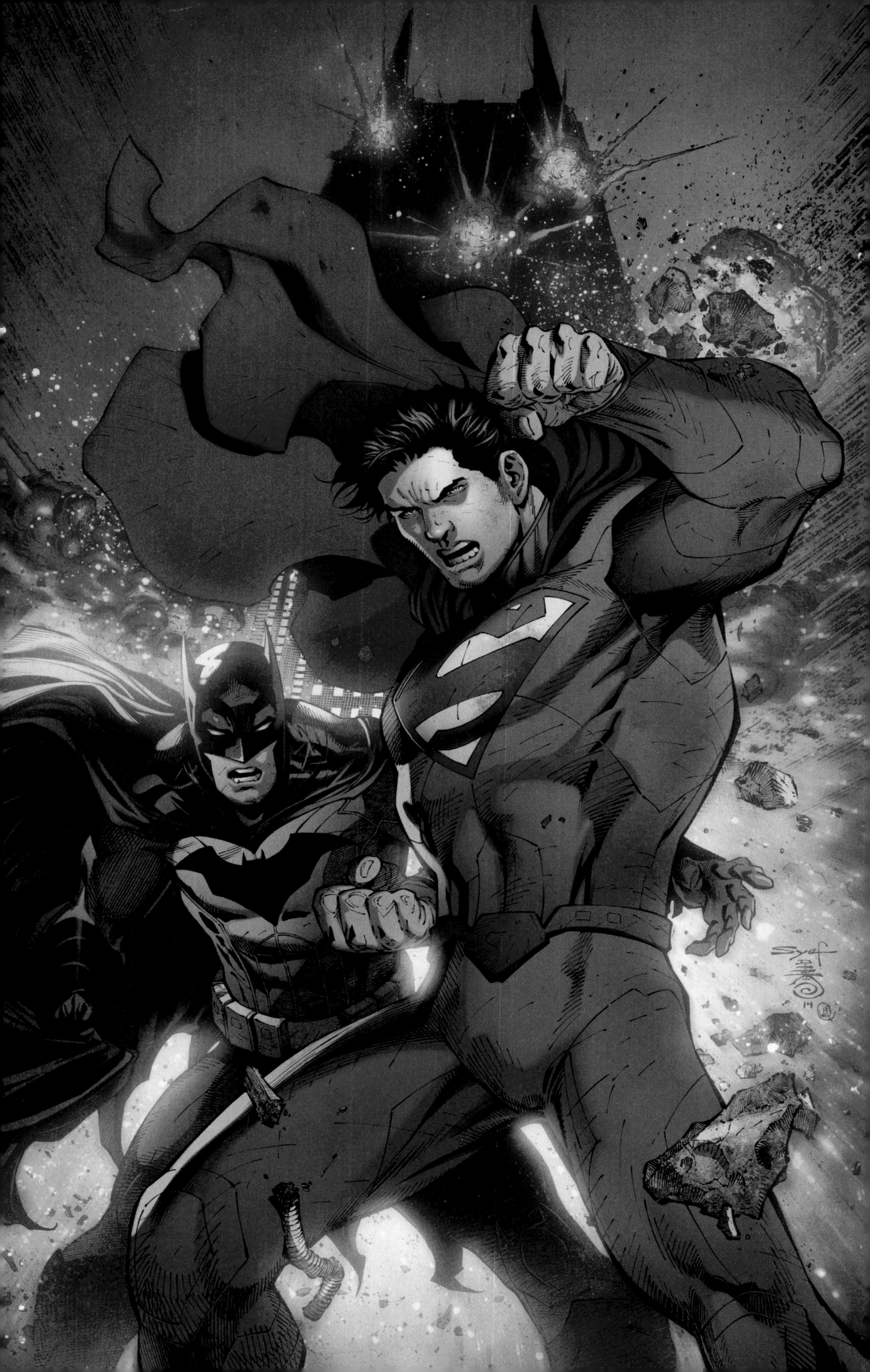

SUPERMAN'S JOKER

GREG PAK writer **ARDIAN SYAF** penciller **SANDRA HOPE ARCHER, DAVID MEIKIS** inkers **ULISES ARREOLA** colorist **ROB LEIGH** letterer
cover by **ARDIAN SYAF, DANNY MIKI** and **WIL QUINTANA**

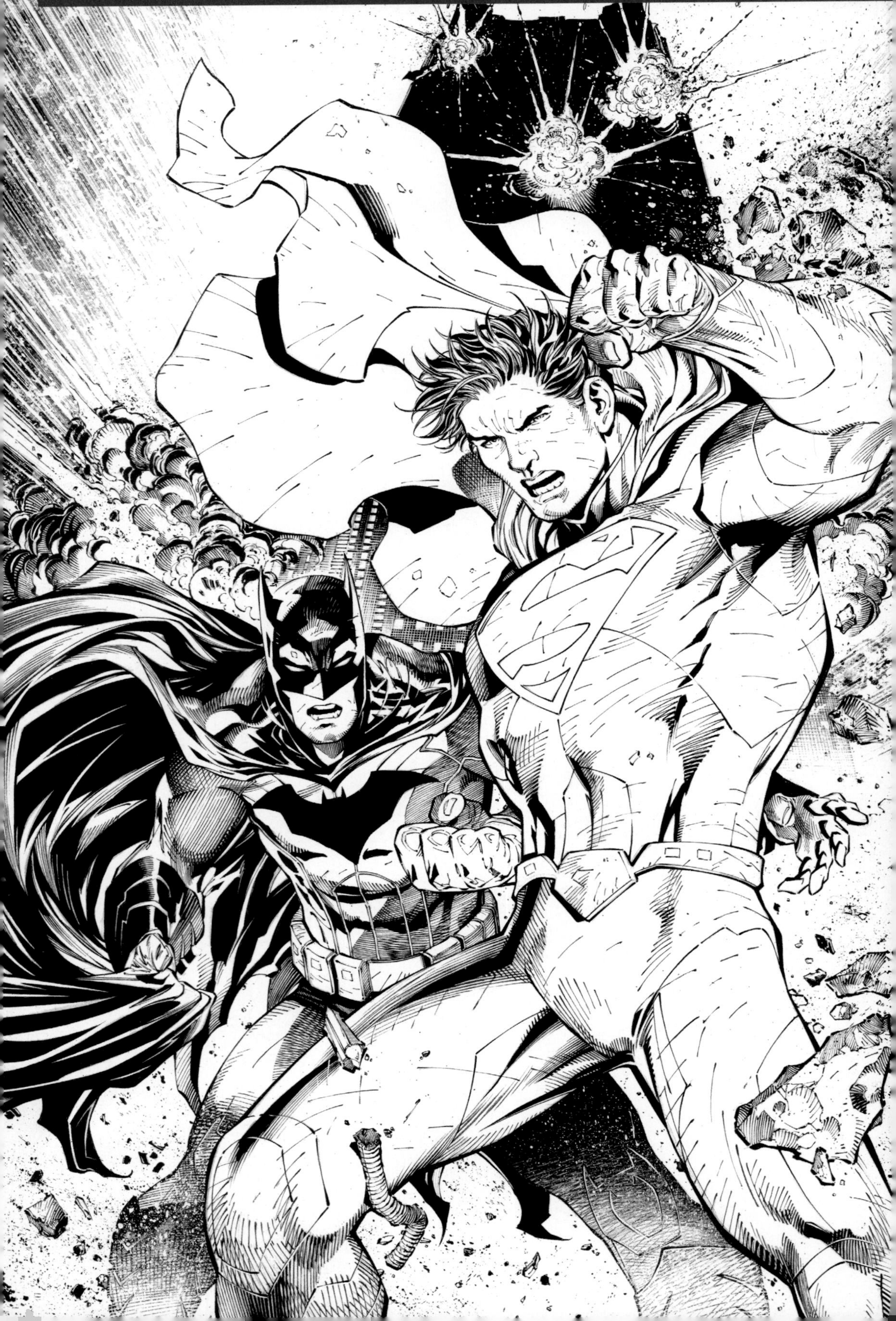

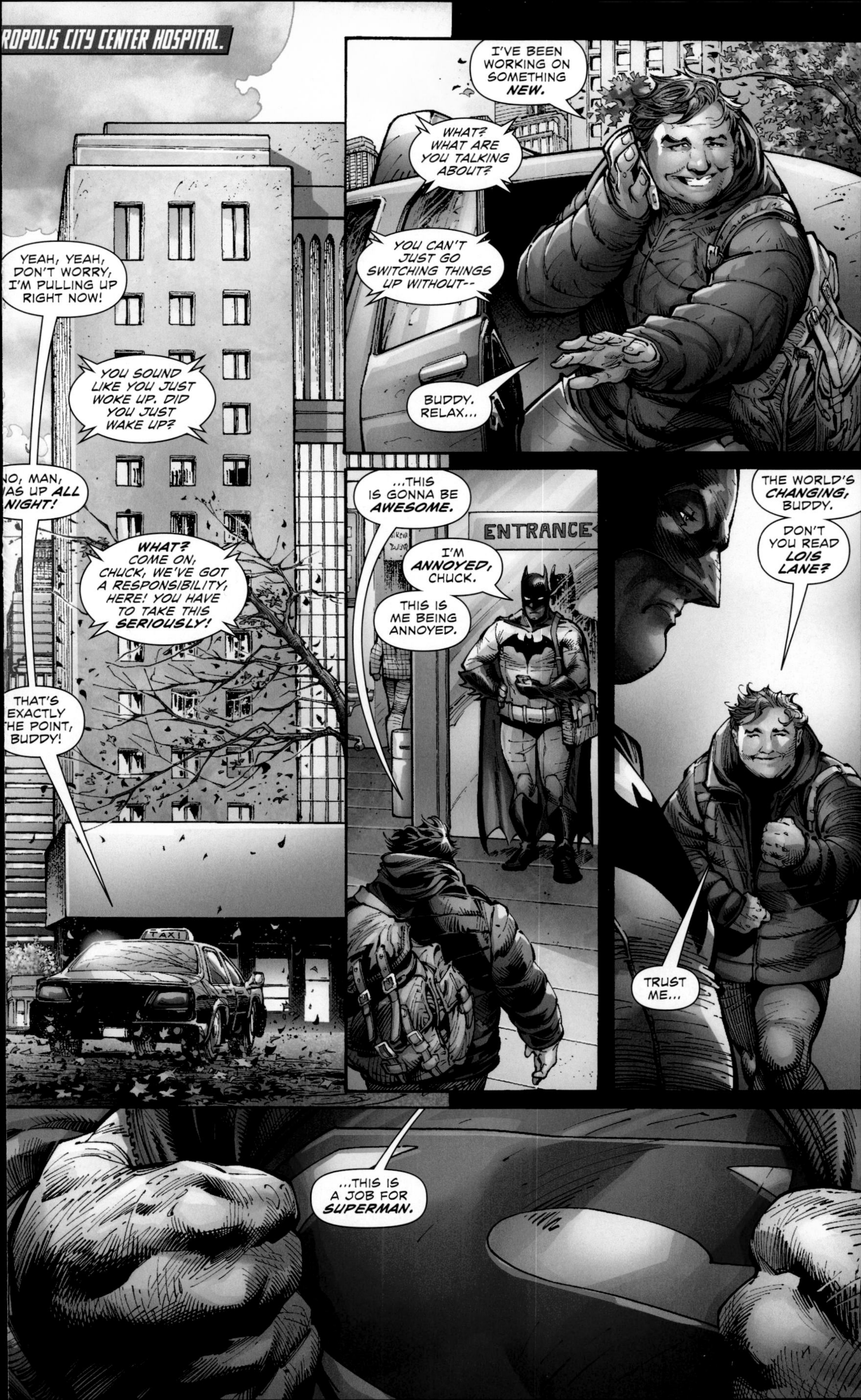
ROPOLIS CITY CENTER HOSPITAL.
YEAH, YEAH, DON'T WORRY, I'M PULLING UP RIGHT NOW!
YOU SOUND LIKE YOU JUST WOKE UP. DID YOU JUST WAKE UP?
NO, MAN, WAS UP ALL NIGHT!
WHAT? COME ON, CHUCK, WE'VE GOT A RESPONSIBILITY, HERE! YOU HAVE TO TAKE THIS SERIOUSLY!
THAT'S EXACTLY THE POINT, BUDDY!
TAXI
I'VE BEEN WORKING ON SOMETHING NEW.
WHAT? WHAT ARE YOU TALKING ABOUT?
YOU CAN'T JUST GO SWITCHING THINGS UP WITHOUT--
BUDDY. RELAX...
...THIS IS GONNA BE AWESOME.
ENTRANCE
I'M ANNOYED, CHUCK.
THIS IS ME BEING ANNOYED.
THE WORLD'S CHANGING, BUDDY.
DON'T YOU READ LOIS LANE?
TRUST ME...
...THIS IS A JOB FOR SUPERMAN.

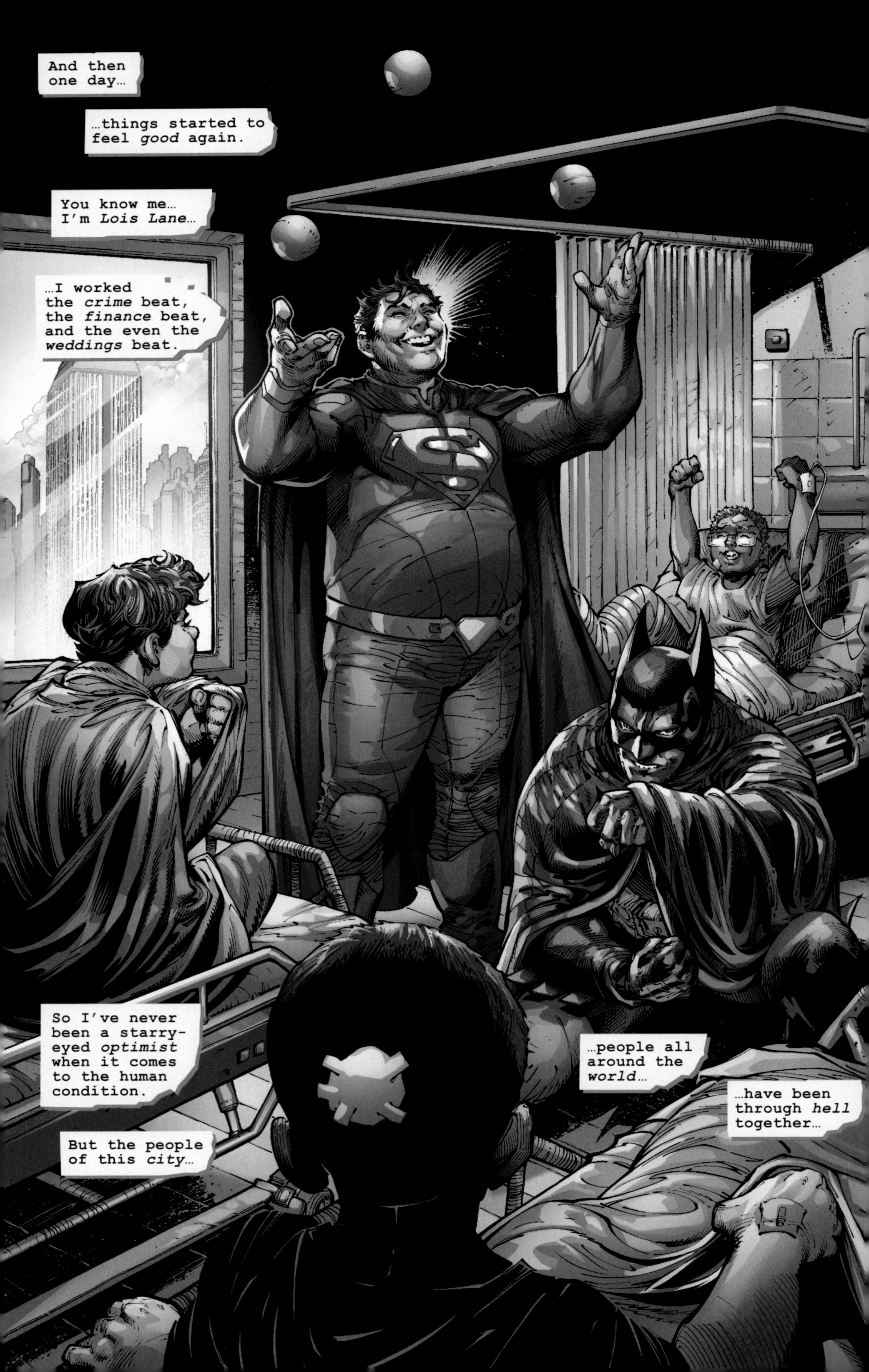
And then one day…
…things started to feel *good* again.
You know me… I'm *Lois Lane*…
…I worked the *crime* beat, the *finance* beat, and the even the *weddings* beat.
So I've never been a starry-eyed *optimist* when it comes to the human condition.
But the people of this *city*…
…people all around the *world*…
…have been through *hell* together…

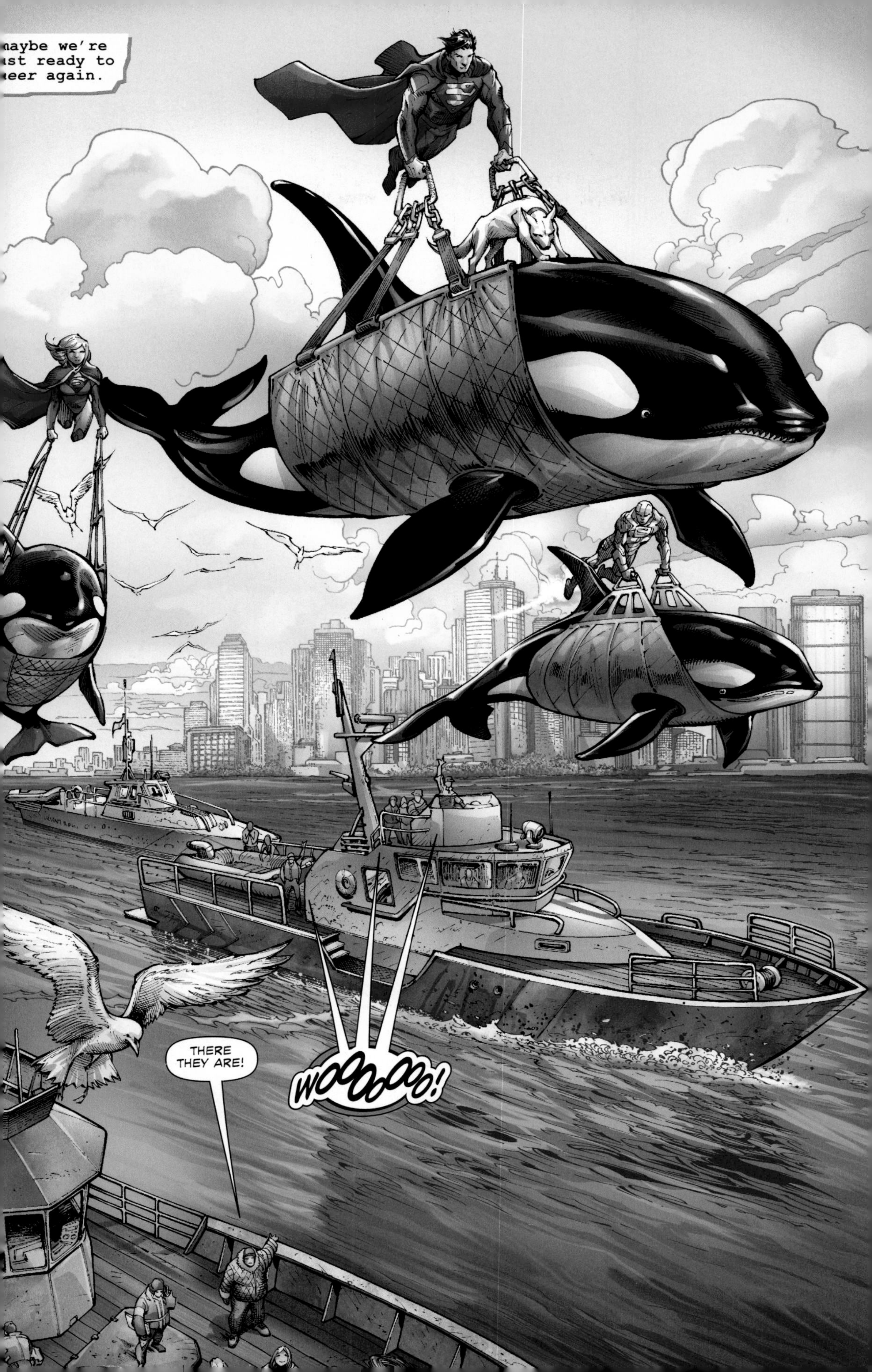
maybe we're
ust ready to
eer again.
THERE THEY ARE!
WOOOOOOO!

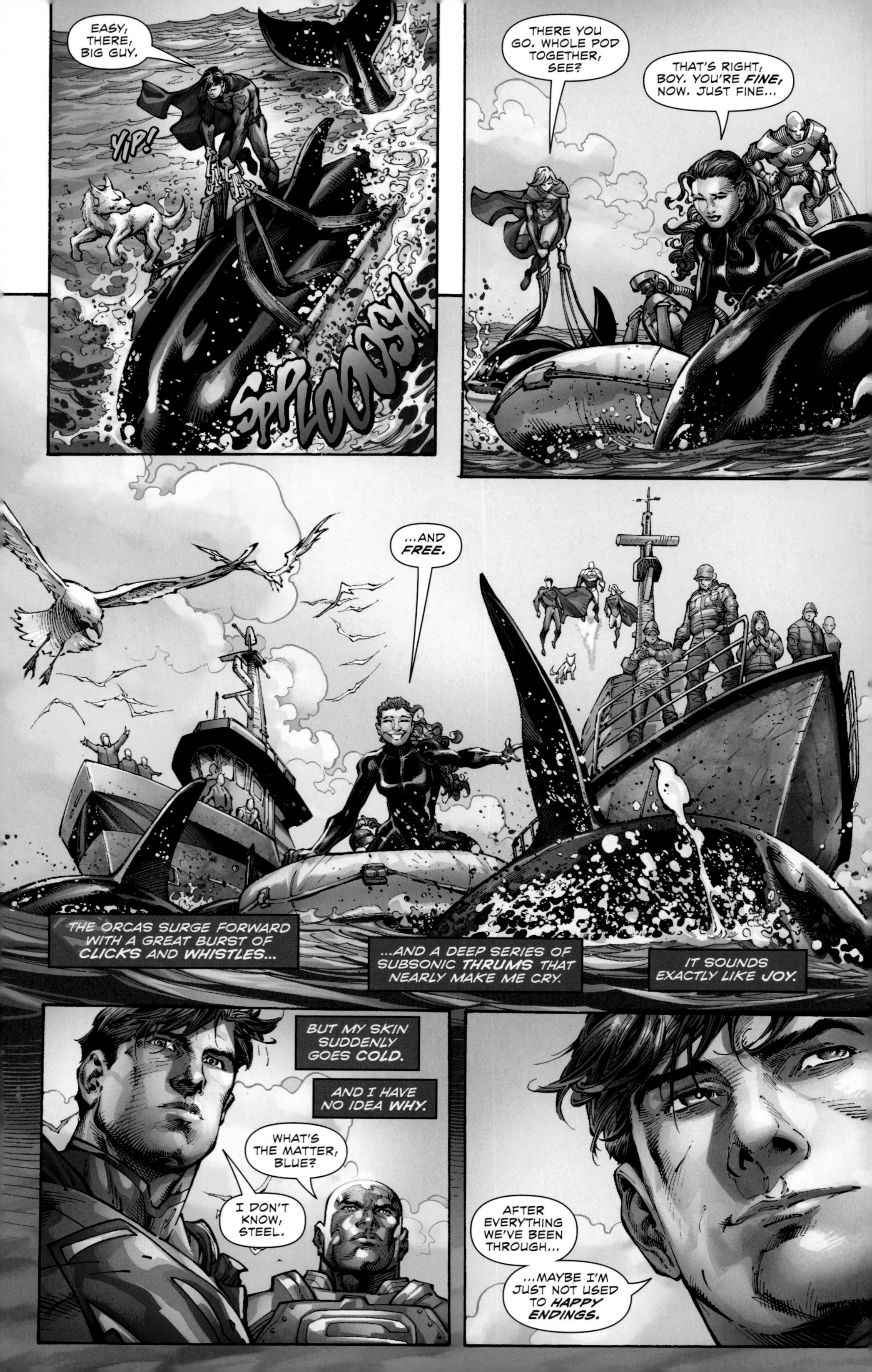
EASY, THERE, BIG GUY.
YIP!
SPLOOOSH
THERE YOU GO. WHOLE POD TOGETHER, SEE?
THAT'S RIGHT, BOY. YOU'RE FINE, NOW. JUST FINE...
...AND FREE.
THE ORCAS SURGE FORWARD WITH A GREAT BURST OF CLICKS AND WHISTLES...
...AND A DEEP SERIES OF SUBSONIC THRUMS THAT NEARLY MAKE ME CRY.
IT SOUNDS EXACTLY LIKE JOY.
BUT MY SKIN SUDDENLY GOES COLD.
AND I HAVE NO IDEA WHY.
WHAT'S THE MATTER, BLUE?
I DON'T KNOW, STEEL.
AFTER EVERYTHING WE'VE BEEN THROUGH...
...MAYBE I'M JUST NOT USED TO HAPPY ENDINGS.

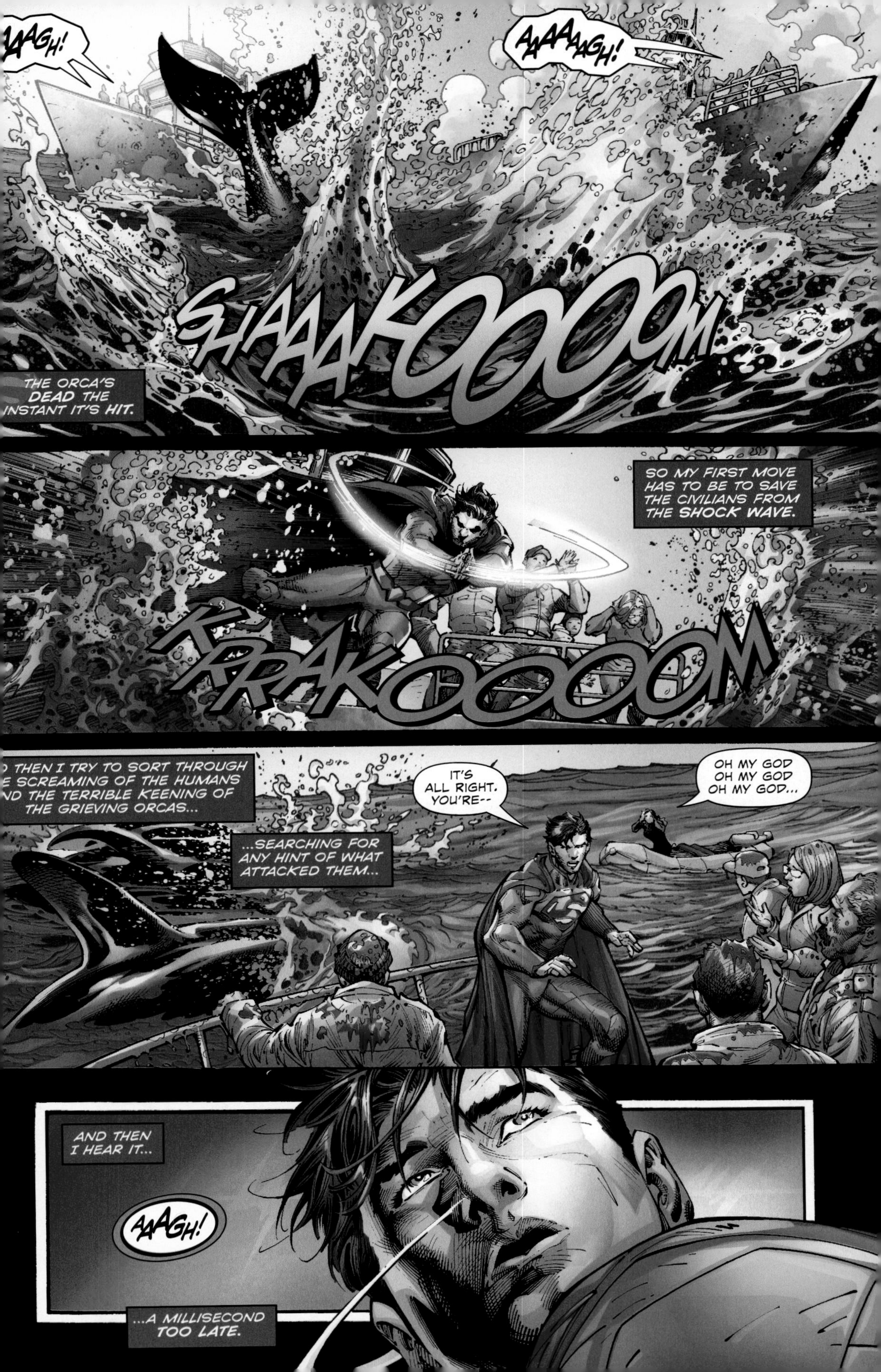
AAGH!
AAAAAAGH!
SHAAAKOOOOOM
THE ORCA'S DEAD THE INSTANT IT'S HIT.
SO MY FIRST MOVE HAS TO BE TO SAVE THE CIVILIANS FROM THE SHOCK WAVE.
KRRAKOOOOOM
THEN I TRY TO SORT THROUGH SCREAMING OF THE HUMANS ND THE TERRIBLE KEENING OF THE GRIEVING ORCAS...
...SEARCHING FOR ANY HINT OF WHAT ATTACKED THEM...
IT'S ALL RIGHT. YOU'RE--
OH MY GOD OH MY GOD OH MY GOD...
AND THEN I HEAR IT...
AAAGH!
...A MILLISECOND TOO LATE.

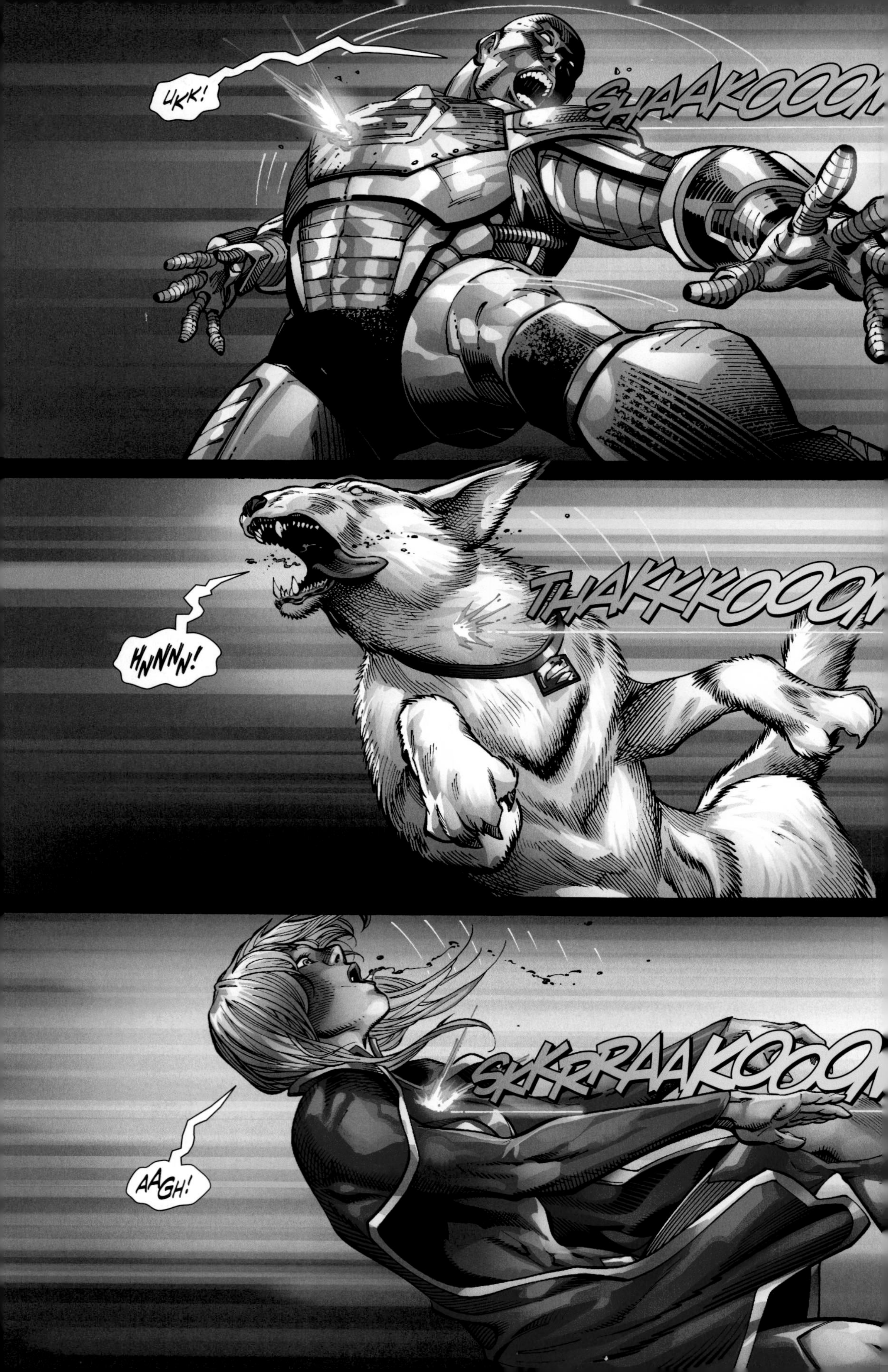
UKK!
SHAAKOOOM
HNNNN!
THAKKOOOM
AAGH!
SKKRRAAKOOOM

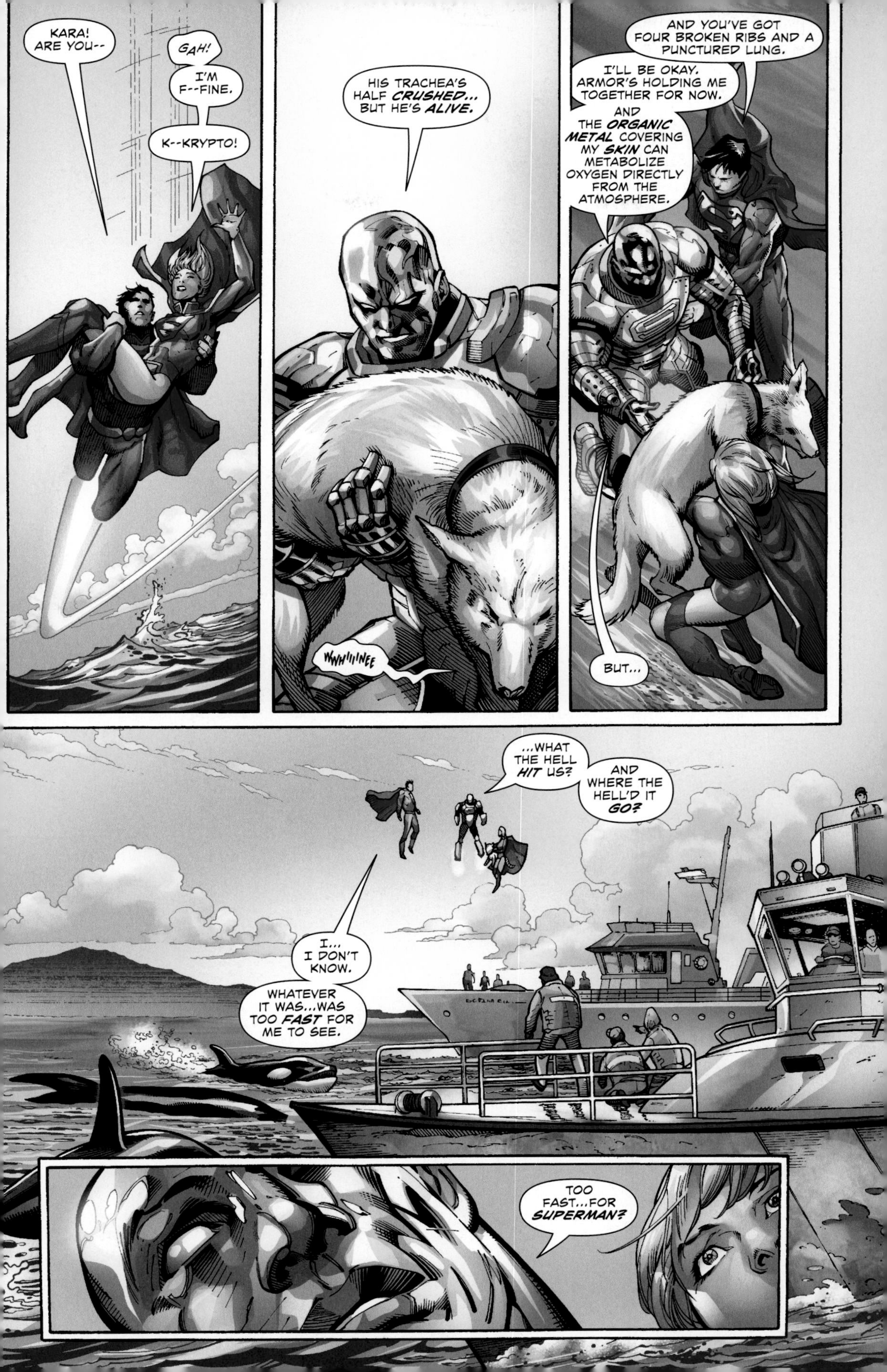
KARA! ARE YOU--
GAH!
I'M F--FINE.
K--KRYPTO!
HIS TRACHEA'S HALF CRUSHED... BUT HE'S ALIVE.
WHHIIINEE
AND YOU'VE GOT FOUR BROKEN RIBS AND A PUNCTURED LUNG.
I'LL BE OKAY. ARMOR'S HOLDING ME TOGETHER FOR NOW.
AND THE ORGANIC METAL COVERING MY SKIN CAN METABOLIZE OXYGEN DIRECTLY FROM THE ATMOSPHERE.
BUT...
...WHAT THE HELL HIT US?
AND WHERE THE HELL'D IT GO?
I... I DON'T KNOW.
WHATEVER IT WAS...WAS TOO FAST FOR ME TO SEE.
TOO FAST...FOR SUPERMAN?

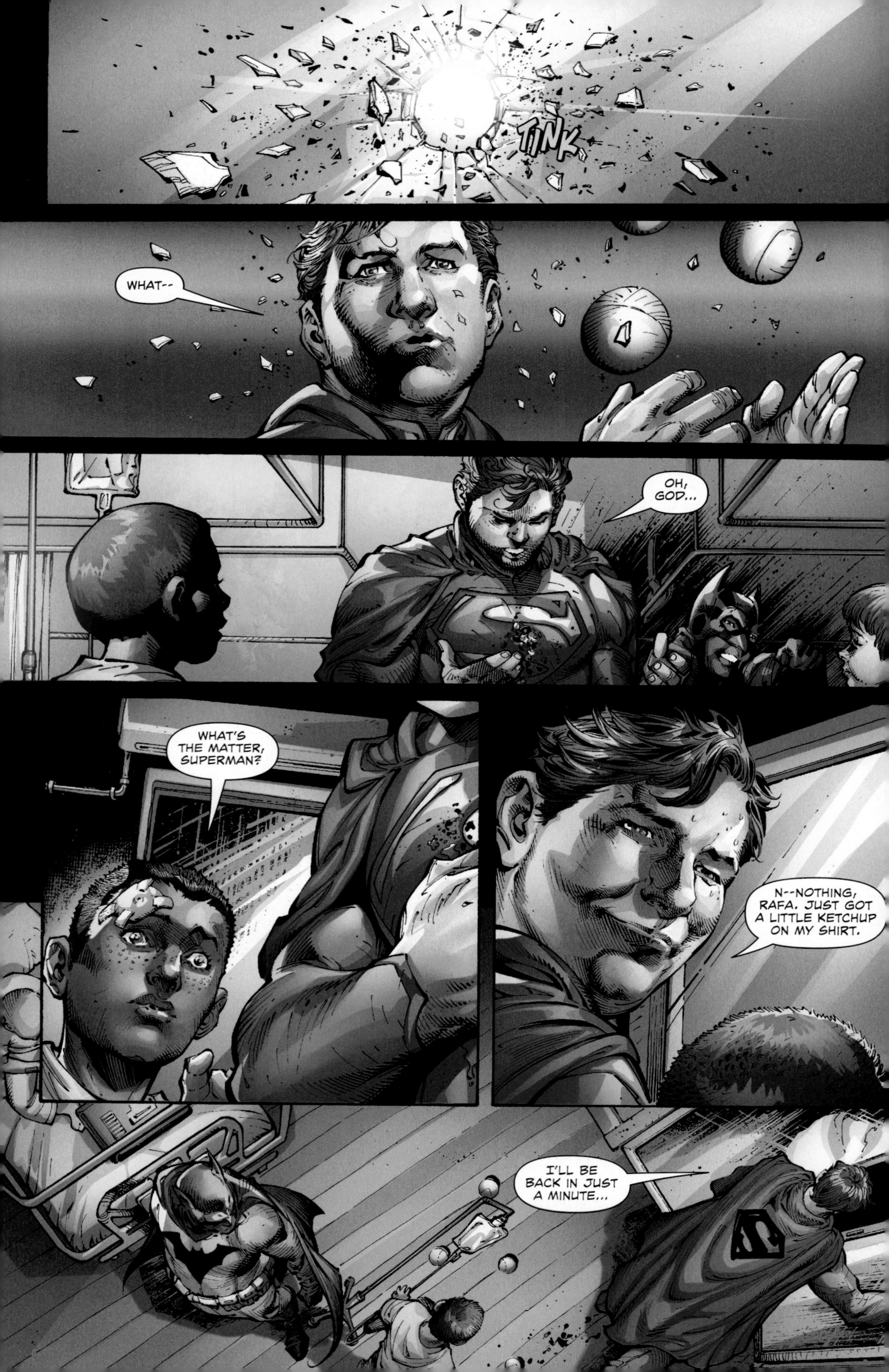
TINK
WHAT--
OH, GOD...
WHAT'S THE MATTER, SUPERMAN?
N--NOTHING, RAFA. JUST GOT A LITTLE KETCHUP ON MY SHIRT.
I'LL BE BACK IN JUST A MINUTE...

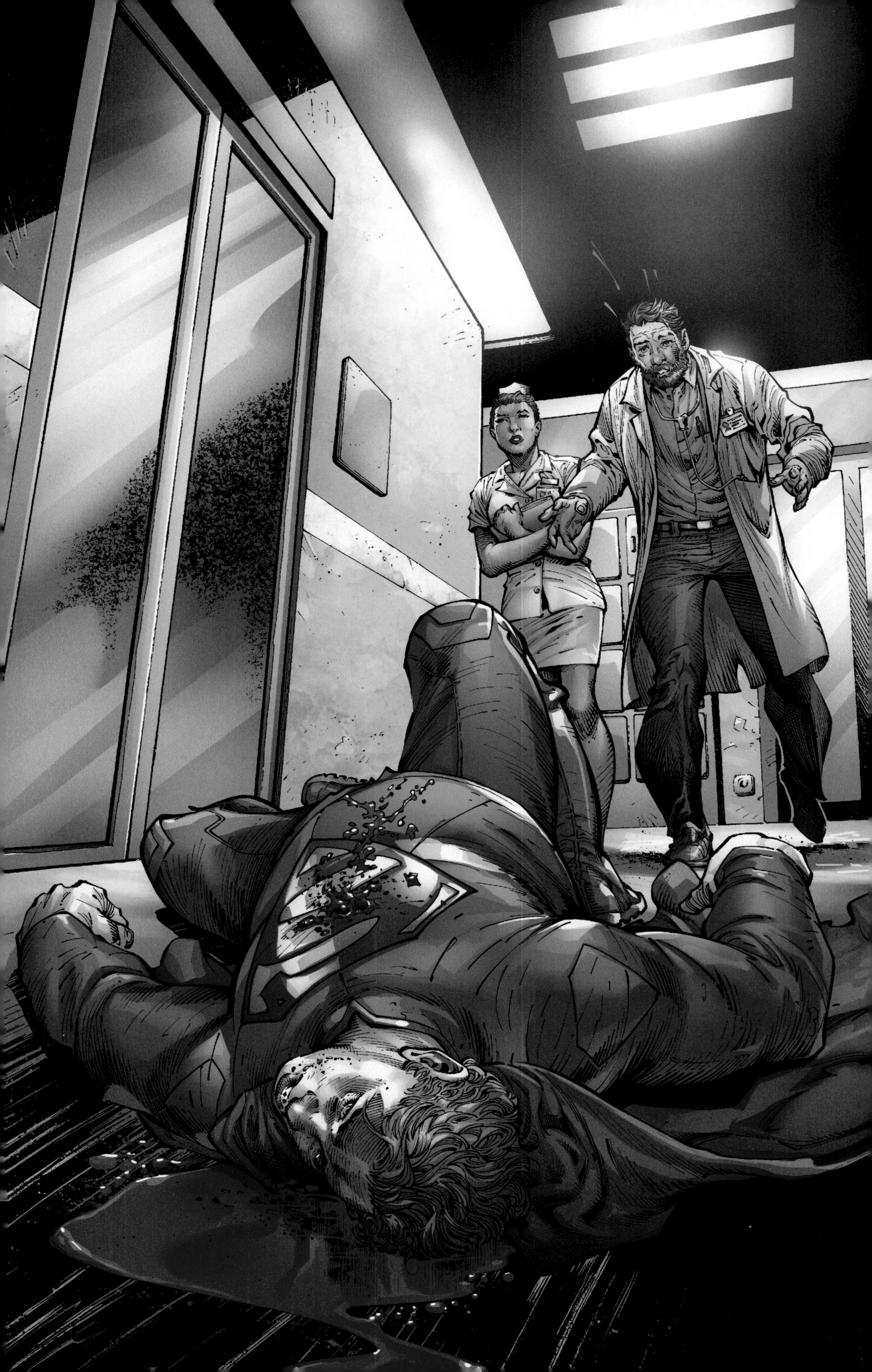

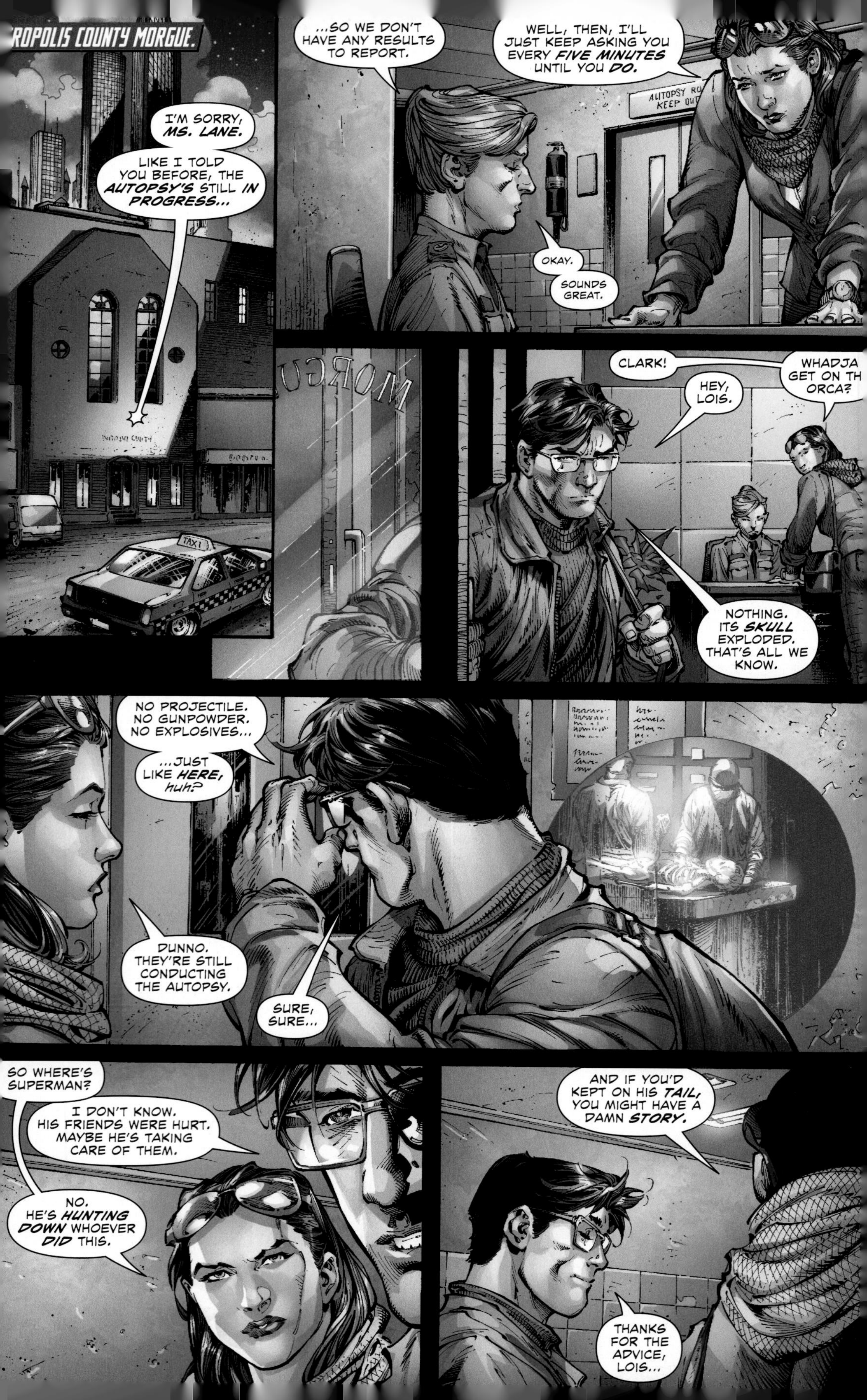

ROPOLIS COUNTY MORGUE.
I'M SORRY, MS. LANE.
LIKE I TOLD YOU BEFORE, THE AUTOPSY'S STILL IN PROGRESS...
...SO WE DON'T HAVE ANY RESULTS TO REPORT.
WELL, THEN, I'LL JUST KEEP ASKING YOU EVERY FIVE MINUTES UNTIL YOU DO.
AUTOPSY R
KEEP OUT
OKAY.
SOUNDS GREAT.
CLARK!
HEY, LOIS.
WHADJA GET ON TH ORCA?
NOTHING. ITS SKULL EXPLODED. THAT'S ALL WE KNOW.
NO PROJECTILE. NO GUNPOWDER. NO EXPLOSIVES...
...JUST LIKE HERE, huh?
DUNNO. THEY'RE STILL CONDUCTING THE AUTOPSY.
SURE, SURE...
SO WHERE'S SUPERMAN?
I DON'T KNOW. HIS FRIENDS WERE HURT. MAYBE HE'S TAKING CARE OF THEM.
NO. HE'S HUNTING DOWN WHOEVER DID THIS.
AND IF YOU'D KEPT ON HIS TAIL, YOU MIGHT HAVE A DAMN STORY.
THANKS FOR THE ADVICE, LOIS...

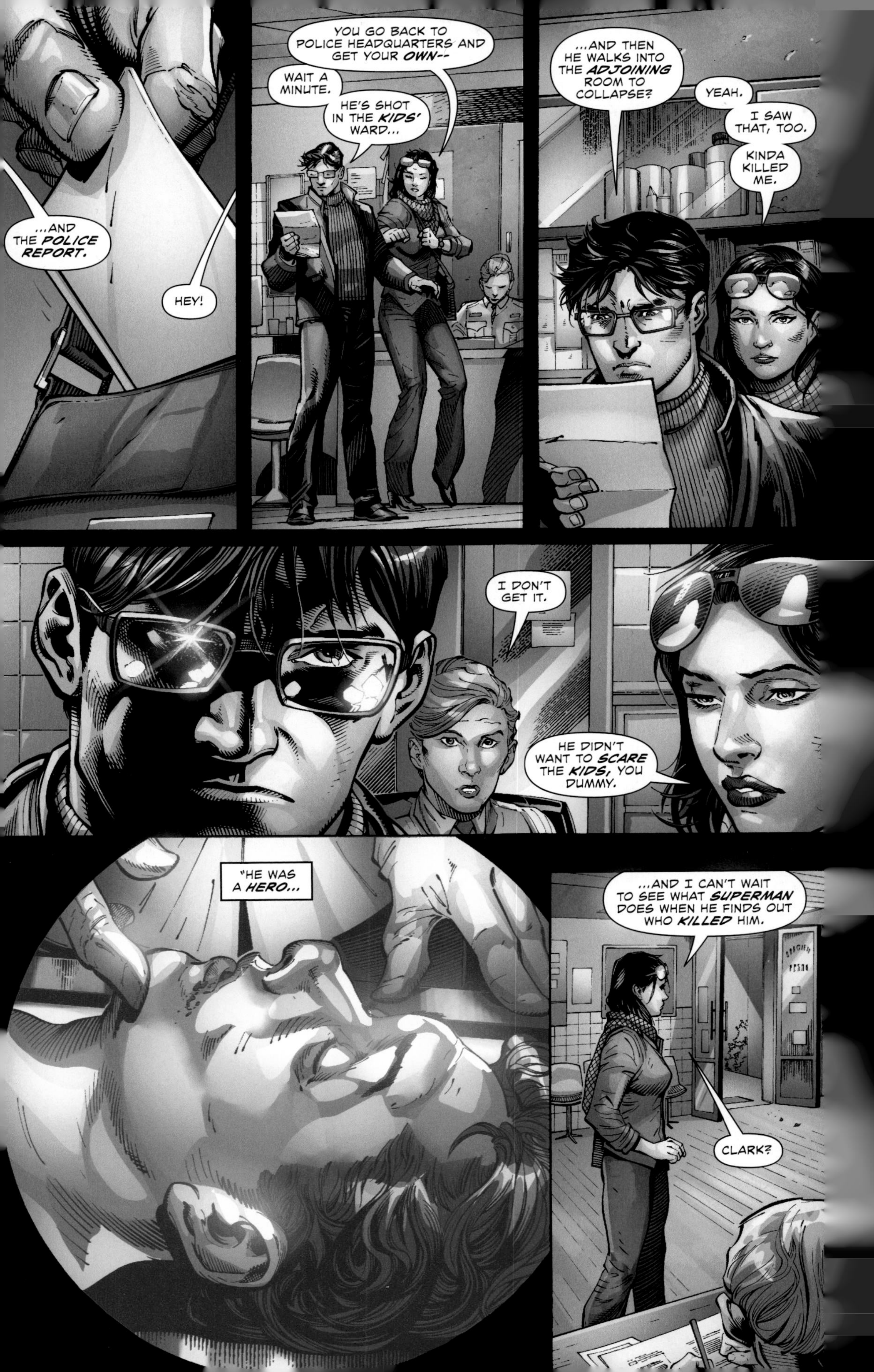
...AND THE POLICE REPORT.
HEY!
YOU GO BACK TO POLICE HEADQUARTERS AND GET YOUR OWN--
WAIT A MINUTE.
HE'S SHOT IN THE KIDS' WARD...
...AND THEN HE WALKS INTO THE ADJOINING ROOM TO COLLAPSE?
YEAH.
I SAW THAT, TOO.
KINDA KILLED ME.
I DON'T GET IT.
HE DIDN'T WANT TO SCARE THE KIDS, YOU DUMMY.
"HE WAS A HERO...
...AND I CAN'T WAIT TO SEE WHAT SUPERMAN DOES WHEN HE FINDS OUT WHO KILLED HIM.
CLARK?

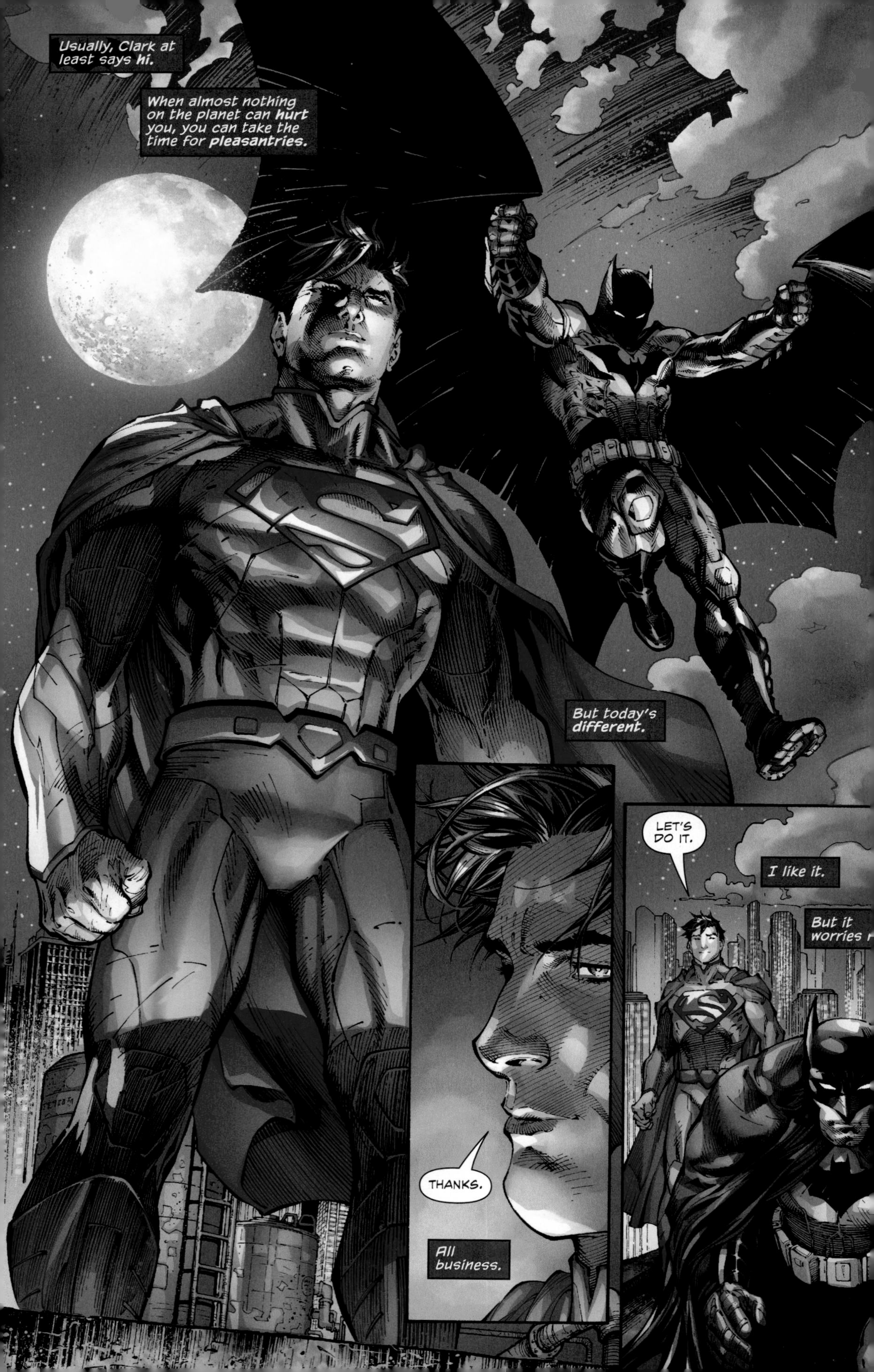
Usually, Clark at least says hi.
When almost nothing on the planet can hurt you, you can take the time for pleasantries.
But today's different.
THANKS.
All business.
LET'S DO IT.
I like it.
But it worries

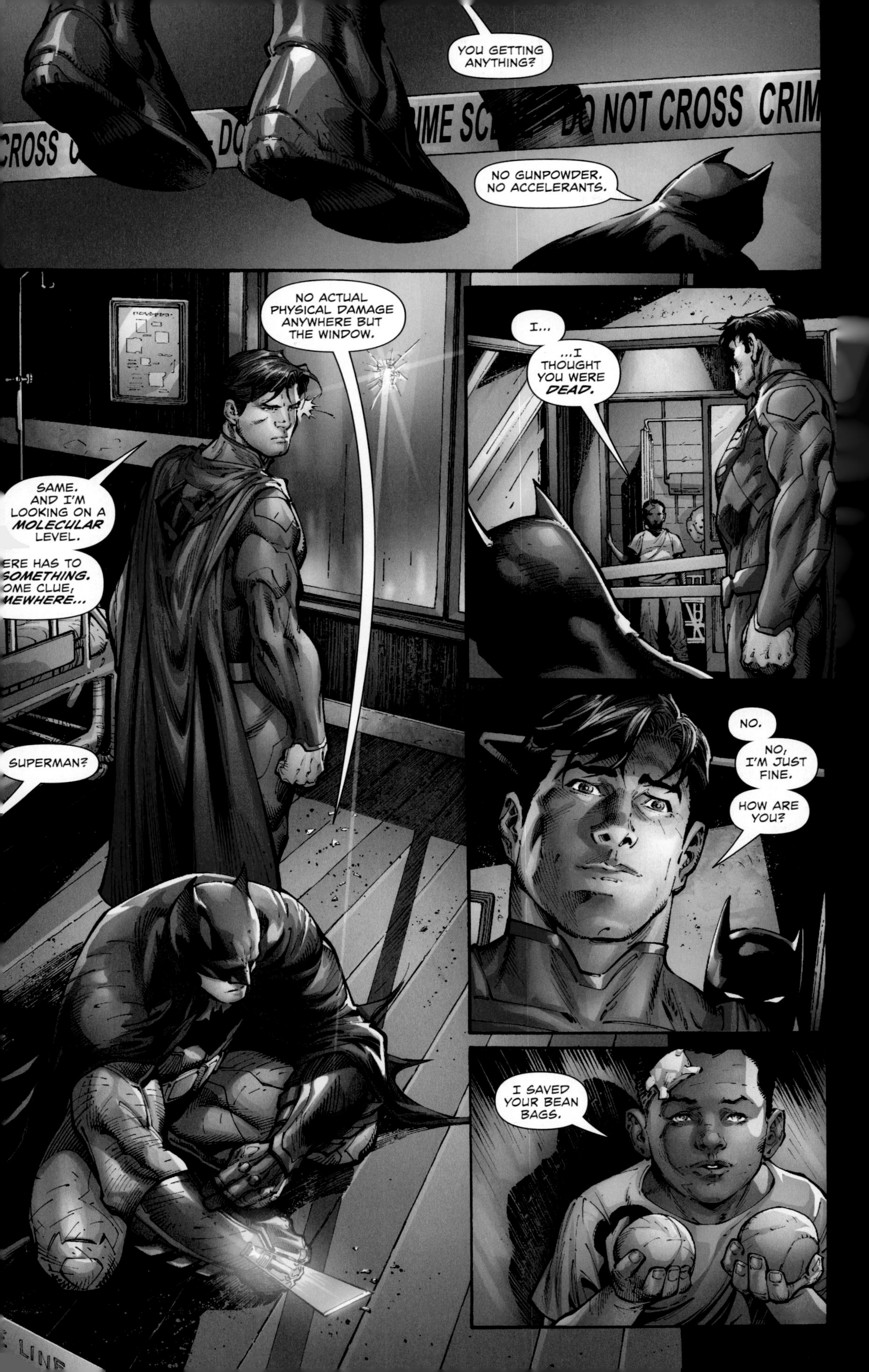
YOU GETTING ANYTHING?
CROSS
DO NOT CROSS CRIM
NO GUNPOWDER. NO ACCELERANTS.
NO ACTUAL PHYSICAL DAMAGE ANYWHERE BUT THE WINDOW.
SAME. AND I'M LOOKING ON A MOLECULAR LEVEL.
ERE HAS TO SOMETHING. OME CLUE, MEWHERE...
SUPERMAN?
I...
...I THOUGHT YOU WERE DEAD.
NO.
NO, I'M JUST FINE.
HOW ARE YOU?
I SAVED YOUR BEAN BAGS.

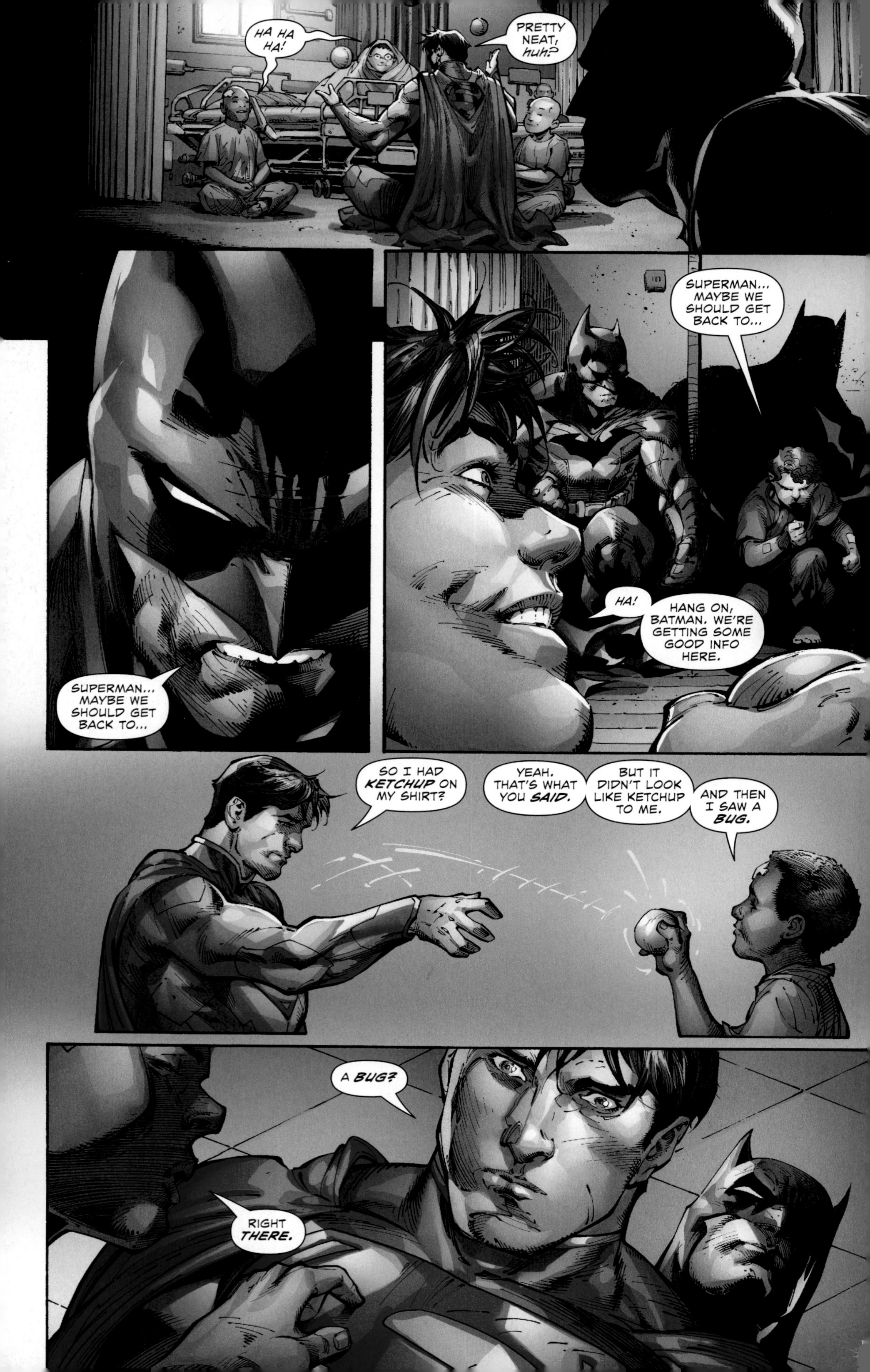
HA HA HA!
PRETTY NEAT, huh?
SUPERMAN... MAYBE WE SHOULD GET BACK TO...
SUPERMAN... MAYBE WE SHOULD GET BACK TO...
HA!
HANG ON, BATMAN. WE'RE GETTING SOME GOOD INFO HERE.
SO I HAD KETCHUP ON MY SHIRT?
YEAH. THAT'S WHAT YOU SAID.
BUT IT DIDN'T LOOK LIKE KETCHUP TO ME.
AND THEN I SAW A BUG.
A BUG?
RIGHT THERE.

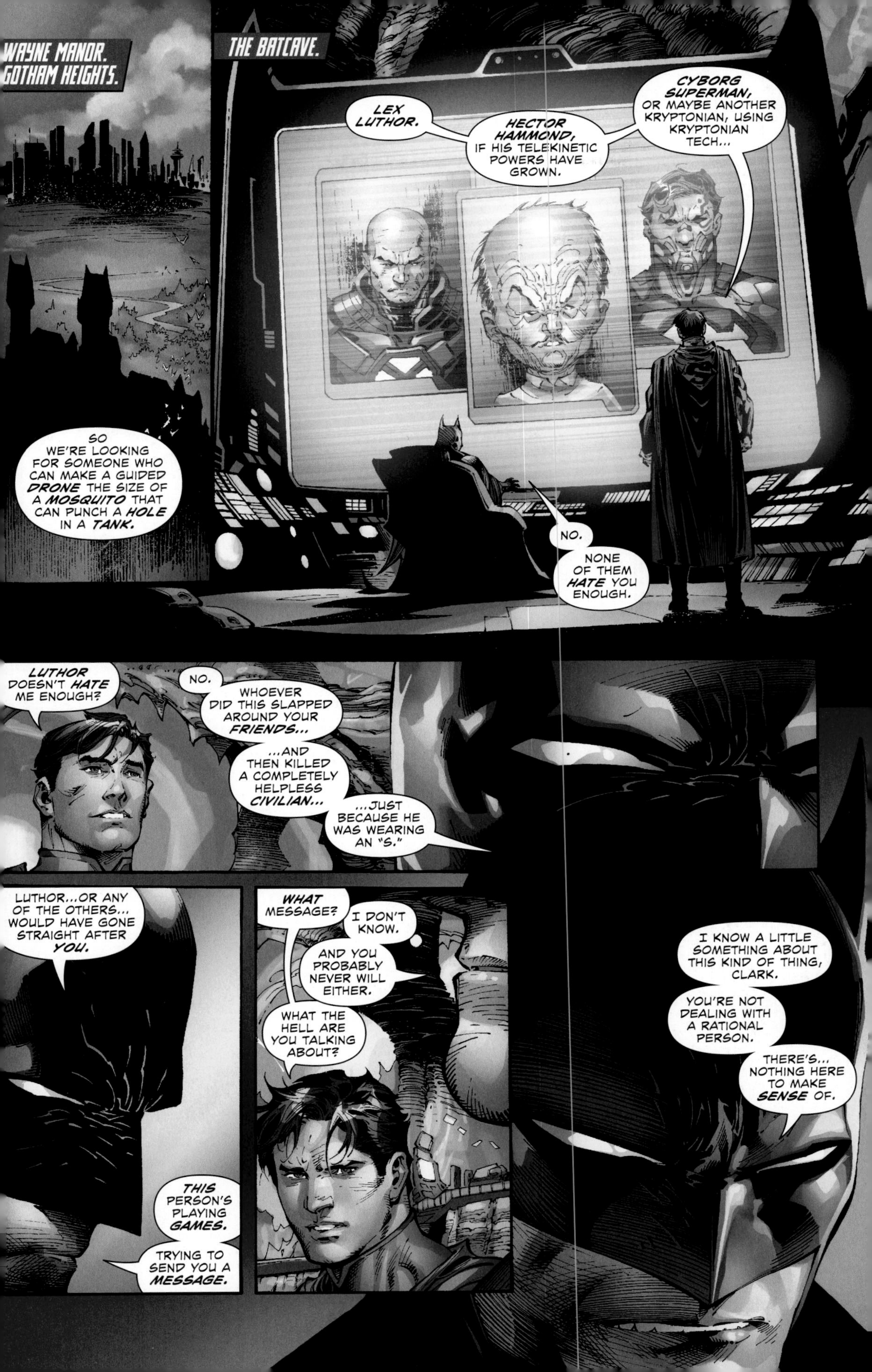

WAYNE MANOR. GOTHAM HEIGHTS.
THE BATCAVE.
SO WE'RE LOOKING FOR SOMEONE WHO CAN MAKE A GUIDED DRONE THE SIZE OF A MOSQUITO THAT CAN PUNCH A HOLE IN A TANK.
LEX LUTHOR.
HECTOR HAMMOND, IF HIS TELEKINETIC POWERS HAVE GROWN.
CYBORG SUPERMAN, OR MAYBE ANOTHER KRYPTONIAN, USING KRYPTONIAN TECH...
NO.
NONE OF THEM HATE YOU ENOUGH.
LUTHOR DOESN'T HATE ME ENOUGH?
NO.
WHOEVER DID THIS SLAPPED AROUND YOUR FRIENDS...
...AND THEN KILLED A COMPLETELY HELPLESS CIVILIAN...
...JUST BECAUSE HE WAS WEARING AN "S."
LUTHOR...OR ANY OF THE OTHERS... WOULD HAVE GONE STRAIGHT AFTER YOU.
THIS PERSON'S PLAYING GAMES.
TRYING TO SEND YOU A MESSAGE.
WHAT MESSAGE?
I DON'T KNOW.
AND YOU PROBABLY NEVER WILL EITHER.
WHAT THE HELL ARE YOU TALKING ABOUT?
I KNOW A LITTLE SOMETHING ABOUT THIS KIND OF THING, CLARK.
YOU'RE NOT DEALING WITH A RATIONAL PERSON.
THERE'S... NOTHING HERE TO MAKE SENSE OF.

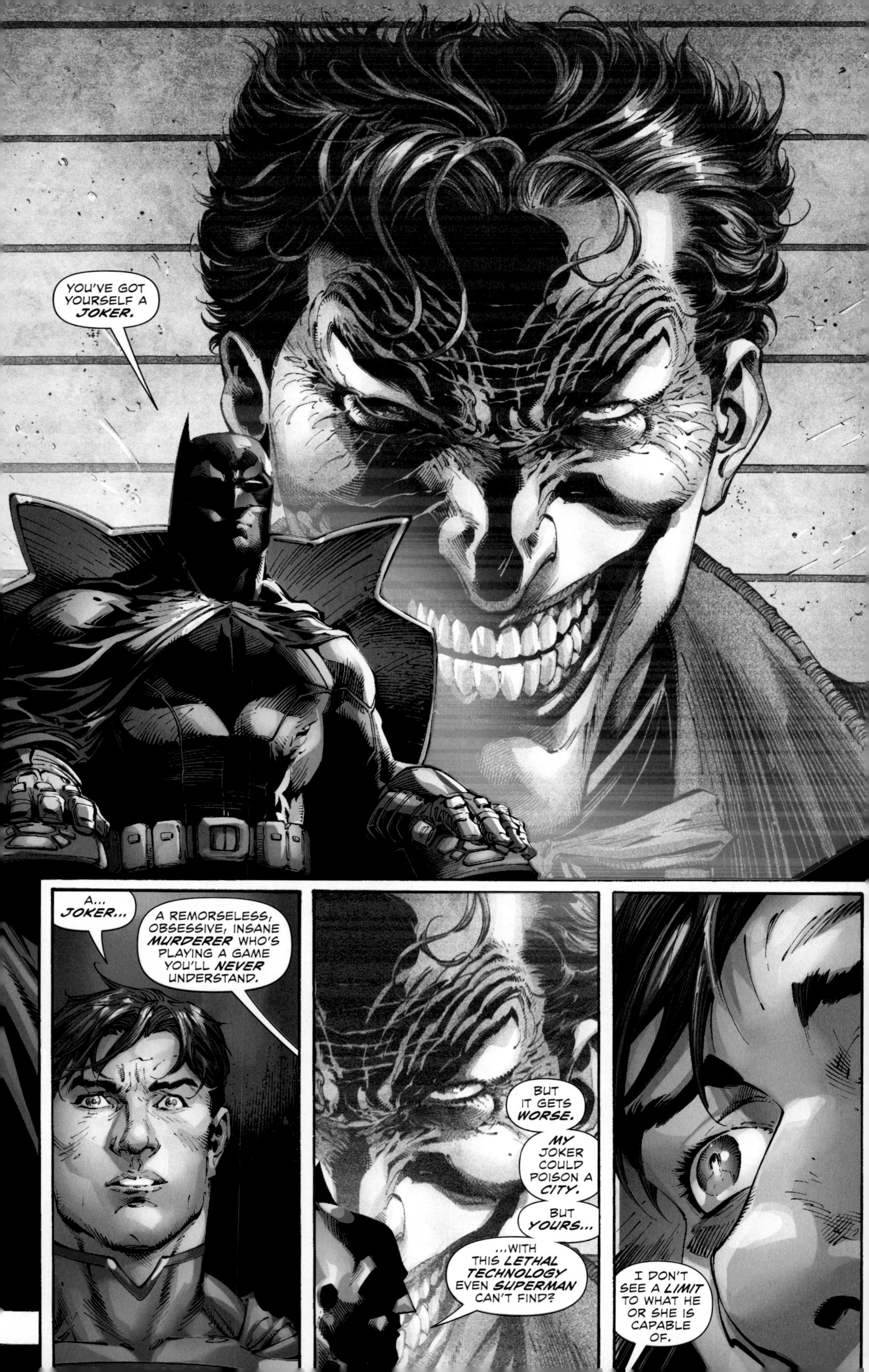
YOU'VE GOT YOURSELF A JOKER.
A... JOKER...
A REMORSELESS, OBSESSIVE, INSANE MURDERER WHO'S PLAYING A GAME YOU'LL NEVER UNDERSTAND.
BUT IT GETS WORSE.
MY JOKER COULD POISON A CITY.
BUT YOURS...
...WITH THIS LETHAL TECHNOLOGY EVEN SUPERMAN CAN'T FIND?
I DON'T SEE A LIMIT TO WHAT HE OR SHE IS CAPABLE OF.

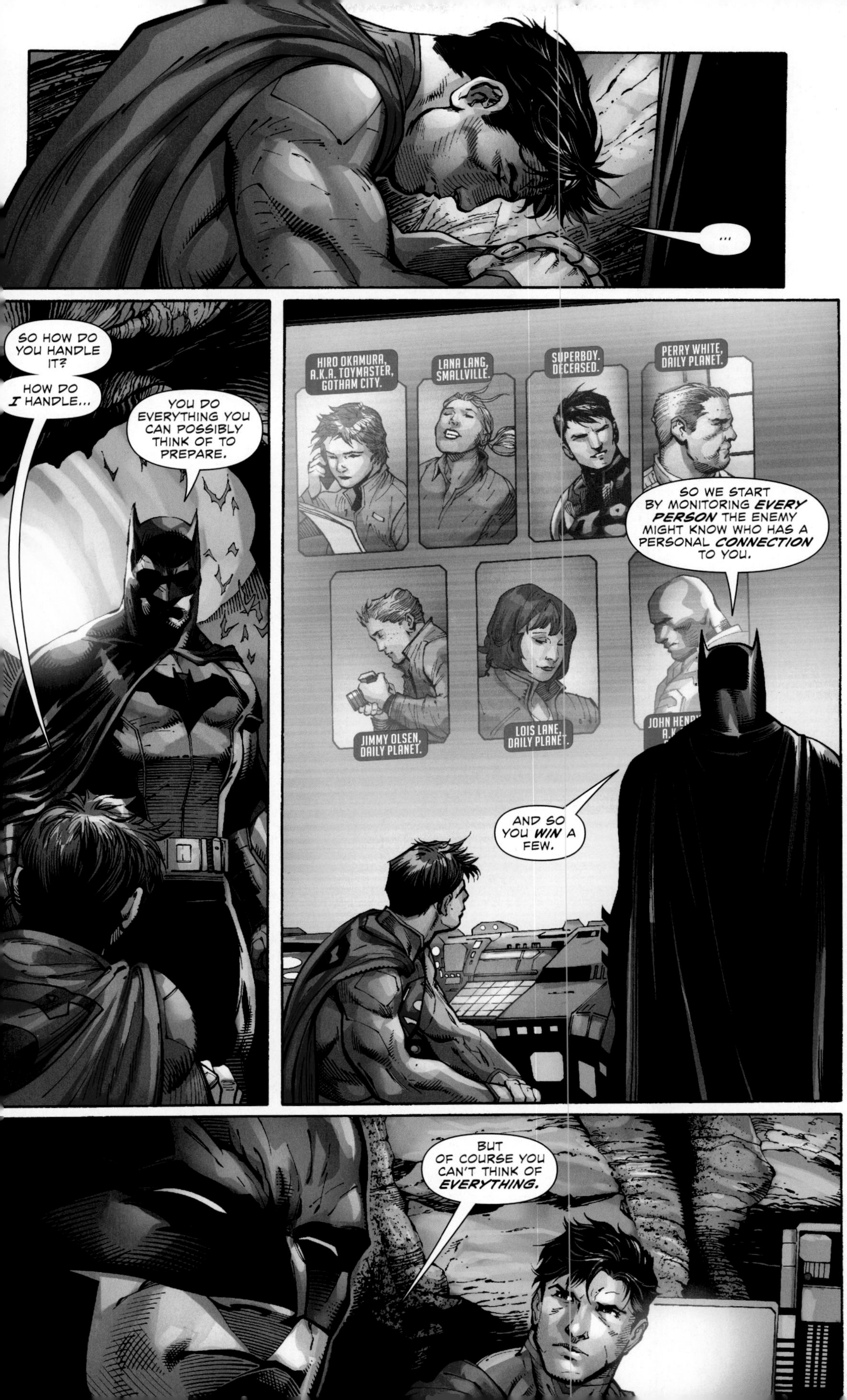
...
SO HOW DO YOU HANDLE IT?
HOW DO I HANDLE...
YOU DO EVERYTHING YOU CAN POSSIBLY THINK OF TO PREPARE.
HIRO OKAMURA, A.K.A. TOYMASTER, GOTHAM CITY.
LANA LANG, SMALLVILLE.
SUPERBOY. DECEASED.
PERRY WHITE, DAILY PLANET.
SO WE START BY MONITORING EVERY PERSON THE ENEMY MIGHT KNOW WHO HAS A PERSONAL CONNECTION TO YOU.
JIMMY OLSEN, DAILY PLANET.
LOIS LANE, DAILY PLANET.
AND SO YOU WIN A FEW.
BUT OF COURSE YOU CAN'T THINK OF EVERYTHING.

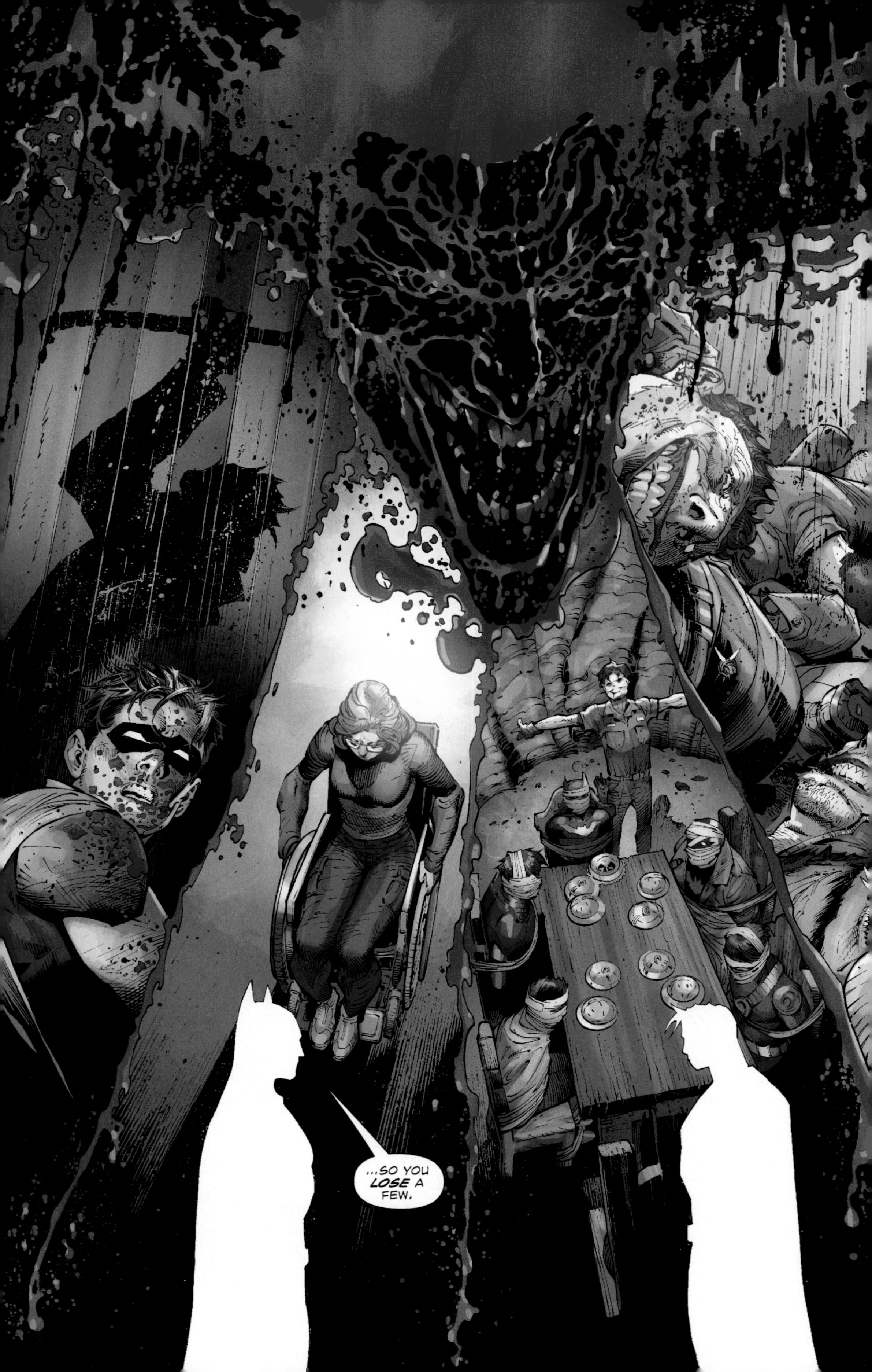
...SO YOU LOSE A FEW.

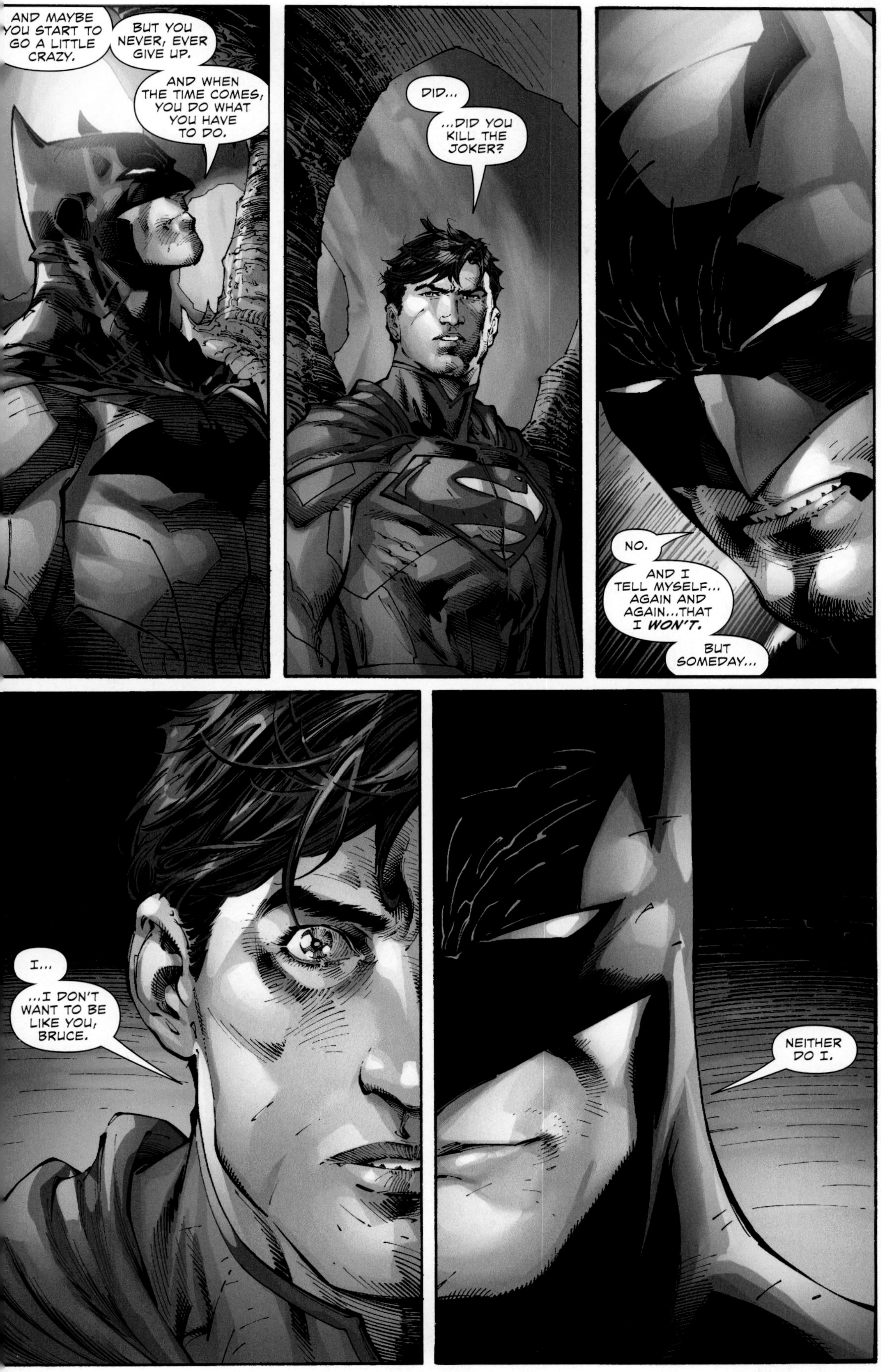
AND MAYBE YOU START TO GO A LITTLE CRAZY.
BUT YOU NEVER, EVER GIVE UP.
AND WHEN THE TIME COMES, YOU DO WHAT YOU HAVE TO DO.
DID...
...DID YOU KILL THE JOKER?
NO.
AND I TELL MYSELF... AGAIN AND AGAIN...THAT I *WON'T*.
BUT SOMEDAY...
I...
...I DON'T WANT TO BE LIKE YOU, BRUCE.
NEITHER DO I.

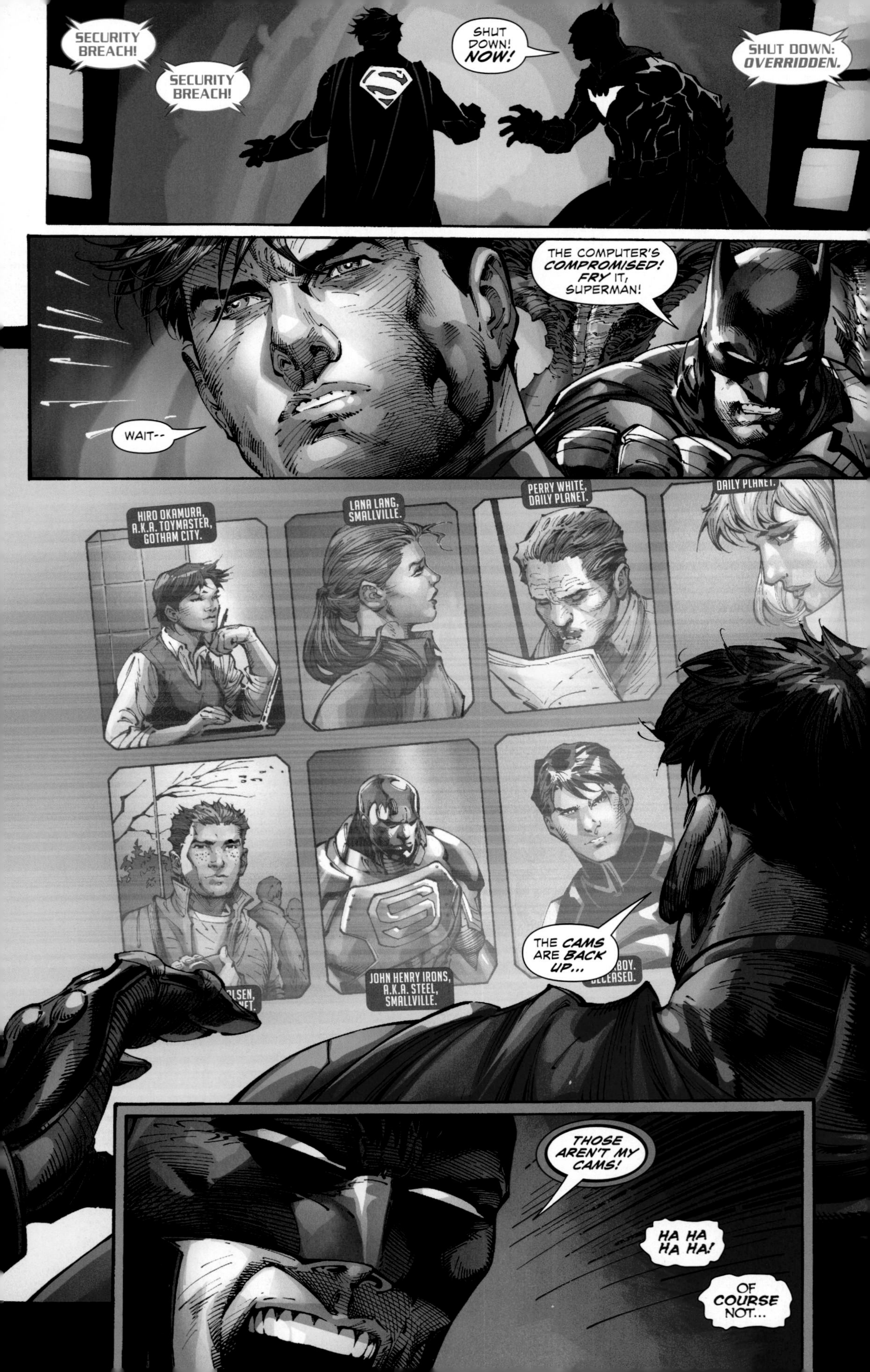
SECURITY BREACH!
SECURITY BREACH!
SHUT DOWN! NOW!
SHUT DOWN: OVERRIDDEN.
THE COMPUTER'S COMPROMISED! FRY IT, SUPERMAN!
WAIT--
HIRO OKAMURA, A.K.A. TOYMASTER, GOTHAM CITY.
LANA LANG, SMALLVILLE.
PERRY WHITE, DAILY PLANET.
DAILY PLANET.
JOHN HENRY IRONS, A.K.A. STEEL, SMALLVILLE.
THE CAMS ARE BACK UP...
THOSE AREN'T MY CAMS!
HA HA HA HA!
OF COURSE NOT...

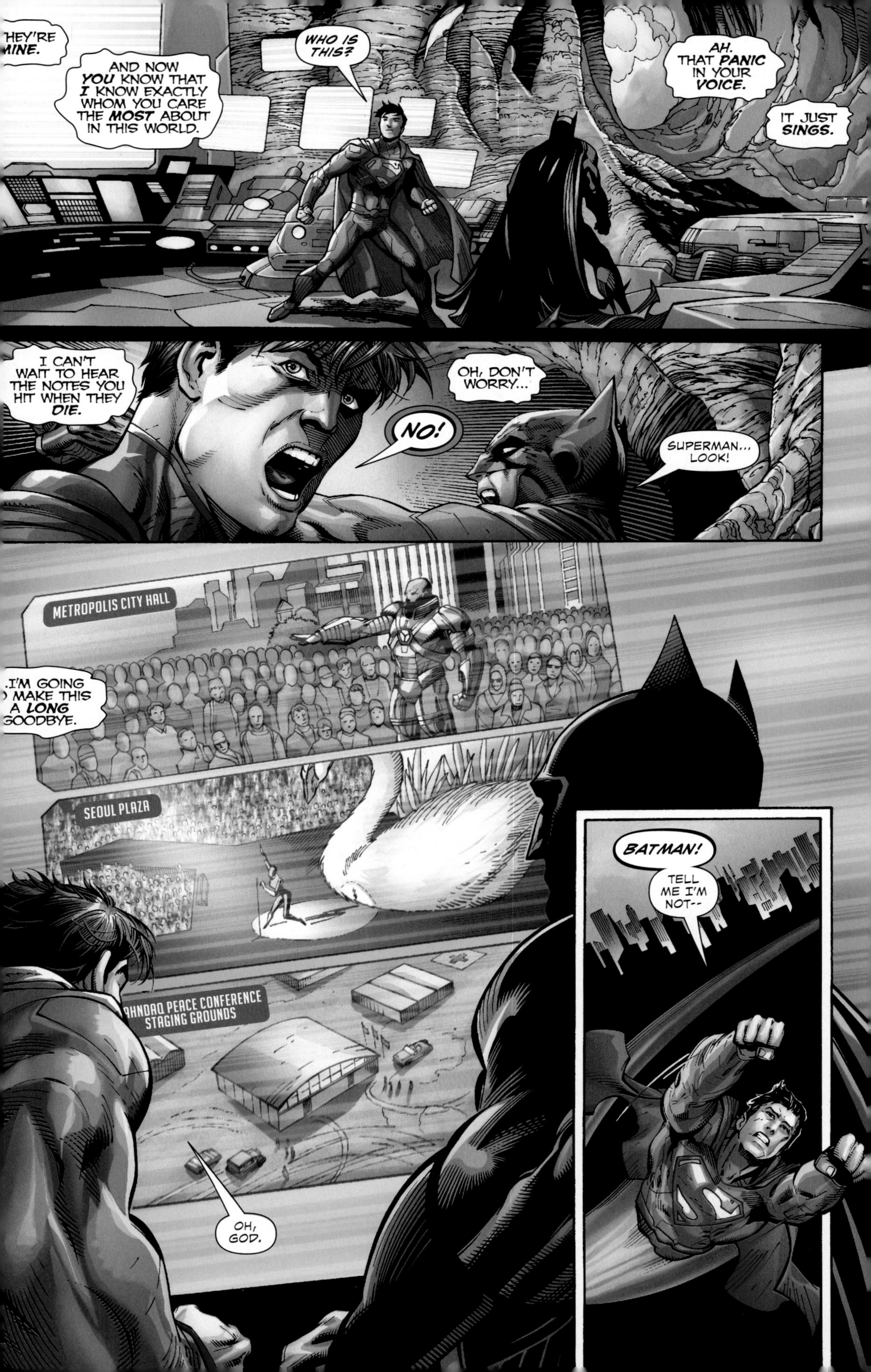
HEY'RE MINE.
AND NOW YOU KNOW THAT I KNOW EXACTLY WHOM YOU CARE THE MOST ABOUT IN THIS WORLD.
WHO IS THIS?
AH. THAT PANIC IN YOUR VOICE.
IT JUST SINGS.
I CAN'T WAIT TO HEAR THE NOTES YOU HIT WHEN THEY DIE.
OH, DON'T WORRY...
NO!
SUPERMAN... LOOK!
METROPOLIS CITY HALL
.I'M GOING MAKE THIS A LONG GOODBYE.
SEOUL PLAZA
HNDAQ PEACE CONFERENCE STAGING GROUNDS
OH, GOD.
BATMAN!
TELL ME I'M NOT--

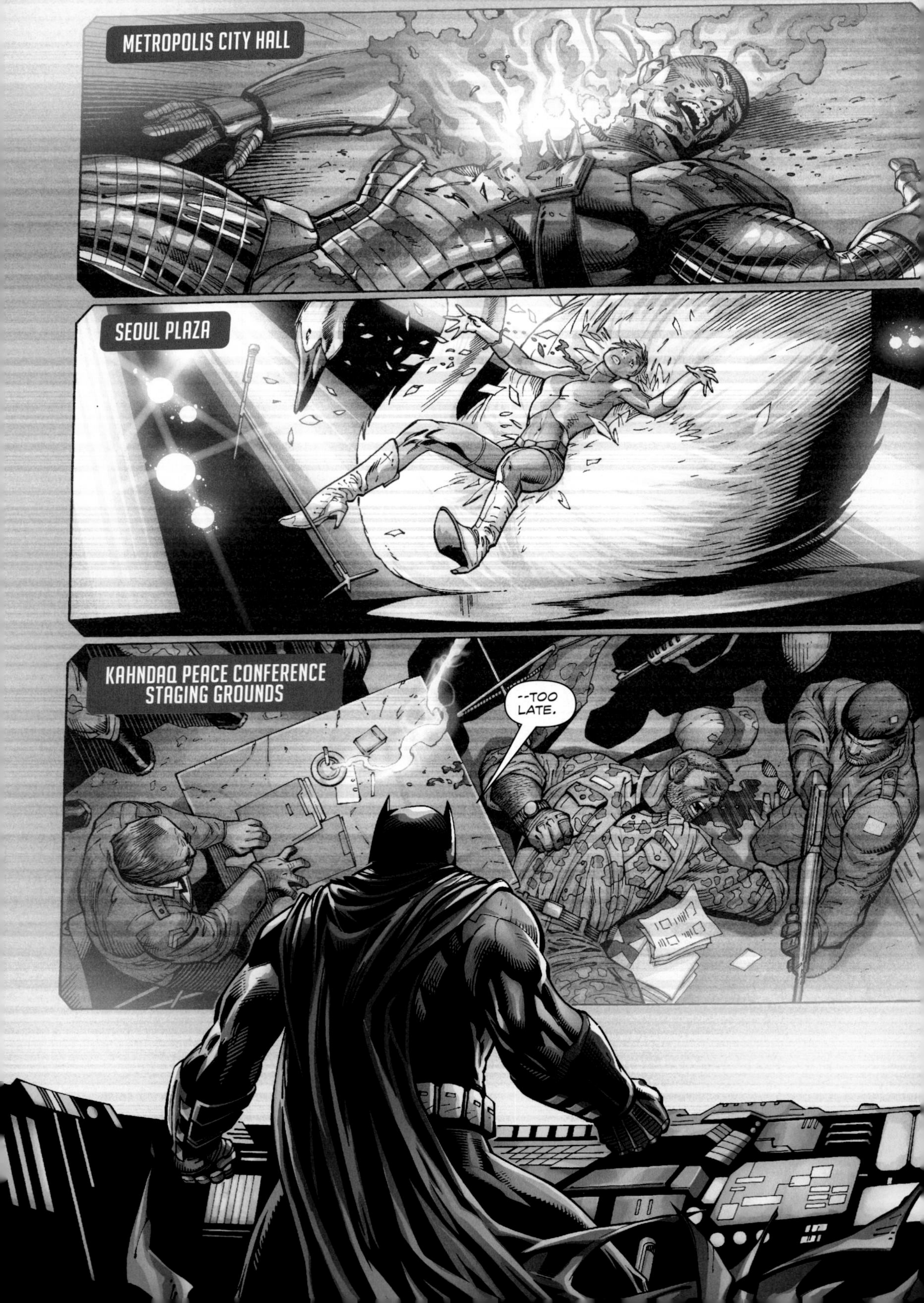
METROPOLIS CITY HALL
SEOUL PLAZA
KAHNDAQ PEACE CONFERENCE STAGING GROUNDS
--TOO LATE.

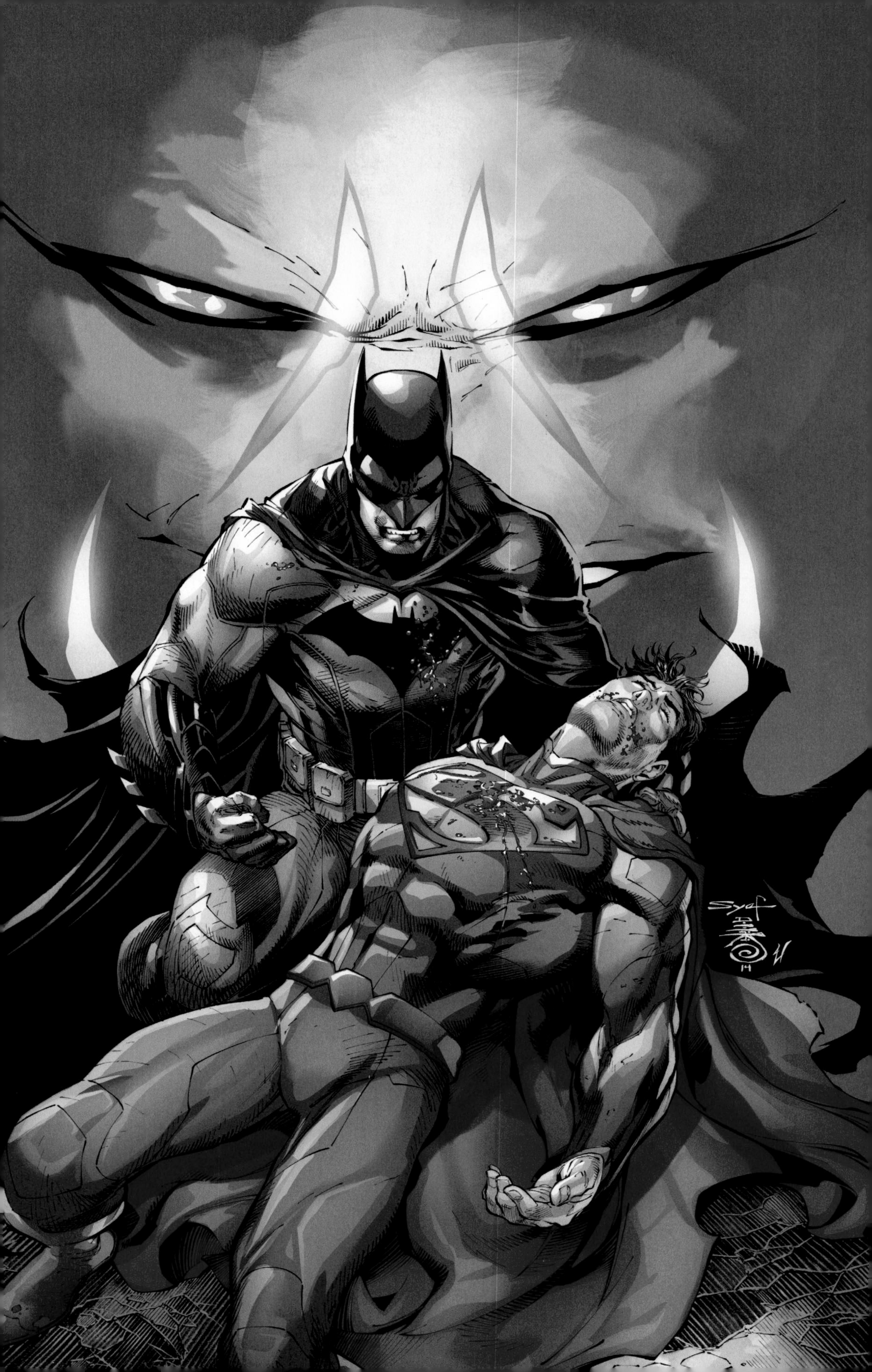

cover by **ARDIAN SYAF, DANNY MIKI** and **ULISES ARREOLA**

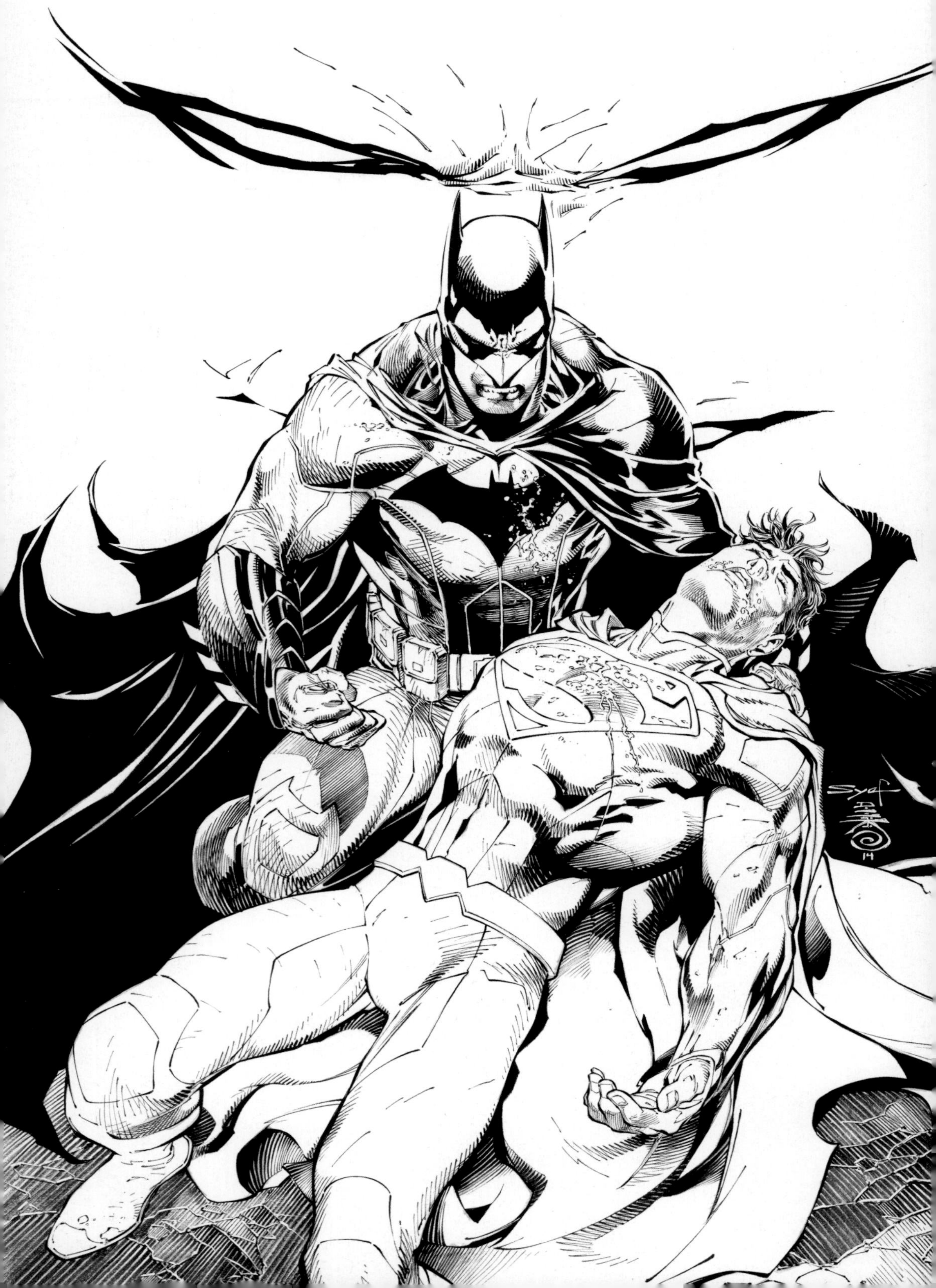

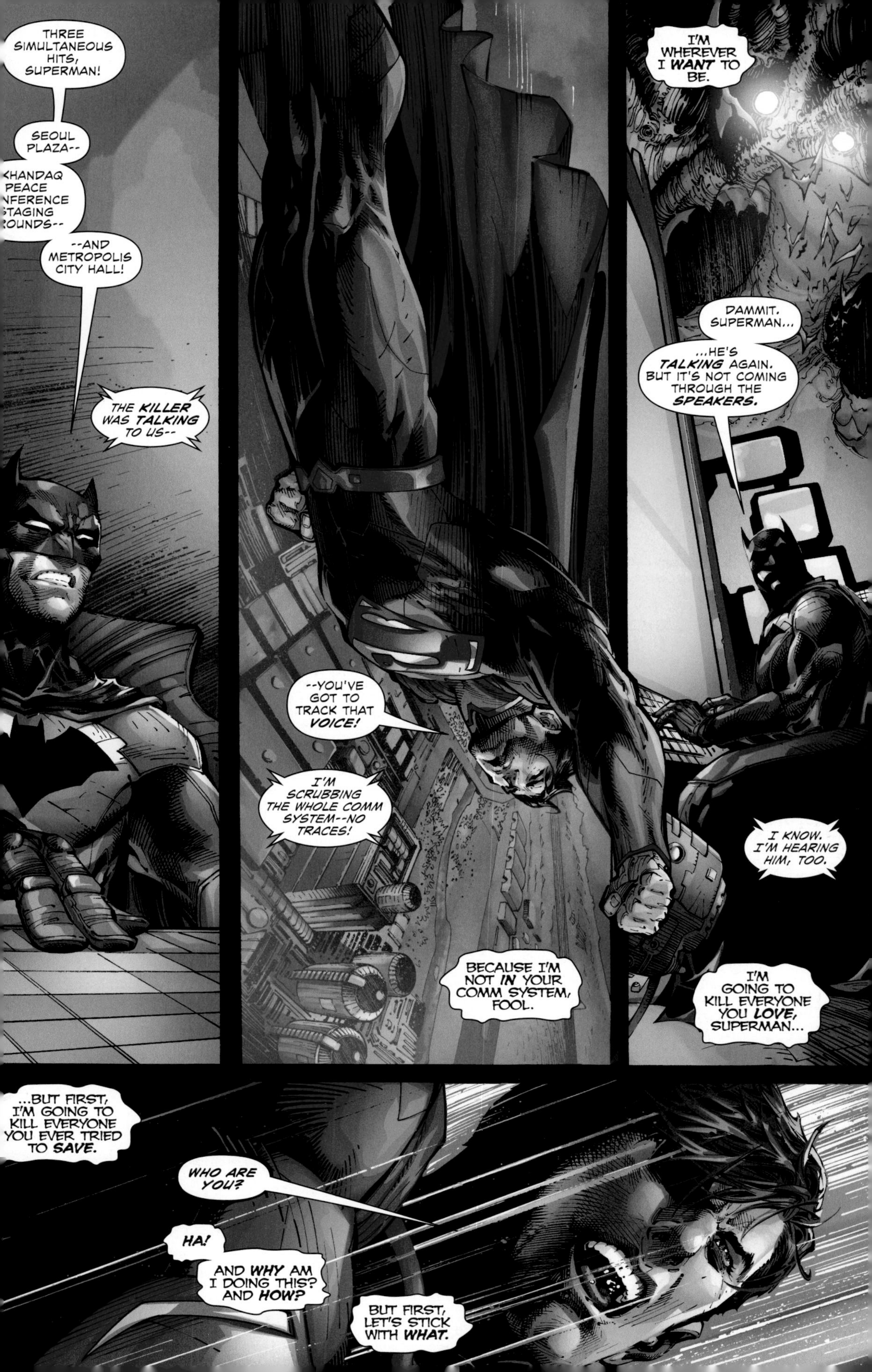

THREE SIMULTANEOUS HITS, SUPERMAN!
SEOUL PLAZA--
KHANDAQ PEACE CONFERENCE STAGING GROUNDS--
--AND METROPOLIS CITY HALL!
THE KILLER WAS TALKING TO US--
--YOU'VE GOT TO TRACK THAT VOICE!
I'M SCRUBBING THE WHOLE COMM SYSTEM--NO TRACES!
BECAUSE I'M NOT IN YOUR COMM SYSTEM, FOOL.
I'M WHEREVER I WANT TO BE.
DAMMIT. SUPERMAN...
...HE'S TALKING AGAIN. BUT IT'S NOT COMING THROUGH THE SPEAKERS.
I KNOW. I'M HEARING HIM, TOO.
I'M GOING TO KILL EVERYONE YOU LOVE, SUPERMAN...
...BUT FIRST, I'M GOING TO KILL EVERYONE YOU EVER TRIED TO SAVE.
WHO ARE YOU?
HA!
AND WHY AM I DOING THIS? AND HOW?
BUT FIRST, LET'S STICK WITH WHAT.

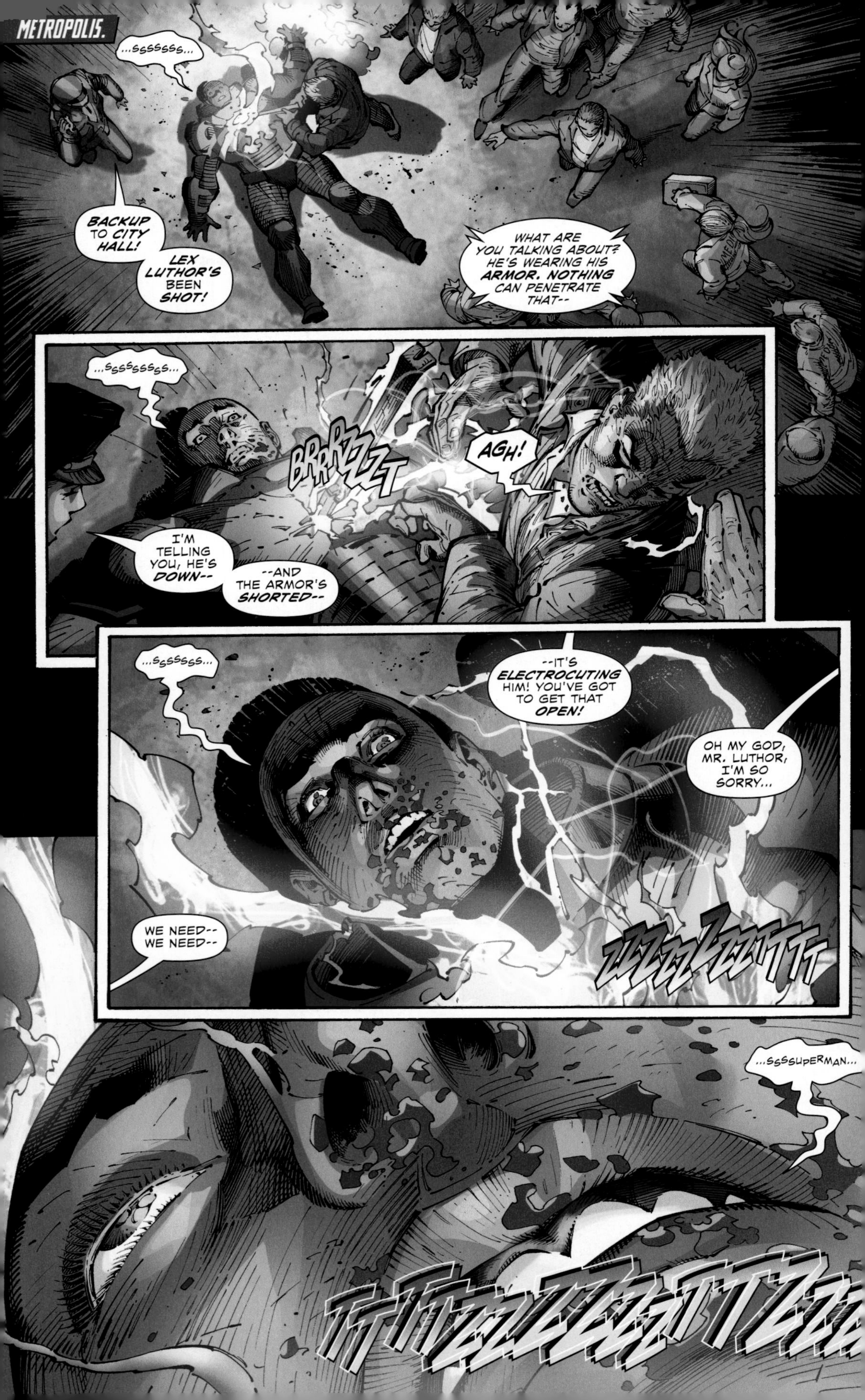
METROPOLIS.
...SSSSSSS...
BACKUP TO CITY HALL!
LEX LUTHOR'S BEEN SHOT!
WHAT ARE YOU TALKING ABOUT? HE'S WEARING HIS ARMOR. NOTHING CAN PENETRATE THAT--
...SSSSSSSSS...
BRRRZZZT
AGH!
I'M TELLING YOU, HE'S DOWN--
--AND THE ARMOR'S SHORTED--
...SSSSSSS...
--IT'S ELECTROCUTING HIM! YOU'VE GOT TO GET THAT OPEN!
OH MY GOD, MR. LUTHOR, I'M SO SORRY...
WE NEED-- WE NEED--
ZZZZZZZZZTTTTT
...SSSSUPERMAN...
TTTTZZZZZZZTTTZZZ

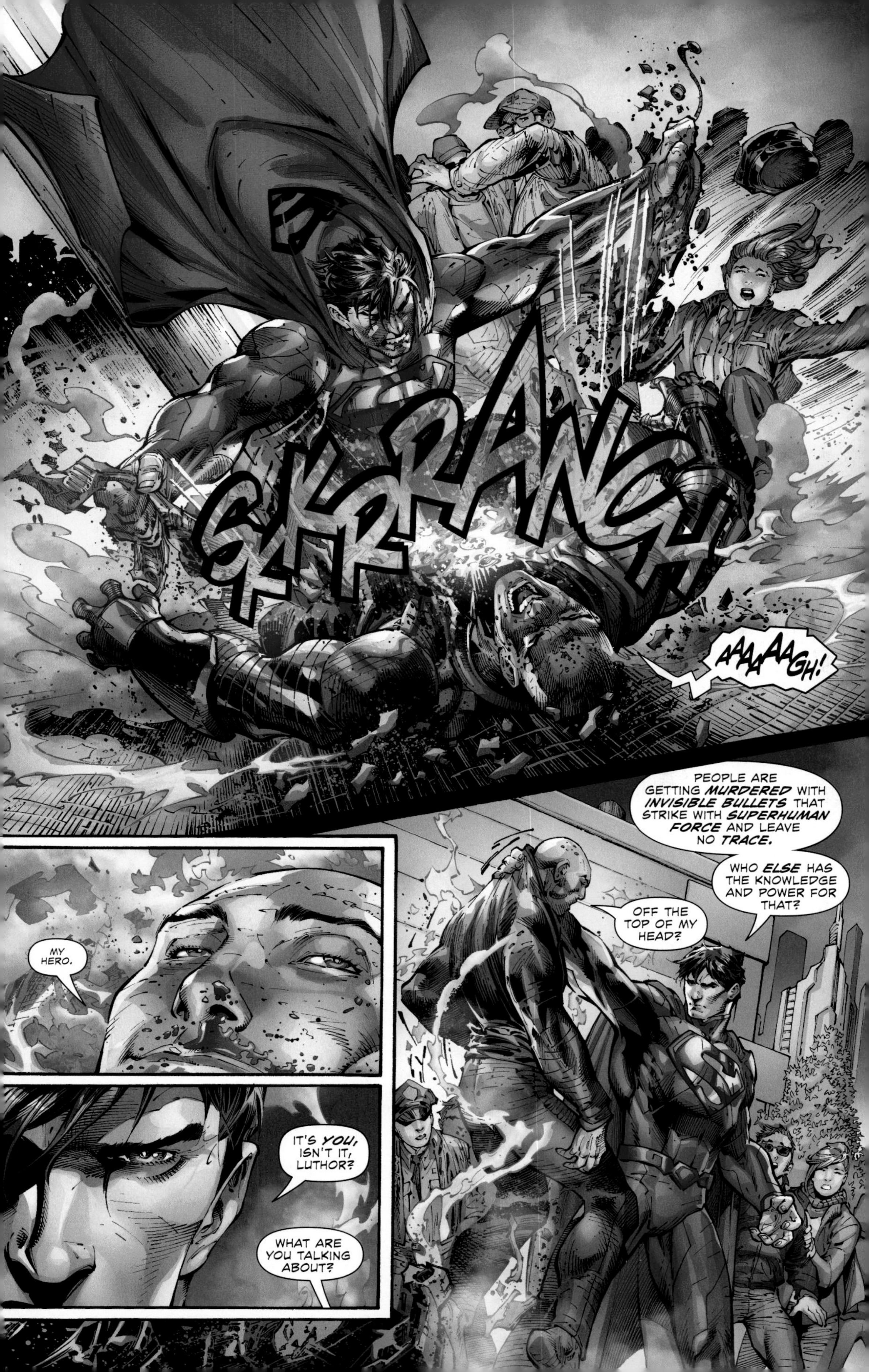
SKRANCH
AAAAAAGH!
MY HERO.
IT'S YOU, ISN'T IT, LUTHOR?
WHAT ARE YOU TALKING ABOUT?
PEOPLE ARE GETTING MURDERED WITH INVISIBLE BULLETS THAT STRIKE WITH SUPERHUMAN FORCE AND LEAVE NO TRACE.
WHO ELSE HAS THE KNOWLEDGE AND POWER FOR THAT?
OFF THE TOP OF MY HEAD?

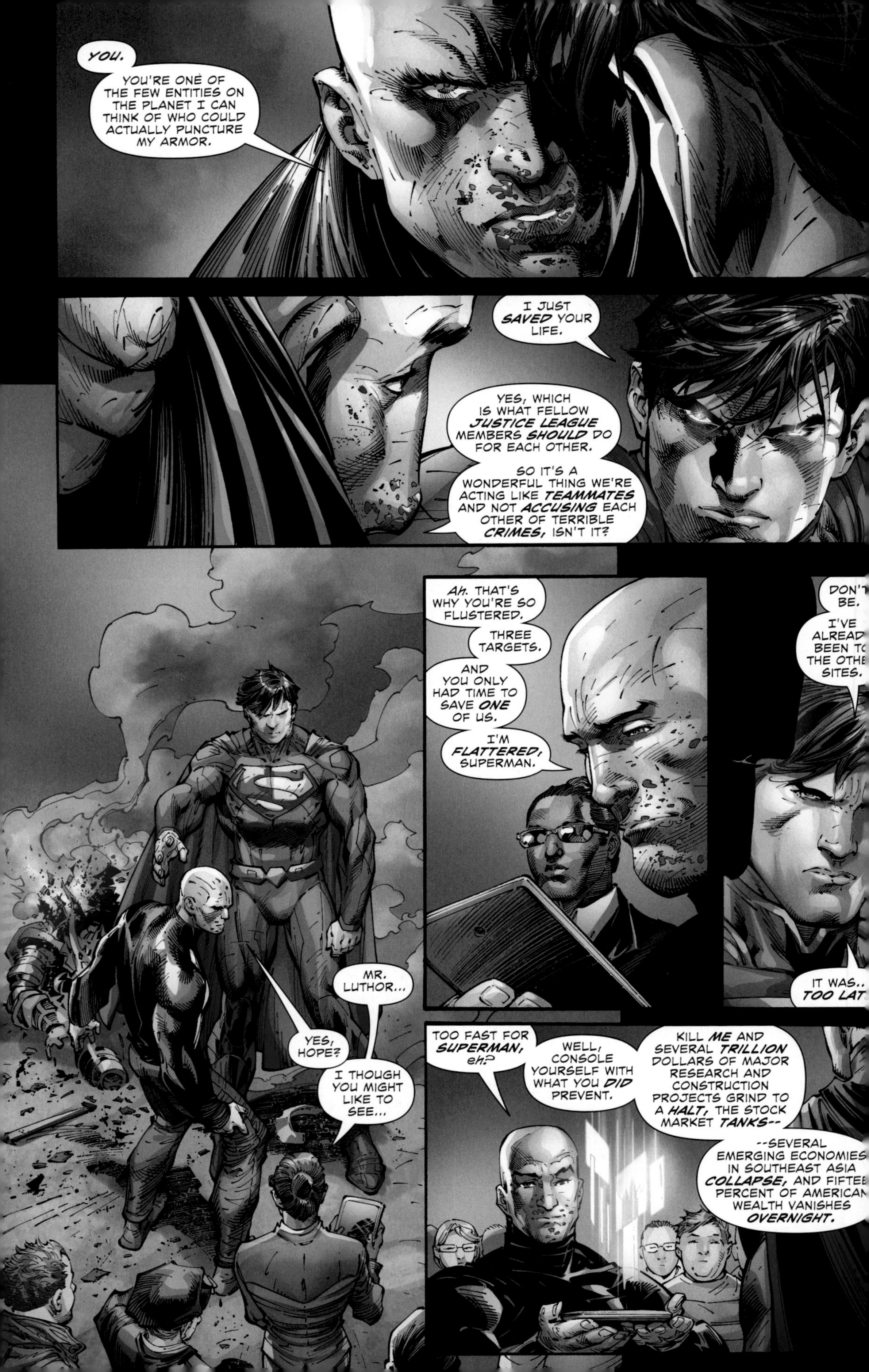
YOU.
YOU'RE ONE OF THE FEW ENTITIES ON THE PLANET I CAN THINK OF WHO COULD ACTUALLY PUNCTURE MY ARMOR.
I JUST SAVED YOUR LIFE.
YES, WHICH IS WHAT FELLOW JUSTICE LEAGUE MEMBERS SHOULD DO FOR EACH OTHER.
SO IT'S A WONDERFUL THING WE'RE ACTING LIKE TEAMMATES AND NOT ACCUSING EACH OTHER OF TERRIBLE CRIMES, ISN'T IT?
MR. LUTHOR...
YES, HOPE?
I THOUGH YOU MIGHT LIKE TO SEE...
Ah. THAT'S WHY YOU'RE SO FLUSTERED.
THREE TARGETS.
AND YOU ONLY HAD TIME TO SAVE ONE OF US.
I'M FLATTERED, SUPERMAN.
DON'T BE.
I'VE ALREAD BEEN TO THE OTHE SITES.
IT WAS... TOO LAT
TOO FAST FOR SUPERMAN, eh?
WELL, CONSOLE YOURSELF WITH WHAT YOU DID PREVENT.
KILL ME AND SEVERAL TRILLION DOLLARS OF MAJOR RESEARCH AND CONSTRUCTION PROJECTS GRIND TO A HALT, THE STOCK MARKET TANKS--
--SEVERAL EMERGING ECONOMIES IN SOUTHEAST ASIA COLLAPSE, AND FIFTEE PERCENT OF AMERICAN WEALTH VANISHES OVERNIGHT.

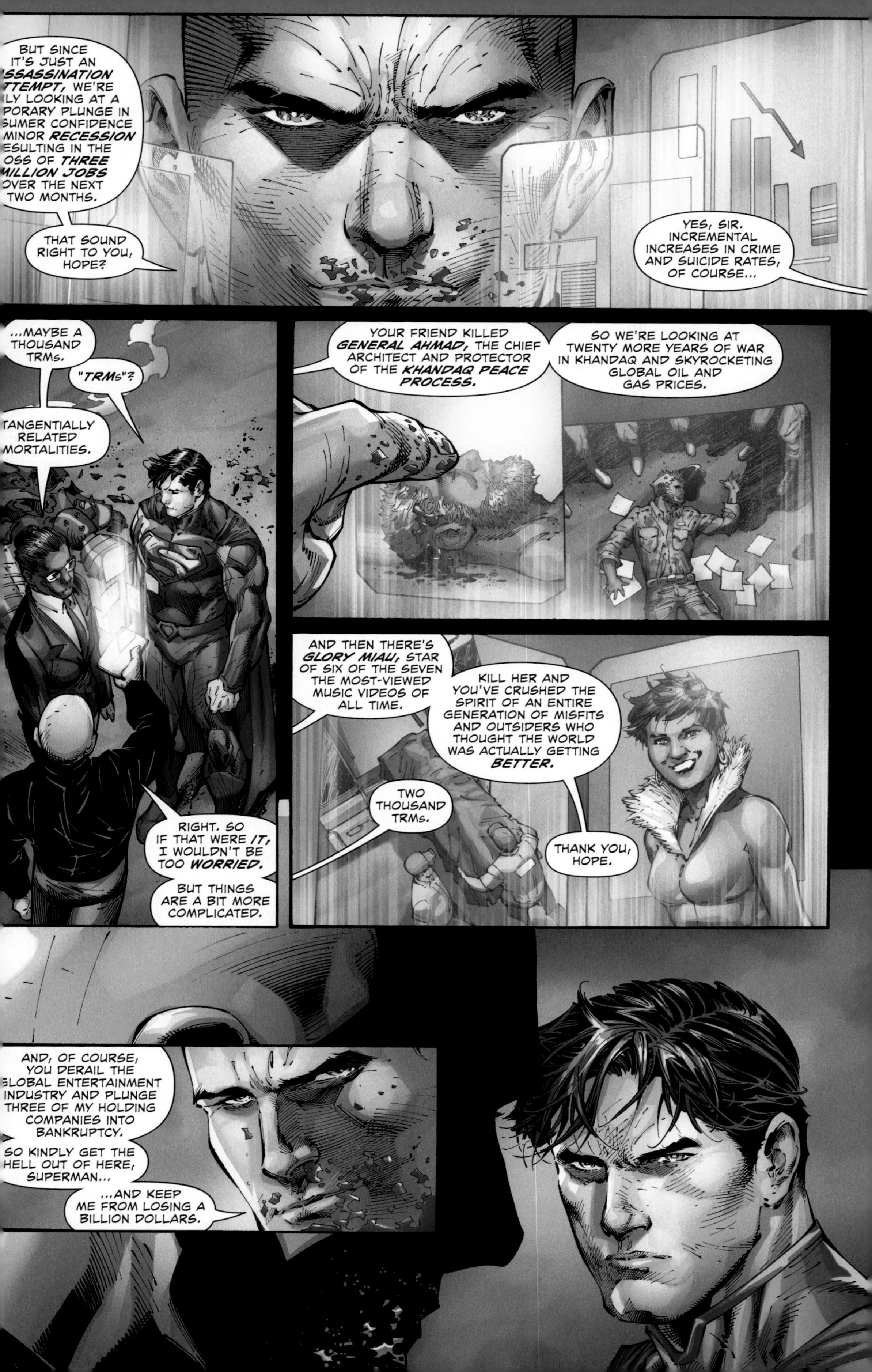
BUT SINCE IT'S JUST AN ASSASSINATION ATTEMPT, WE'RE ...LY LOOKING AT A ...PORARY PLUNGE IN ...SUMER CONFIDENCE ...MINOR RECESSION ...ESULTING IN THE ...OSS OF THREE MILLION JOBS OVER THE NEXT TWO MONTHS.
THAT SOUND RIGHT TO YOU, HOPE?
YES, SIR. INCREMENTAL INCREASES IN CRIME AND SUICIDE RATES, OF COURSE...
...MAYBE A THOUSAND TRMs.
"TRMs"?
TANGENTIALLY RELATED MORTALITIES.
YOUR FRIEND KILLED GENERAL AHMAD, THE CHIEF ARCHITECT AND PROTECTOR OF THE KHANDAQ PEACE PROCESS.
SO WE'RE LOOKING AT TWENTY MORE YEARS OF WAR IN KHANDAQ AND SKYROCKETING GLOBAL OIL AND GAS PRICES.
AND THEN THERE'S GLORY MIAU, STAR OF SIX OF THE SEVEN THE MOST-VIEWED MUSIC VIDEOS OF ALL TIME.
KILL HER AND YOU'VE CRUSHED THE SPIRIT OF AN ENTIRE GENERATION OF MISFITS AND OUTSIDERS WHO THOUGHT THE WORLD WAS ACTUALLY GETTING BETTER.
TWO THOUSAND TRMs.
THANK YOU, HOPE.
RIGHT. SO IF THAT WERE IT, I WOULDN'T BE TOO WORRIED.
BUT THINGS ARE A BIT MORE COMPLICATED.
AND, OF COURSE, YOU DERAIL THE GLOBAL ENTERTAINMENT INDUSTRY AND PLUNGE THREE OF MY HOLDING COMPANIES INTO BANKRUPTCY.
SO KINDLY GET THE HELL OUT OF HERE, SUPERMAN...
...AND KEEP ME FROM LOSING A BILLION DOLLARS.

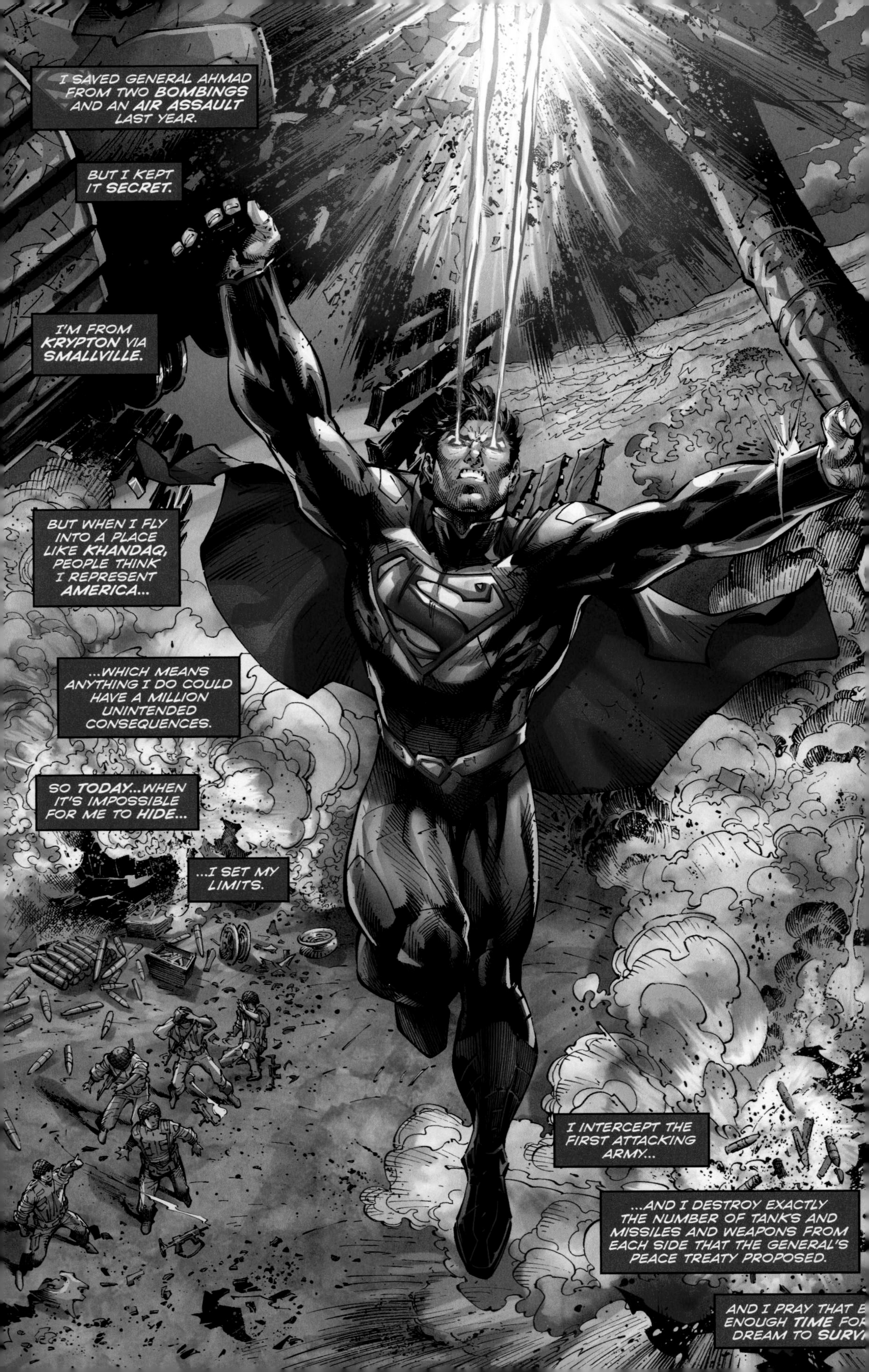
I SAVED GENERAL AHMAD FROM TWO BOMBINGS AND AN AIR ASSAULT LAST YEAR.
BUT I KEPT IT SECRET.
I'M FROM KRYPTON VIA SMALLVILLE.
BUT WHEN I FLY INTO A PLACE LIKE KHANDAQ, PEOPLE THINK I REPRESENT AMERICA...
...WHICH MEANS ANYTHING I DO COULD HAVE A MILLION UNINTENDED CONSEQUENCES.
SO TODAY...WHEN IT'S IMPOSSIBLE FOR ME TO HIDE...
...I SET MY LIMITS.
I INTERCEPT THE FIRST ATTACKING ARMY...
...AND I DESTROY EXACTLY THE NUMBER OF TANKS AND MISSILES AND WEAPONS FROM EACH SIDE THAT THE GENERAL'S PEACE TREATY PROPOSED.
AND I PRAY THAT
ENOUGH TIME
DREAM TO

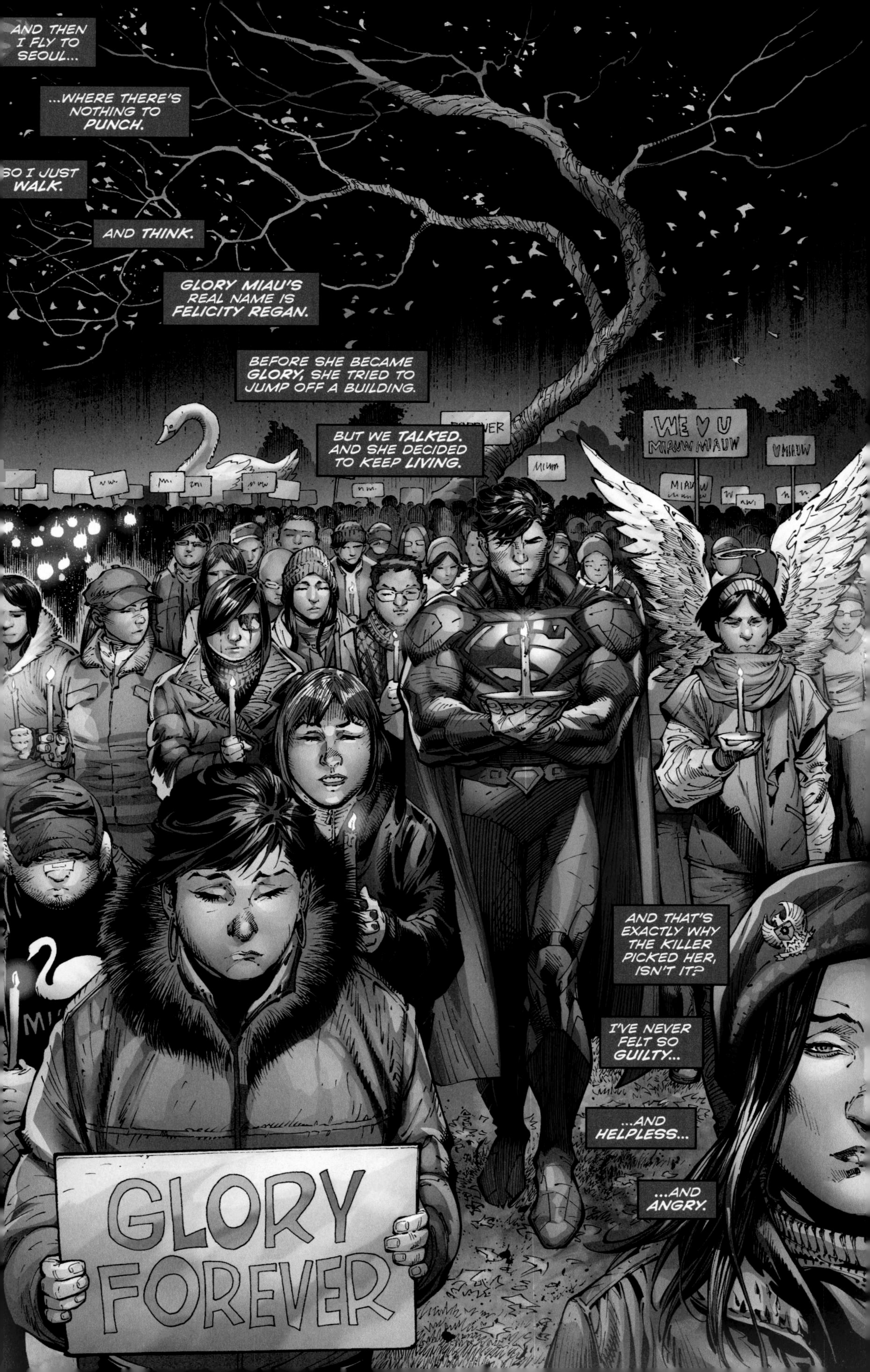
AND THEN I FLY TO SEOUL...
...WHERE THERE'S NOTHING TO PUNCH.
SO I JUST WALK.
AND THINK.
GLORY MIAU'S REAL NAME IS FELICITY REGAN.
BEFORE SHE BECAME GLORY, SHE TRIED TO JUMP OFF A BUILDING.
BUT WE TALKED. AND SHE DECIDED TO KEEP LIVING.
WE ♥ U MIAUW MIAUW
AND THAT'S EXACTLY WHY THE KILLER PICKED HER, ISN'T IT?
I'VE NEVER FELT SO GUILTY...
...AND HELPLESS...
...AND ANGRY.
GLORY FOREVER

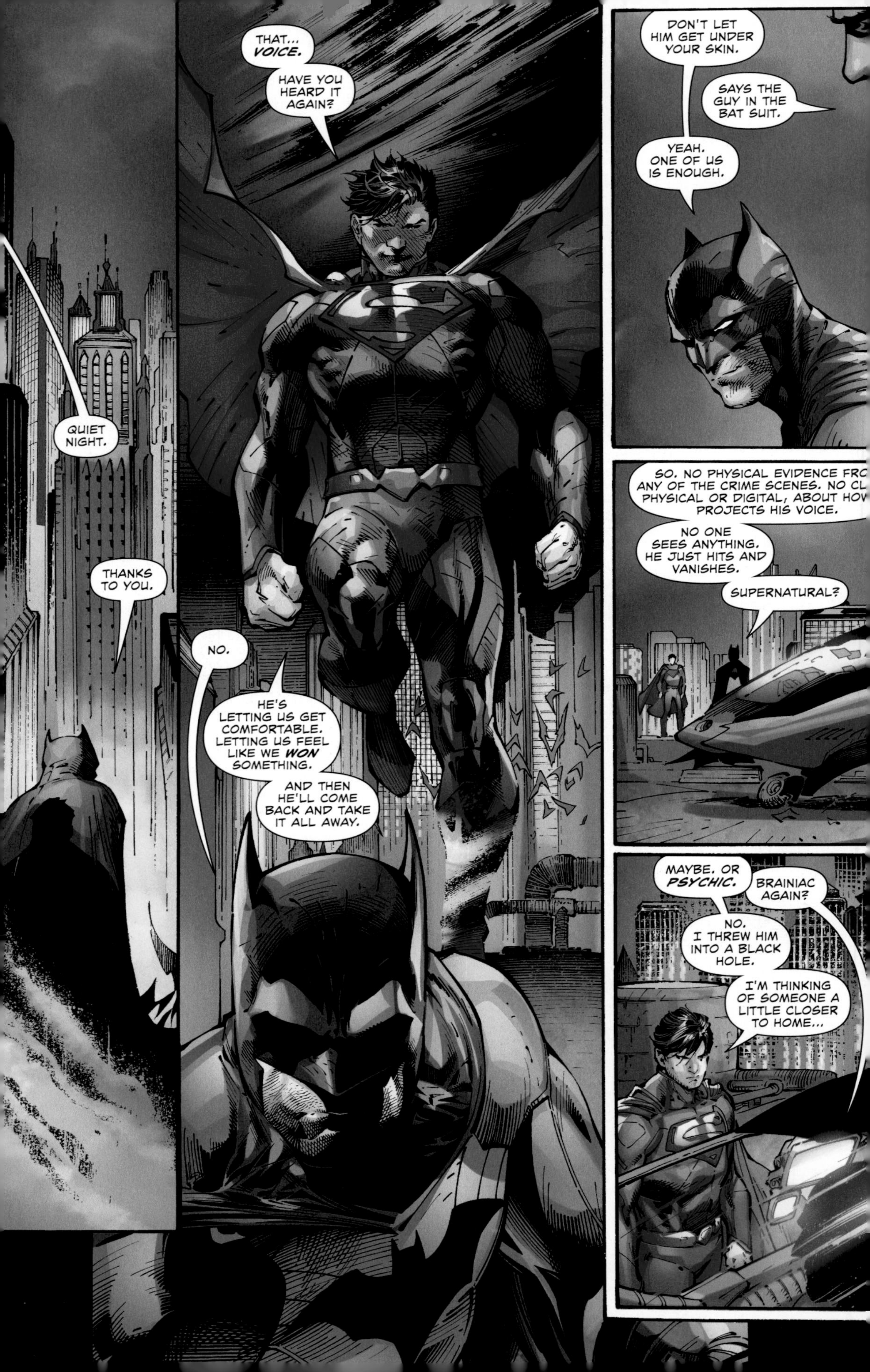

THAT... VOICE.
HAVE YOU HEARD IT AGAIN?
QUIET NIGHT.
THANKS TO YOU.
NO.
HE'S LETTING US GET COMFORTABLE. LETTING US FEEL LIKE WE WON SOMETHING.
AND THEN HE'LL COME BACK AND TAKE IT ALL AWAY.
DON'T LET HIM GET UNDER YOUR SKIN.
SAYS THE GUY IN THE BAT SUIT.
YEAH. ONE OF US IS ENOUGH.
SO. NO PHYSICAL EVIDENCE FRO ANY OF THE CRIME SCENES. NO CL PHYSICAL OR DIGITAL, ABOUT HOW PROJECTS HIS VOICE.
NO ONE SEES ANYTHING. HE JUST HITS AND VANISHES.
SUPERNATURAL?
MAYBE. OR PSYCHIC.
BRAINIAC AGAIN?
NO. I THREW HIM INTO A BLACK HOLE.
I'M THINKING OF SOMEONE A LITTLE CLOSER TO HOME...

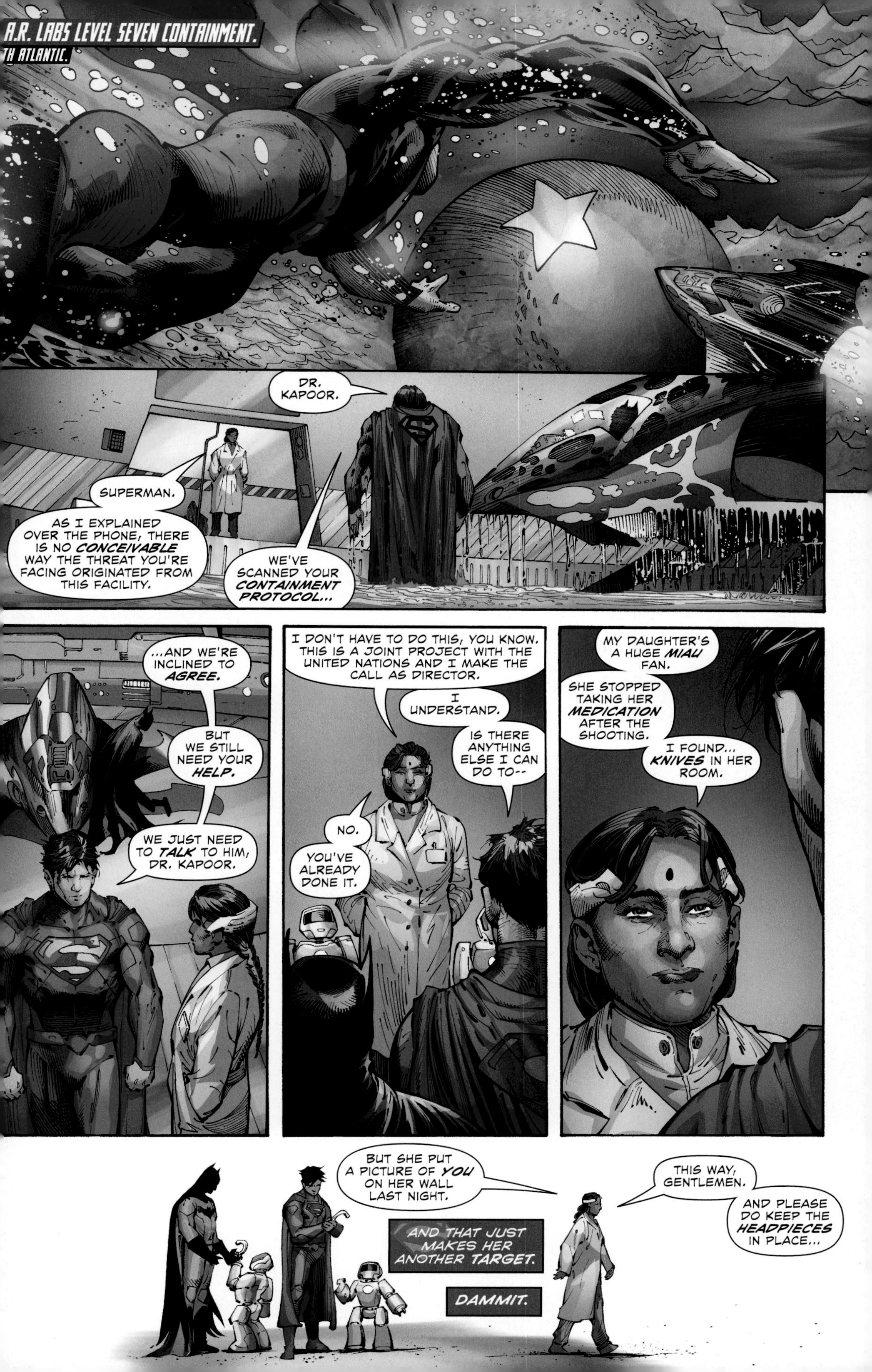
A.R. LABS LEVEL SEVEN CONTAINMENT.
TH ATLANTIC.
DR. KAPOOR.
SUPERMAN.
AS I EXPLAINED OVER THE PHONE, THERE IS NO CONCEIVABLE WAY THE THREAT YOU'RE FACING ORIGINATED FROM THIS FACILITY.
WE'VE SCANNED YOUR CONTAINMENT PROTOCOL...
...AND WE'RE INCLINED TO AGREE.
BUT WE STILL NEED YOUR HELP.
WE JUST NEED TO TALK TO HIM, DR. KAPOOR.
I DON'T HAVE TO DO THIS, YOU KNOW. THIS IS A JOINT PROJECT WITH THE UNITED NATIONS AND I MAKE THE CALL AS DIRECTOR.
I UNDERSTAND.
IS THERE ANYTHING ELSE I CAN DO TO--
NO.
YOU'VE ALREADY DONE IT.
MY DAUGHTER'S A HUGE MIAU FAN.
SHE STOPPED TAKING HER MEDICATION AFTER THE SHOOTING.
I FOUND... KNIVES IN HER ROOM.
BUT SHE PUT A PICTURE OF YOU ON HER WALL LAST NIGHT.
AND THAT JUST MAKES HER ANOTHER TARGET.
DAMMIT.
THIS WAY, GENTLEMEN.
AND PLEASE DO KEEP THE HEADPIECES IN PLACE...

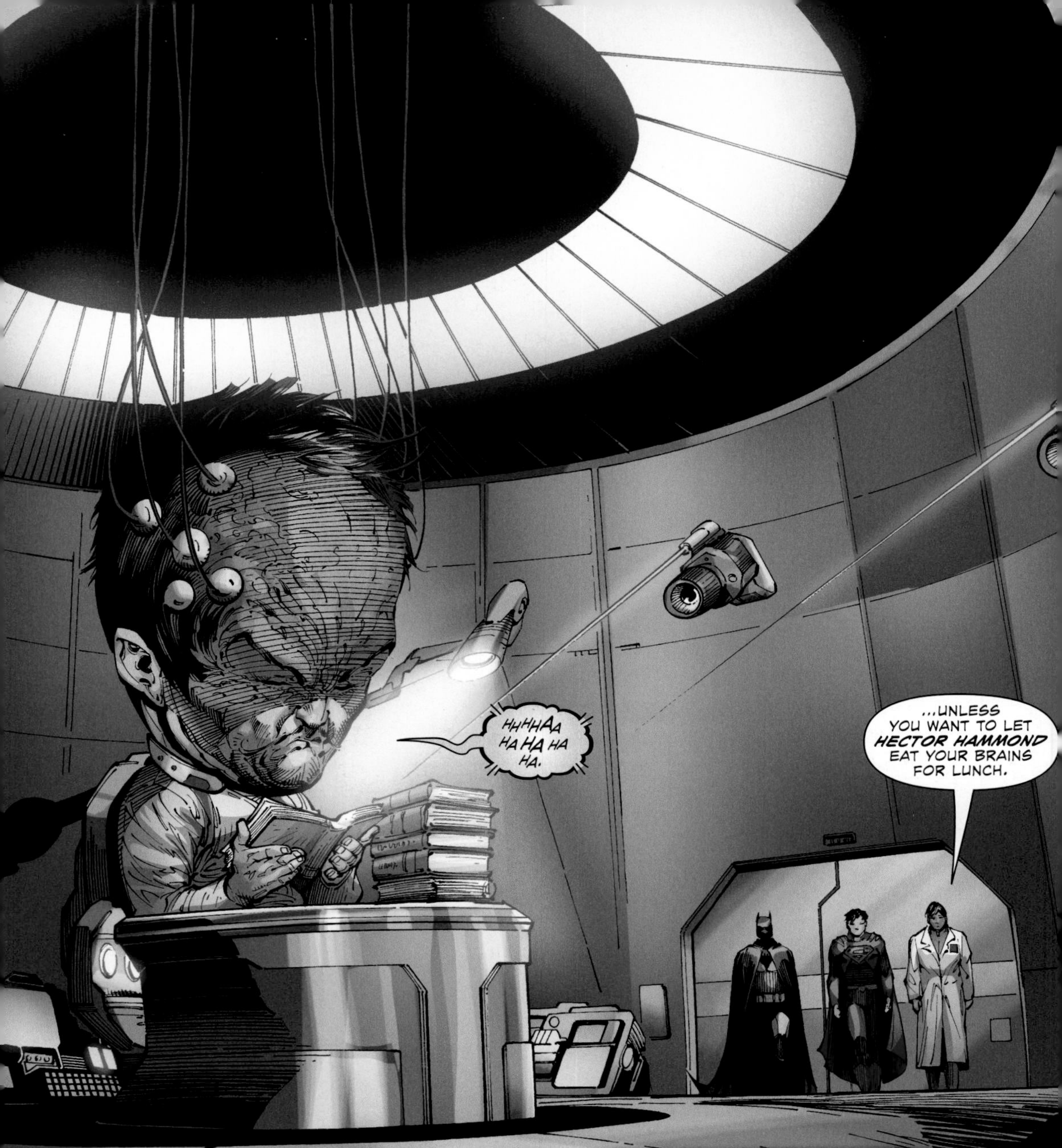
HHHHAA HA HA HA HA HA.
...UNLESS YOU WANT TO LET HECTOR HAMMOND EAT YOUR BRAINS FOR LUNCH.

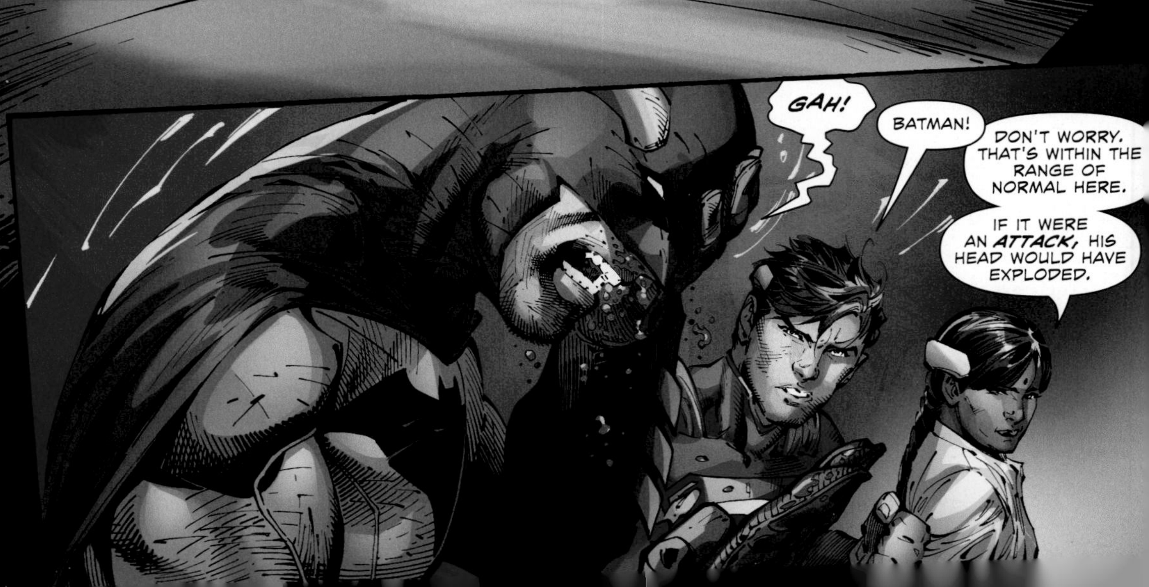
GAH!
BATMAN!
DON'T WORRY. THAT'S WITHIN THE RANGE OF NORMAL HERE.
IF IT WERE AN ATTACK, HIS HEAD WOULD HAVE EXPLODED.

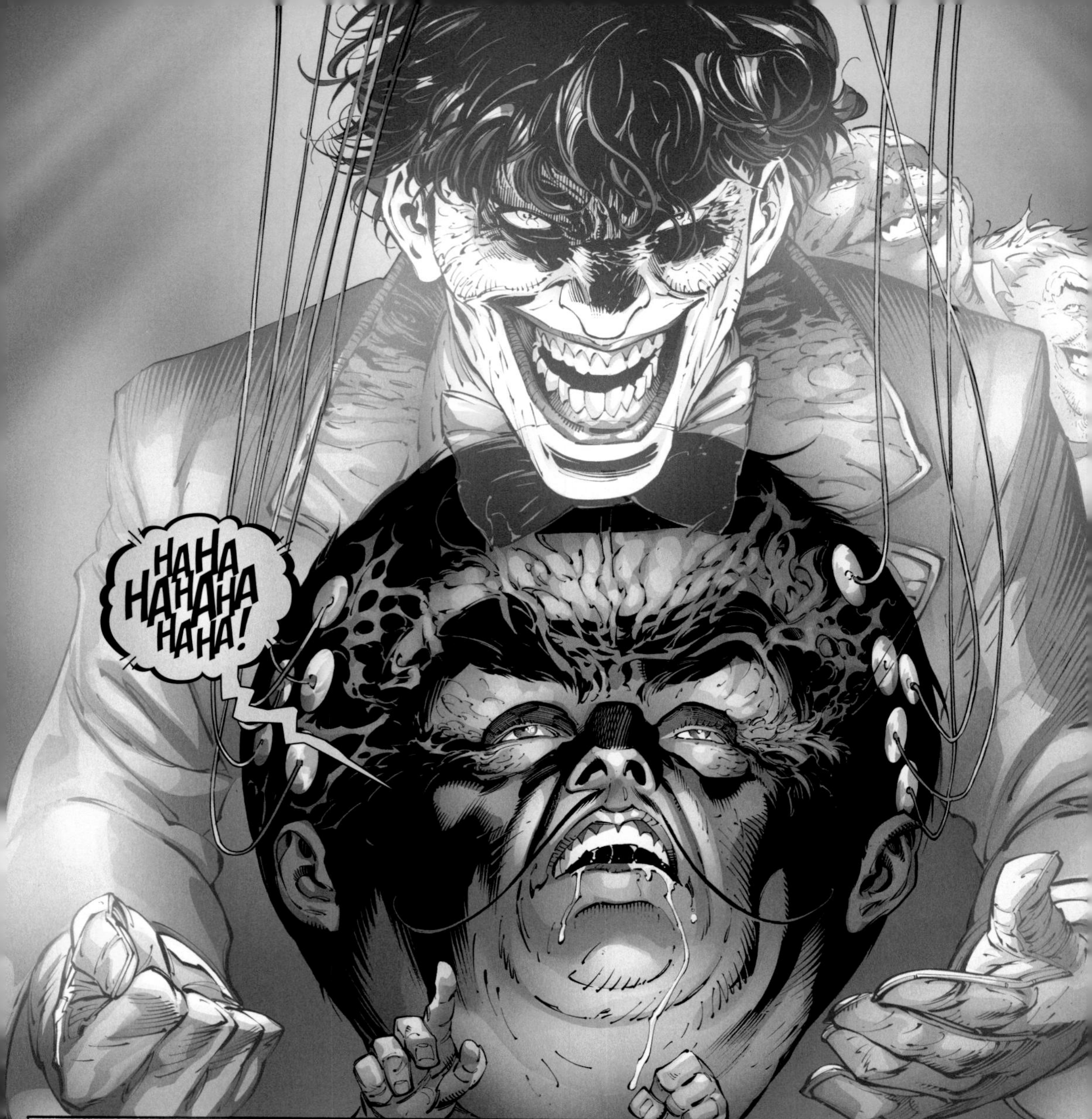
HAHA HAHAHA HAHA!

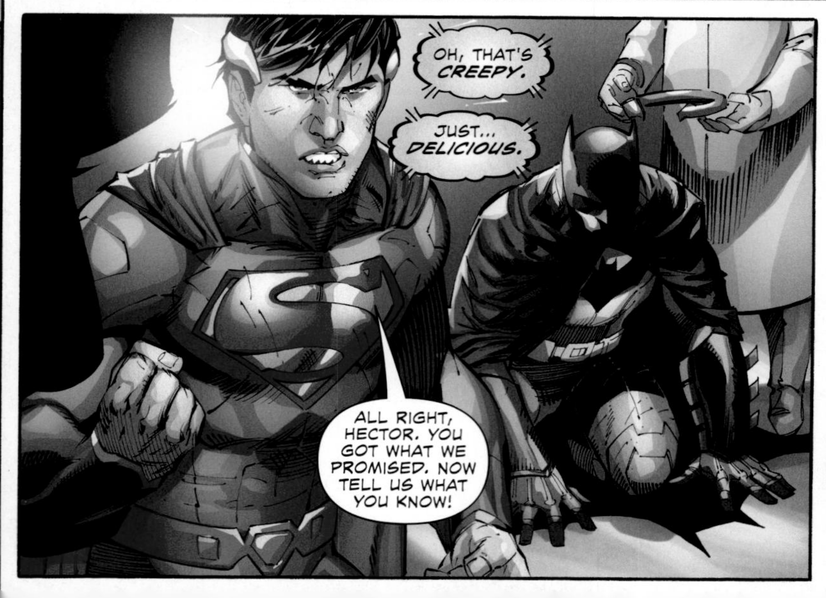
OH, THAT'S CREEPY.
JUST... DELICIOUS.
ALL RIGHT, HECTOR. YOU GOT WHAT WE PROMISED. NOW TELL US WHAT YOU KNOW!

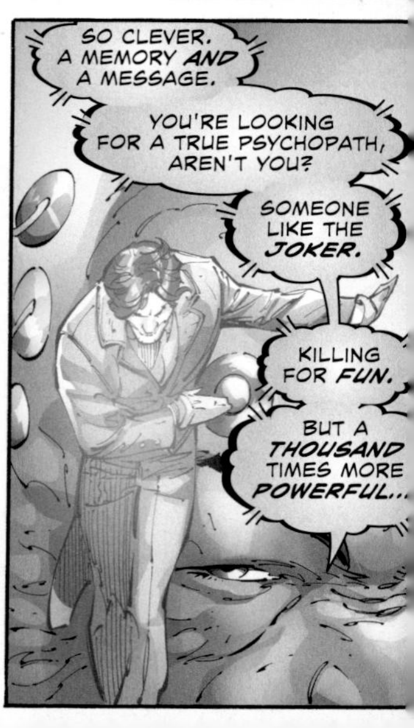
SO CLEVER. A MEMORY AND A MESSAGE.
YOU'RE LOOKING FOR A TRUE PSYCHOPATH, AREN'T YOU?
SOMEONE LIKE THE JOKER.
KILLING FOR FUN.
BUT A THOUSAND TIMES MORE POWERFUL...

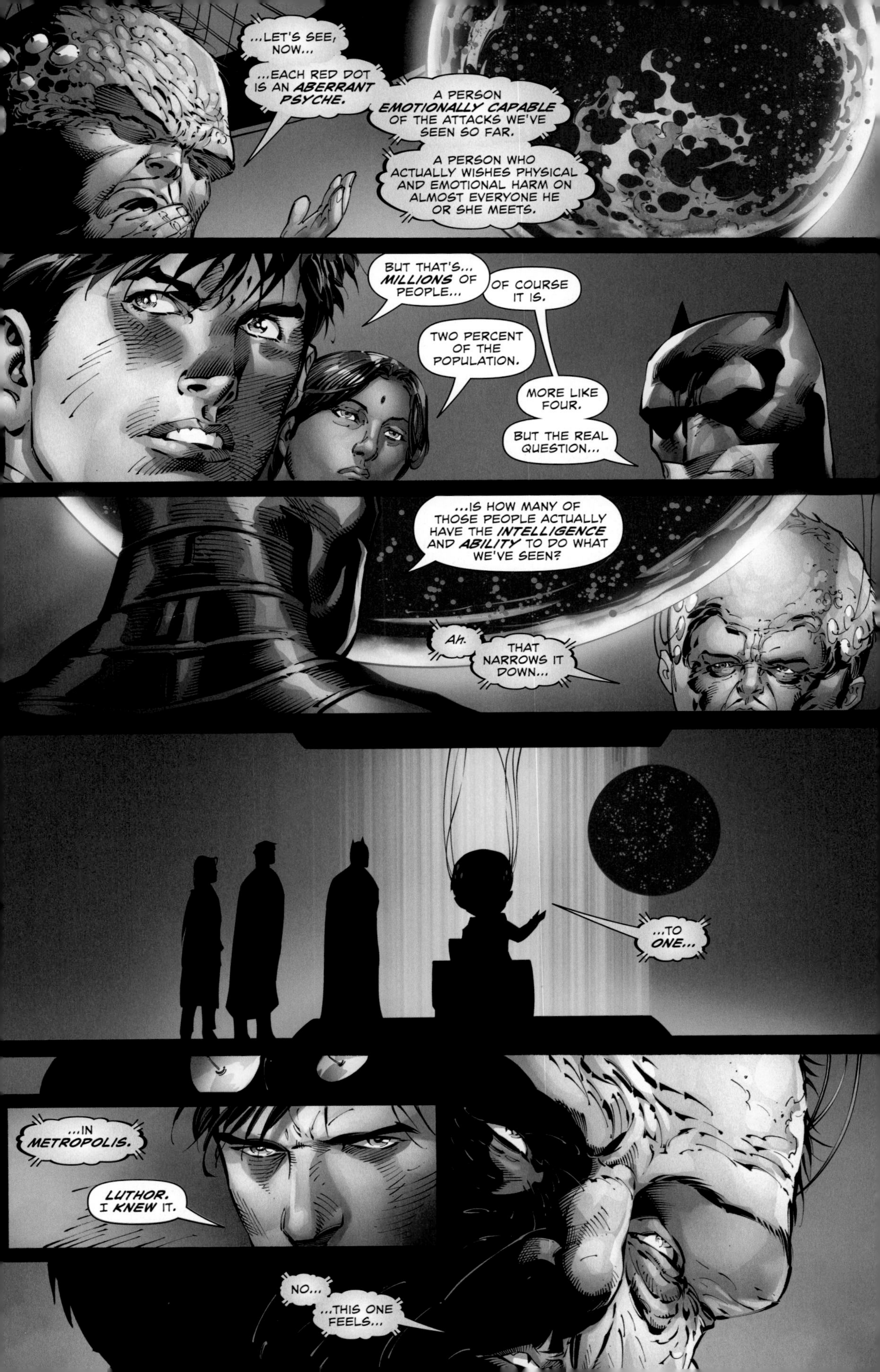
...LET'S SEE, NOW...
...EACH RED DOT IS AN ABERRANT PSYCHE.
A PERSON EMOTIONALLY CAPABLE OF THE ATTACKS WE'VE SEEN SO FAR.
A PERSON WHO ACTUALLY WISHES PHYSICAL AND EMOTIONAL HARM ON ALMOST EVERYONE HE OR SHE MEETS.
BUT THAT'S... MILLIONS OF PEOPLE...
OF COURSE IT IS.
TWO PERCENT OF THE POPULATION.
MORE LIKE FOUR.
BUT THE REAL QUESTION...
...IS HOW MANY OF THOSE PEOPLE ACTUALLY HAVE THE INTELLIGENCE AND ABILITY TO DO WHAT WE'VE SEEN?
Ah.
THAT NARROWS IT DOWN...
...TO ONE...
...IN METROPOLIS.
LUTHOR. I KNEW IT.
NO...
...THIS ONE FEELS...

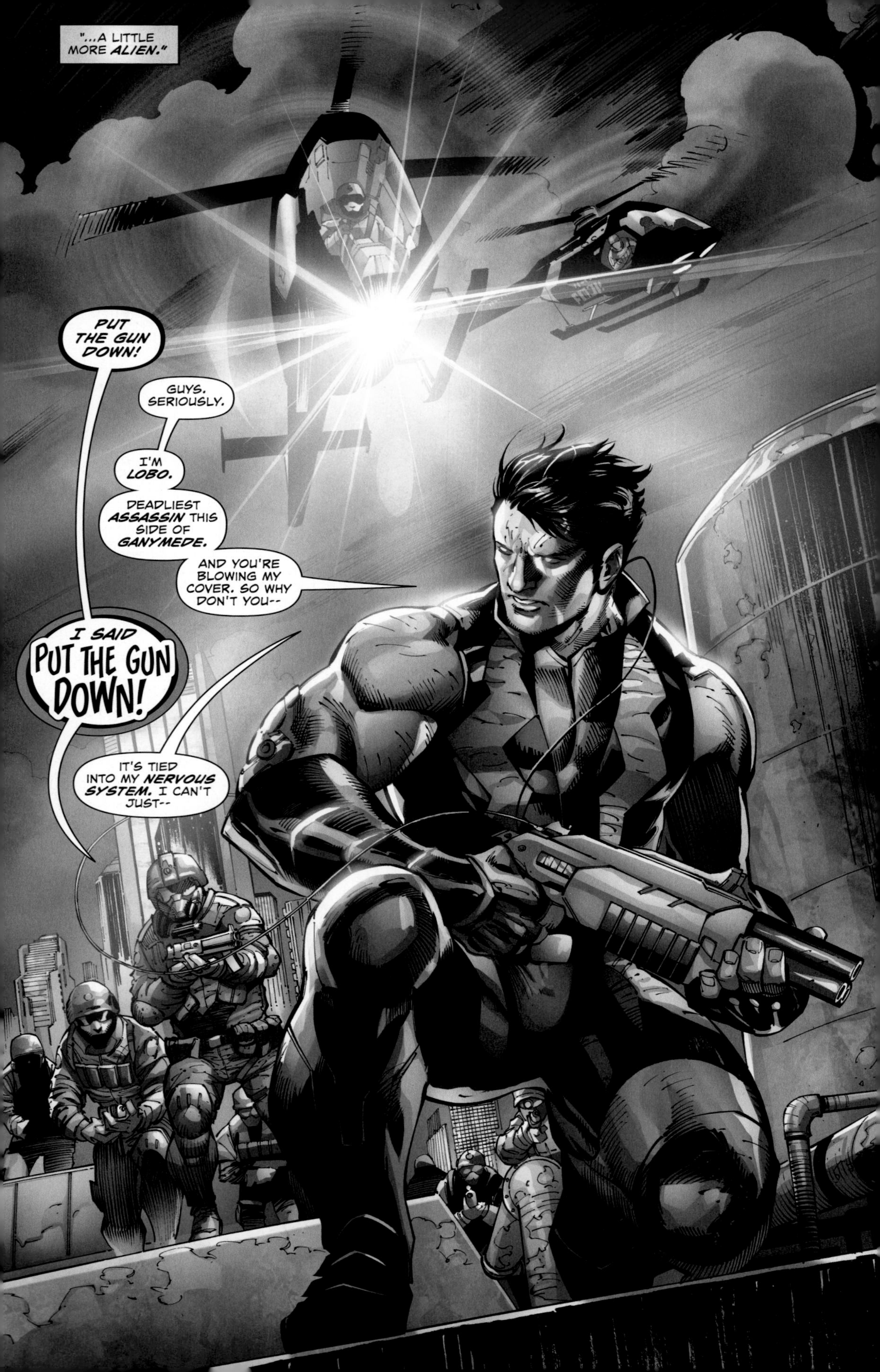
"...A LITTLE MORE ALIEN."
PUT THE GUN DOWN!
GUYS. SERIOUSLY.
I'M LOBO.
DEADLIEST ASSASSIN THIS SIDE OF GANYMEDE.
AND YOU'RE BLOWING MY COVER. SO WHY DON'T YOU--
I SAID PUT THE GUN DOWN!
IT'S TIED INTO MY NERVOUS SYSTEM. I CAN'T JUST--

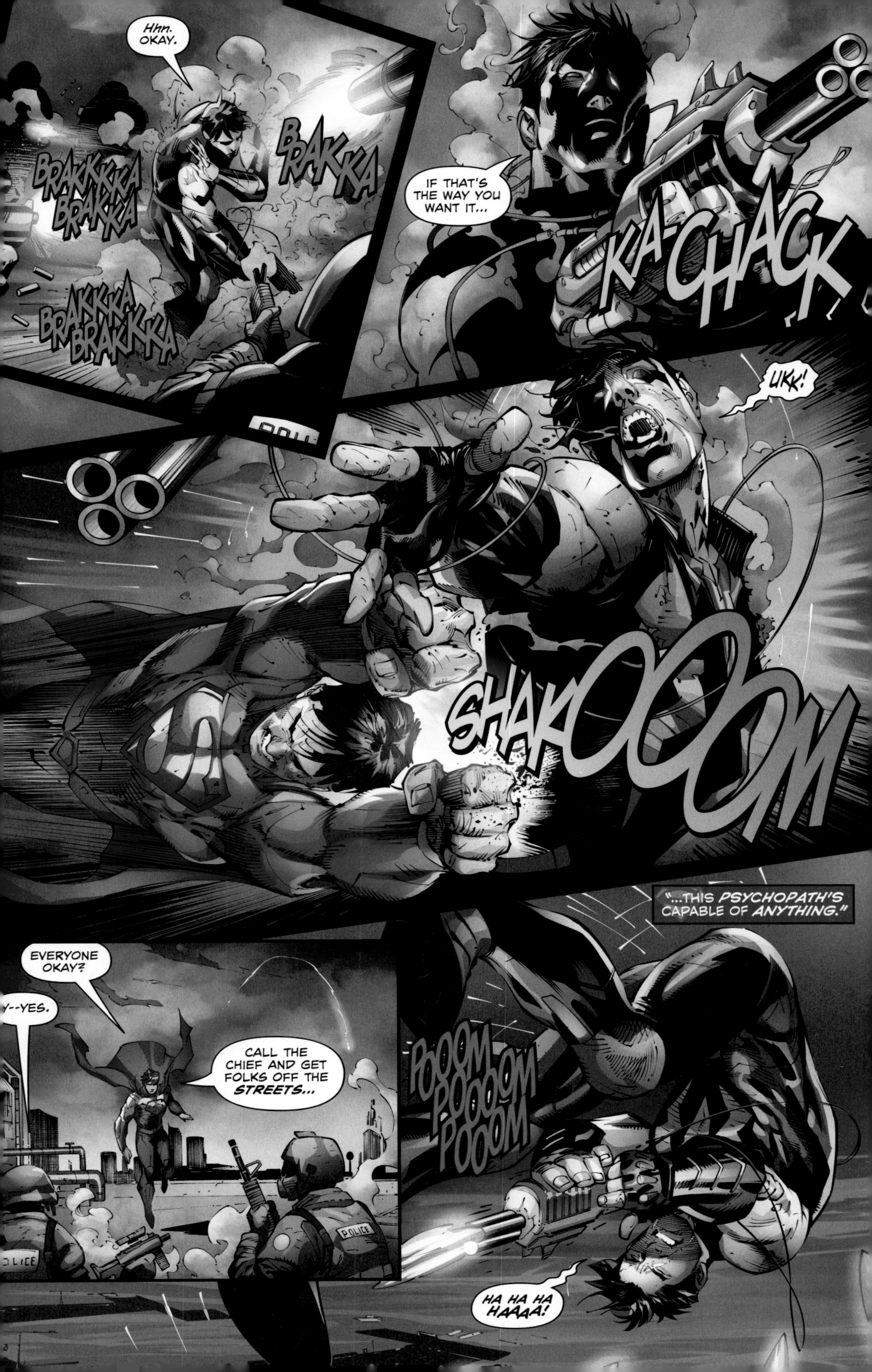

Hhn. OKAY.
BRAKKKA BRAKKA
BRAKKA
BRAKKKA BRAKKKA
IF THAT'S THE WAY YOU WANT IT...
KA-CHACK
UKK!
SHAKOOOOM
"...THIS PSYCHOPATH'S CAPABLE OF ANYTHING."
EVERYONE OKAY?
Y--YES.
CALL THE CHIEF AND GET FOLKS OFF THE STREETS...
POOOM POOOOM POOOM
HA HA HA HAAAA!

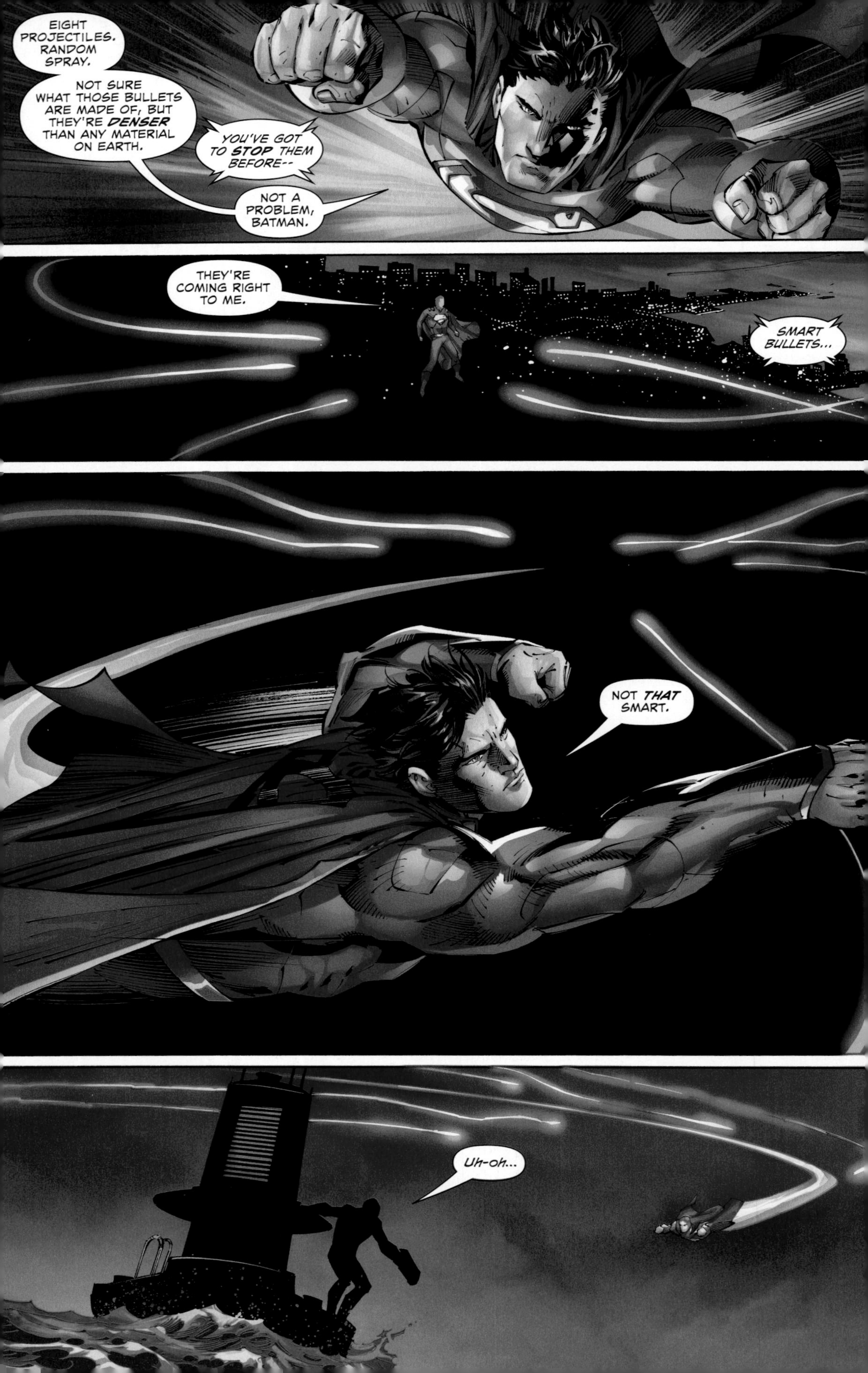
EIGHT PROJECTILES. RANDOM SPRAY.
NOT SURE WHAT THOSE BULLETS ARE MADE OF, BUT THEY'RE DENSER THAN ANY MATERIAL ON EARTH.
YOU'VE GOT TO STOP THEM BEFORE--
NOT A PROBLEM, BATMAN.
THEY'RE COMING RIGHT TO ME.
SMART BULLETS...
NOT THAT SMART.
Uh-oh...

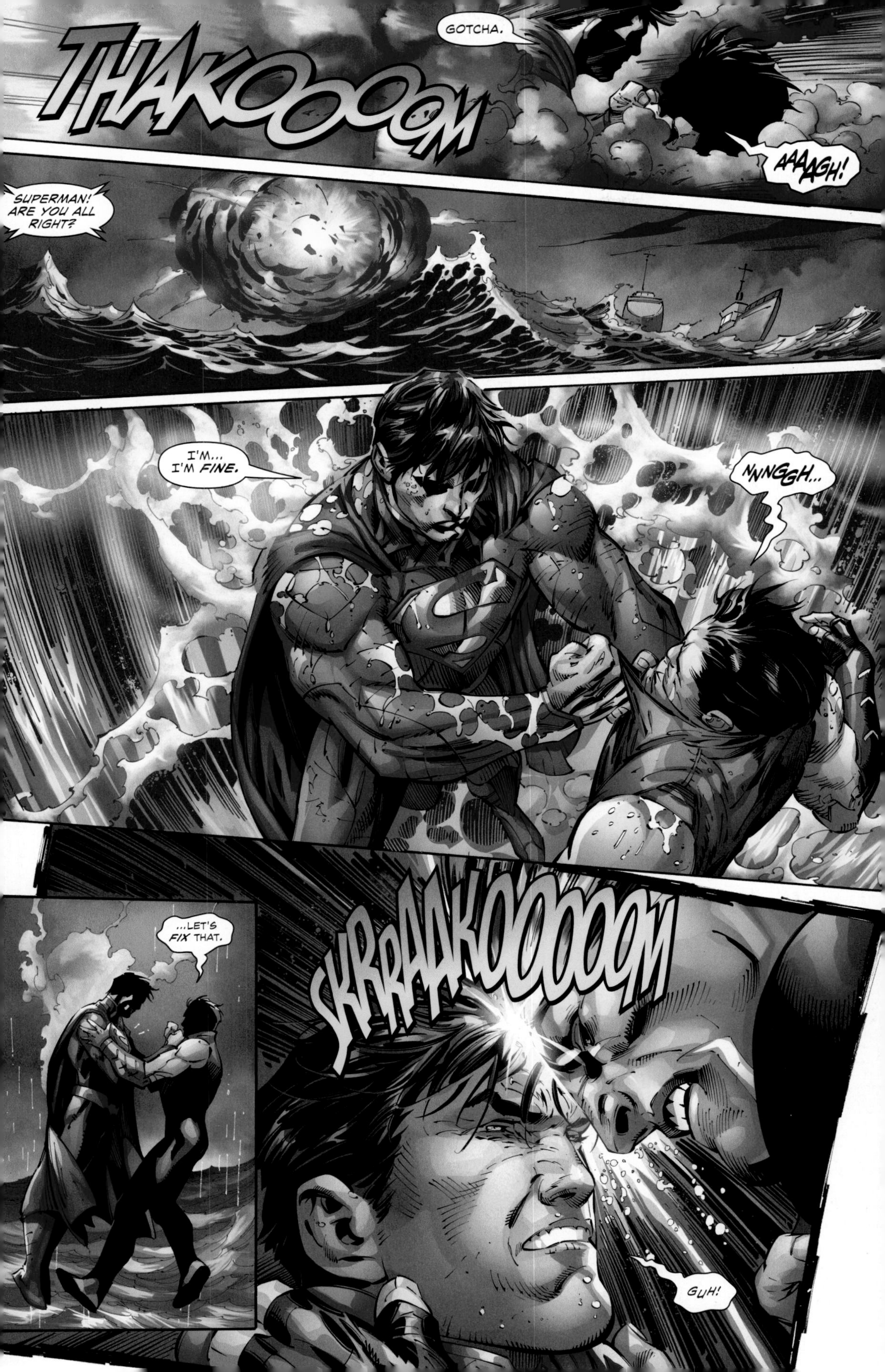
THAKOOOOM
GOTCHA.
AAAAGH!
SUPERMAN! ARE YOU ALL RIGHT?
I'M... I'M *FINE.*
NNNGGH...
...LET'S *FIX* THAT.
SKRAAKOOOOOM
GUH!

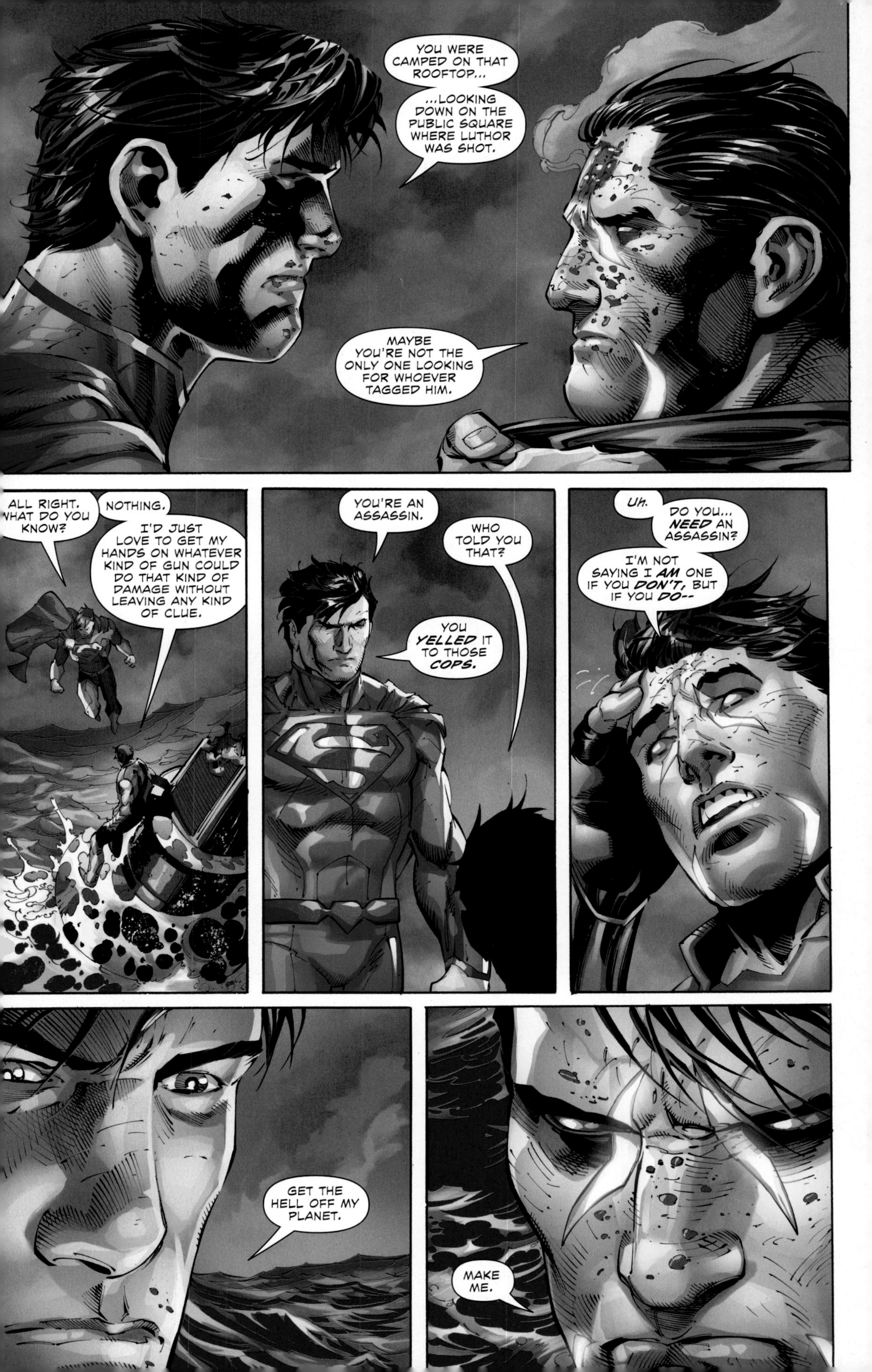
YOU WERE CAMPED ON THAT ROOFTOP...
...LOOKING DOWN ON THE PUBLIC SQUARE WHERE LUTHOR WAS SHOT.
MAYBE YOU'RE NOT THE ONLY ONE LOOKING FOR WHOEVER TAGGED HIM.
ALL RIGHT. WHAT DO YOU KNOW?
NOTHING.
I'D JUST LOVE TO GET MY HANDS ON WHATEVER KIND OF GUN COULD DO THAT KIND OF DAMAGE WITHOUT LEAVING ANY KIND OF CLUE.
YOU'RE AN ASSASSIN.
WHO TOLD YOU THAT?
YOU *YELLED* IT TO THOSE *COPS.*
Uh.
DO YOU... *NEED* AN ASSASSIN?
I'M NOT SAYING I *AM* ONE IF YOU *DON'T,* BUT IF YOU *DO--*
GET THE HELL OFF MY PLANET.
MAKE ME.

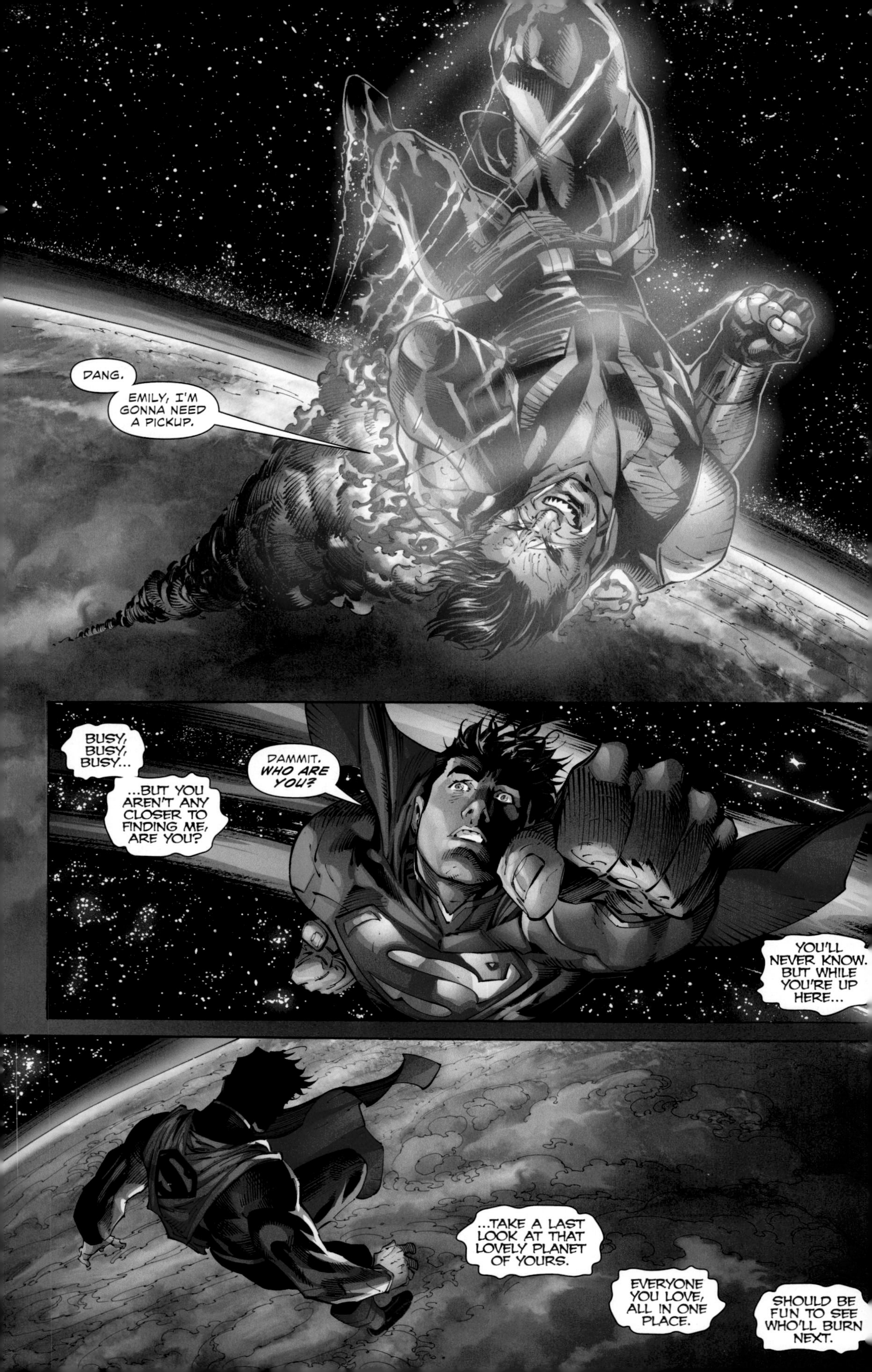
DANG.
EMILY, I'M GONNA NEED A PICKUP.
BUSY, BUSY, BUSY...
...BUT YOU AREN'T ANY CLOSER TO FINDING ME, ARE YOU?
DAMMIT. *WHO ARE YOU?*
YOU'LL NEVER KNOW. BUT WHILE YOU'RE UP HERE...
...TAKE A LAST LOOK AT THAT LOVELY PLANET OF YOURS.
EVERYONE YOU LOVE, ALL IN ONE PLACE.
SHOULD BE FUN TO SEE WHO'LL BURN NEXT.

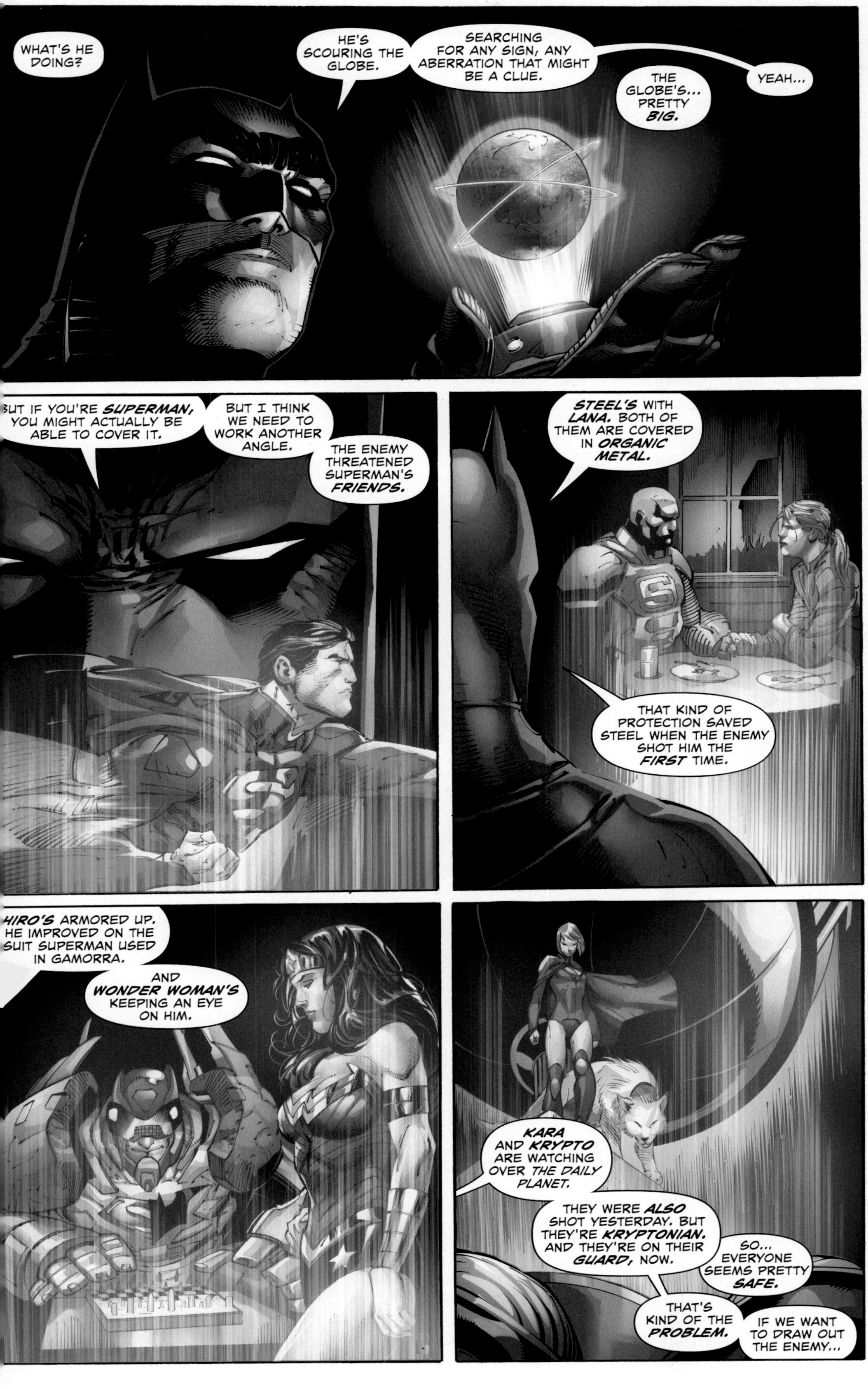

WHAT'S HE DOING?
HE'S SCOURING THE GLOBE.
SEARCHING FOR ANY SIGN, ANY ABERRATION THAT MIGHT BE A CLUE.
THE GLOBE'S... PRETTY BIG.
YEAH...
BUT IF YOU'RE SUPERMAN, YOU MIGHT ACTUALLY BE ABLE TO COVER IT.
BUT I THINK WE NEED TO WORK ANOTHER ANGLE.
THE ENEMY THREATENED SUPERMAN'S FRIENDS.
STEEL'S WITH LANA. BOTH OF THEM ARE COVERED IN ORGANIC METAL.
THAT KIND OF PROTECTION SAVED STEEL WHEN THE ENEMY SHOT HIM THE FIRST TIME.
HIRO'S ARMORED UP. HE IMPROVED ON THE SUIT SUPERMAN USED IN GAMORRA.
AND WONDER WOMAN'S KEEPING AN EYE ON HIM.
KARA AND KRYPTO ARE WATCHING OVER THE DAILY PLANET.
THEY WERE ALSO SHOT YESTERDAY. BUT THEY'RE KRYPTONIAN. AND THEY'RE ON THEIR GUARD, NOW.
SO... EVERYONE SEEMS PRETTY SAFE.
THAT'S KIND OF THE PROBLEM.
IF WE WANT TO DRAW OUT THE ENEMY...

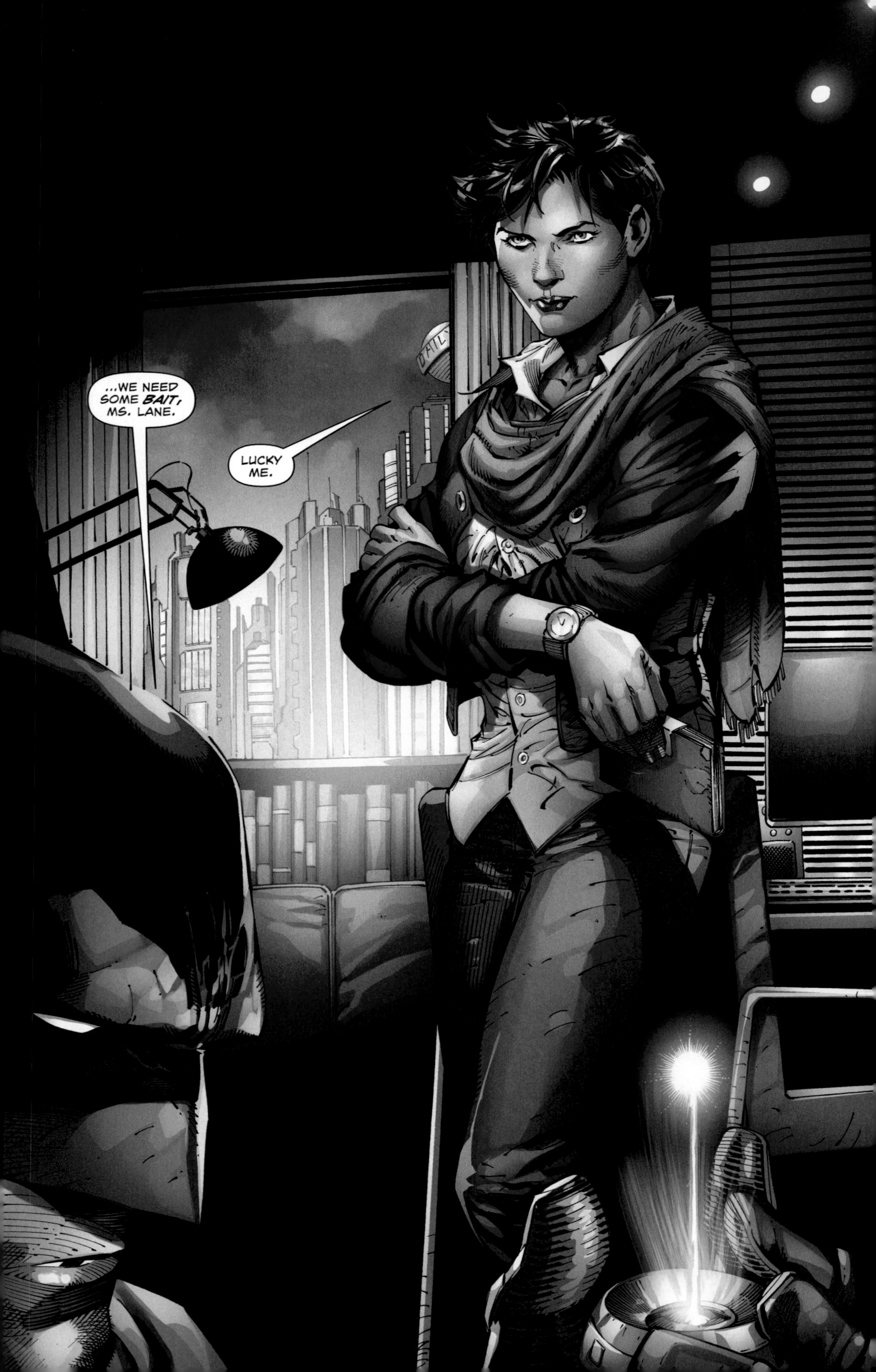
...WE NEED SOME BAIT, MS. LANE.
LUCKY ME.

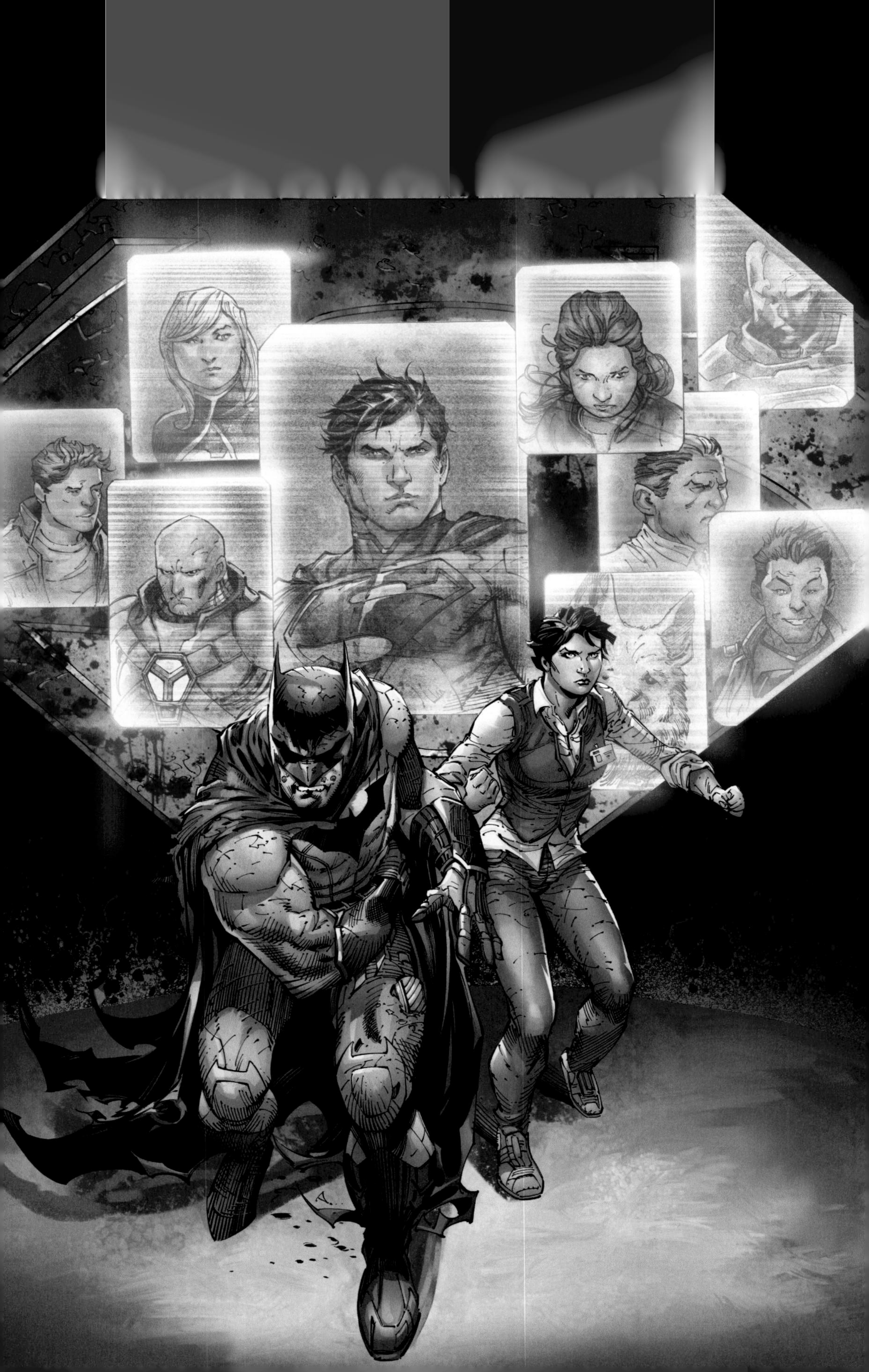

GREG PAK writer ARDIAN SYAF penciller JONATHAN GLAPION, SANDRA HOPE ARCHER, JAIME MENDOZA inkers ULISES ARREOLA colorist ROB LEIGH letterer
cover by ARDIAN SYAF, JONATHAN GLAPION and ULISES ARREOLA

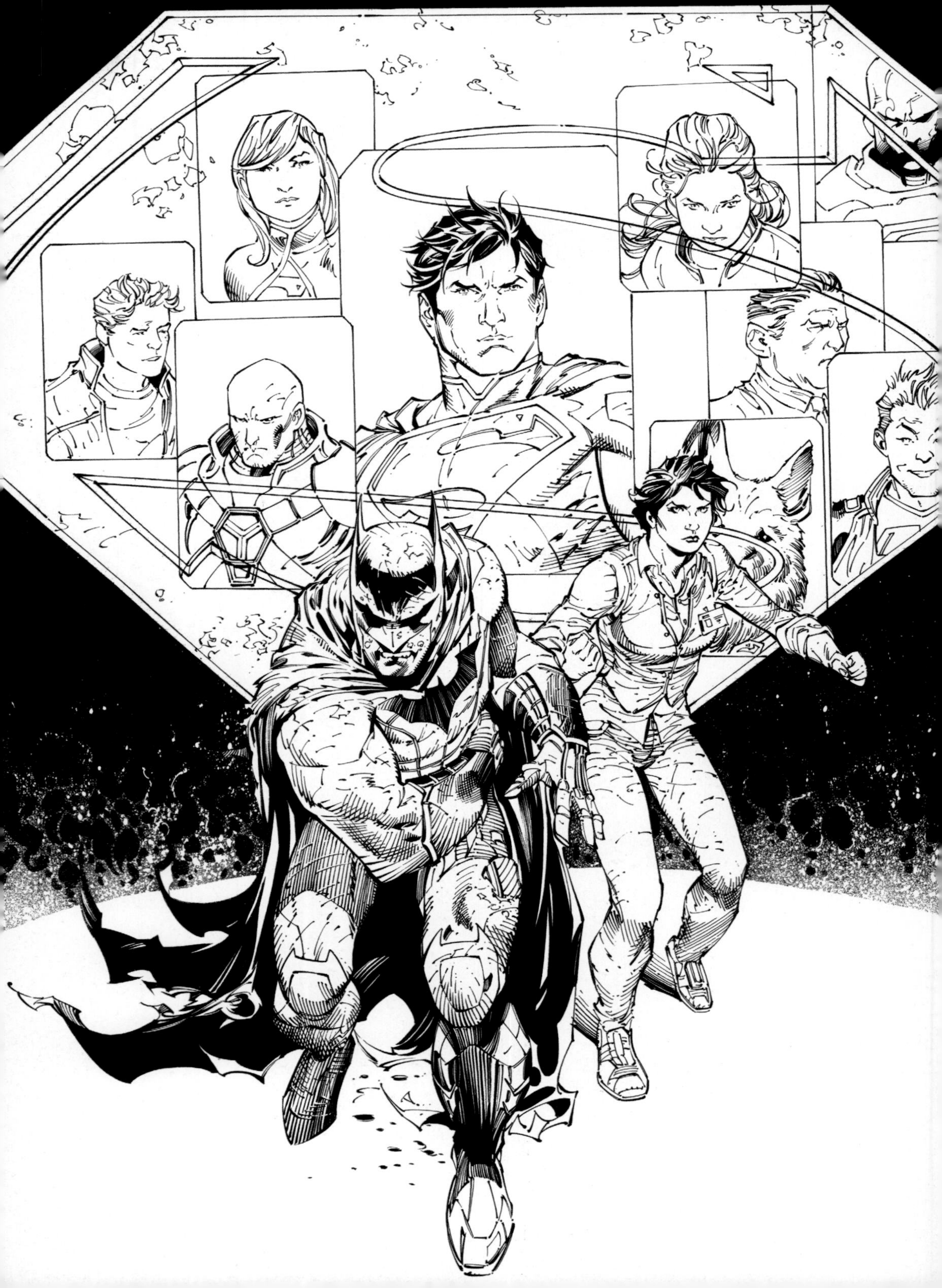

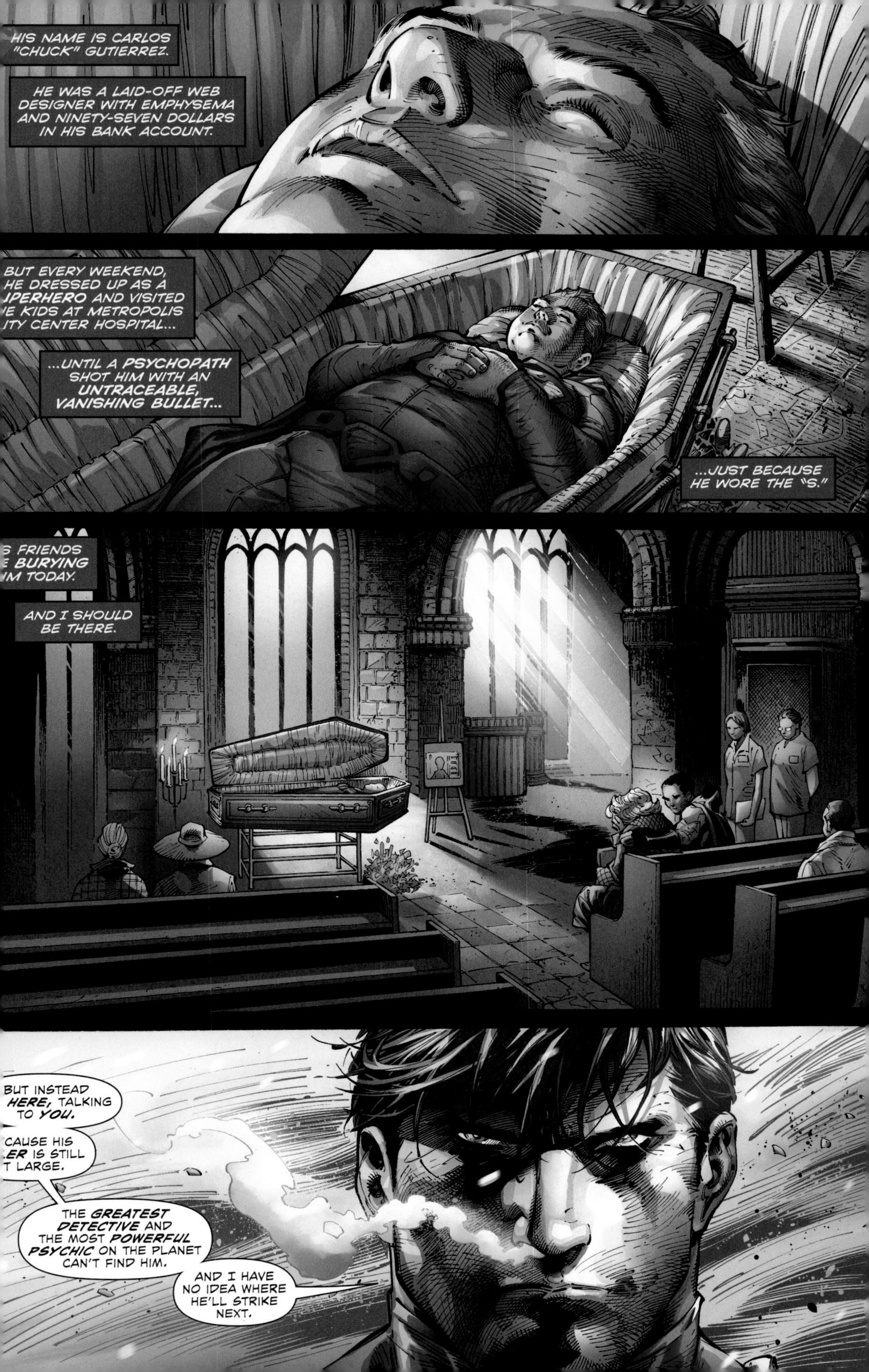
HIS NAME IS CARLOS "CHUCK" GUTIERREZ.
HE WAS A LAID-OFF WEB DESIGNER WITH EMPHYSEMA AND NINETY-SEVEN DOLLARS IN HIS BANK ACCOUNT.
BUT EVERY WEEKEND, HE DRESSED UP AS A UPERHERO AND VISITED E KIDS AT METROPOLIS ITY CENTER HOSPITAL...
...UNTIL A PSYCHOPATH SHOT HIM WITH AN UNTRACEABLE, VANISHING BULLET...
...JUST BECAUSE HE WORE THE "S."
S FRIENDS E BURYING IM TODAY.
AND I SHOULD BE THERE.
BUT INSTEAD HERE, TALKING TO YOU.
CAUSE HIS ER IS STILL T LARGE.
THE GREATEST DETECTIVE AND THE MOST POWERFUL PSYCHIC ON THE PLANET CAN'T FIND HIM.
AND I HAVE NO IDEA WHERE HE'LL STRIKE NEXT.

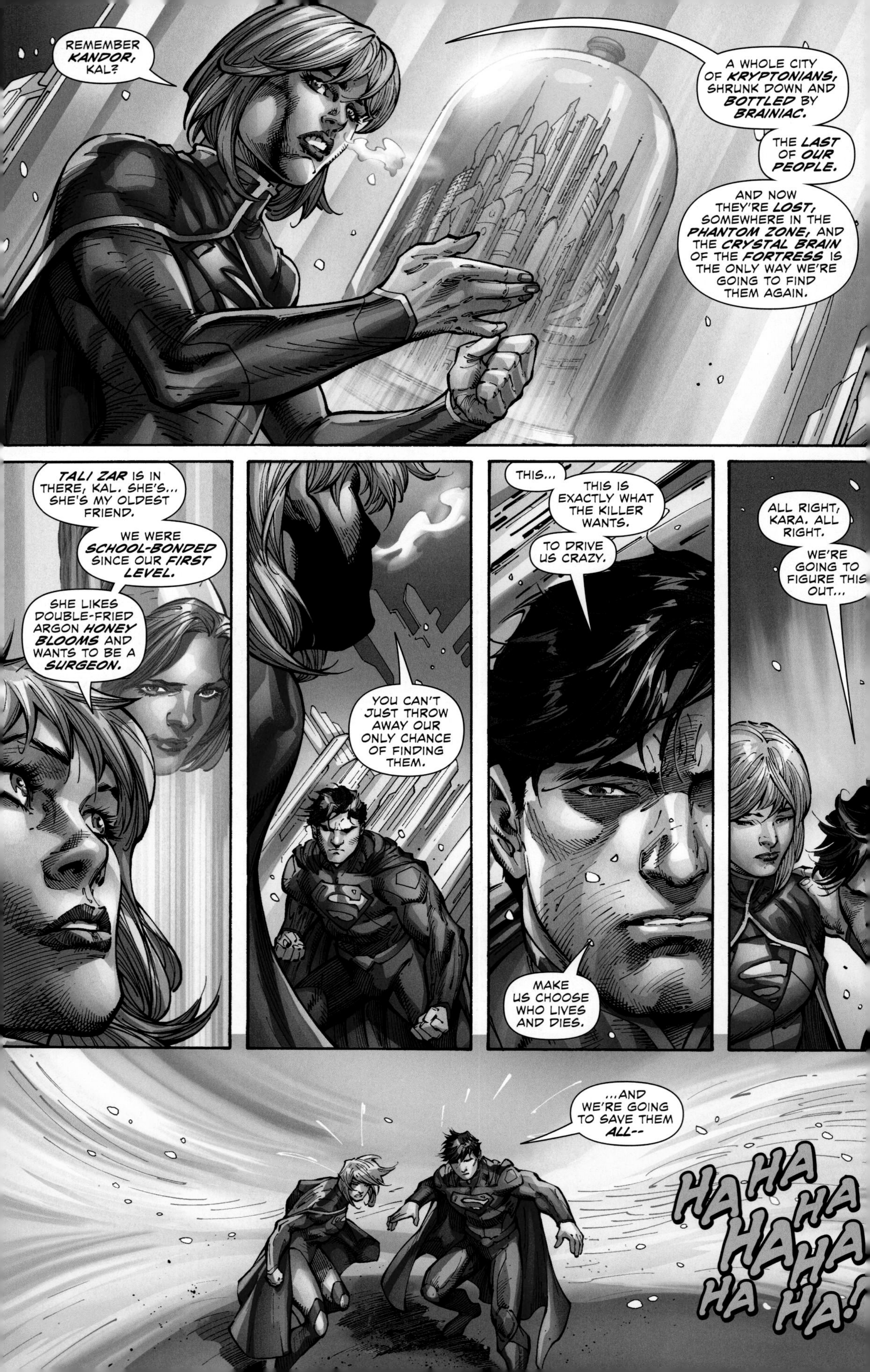
REMEMBER KANDOR, KAL?
A WHOLE CITY OF KRYPTONIANS, SHRUNK DOWN AND BOTTLED BY BRAINIAC.
THE LAST OF OUR PEOPLE.
AND NOW THEY'RE LOST, SOMEWHERE IN THE PHANTOM ZONE, AND THE CRYSTAL BRAIN OF THE FORTRESS IS THE ONLY WAY WE'RE GOING TO FIND THEM AGAIN.
TALI ZAR IS IN THERE, KAL. SHE'S... SHE'S MY OLDEST FRIEND.
WE WERE SCHOOL-BONDED SINCE OUR FIRST LEVEL.
SHE LIKES DOUBLE-FRIED ARGON HONEY BLOOMS AND WANTS TO BE A SURGEON.
YOU CAN'T JUST THROW AWAY OUR ONLY CHANCE OF FINDING THEM.
THIS...
THIS IS EXACTLY WHAT THE KILLER WANTS.
TO DRIVE US CRAZY.
MAKE US CHOOSE WHO LIVES AND DIES.
ALL RIGHT, KARA. ALL RIGHT.
WE'RE GOING TO FIGURE THIS OUT...
...AND WE'RE GOING TO SAVE THEM ALL--
HA HA HA HA HA HA HA HA HA HA HA!

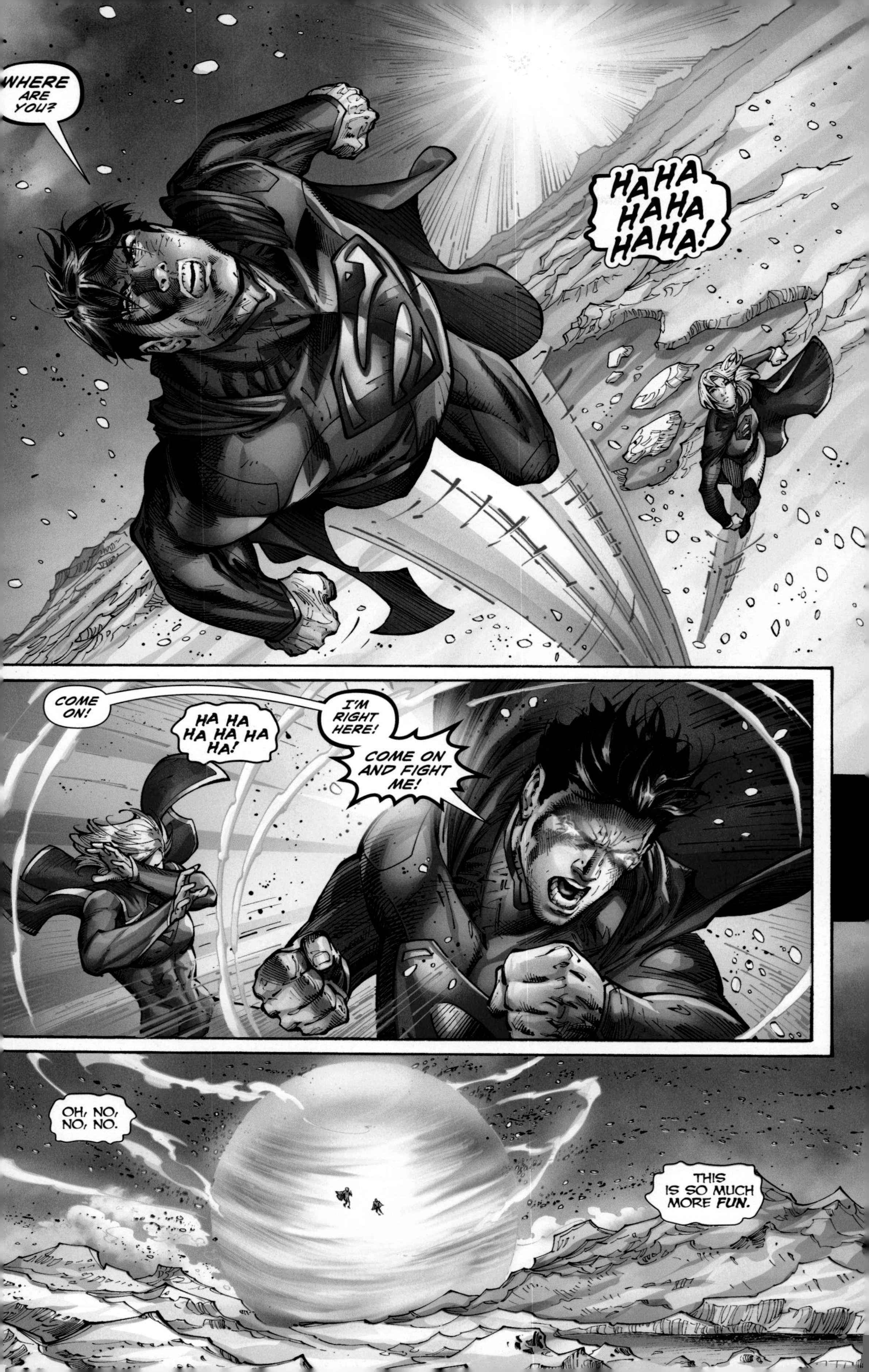
WHERE ARE YOU?
HAHA HAHA HAHA!
COME ON!
HA HA HA HA HA HA!
I'M RIGHT HERE!
COME ON AND FIGHT ME!
OH, NO, NO, NO.
THIS IS SO MUCH MORE FUN.

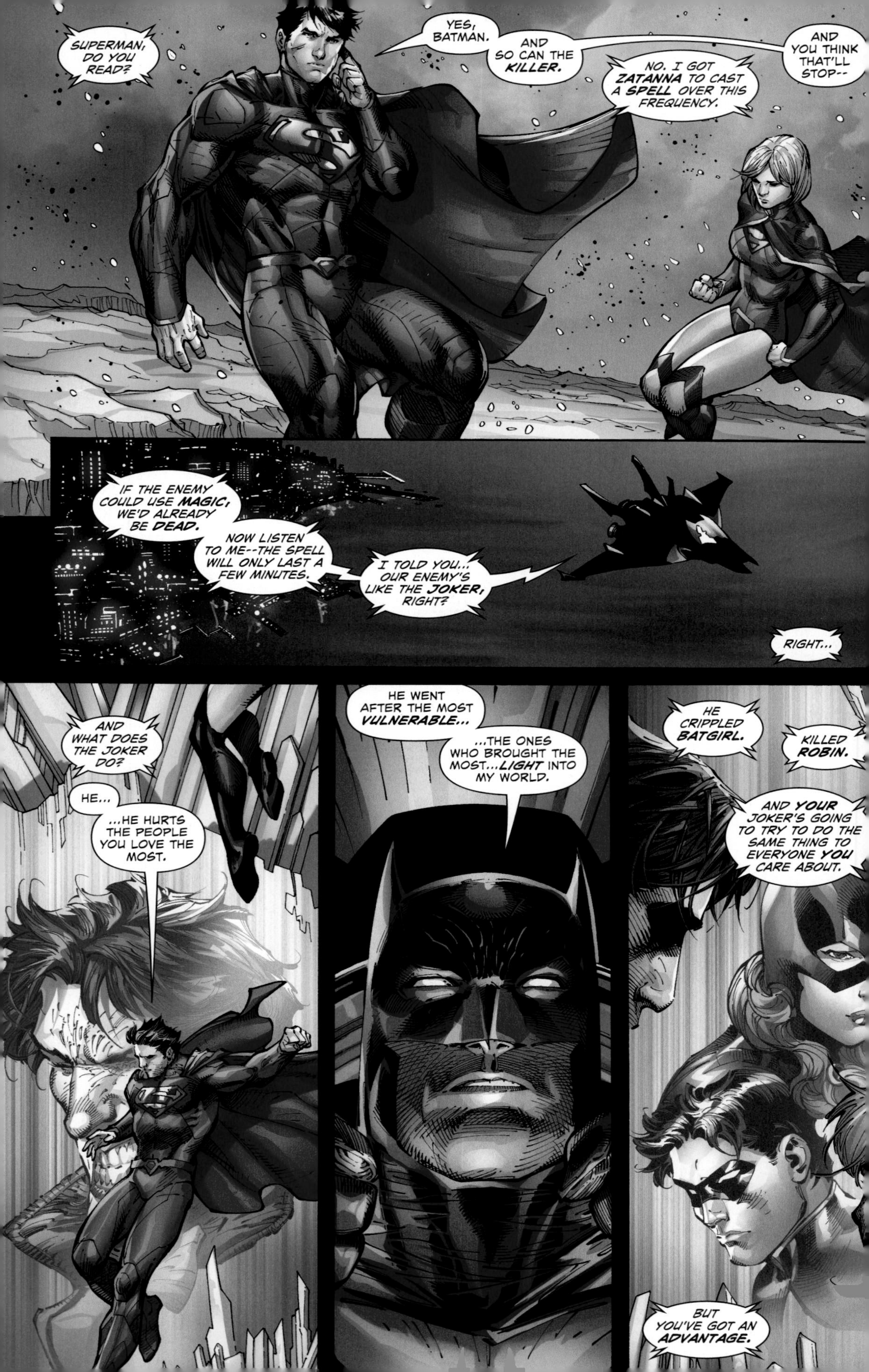
SUPERMAN, DO YOU READ?
YES, BATMAN.
AND SO CAN THE KILLER.
NO. I GOT ZATANNA TO CAST A SPELL OVER THIS FREQUENCY.
AND YOU THINK THAT'LL STOP--
IF THE ENEMY COULD USE MAGIC, WE'D ALREADY BE DEAD.
NOW LISTEN TO ME--THE SPELL WILL ONLY LAST A FEW MINUTES.
I TOLD YOU... OUR ENEMY'S LIKE THE JOKER, RIGHT?
RIGHT...
AND WHAT DOES THE JOKER DO?
HE...
...HE HURTS THE PEOPLE YOU LOVE THE MOST.
HE WENT AFTER THE MOST VULNERABLE...
...THE ONES WHO BROUGHT THE MOST...LIGHT INTO MY WORLD.
HE CRIPPLED BATGIRL.
KILLED ROBIN.
AND YOUR JOKER'S GOING TO TRY TO DO THE SAME THING TO EVERYONE YOU CARE ABOUT.
BUT YOU'VE GOT AN ADVANTAGE.

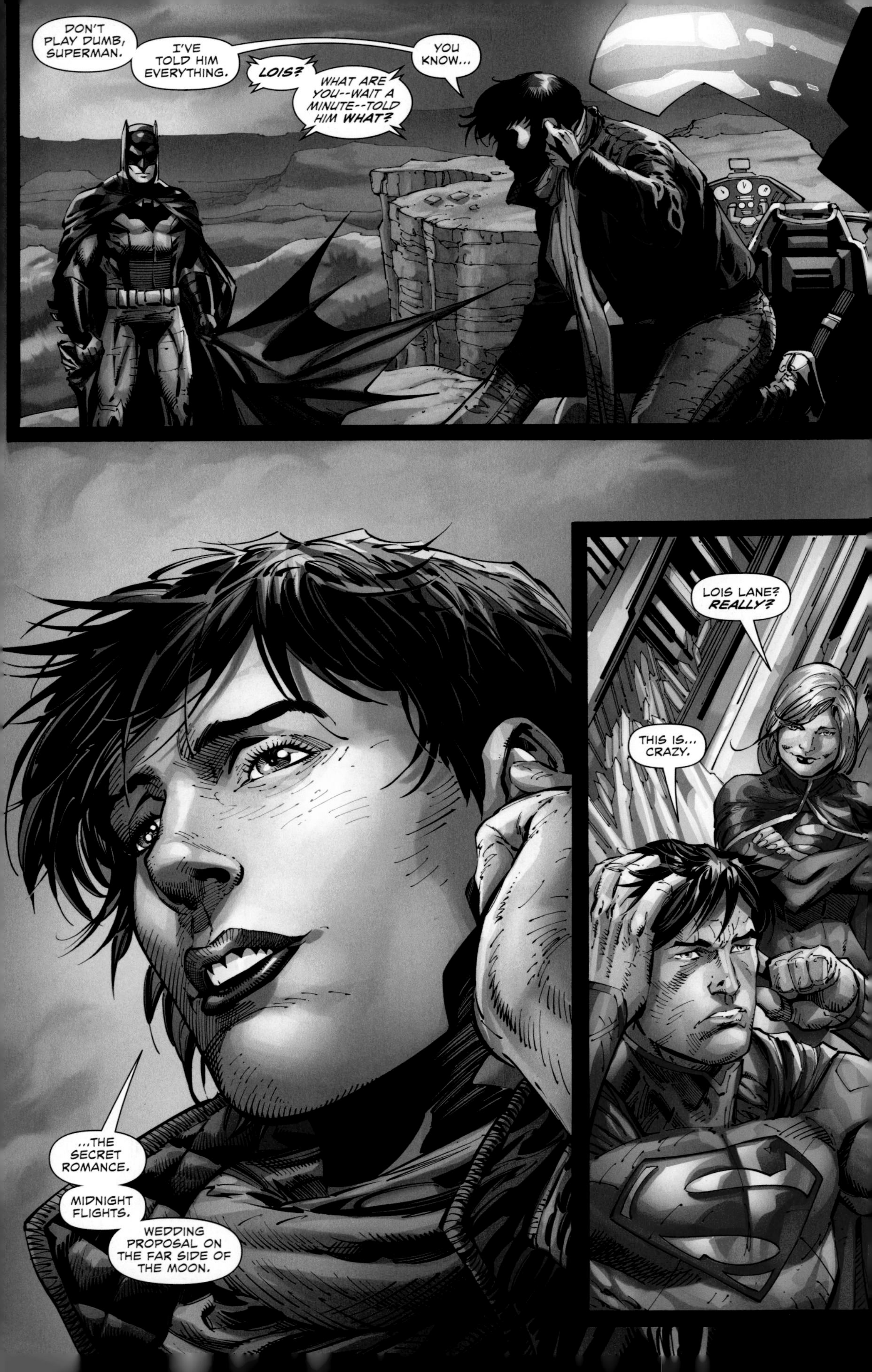
DON'T PLAY DUMB, SUPERMAN.
I'VE TOLD HIM EVERYTHING.
YOU KNOW...
LOIS?
WHAT ARE YOU--WAIT A MINUTE--TOLD HIM WHAT?
...THE SECRET ROMANCE.
MIDNIGHT FLIGHTS.
WEDDING PROPOSAL ON THE FAR SIDE OF THE MOON.
LOIS LANE? REALLY?
THIS IS... CRAZY.

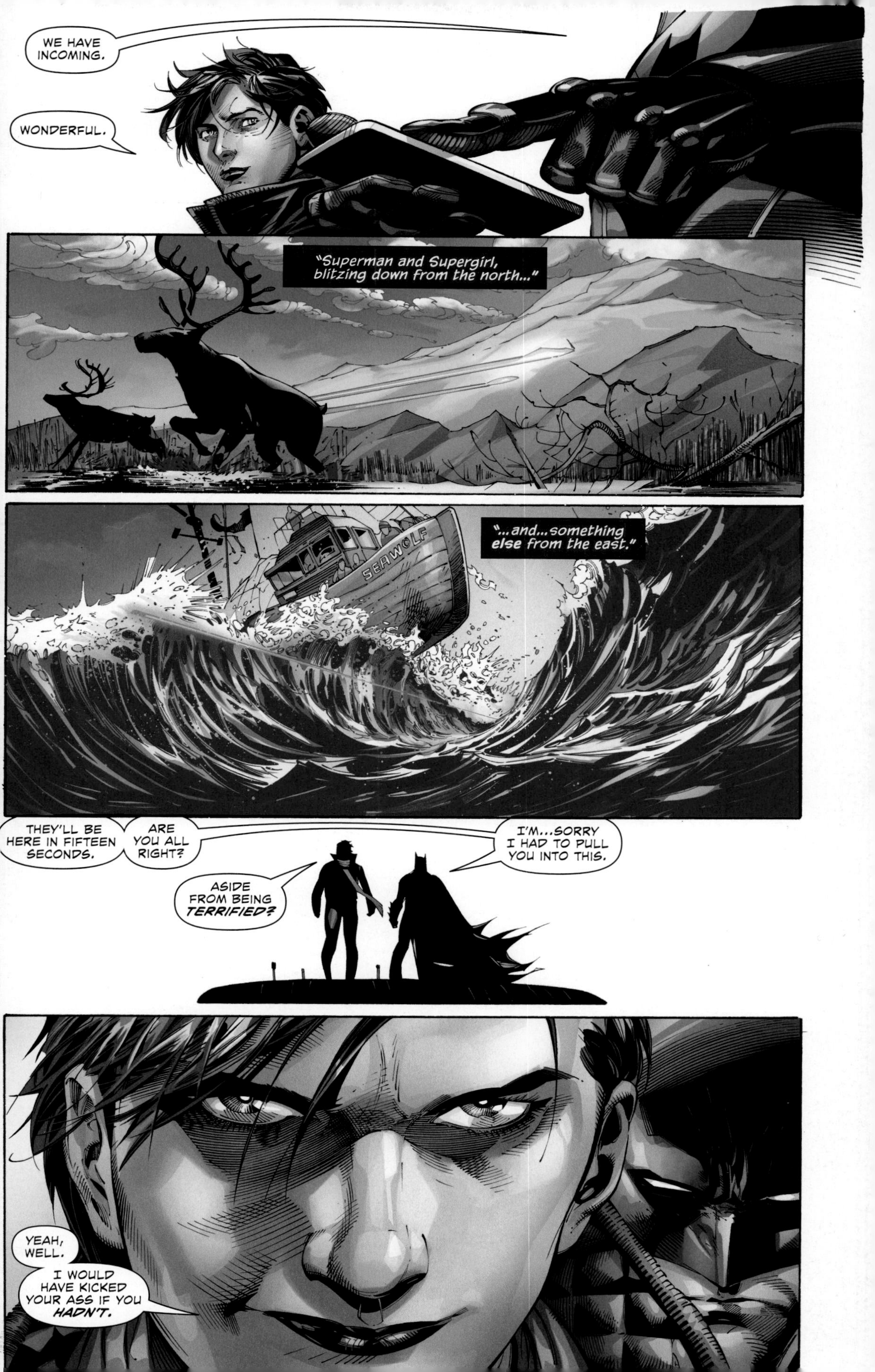
WE HAVE INCOMING.
WONDERFUL.
"Superman and Supergirl, blitzing down from the north..."
SEAWOLF
"...and...something else from the east."
THEY'LL BE HERE IN FIFTEEN SECONDS.
ARE YOU ALL RIGHT?
ASIDE FROM BEING TERRIFIED?
I'M...SORRY I HAD TO PULL YOU INTO THIS.
YEAH, WELL.
I WOULD HAVE KICKED YOUR ASS IF YOU HADN'T.

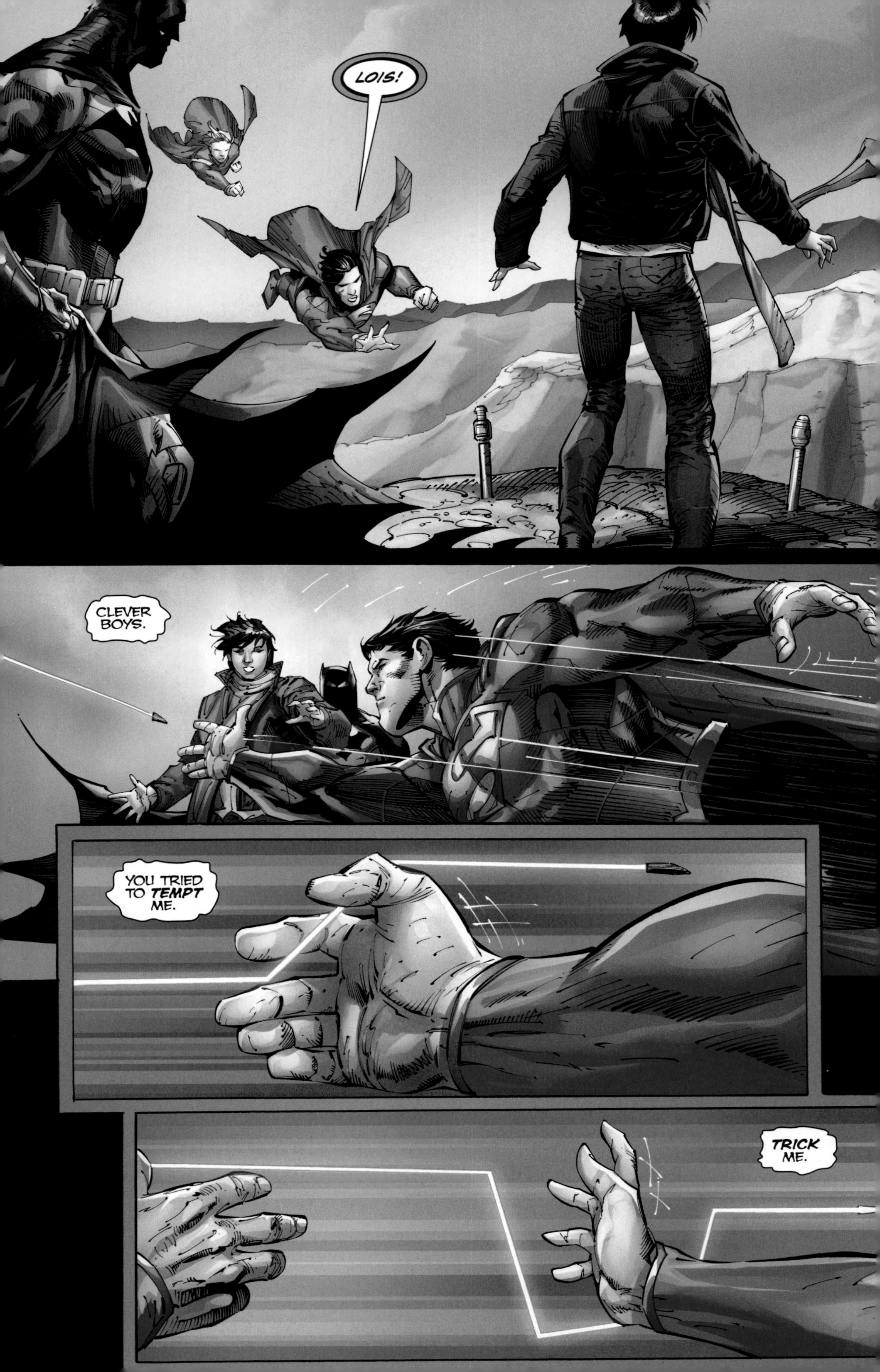
LOIS!
CLEVER BOYS.
YOU TRIED TO TEMPT ME.
TRICK ME.

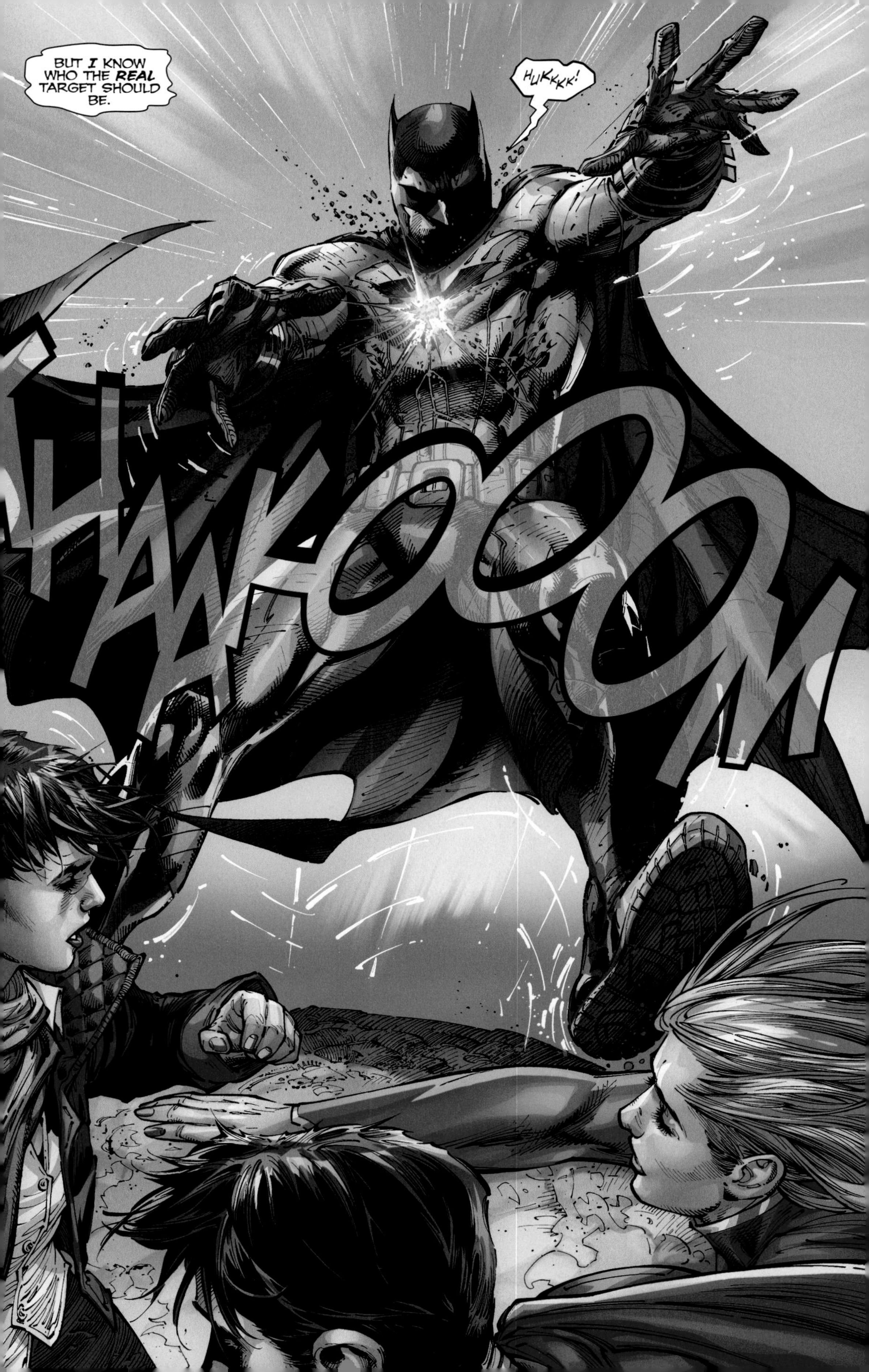
BUT *I* KNOW WHO THE *REAL* TARGET SHOULD BE.
HUKKKK!
KAWOOOM

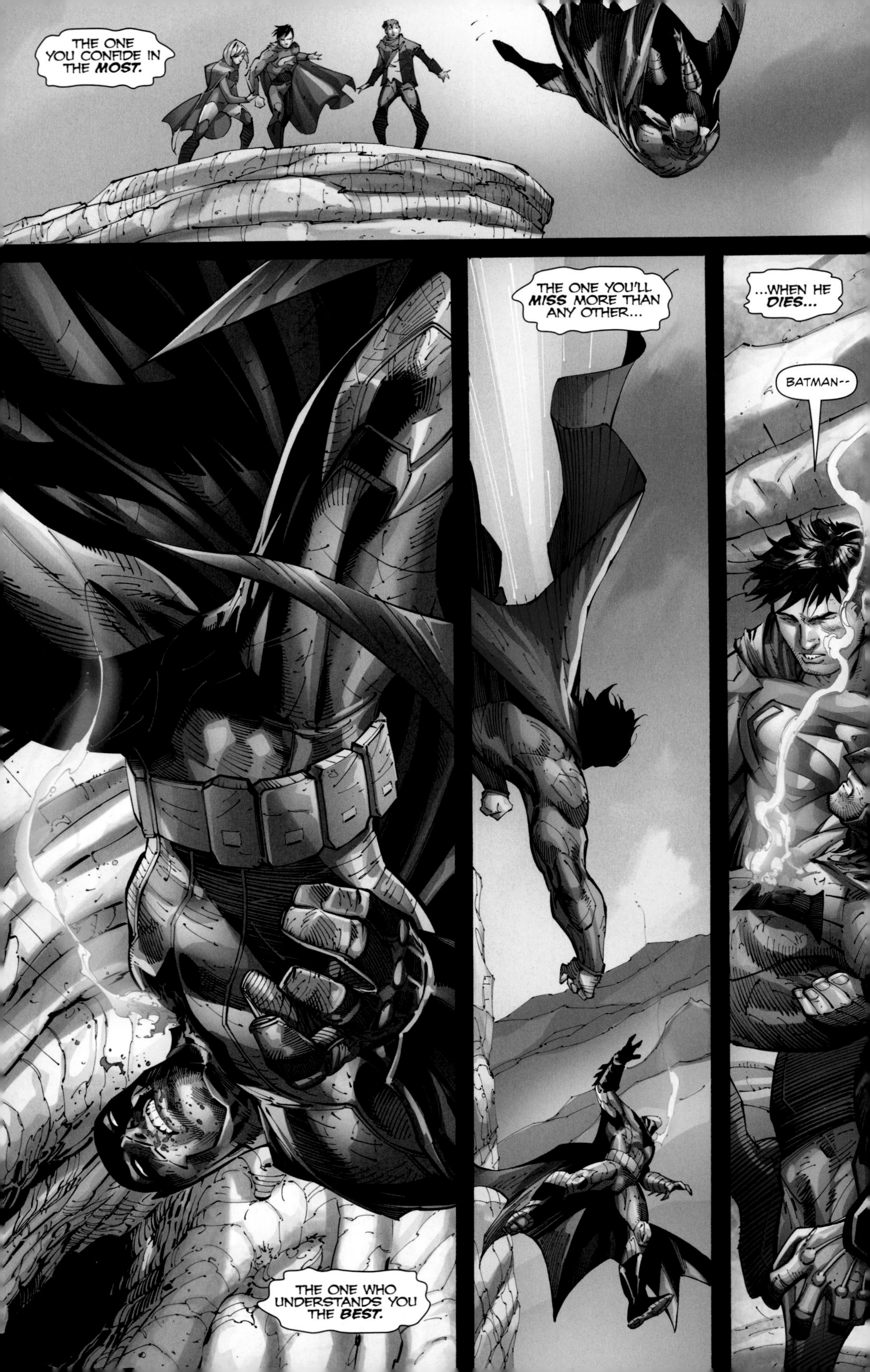
THE ONE YOU CONFIDE IN THE MOST.
THE ONE WHO UNDERSTANDS YOU THE BEST.
THE ONE YOU'LL MISS MORE THAN ANY OTHER...
...WHEN HE DIES...
BATMAN--

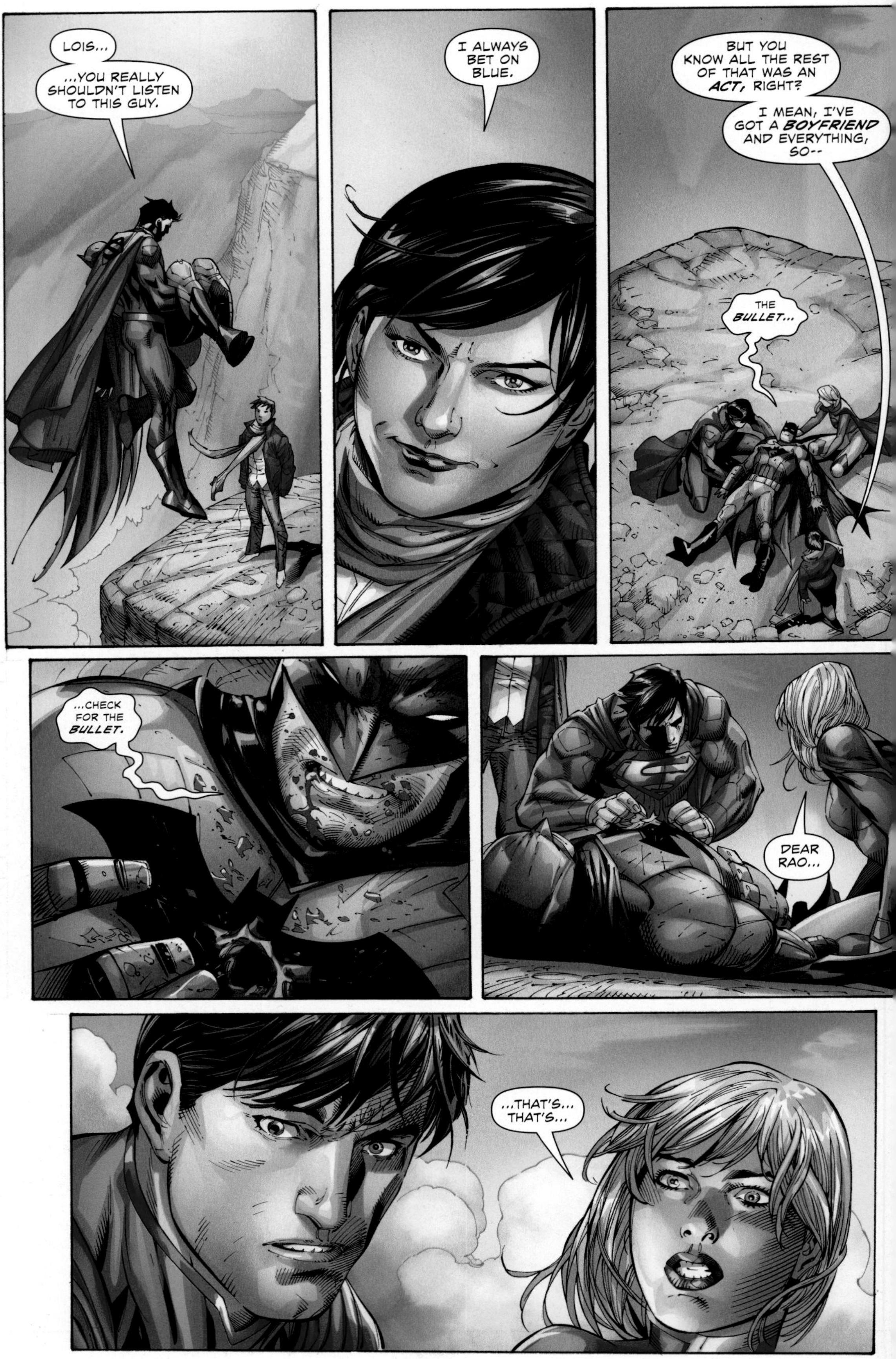
LOIS...
...YOU REALLY SHOULDN'T LISTEN TO THIS GUY.
I ALWAYS BET ON BLUE.
BUT YOU KNOW ALL THE REST OF THAT WAS AN ACT, RIGHT?
I MEAN, I'VE GOT A BOYFRIEND AND EVERYTHING, SO--
THE BULLET...
...CHECK FOR THE BULLET.
DEAR RAO...
...THAT'S... THAT'S...

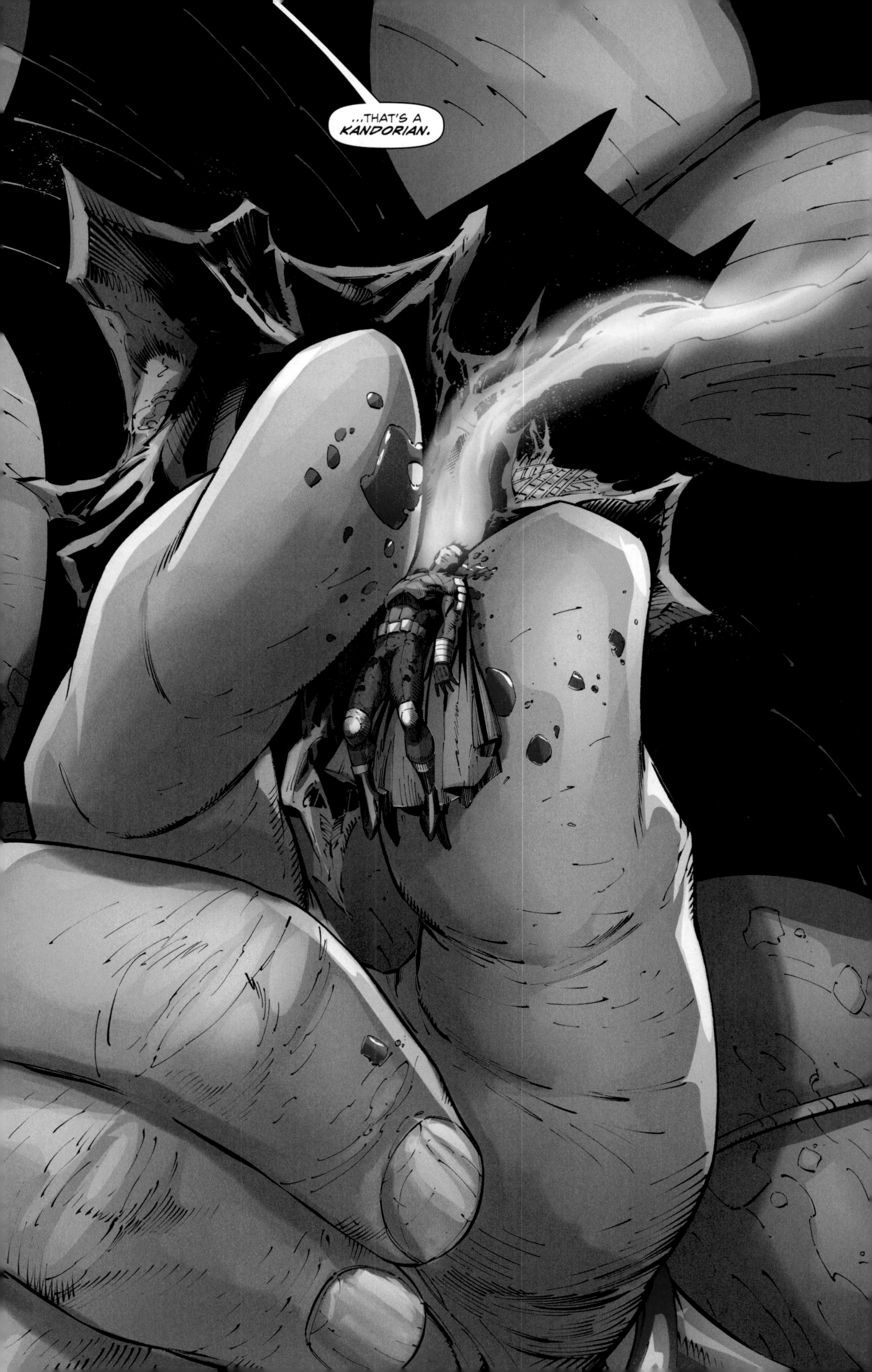
...THAT'S A KANDORIAN.

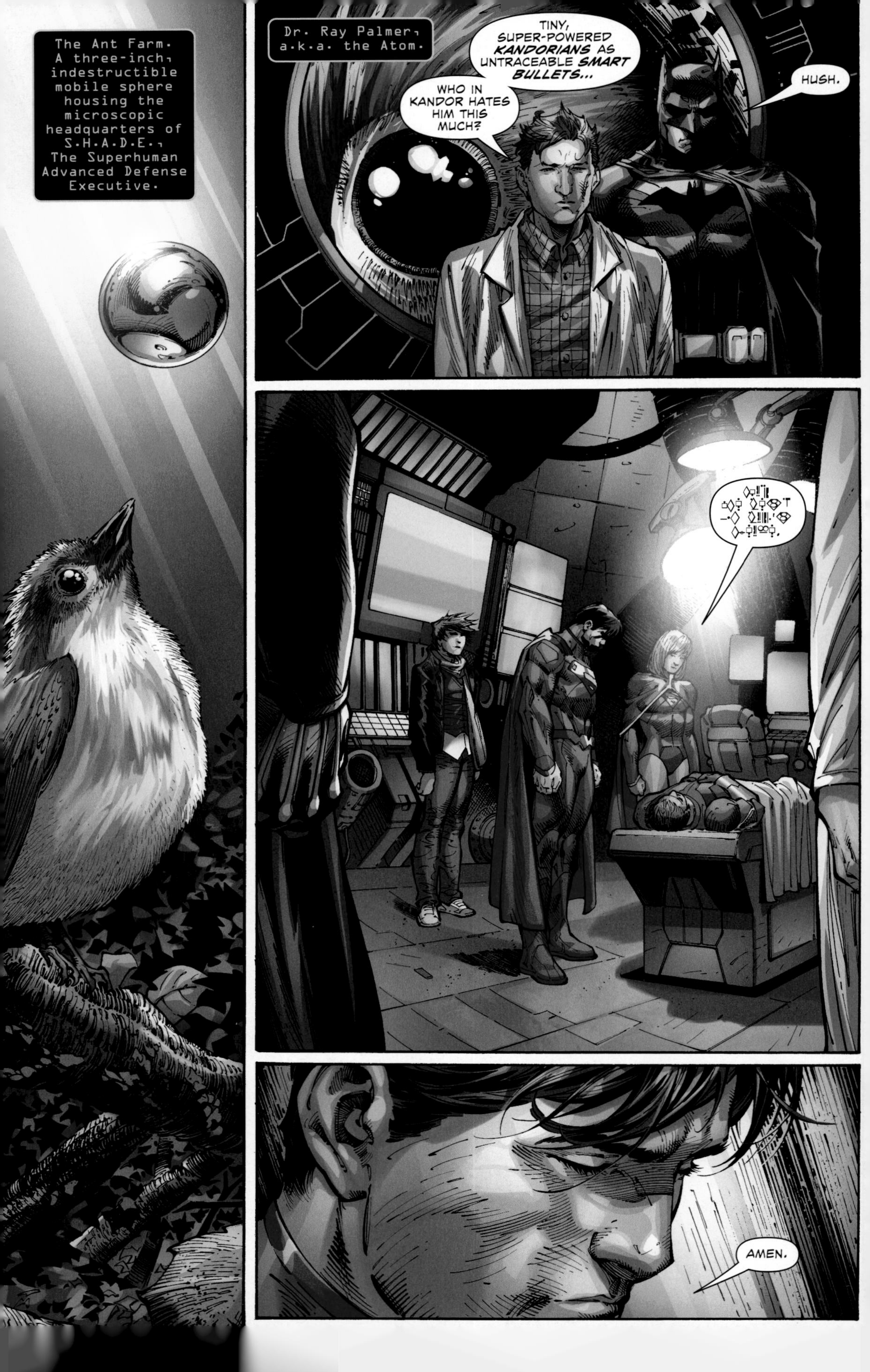

The Ant Farm. A three-inch, indestructible mobile sphere housing the microscopic headquarters of S.H.A.D.E., The Superhuman Advanced Defense Executive.
Dr. Ray Palmer, a.k.a. the Atom.
TINY, SUPER-POWERED KANDORIANS AS UNTRACEABLE SMART BULLETS...
WHO IN KANDOR HATES HIM THIS MUCH?
HUSH.
AMEN.

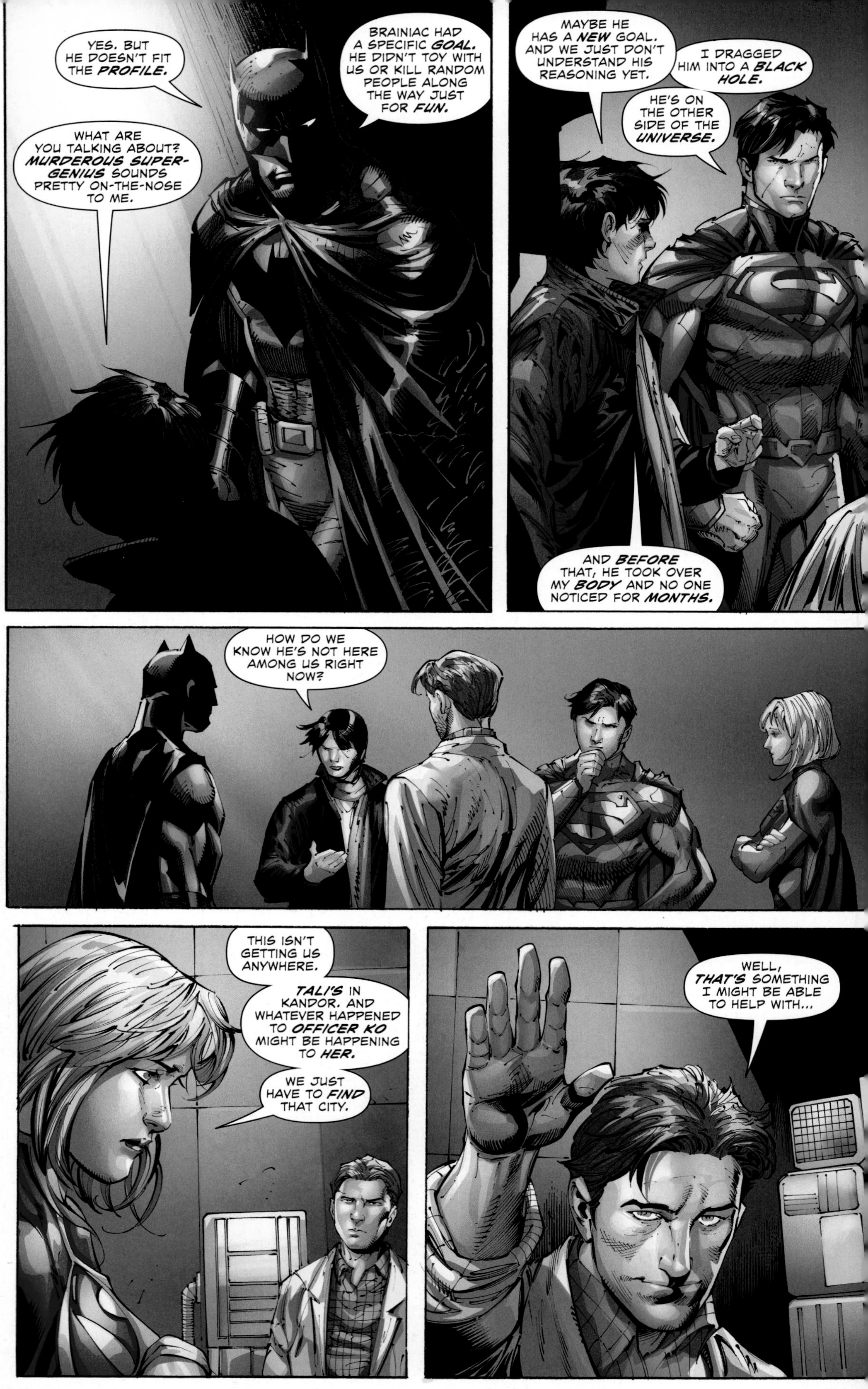
YES. BUT HE DOESN'T FIT THE PROFILE.
BRAINIAC HAD A SPECIFIC GOAL. HE DIDN'T TOY WITH US OR KILL RANDOM PEOPLE ALONG THE WAY JUST FOR FUN.
WHAT ARE YOU TALKING ABOUT? MURDEROUS SUPER-GENIUS SOUNDS PRETTY ON-THE-NOSE TO ME.
MAYBE HE HAS A NEW GOAL. AND WE JUST DON'T UNDERSTAND HIS REASONING YET.
I DRAGGED HIM INTO A BLACK HOLE.
HE'S ON THE OTHER SIDE OF THE UNIVERSE.
AND BEFORE THAT, HE TOOK OVER MY BODY AND NO ONE NOTICED FOR MONTHS.
HOW DO WE KNOW HE'S NOT HERE AMONG US RIGHT NOW?
THIS ISN'T GETTING US ANYWHERE.
TALI'S IN KANDOR. AND WHATEVER HAPPENED TO OFFICER KO MIGHT BE HAPPENING TO HER.
WE JUST HAVE TO FIND THAT CITY.
WELL, THAT'S SOMETHING I MIGHT BE ABLE TO HELP WITH...

BATMAN'S *TRACKERS* COLLECTED SOME PRETTY GOOD *DATA.*

"I WAS ABLE TO CROSS-*REFERENCE* IT WITH UNEXPLAINED *WEATHER PATTERNS* AND *TIDAL IRREGULARITIES* ACROSS THE ATLANTIC.

"THAT BRINGS US TO THE *BLACK SAND DESERT* OF *ICELAND...*

"...IN THE MIDDLE OF WHICH WE'VE LOCATED A MELTED CIRCLE OF *STRANGE GLASS* TWO MILES ACROSS.

"THE GLASS HAS SPECIAL PROPERTIES...

"...IT *ABSORBS LIGHT* AND FOILS *RADAR* AND *CAMERAS.*

"BUT WE CAN MAKE OUT SOMETHING AT ITS CENTER...

"...SHAPED NOT UNLIKE...

"...A *BOTTLE.*

"AND THAT'S AS MUCH AS WE CAN SEE.

"TO FIND OUT MORE, WE'LL HAVE TO APPROACH IN PERSON.

"BUT GIVEN THE CIRCUMSTANCES, I RECOMMEND AN *INFILTRATION* RATHER THAN FULL-ON *ASSAULT...*

"...SINCE WE HAVE

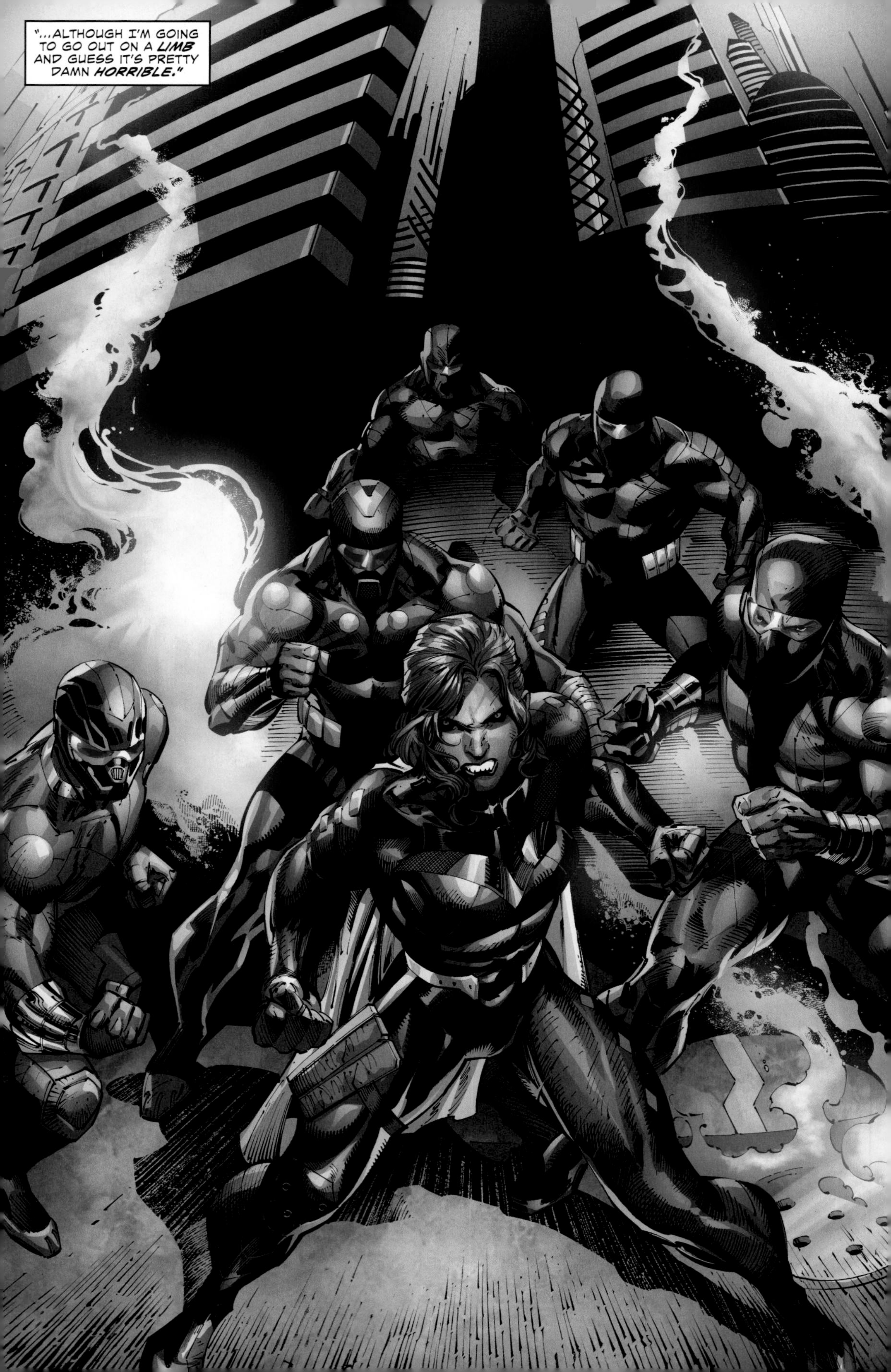
"...ALTHOUGH I'M GOING TO GO OUT ON A *LIMB* AND GUESS IT'S PRETTY DAMN *HORRIBLE.*"

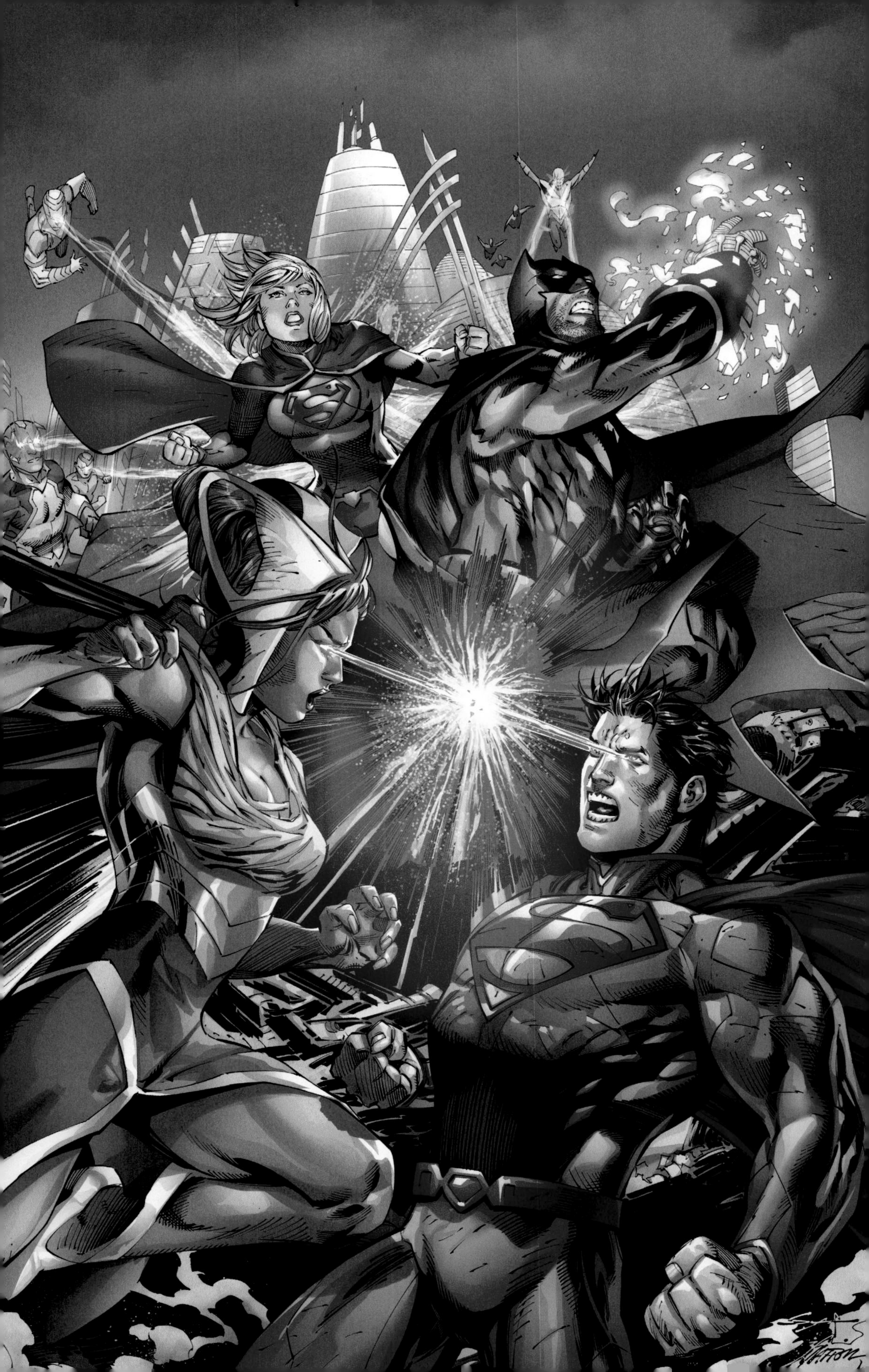

PHANTOMS

GREG PAK writer **ARDIAN SYAF** penciller **MARK MORALES, JAIME MENDOZA, DON HO, VICENTE CIFUENTES** inkers **ULISES ARREOLA** colorist **ROB LEIGH** letterer
cover by **ARDIAN SYAF, JONATHAN GLAPION** and **ULISES ARREOLA**

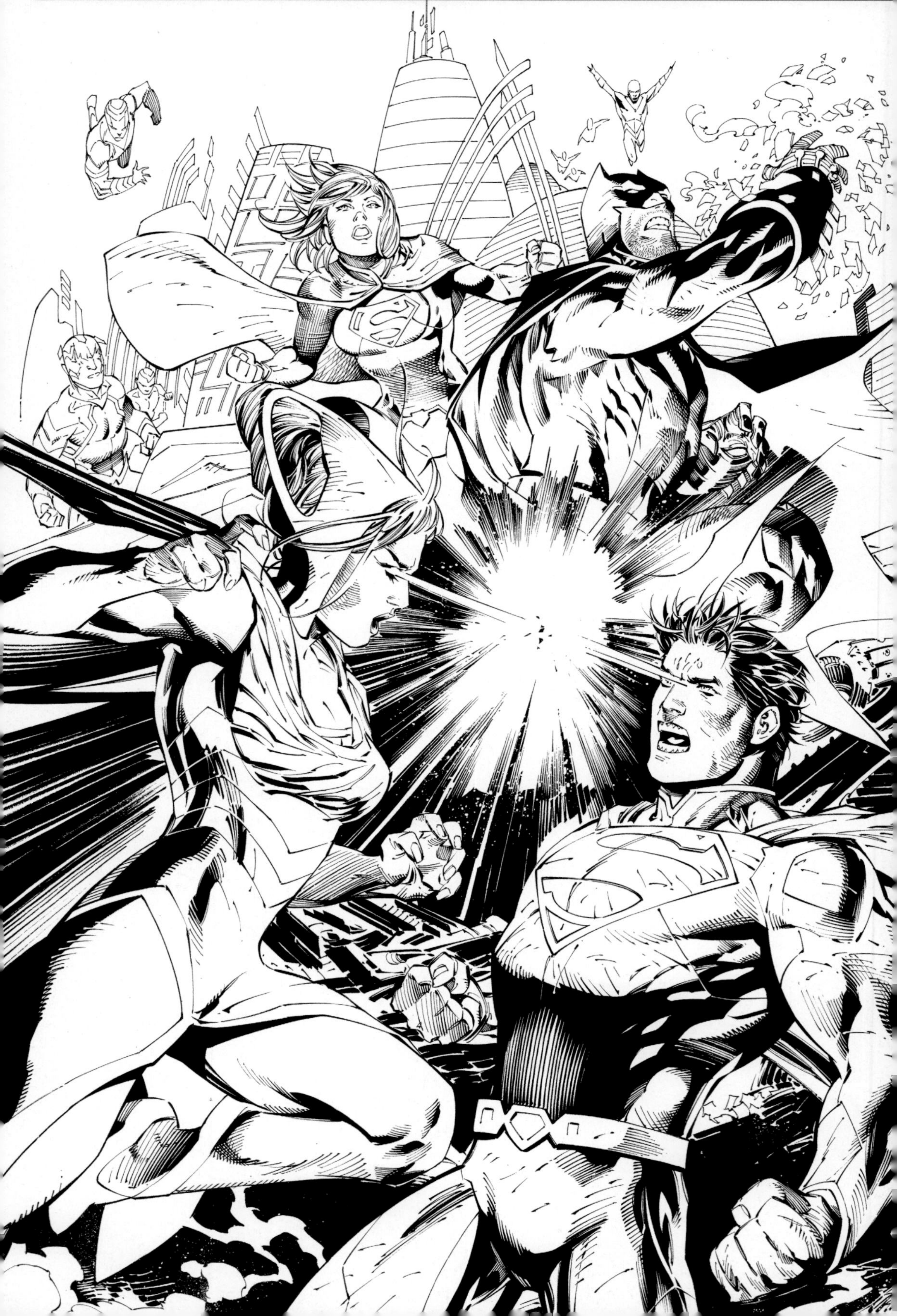

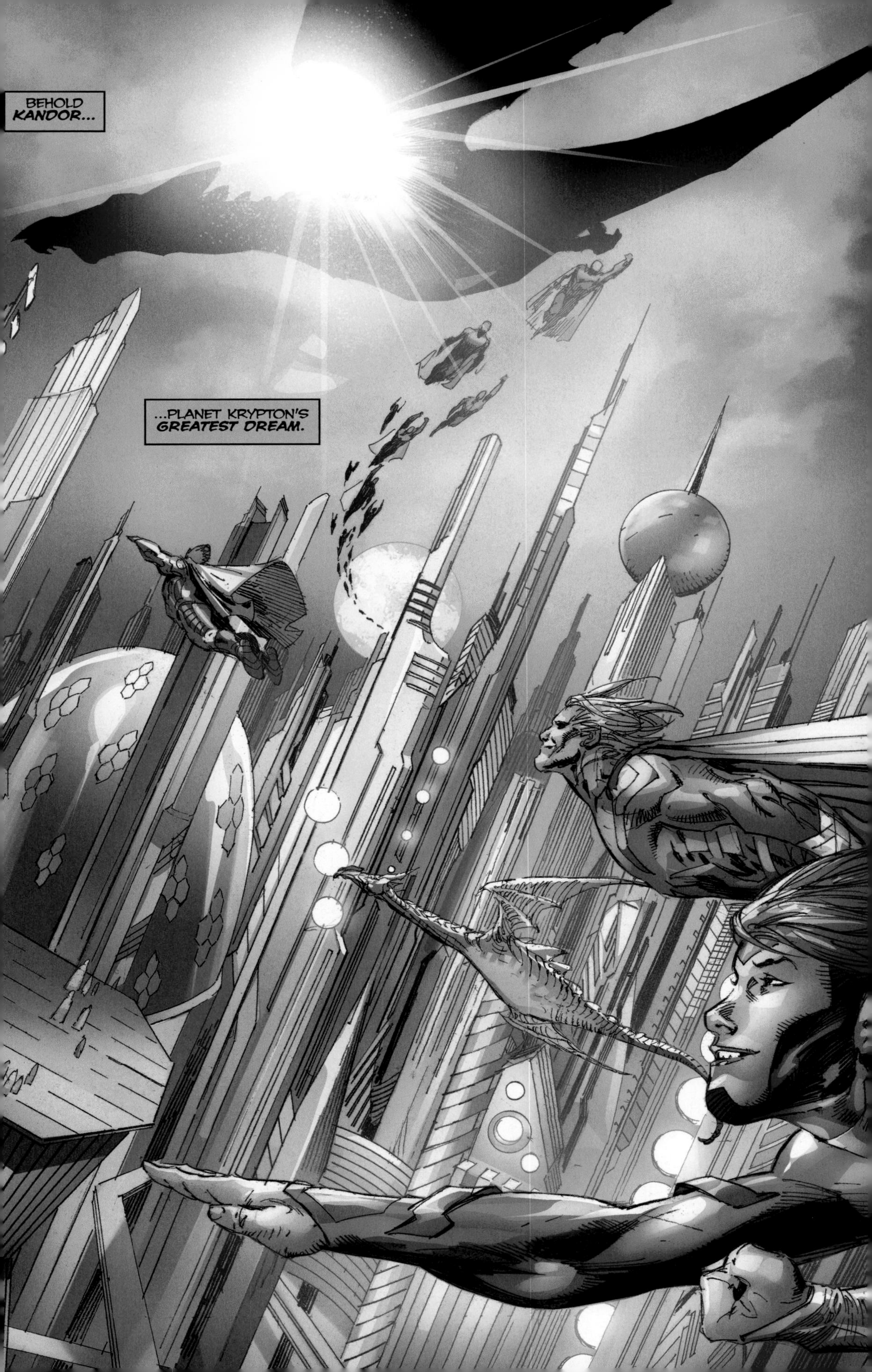
BEHOLD KANDOR...
...PLANET KRYPTON'S GREATEST DREAM.

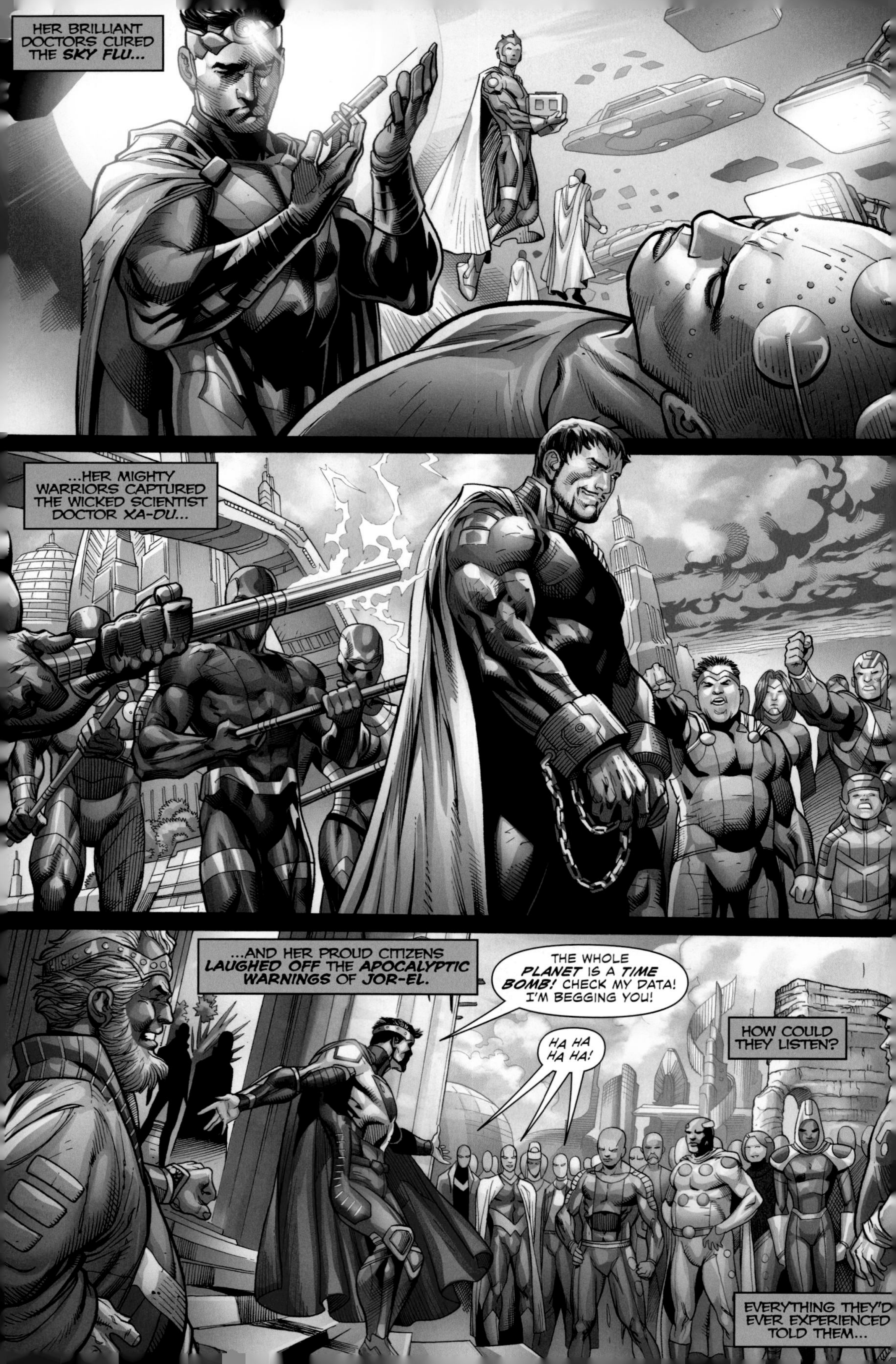
HER BRILLIANT DOCTORS CURED THE SKY FLU...
...HER MIGHTY WARRIORS CAPTURED THE WICKED SCIENTIST DOCTOR XA-DU...
...AND HER PROUD CITIZENS LAUGHED OFF THE APOCALYPTIC WARNINGS OF JOR-EL.
THE WHOLE PLANET IS A TIME BOMB! CHECK MY DATA! I'M BEGGING YOU!
HA HA HA HA!
HOW COULD THEY LISTEN?
EVERYTHING THEY'D EVER EXPERIENCED TOLD THEM...

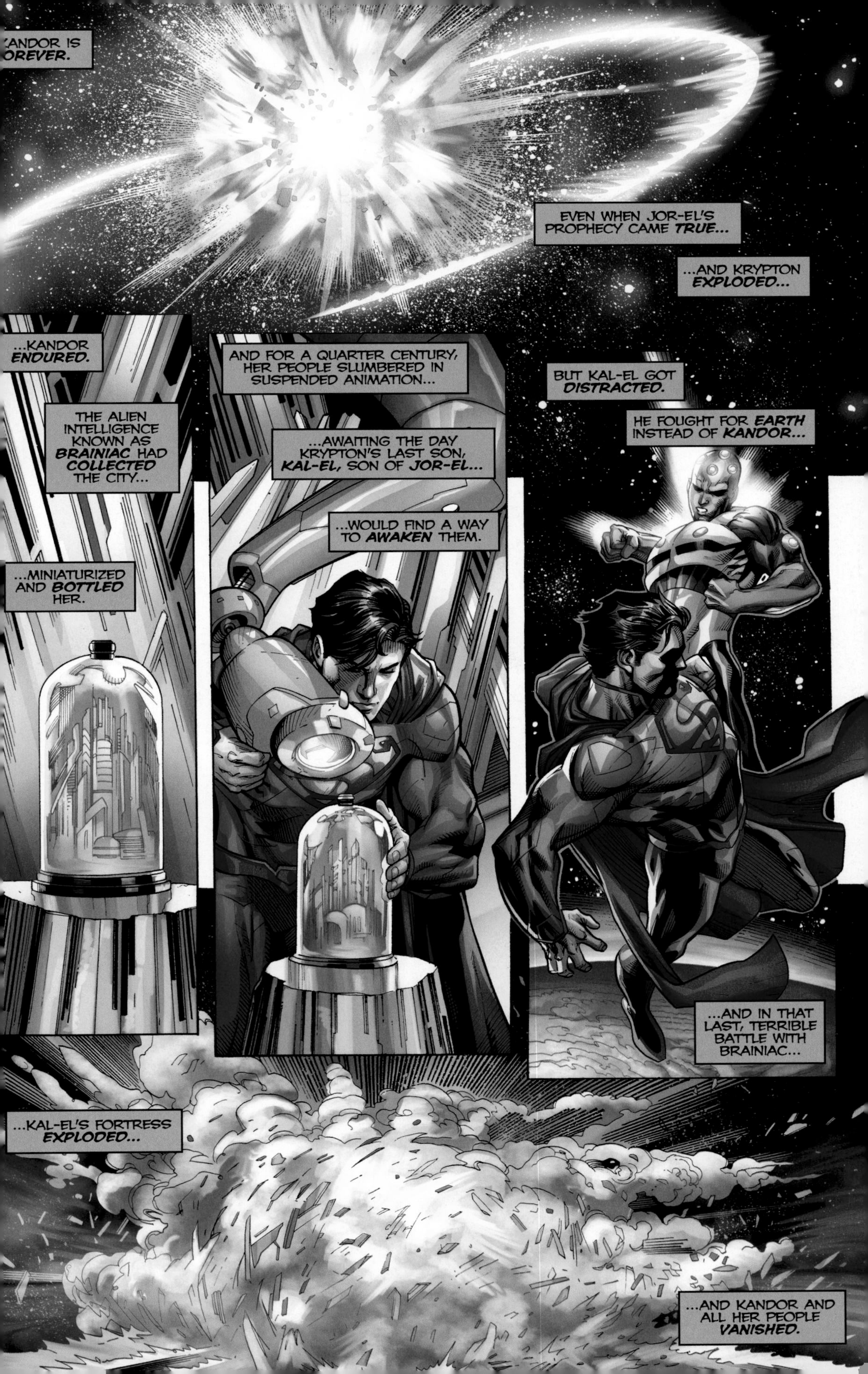
KANDOR IS
FOREVER.
EVEN WHEN JOR-EL'S PROPHECY CAME TRUE...
...AND KRYPTON EXPLODED...
...KANDOR ENDURED.
THE ALIEN INTELLIGENCE KNOWN AS BRAINIAC HAD COLLECTED THE CITY...
...MINIATURIZED AND BOTTLED HER.
AND FOR A QUARTER CENTURY, HER PEOPLE SLUMBERED IN SUSPENDED ANIMATION...
...AWAITING THE DAY KRYPTON'S LAST SON, KAL-EL, SON OF JOR-EL...
...WOULD FIND A WAY TO AWAKEN THEM.
BUT KAL-EL GOT DISTRACTED.
HE FOUGHT FOR EARTH INSTEAD OF KANDOR...
...AND IN THAT LAST, TERRIBLE BATTLE WITH BRAINIAC...
...KAL-EL'S FORTRESS EXPLODED...
...AND KANDOR AND ALL HER PEOPLE VANISHED.

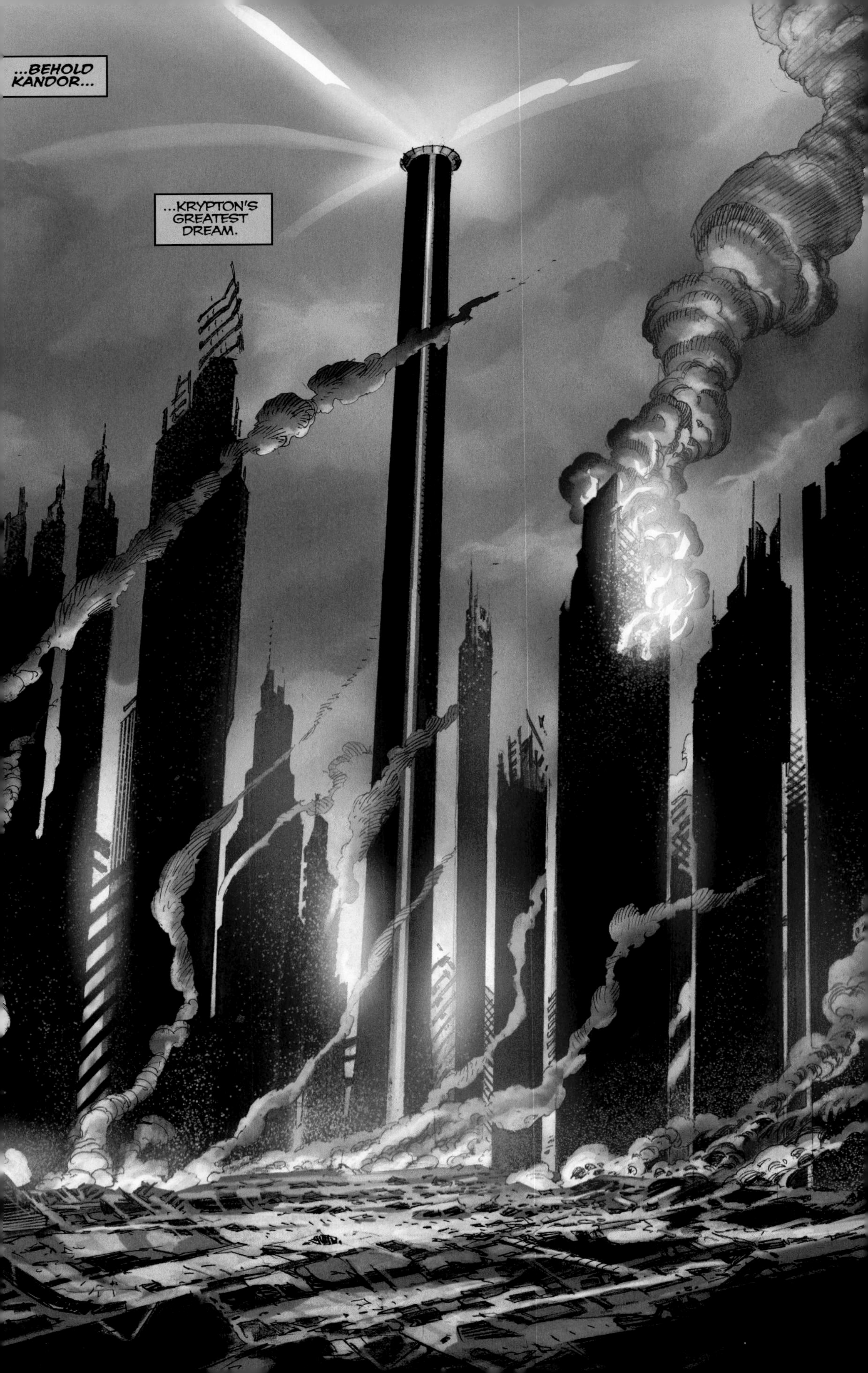
...BEHOLD KANDOR...
...KRYPTON'S GREATEST DREAM.

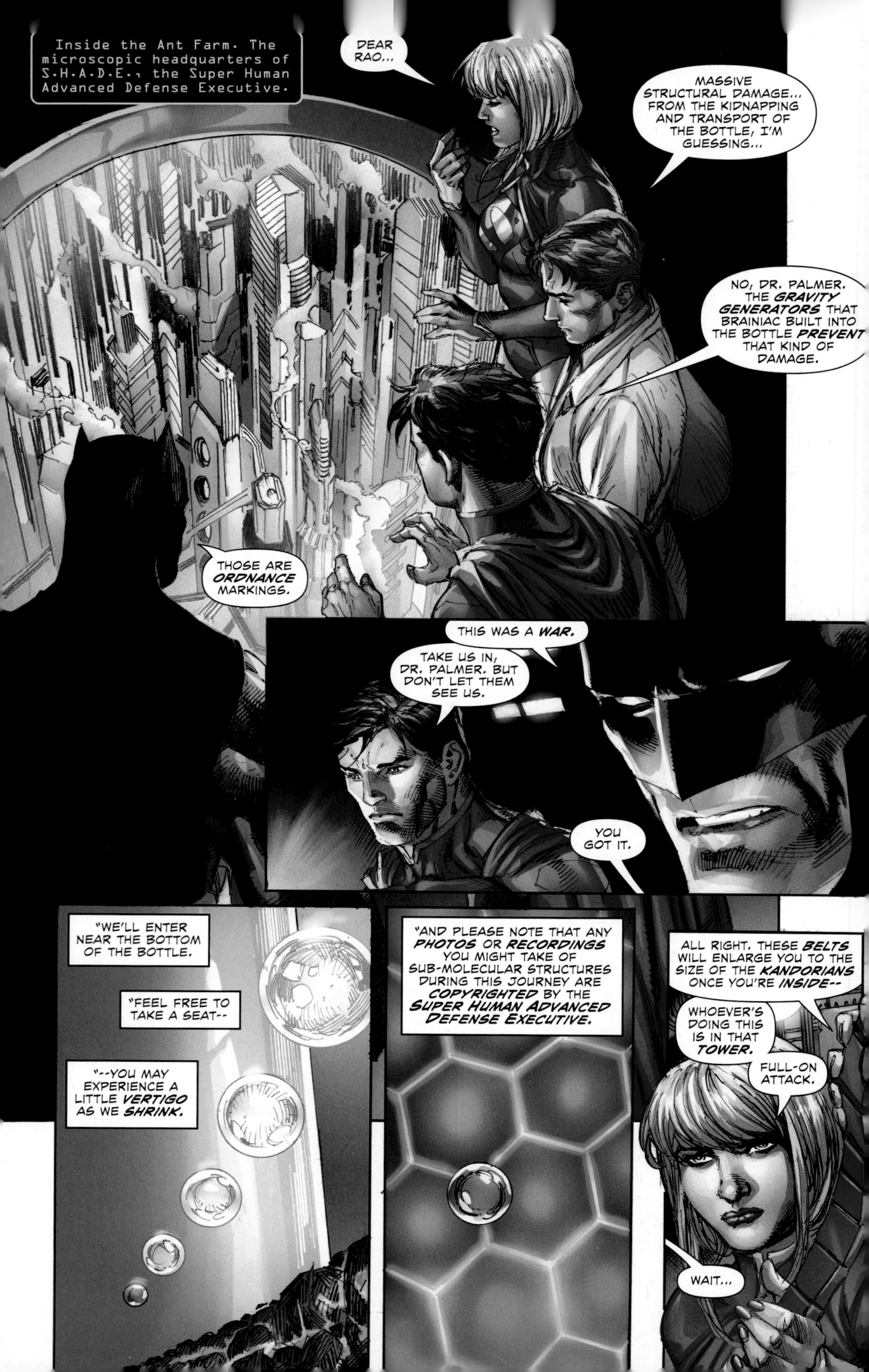
Inside the Ant Farm. The microscopic headquarters of S.H.A.D.E., the Super Human Advanced Defense Executive.
DEAR RAO...
MASSIVE STRUCTURAL DAMAGE... FROM THE KIDNAPPING AND TRANSPORT OF THE BOTTLE, I'M GUESSING...
NO, DR. PALMER. THE GRAVITY GENERATORS THAT BRAINIAC BUILT INTO THE BOTTLE PREVENT THAT KIND OF DAMAGE.
THOSE ARE ORDNANCE MARKINGS.
THIS WAS A WAR.
TAKE US IN, DR. PALMER. BUT DON'T LET THEM SEE US.
YOU GOT IT.
"WE'LL ENTER NEAR THE BOTTOM OF THE BOTTLE.
"FEEL FREE TO TAKE A SEAT--
"--YOU MAY EXPERIENCE A LITTLE VERTIGO AS WE SHRINK.
"AND PLEASE NOTE THAT ANY PHOTOS OR RECORDINGS YOU MIGHT TAKE OF SUB-MOLECULAR STRUCTURES DURING THIS JOURNEY ARE COPYRIGHTED BY THE SUPER HUMAN ADVANCED DEFENSE EXECUTIVE.
ALL RIGHT. THESE BELTS WILL ENLARGE YOU TO THE SIZE OF THE KANDORIANS ONCE YOU'RE INSIDE--
WHOEVER'S DOING THIS IS IN THAT TOWER.
FULL-ON ATTACK.
WAIT...

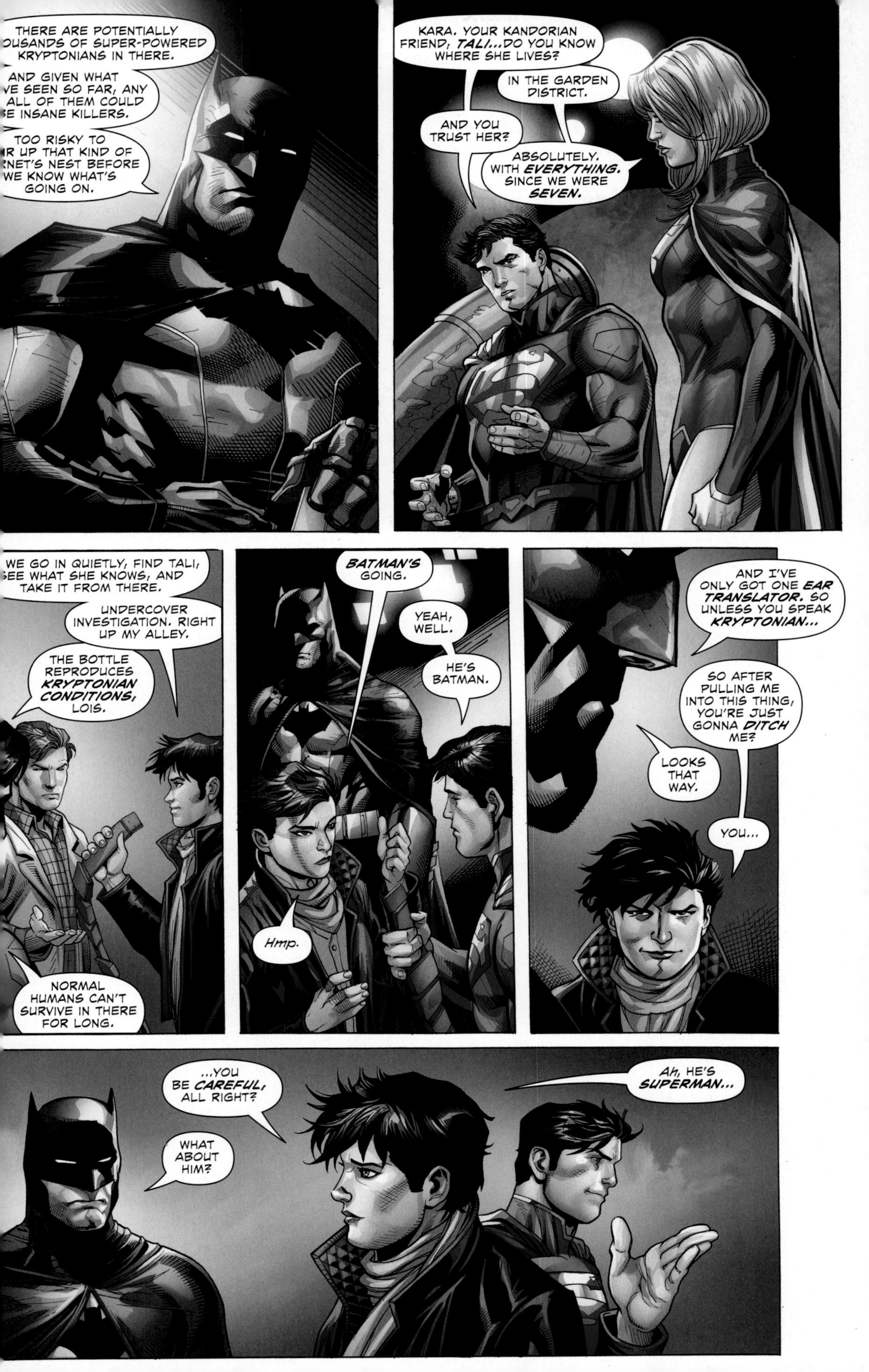

THERE ARE POTENTIALLY OUSANDS OF SUPER-POWERED KRYPTONIANS IN THERE.
AND GIVEN WHAT VE SEEN SO FAR, ANY ALL OF THEM COULD E INSANE KILLERS.
TOO RISKY TO R UP THAT KIND OF RNET'S NEST BEFORE WE KNOW WHAT'S GOING ON.
KARA. YOUR KANDORIAN FRIEND, TALI...DO YOU KNOW WHERE SHE LIVES?
IN THE GARDEN DISTRICT.
AND YOU TRUST HER?
ABSOLUTELY. WITH EVERYTHING. SINCE WE WERE SEVEN.
WE GO IN QUIETLY, FIND TALI, EE WHAT SHE KNOWS, AND TAKE IT FROM THERE.
UNDERCOVER INVESTIGATION. RIGHT UP MY ALLEY.
THE BOTTLE REPRODUCES KRYPTONIAN CONDITIONS, LOIS.
NORMAL HUMANS CAN'T SURVIVE IN THERE FOR LONG.
BATMAN'S GOING.
YEAH, WELL.
HE'S BATMAN.
Hmp.
AND I'VE ONLY GOT ONE EAR TRANSLATOR. SO UNLESS YOU SPEAK KRYPTONIAN...
SO AFTER PULLING ME INTO THIS THING, YOU'RE JUST GONNA DITCH ME?
LOOKS THAT WAY.
YOU...
...YOU BE CAREFUL, ALL RIGHT?
WHAT ABOUT HIM?
Ah, HE'S SUPERMAN...

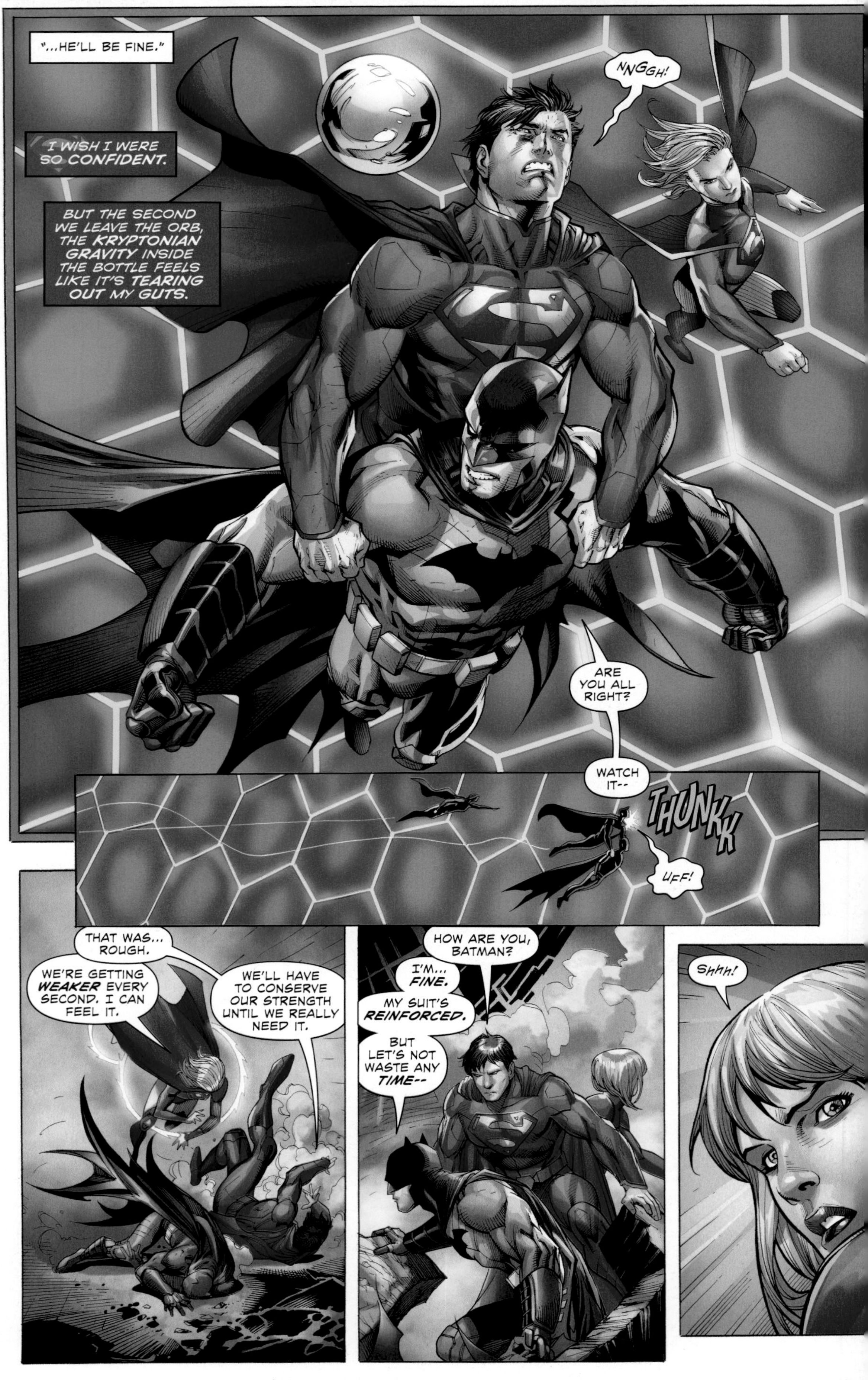
"...HE'LL BE FINE."
NNGGH!
I WISH I WERE SO CONFIDENT.
BUT THE SECOND WE LEAVE THE ORB, THE KRYPTONIAN GRAVITY INSIDE THE BOTTLE FEELS LIKE IT'S TEARING OUT MY GUTS.
ARE YOU ALL RIGHT?
WATCH IT--
THUNKK
UFF!
THAT WAS... ROUGH.
WE'RE GETTING WEAKER EVERY SECOND. I CAN FEEL IT.
WE'LL HAVE TO CONSERVE OUR STRENGTH UNTIL WE REALLY NEED IT.
HOW ARE YOU, BATMAN?
I'M... FINE.
MY SUIT'S REINFORCED.
BUT LET'S NOT WASTE ANY TIME--
Shhh!

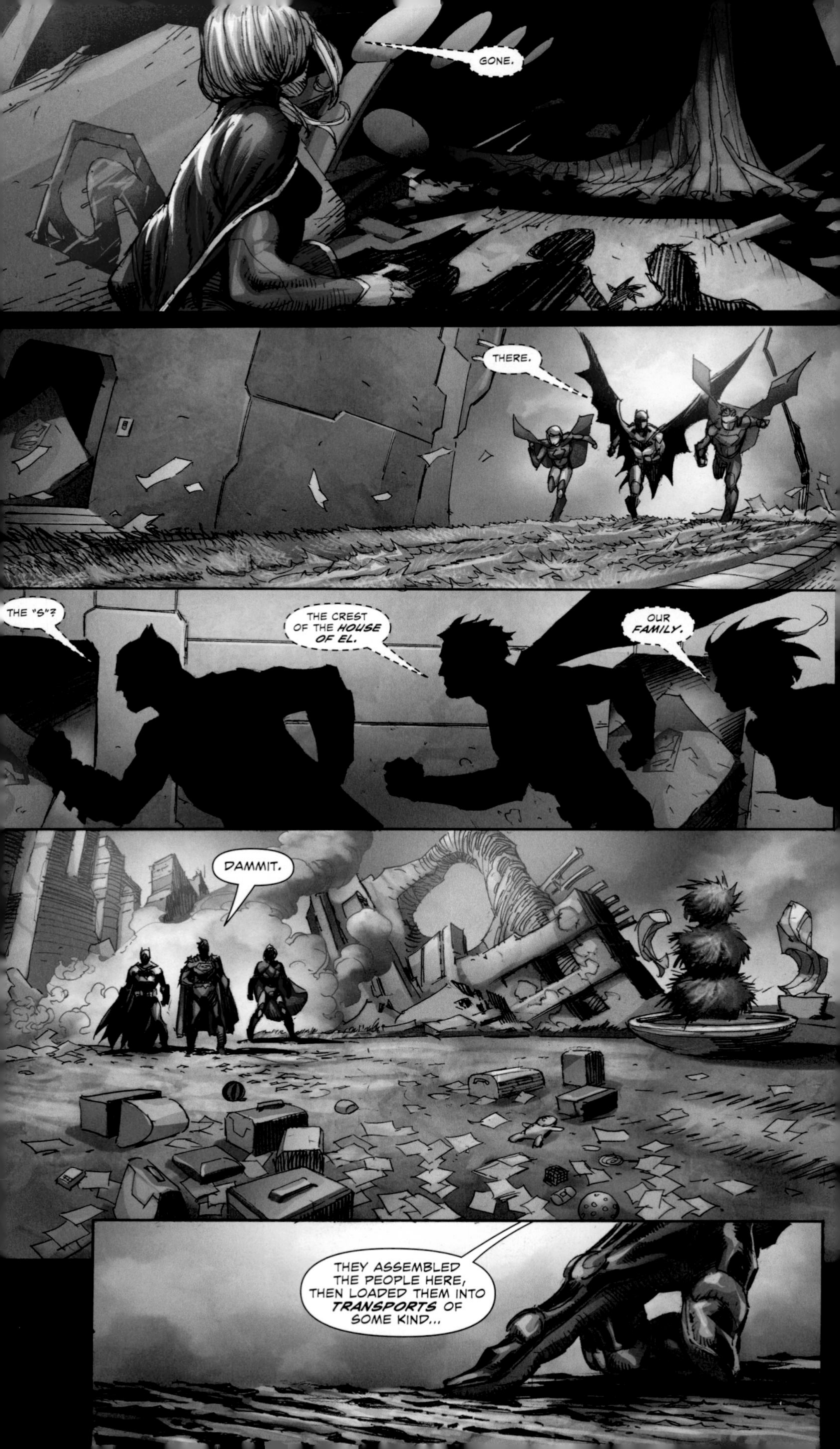
GONE.
THERE.
THE "S"?
THE CREST OF THE HOUSE OF EL.
OUR FAMILY.
DAMMIT.
THEY ASSEMBLED THE PEOPLE HERE, THEN LOADED THEM INTO TRANSPORTS OF SOME KIND...

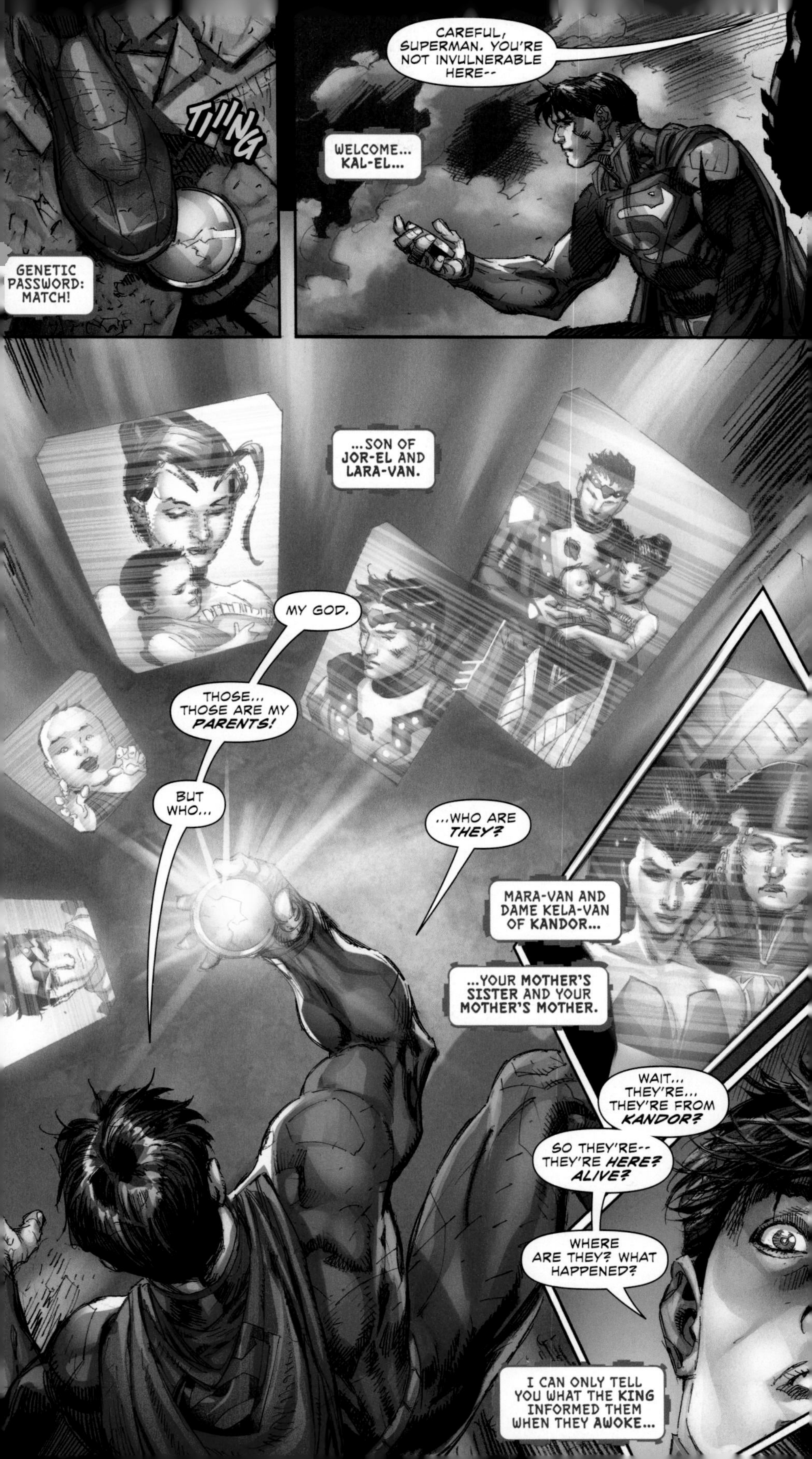

TIING
GENETIC PASSWORD: MATCH!
CAREFUL, SUPERMAN. YOU'RE NOT INVULNERABLE HERE--
WELCOME... KAL-EL...
...SON OF JOR-EL AND LARA-VAN.
MY GOD.
THOSE... THOSE ARE MY PARENTS!
BUT WHO...
...WHO ARE THEY?
MARA-VAN AND DAME KELA-VAN OF KANDOR...
...YOUR MOTHER'S SISTER AND YOUR MOTHER'S MOTHER.
WAIT... THEY'RE... THEY'RE FROM KANDOR?
SO THEY'RE-- THEY'RE HERE? ALIVE?
WHERE ARE THEY? WHAT HAPPENED?
I CAN ONLY TELL YOU WHAT THE KING INFORMED THEM WHEN THEY AWOKE...

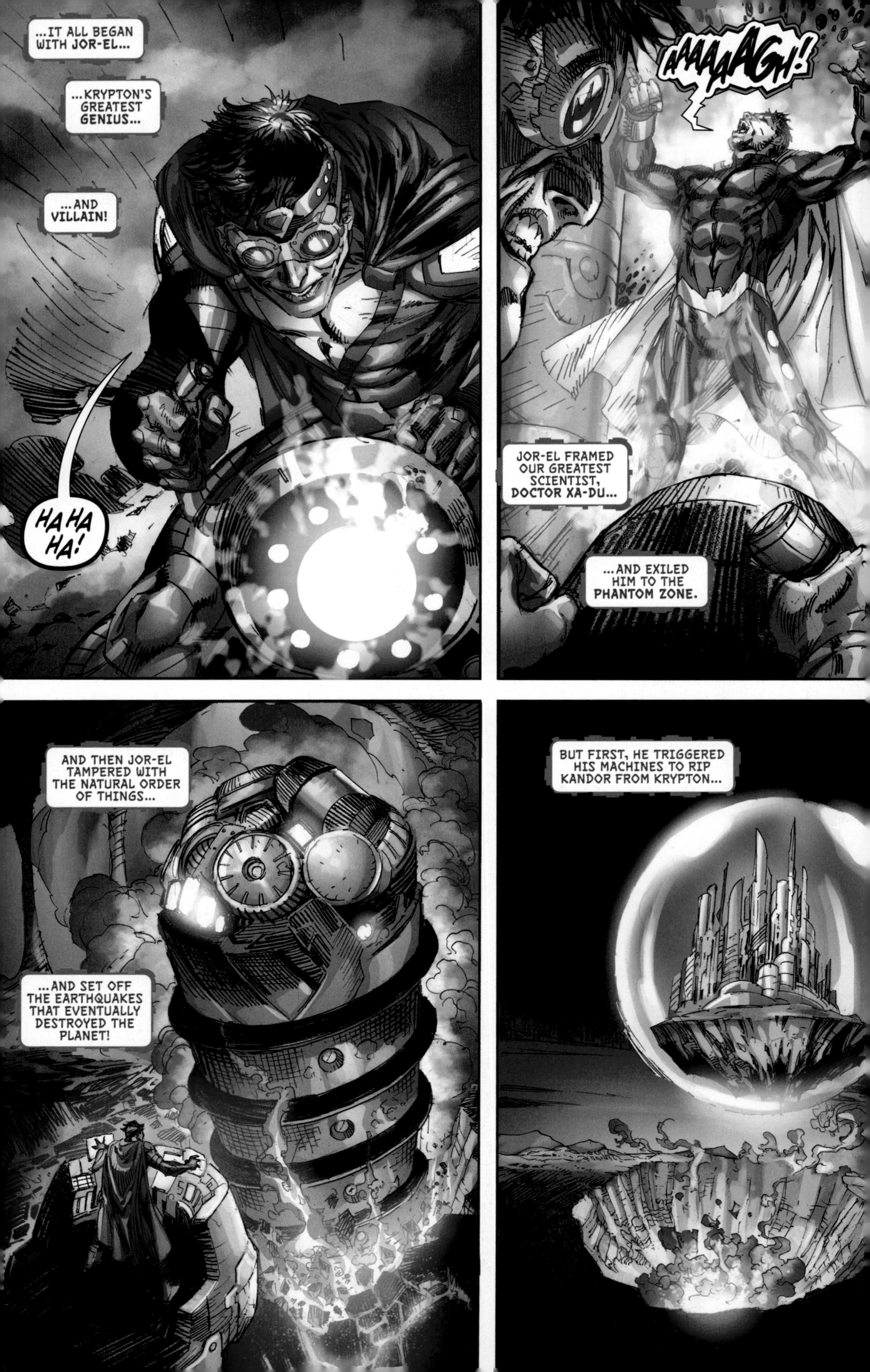
...IT ALL BEGAN WITH JOR-EL...
...KRYPTON'S GREATEST GENIUS...
...AND VILLAIN!
HA HA HA!
AAAAAAGH!
JOR-EL FRAMED OUR GREATEST SCIENTIST, DOCTOR XA-DU...
...AND EXILED HIM TO THE PHANTOM ZONE.
AND THEN JOR-EL TAMPERED WITH THE NATURAL ORDER OF THINGS...
...AND SET OFF THE EARTHQUAKES THAT EVENTUALLY DESTROYED THE PLANET!
BUT FIRST, HE TRIGGERED HIS MACHINES TO RIP KANDOR FROM KRYPTON...

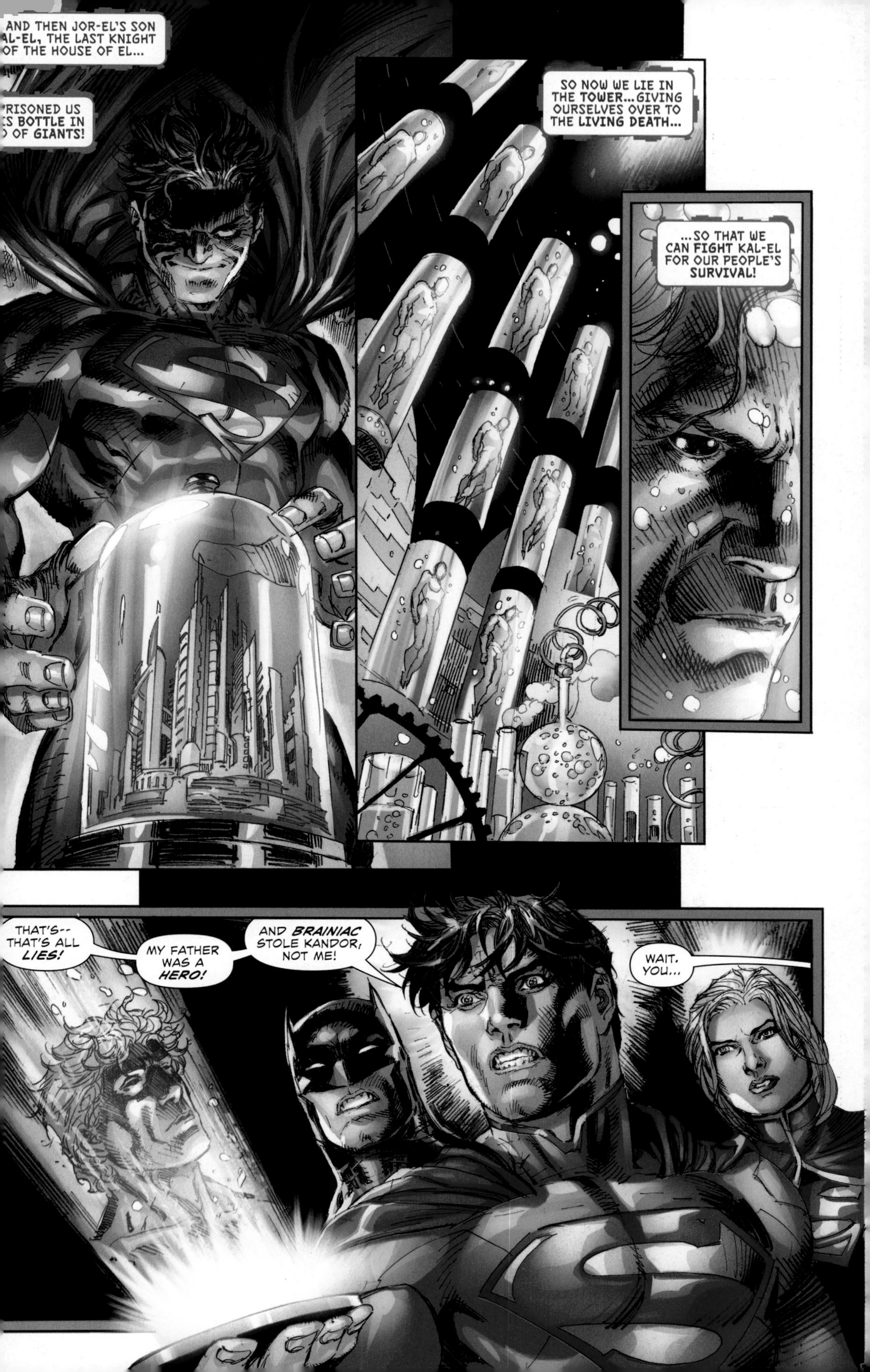
AND THEN JOR-EL'S SON AL-EL, THE LAST KNIGHT OF THE HOUSE OF EL...
RISONED US S BOTTLE IN D OF GIANTS!
SO NOW WE LIE IN THE TOWER... GIVING OURSELVES OVER TO THE LIVING DEATH...
...SO THAT WE CAN FIGHT KAL-EL FOR OUR PEOPLE'S SURVIVAL!
THAT'S-- THAT'S ALL LIES!
MY FATHER WAS A HERO!
AND BRAINIAC STOLE KANDOR, NOT ME!
WAIT. YOU...

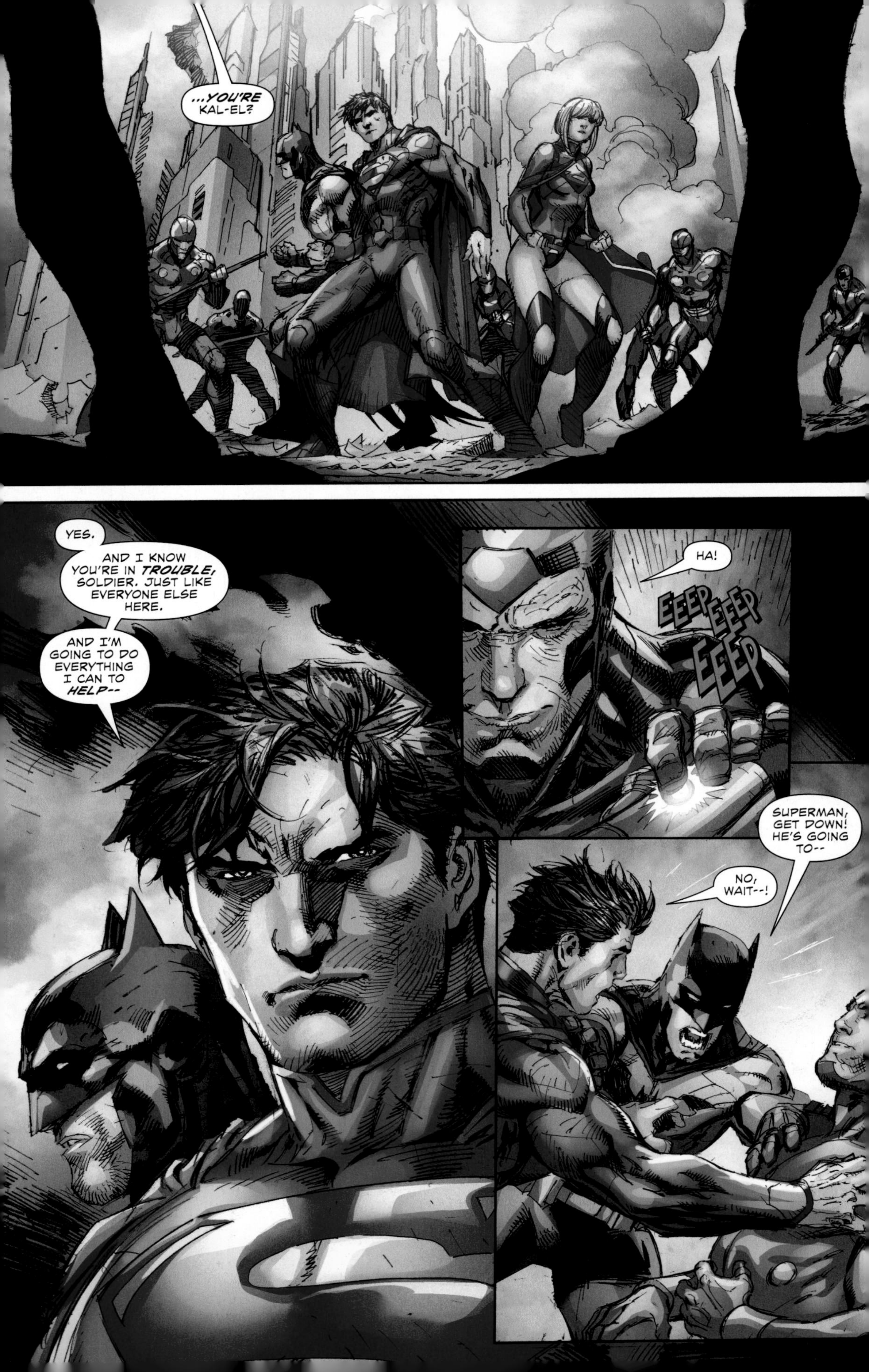
...YOU'RE KAL-EL?
YES.
AND I KNOW YOU'RE IN TROUBLE, SOLDIER. JUST LIKE EVERYONE ELSE HERE.
AND I'M GOING TO DO EVERYTHING I CAN TO HELP--
HA!
EEEP EEEP EEEP
SUPERMAN, GET DOWN! HE'S GOING TO--
NO, WAIT--!

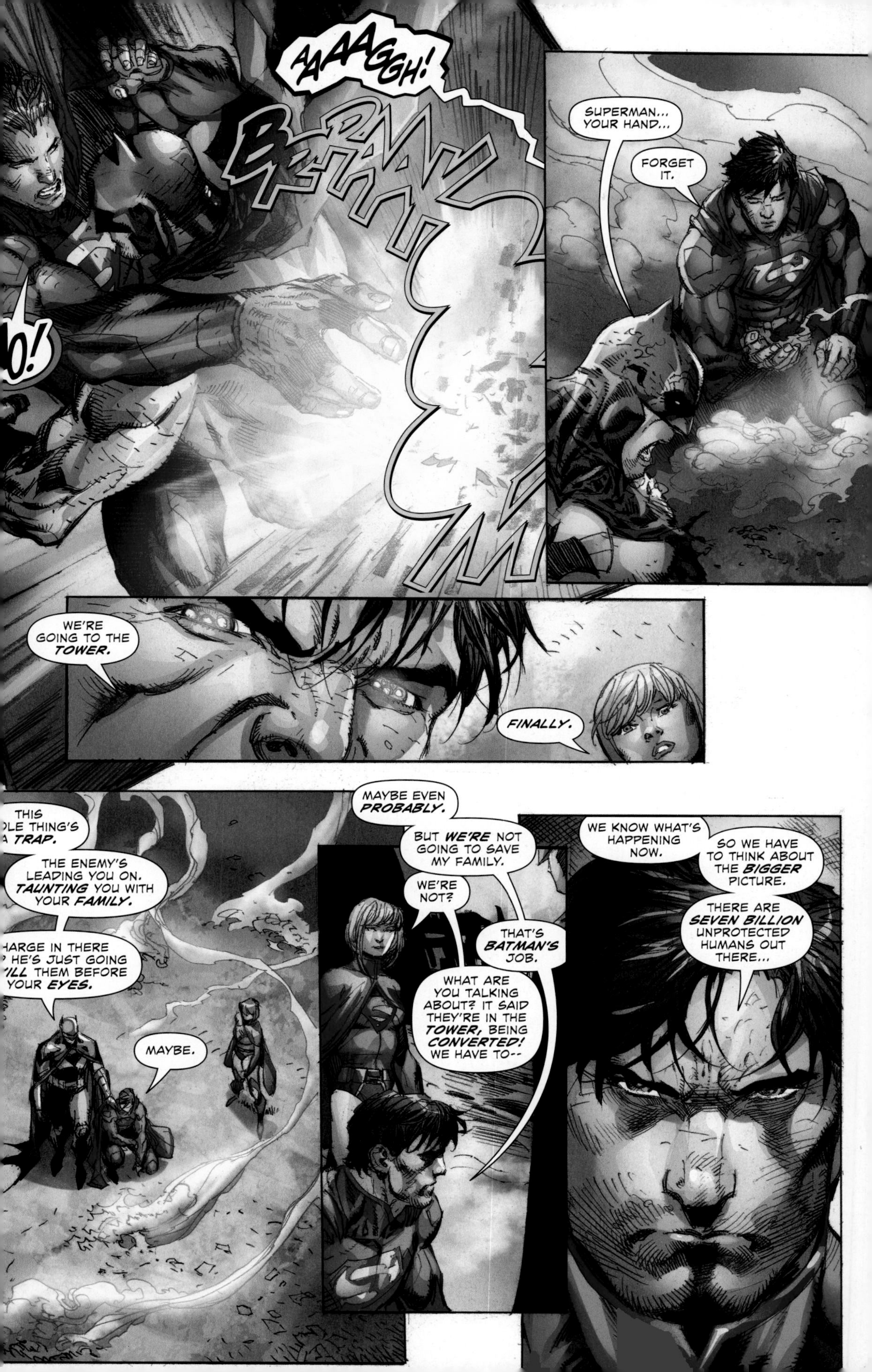
AAAAGGH!
BRRNAKK
...O!
SUPERMAN... YOUR HAND...
FORGET IT.
WE'RE GOING TO THE *TOWER.*
FINALLY.
THIS ...OLE THING'S ...A *TRAP.*
THE ENEMY'S LEADING YOU ON. *TAUNTING* YOU WITH YOUR *FAMILY.*
...HARGE IN THERE ... HE'S JUST GOING ...ILL THEM BEFORE YOUR *EYES.*
MAYBE.
MAYBE EVEN *PROBABLY.*
BUT *WE'RE* NOT GOING TO SAVE MY FAMILY.
WE'RE NOT?
THAT'S *BATMAN'S* JOB.
WHAT ARE YOU TALKING ABOUT? IT SAID THEY'RE IN THE *TOWER,* BEING *CONVERTED!* WE HAVE TO--
WE KNOW WHAT'S HAPPENING NOW.
SO WE HAVE TO THINK ABOUT THE *BIGGER* PICTURE.
THERE ARE *SEVEN BILLION* UNPROTECTED HUMANS OUT THERE...

"...SO BEFORE *ANYTHING ELSE*, WE HAVE TO DESTROY THAT *EXIT RAMP* AT THE TOP OF THE TOWER."

GRRAAAAAAA!

BRRRA KOOOOM

KTHOKK

UKK!

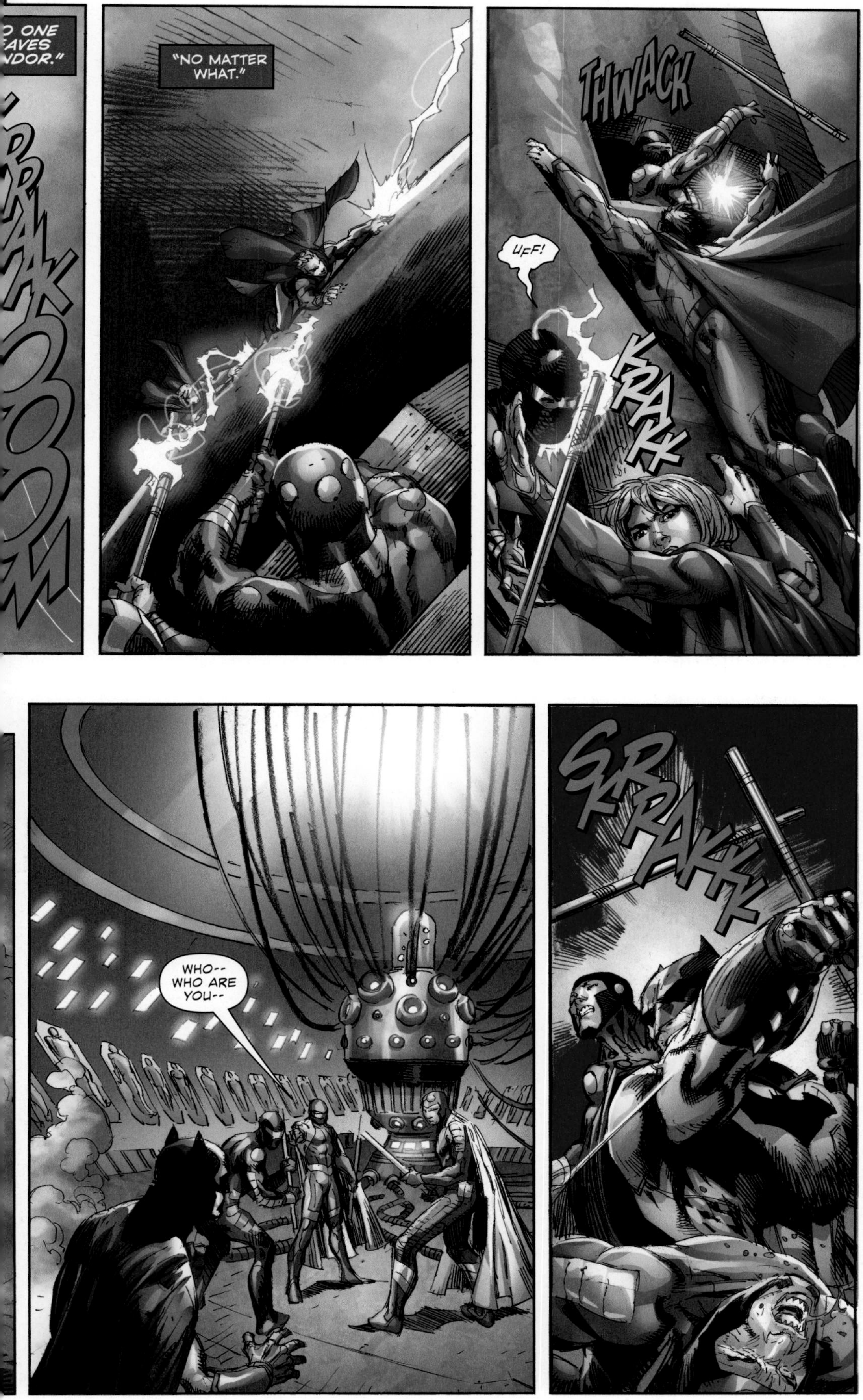
O ONE
EAVES
NDOR."
"NO MATTER WHAT."
THWACK
UFF!
KRAKK
WHO-- WHO ARE YOU--

BRRAKOOOM BA

HA HA HA HA HA HA

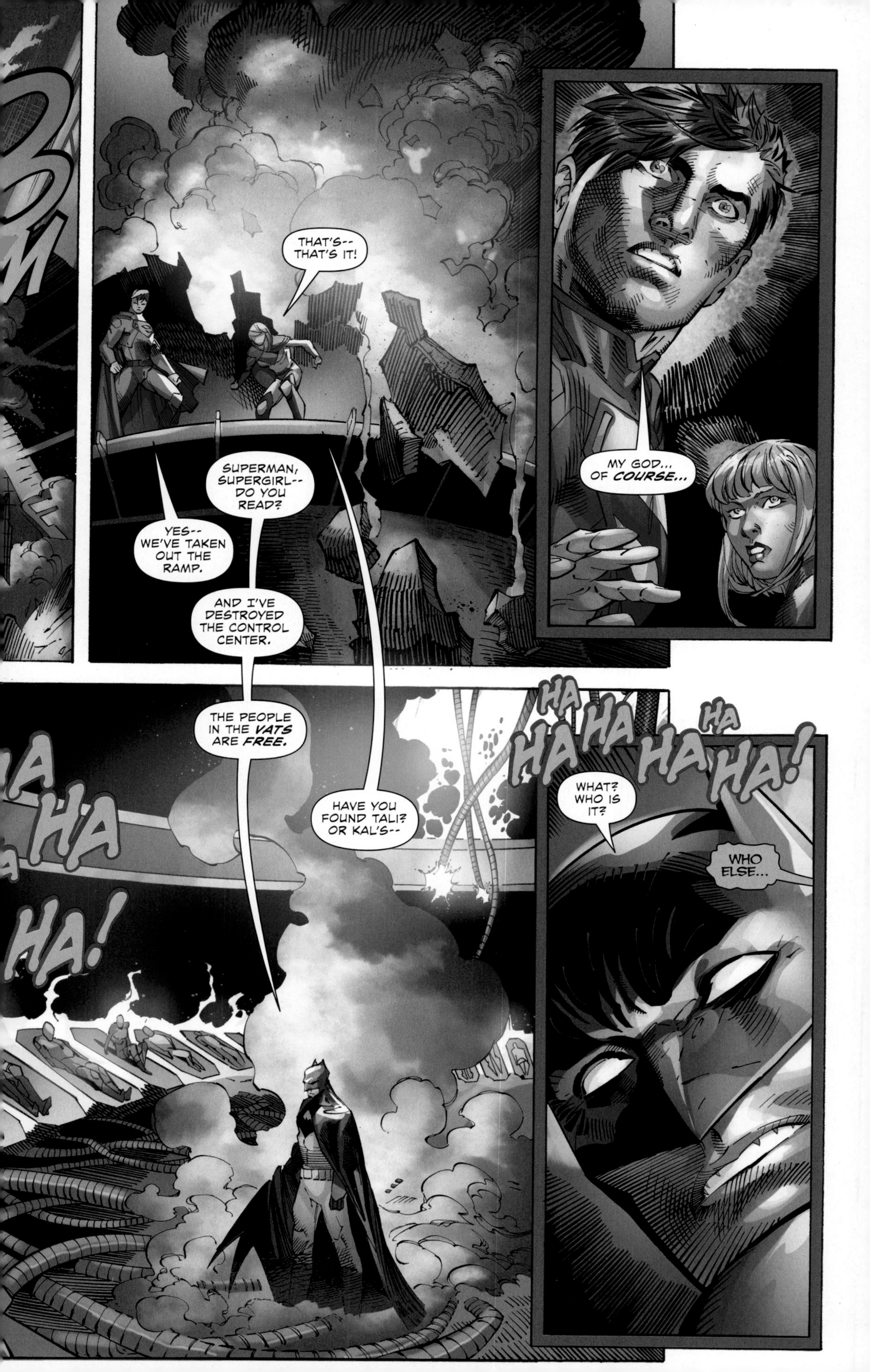

THAT'S--
THAT'S IT!
MY GOD... OF COURSE...
SUPERMAN, SUPERGIRL-- DO YOU READ?
YES-- WE'VE TAKEN OUT THE RAMP.
AND I'VE DESTROYED THE CONTROL CENTER.
THE PEOPLE IN THE VATS ARE FREE.
HAVE YOU FOUND TALI? OR KAL'S--
HA HA HA HA HA HA HA!
WHAT? WHO IS IT?
WHO ELSE...
HA HA HA HA!

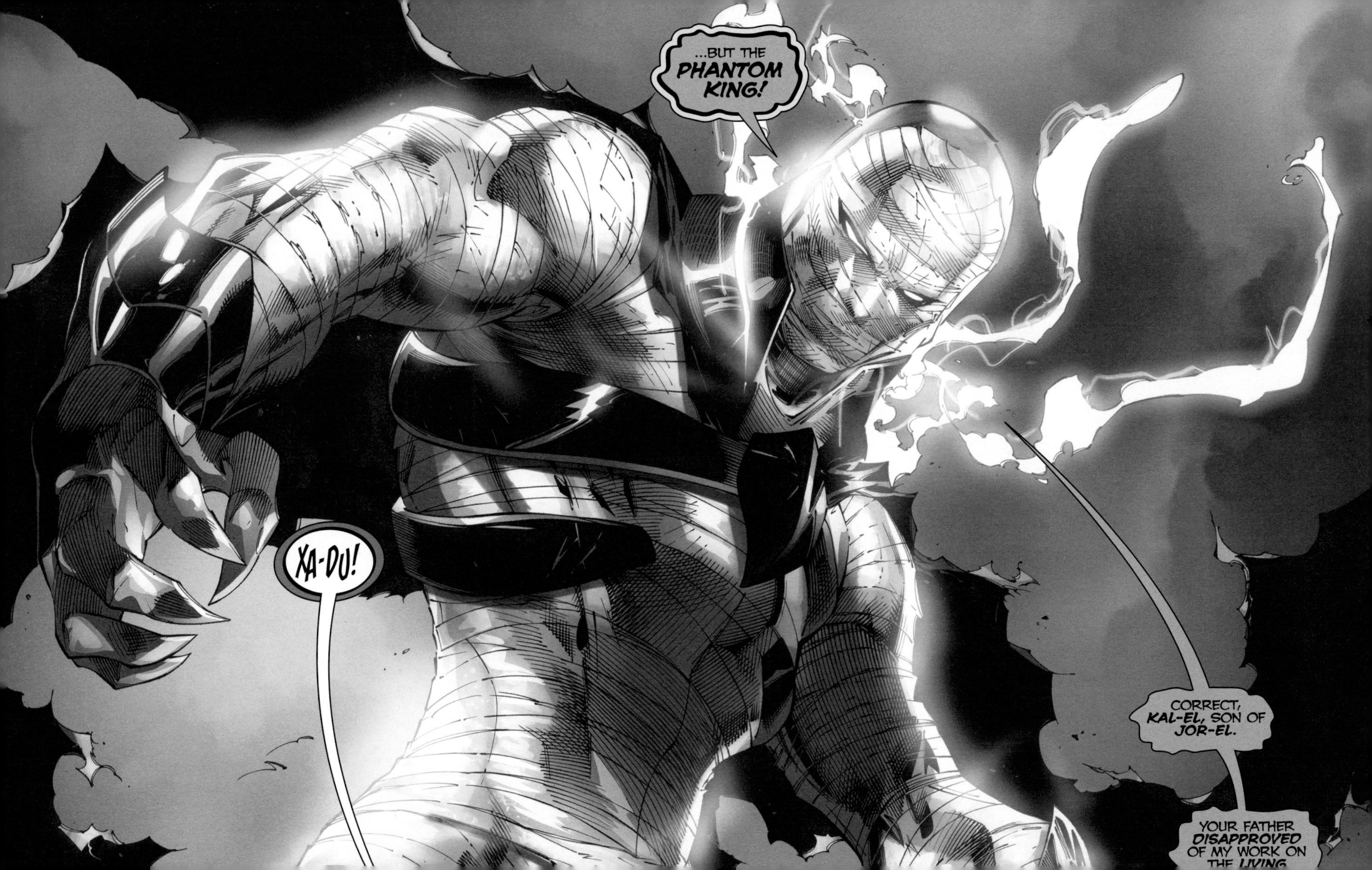
...BUT THE PHANTOM KING!
XA-DU!
CORRECT, KAL-EL, SON OF JOR-EL.
YOUR FATHER DISAPPROVED OF MY WORK ON THE LIVING

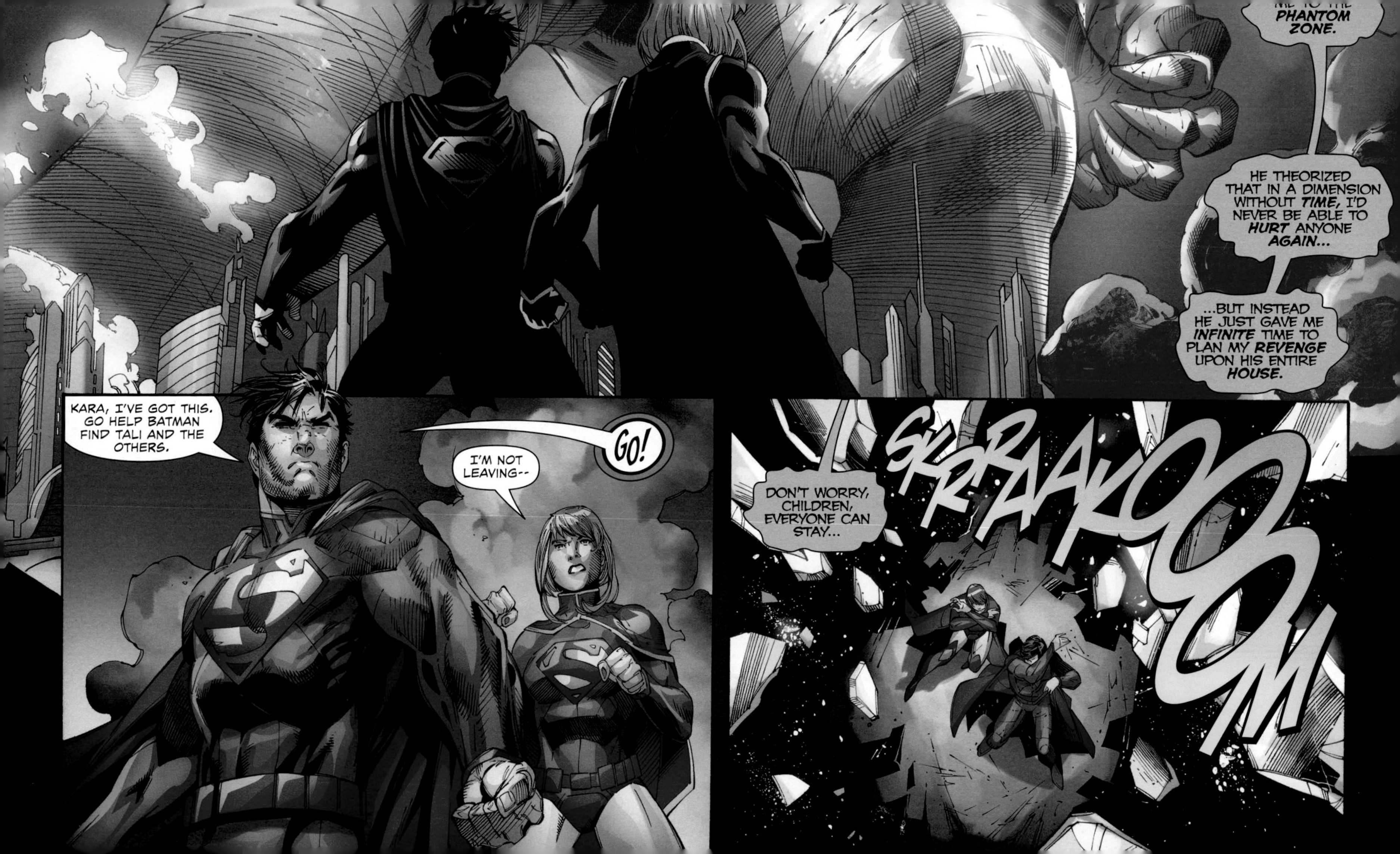
PHANTOM ZONE.
HE THEORIZED THAT IN A DIMENSION WITHOUT TIME, I'D NEVER BE ABLE TO HURT ANYONE AGAIN...
...BUT INSTEAD HE JUST GAVE ME INFINITE TIME TO PLAN MY REVENGE UPON HIS ENTIRE HOUSE.
KARA, I'VE GOT THIS. GO HELP BATMAN FIND TALI AND THE OTHERS.
GO!
I'M NOT LEAVING--
DON'T WORRY, CHILDREN, EVERYONE CAN STAY...
SKRRAAKOOOM

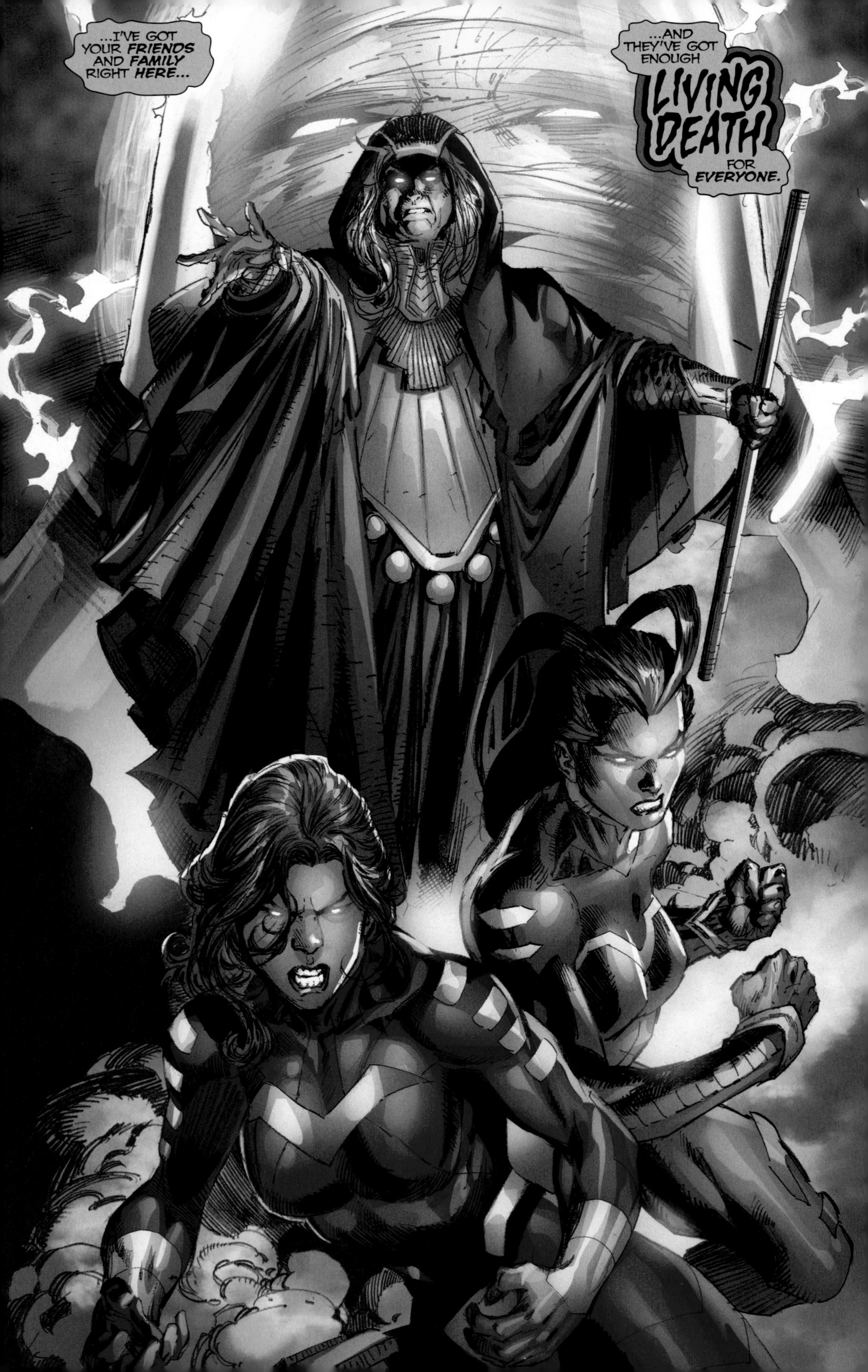
...I'VE GOT YOUR FRIENDS AND FAMILY RIGHT HERE...
...AND THEY'VE GOT ENOUGH LIVING DEATH FOR EVERYONE.

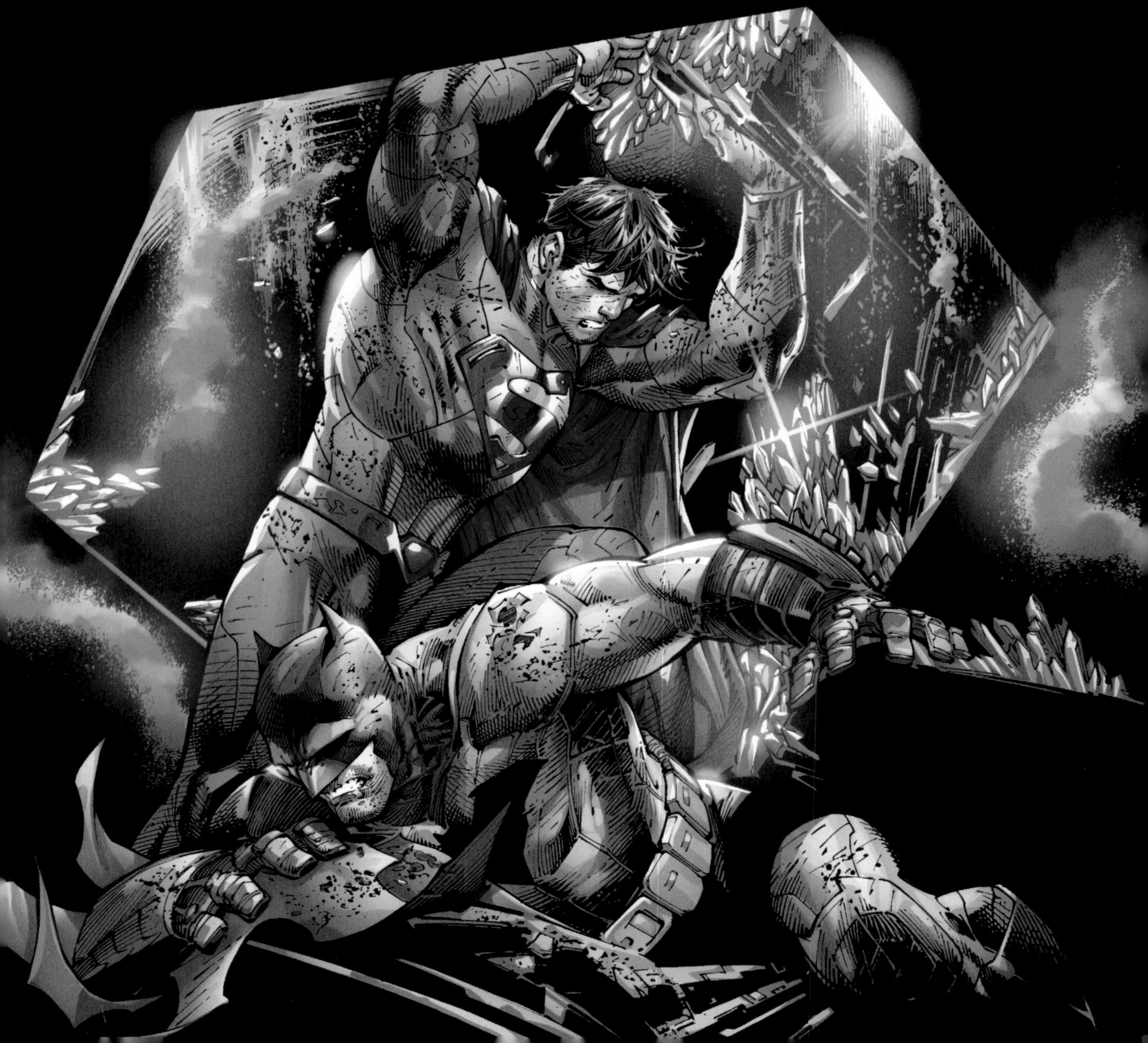

FAMILY MATTERS

GREG PAK writer ARDIAN SYAF penciller VICENTE CIFUENTES, MARK MORALES inkers ULISES ARREOLA colorist ROB LEIGH letterer

cover by ARDIAN SYAF, SANDRA HOPE ARCHER and ULISES ARREOLA

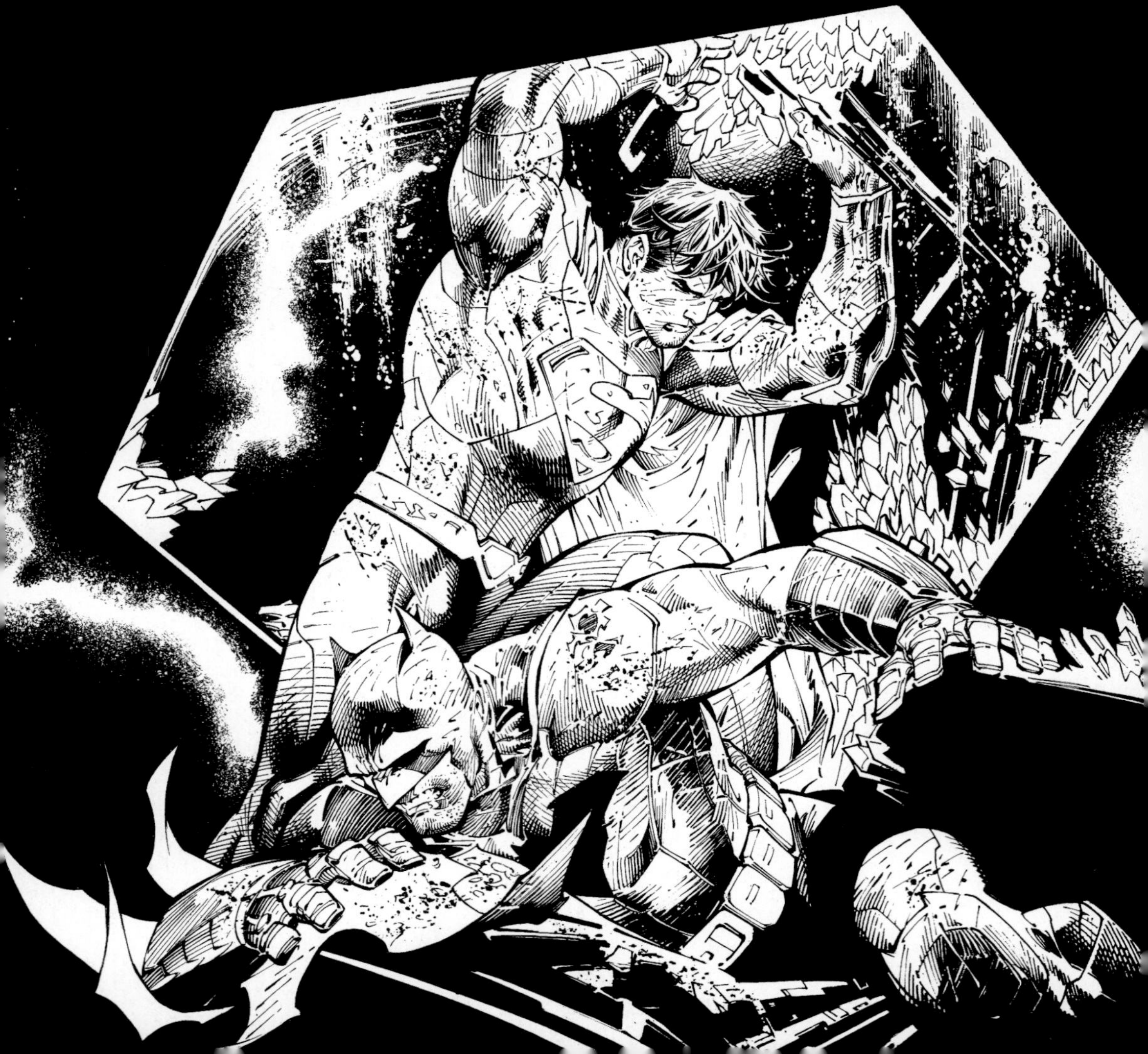

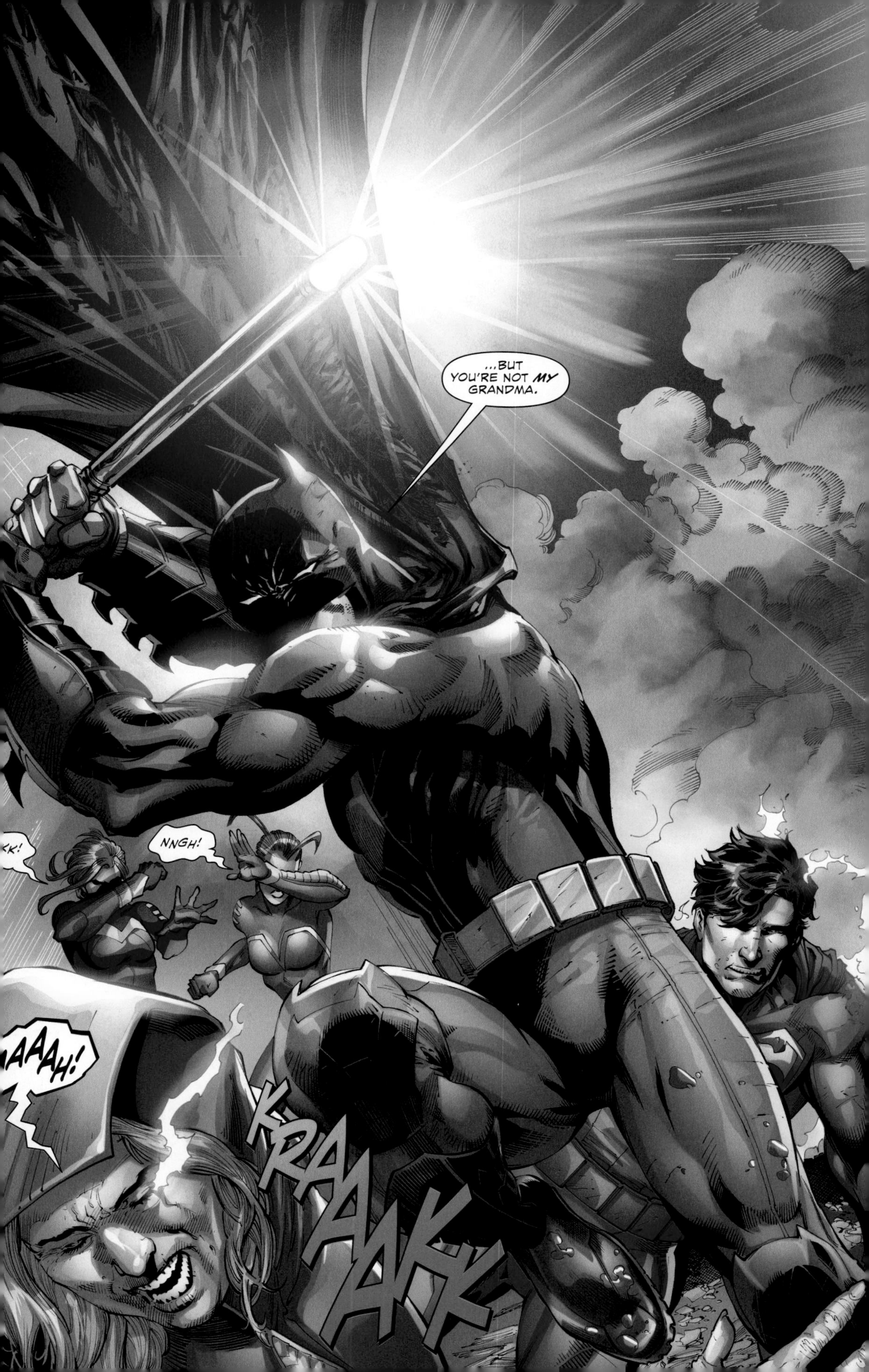

...BUT YOU'RE NOT MY GRANDMA.
NNGH!
KRAAAKK

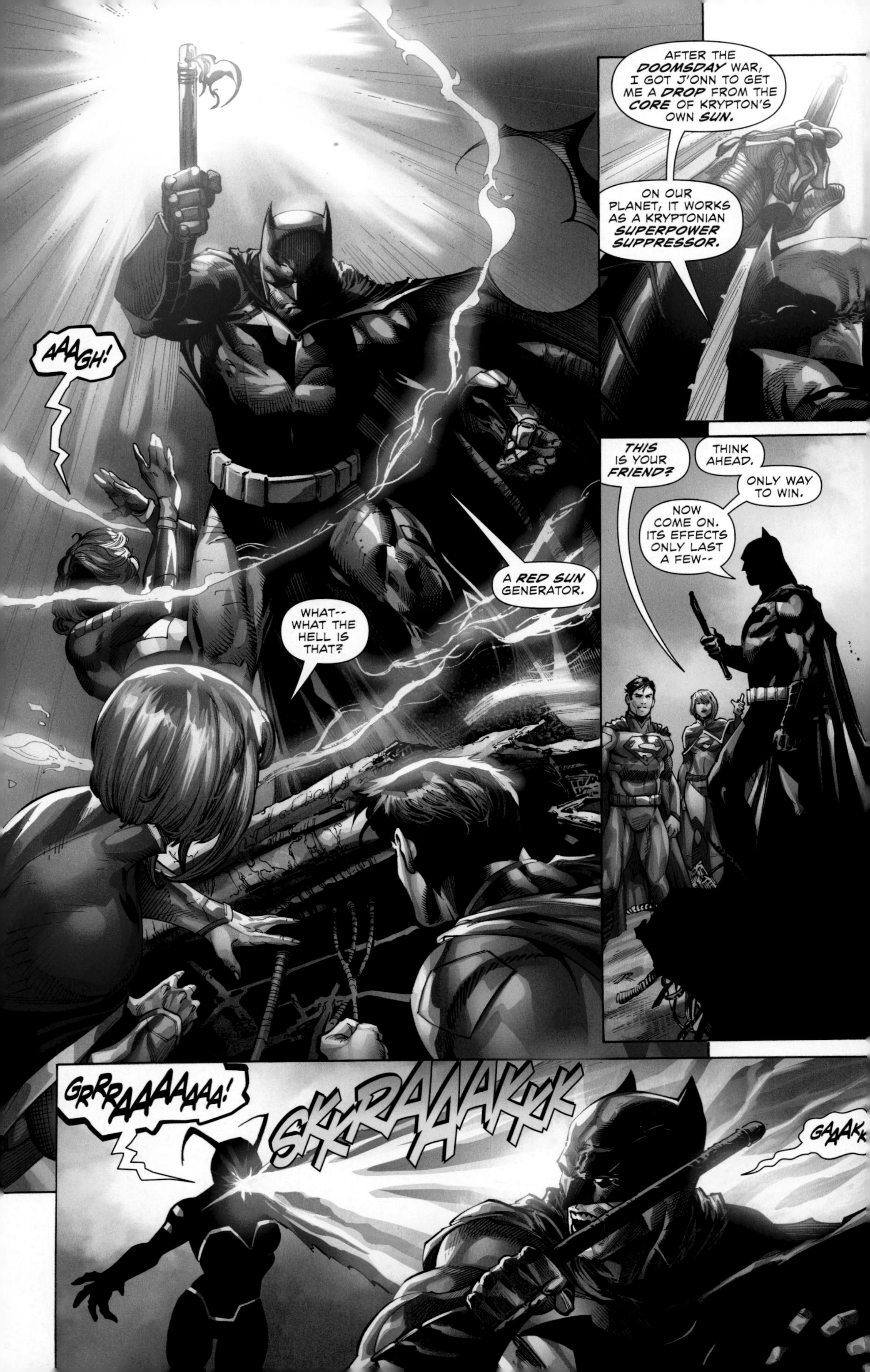
AAAGH!
WHAT--
WHAT THE
HELL IS
THAT?
A RED SUN
GENERATOR.
AFTER THE
DOOMSDAY WAR,
I GOT J'ONN TO GET
ME A DROP FROM THE
CORE OF KRYPTON'S
OWN SUN.
ON OUR
PLANET, IT WORKS
AS A KRYPTONIAN
SUPERPOWER
SUPPRESSOR.
THIS
IS YOUR
FRIEND?
THINK
AHEAD.
ONLY WAY
TO WIN.
NOW
COME ON.
ITS EFFECTS
ONLY LAST
A FEW--
GRRRAAAAAAA!
SKKRAAAKKK
GAAAKK

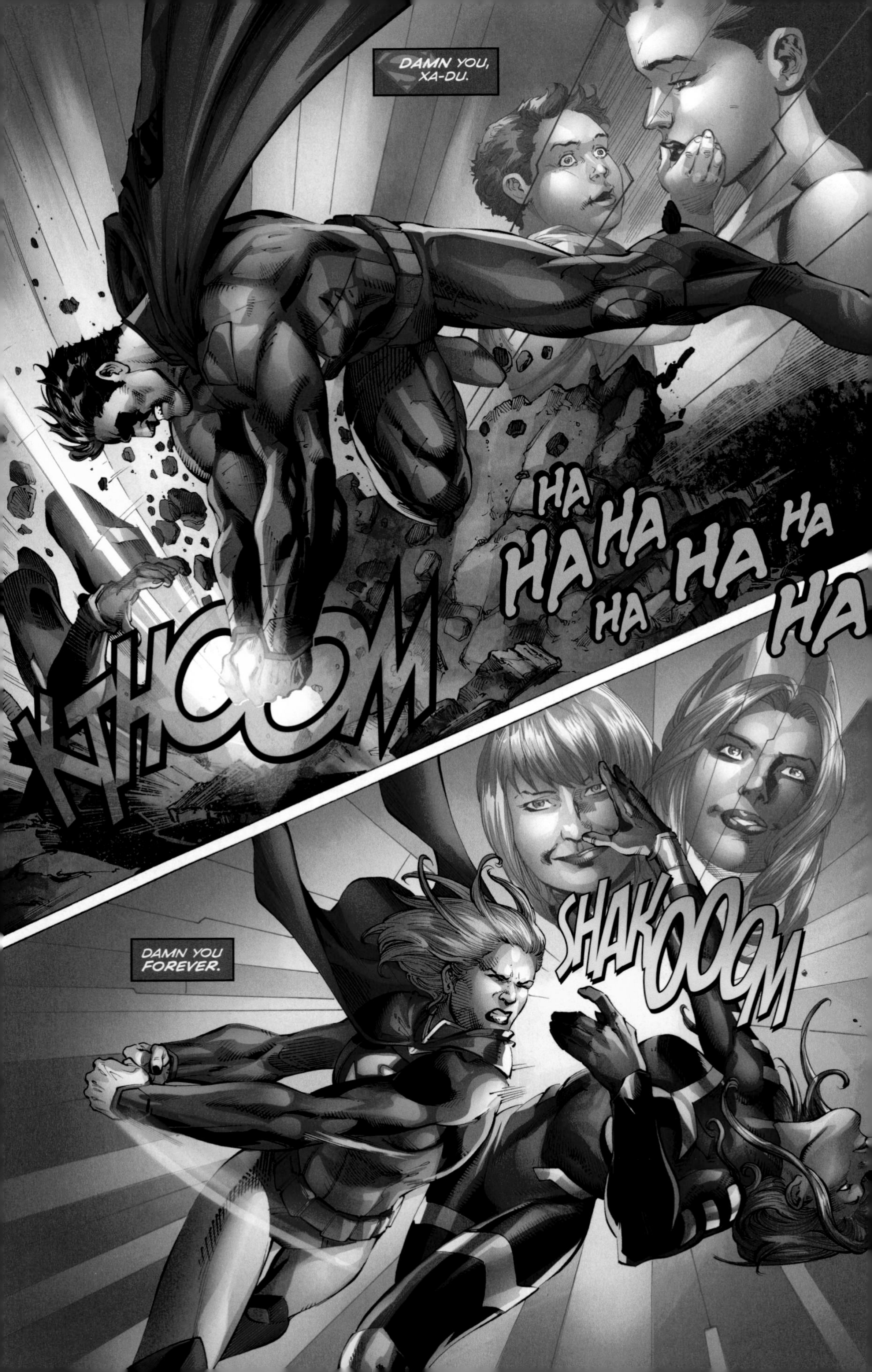
DAMN YOU, XA-DU.
KTHOOM
HA HA HA HA HA HA HA HA
DAMN YOU FOREVER.
SHAKOOOM

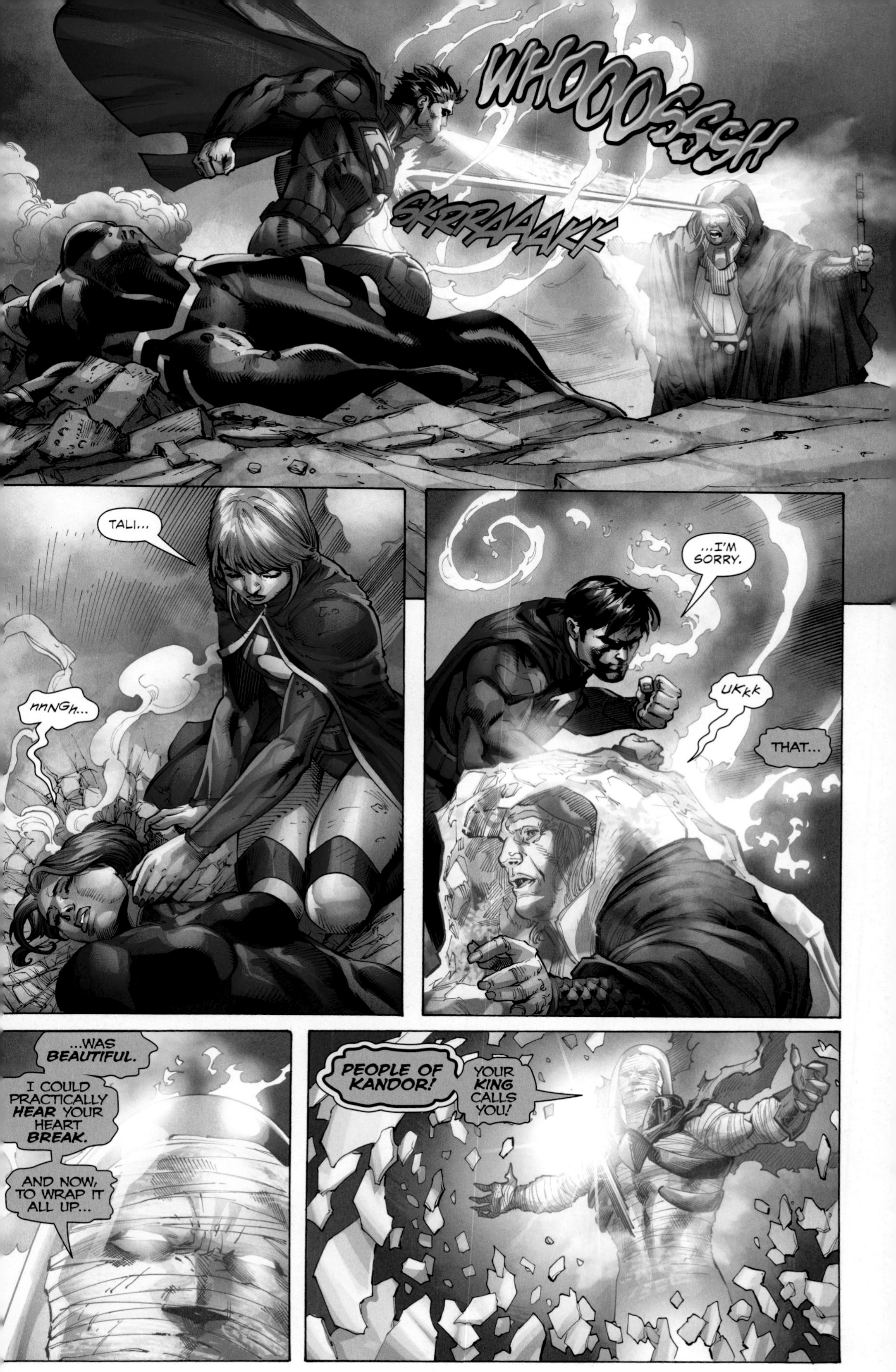
WHOOOOSSSH
SKRRAAAKK
TALI...
nnNGh...
...I'M SORRY.
UKkk
THAT...
...WAS BEAUTIFUL.
I COULD PRACTICALLY HEAR YOUR HEART BREAK.
AND NOW, TO WRAP IT ALL UP...
PEOPLE OF KANDOR!
YOUR KING CALLS YOU!

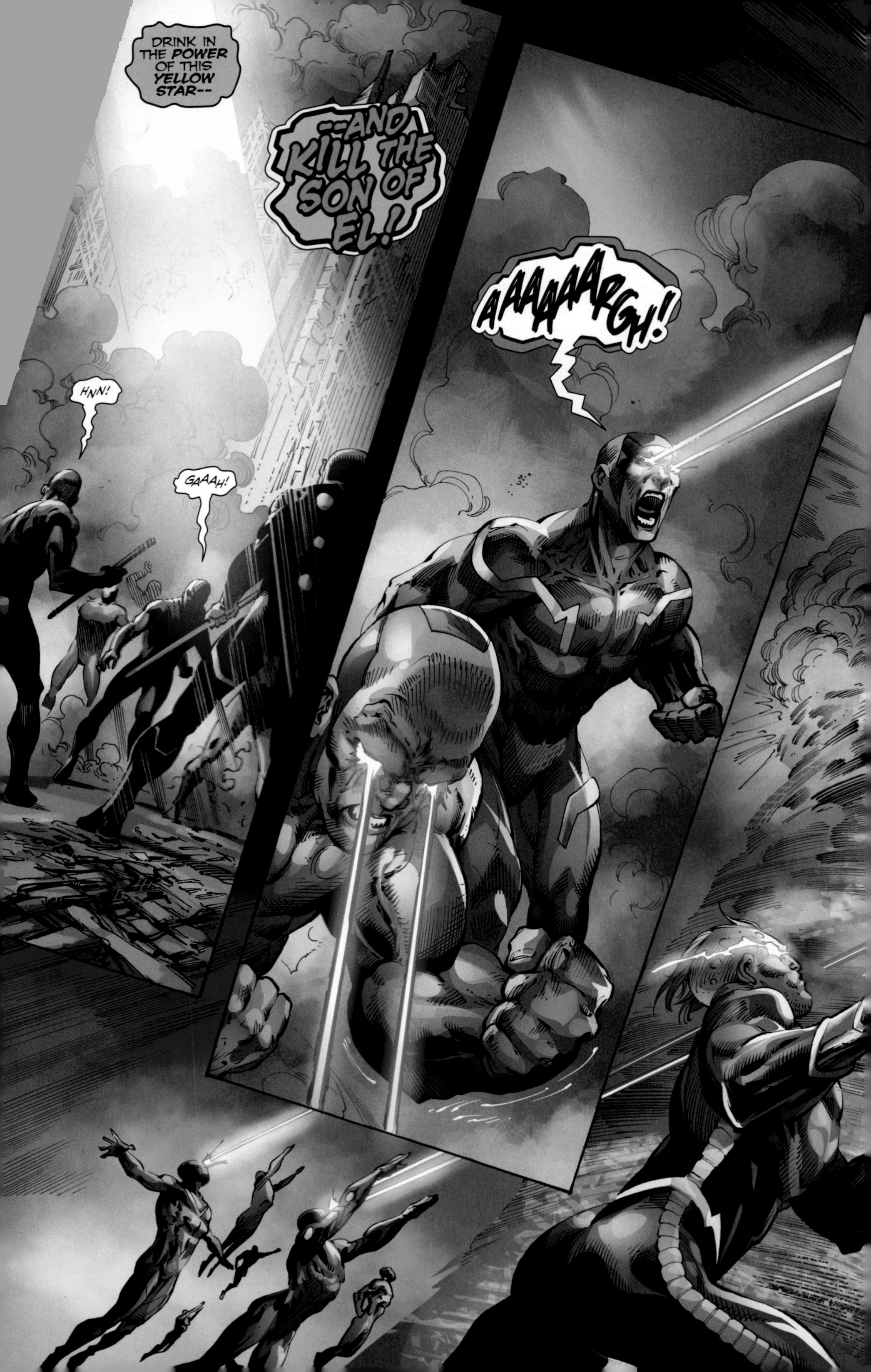
DRINK IN THE POWER OF THIS YELLOW STAR--
--AND KILL THE SON OF EL!
HNN!
GAAAH!
AAAAAAARGH!

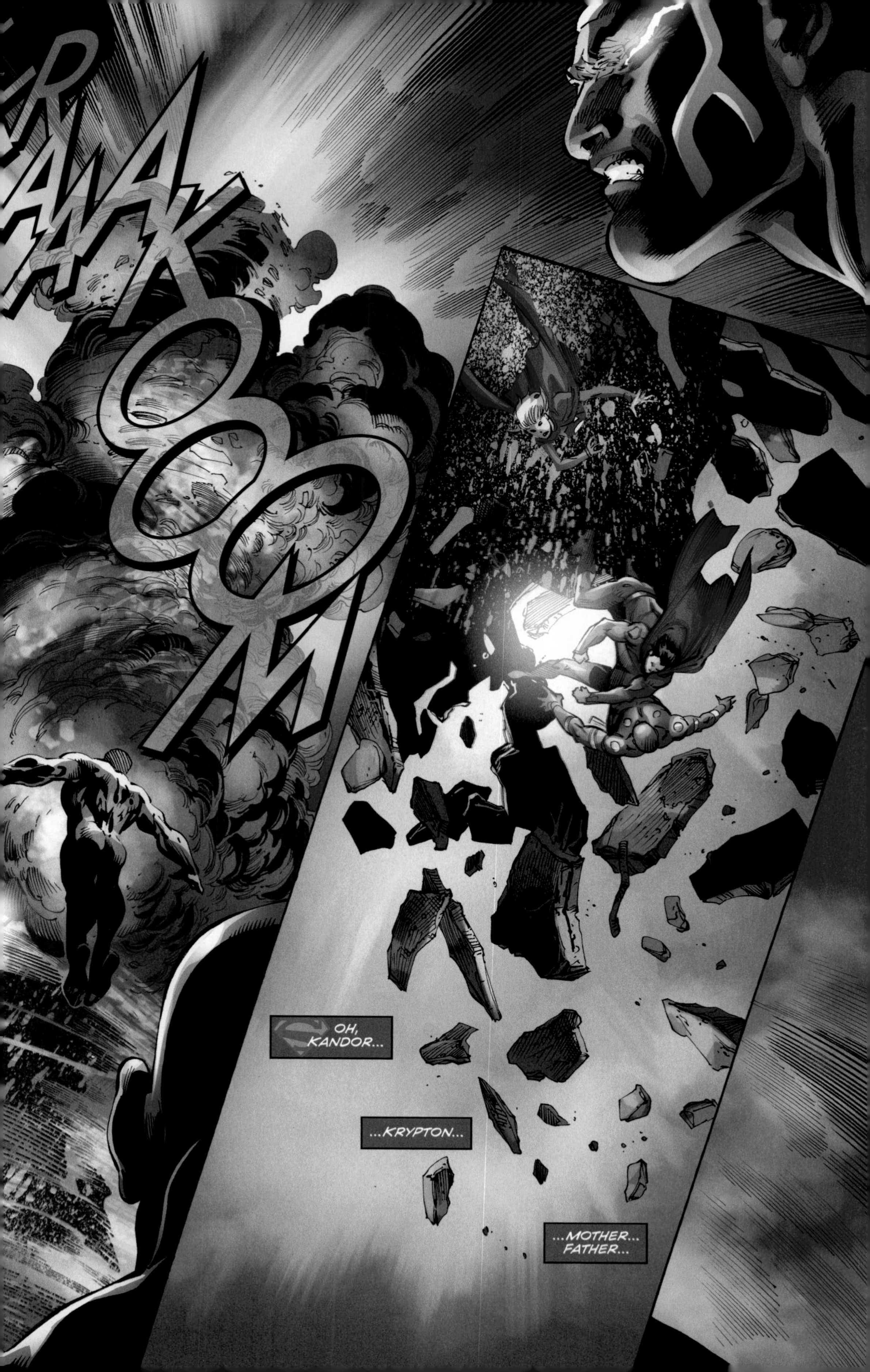

KRAWAKOOOM
OH, KANDOR...
...KRYPTON...
...MOTHER... FATHER...

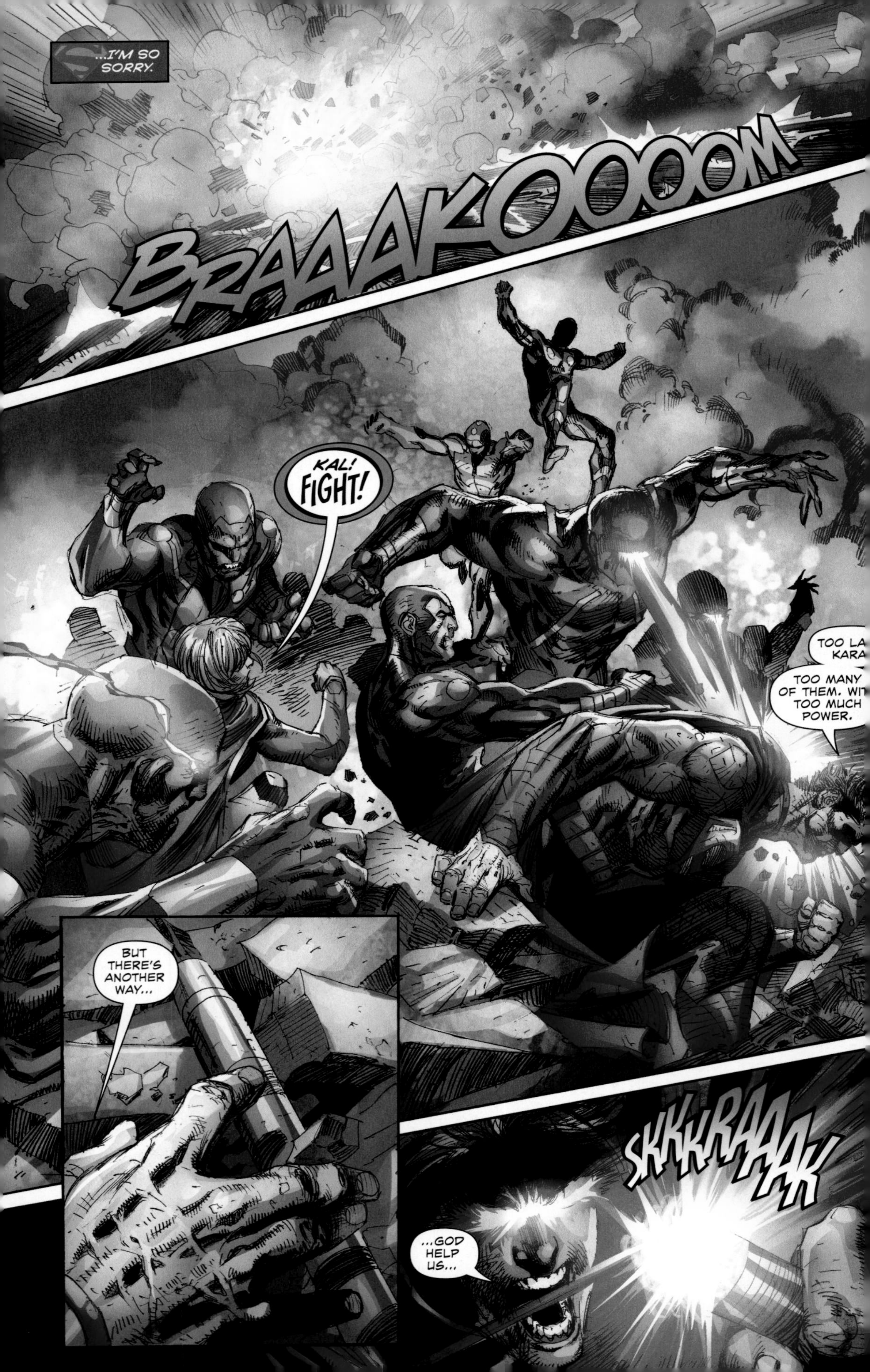
...I'M SO SORRY.
BRAAAKOOOOOM
KAL! FIGHT!
TOO MANY OF THEM.
TOO MUCH POWER.
BUT THERE'S ANOTHER WAY...
SKKKRAAAK
...GOD HELP US...

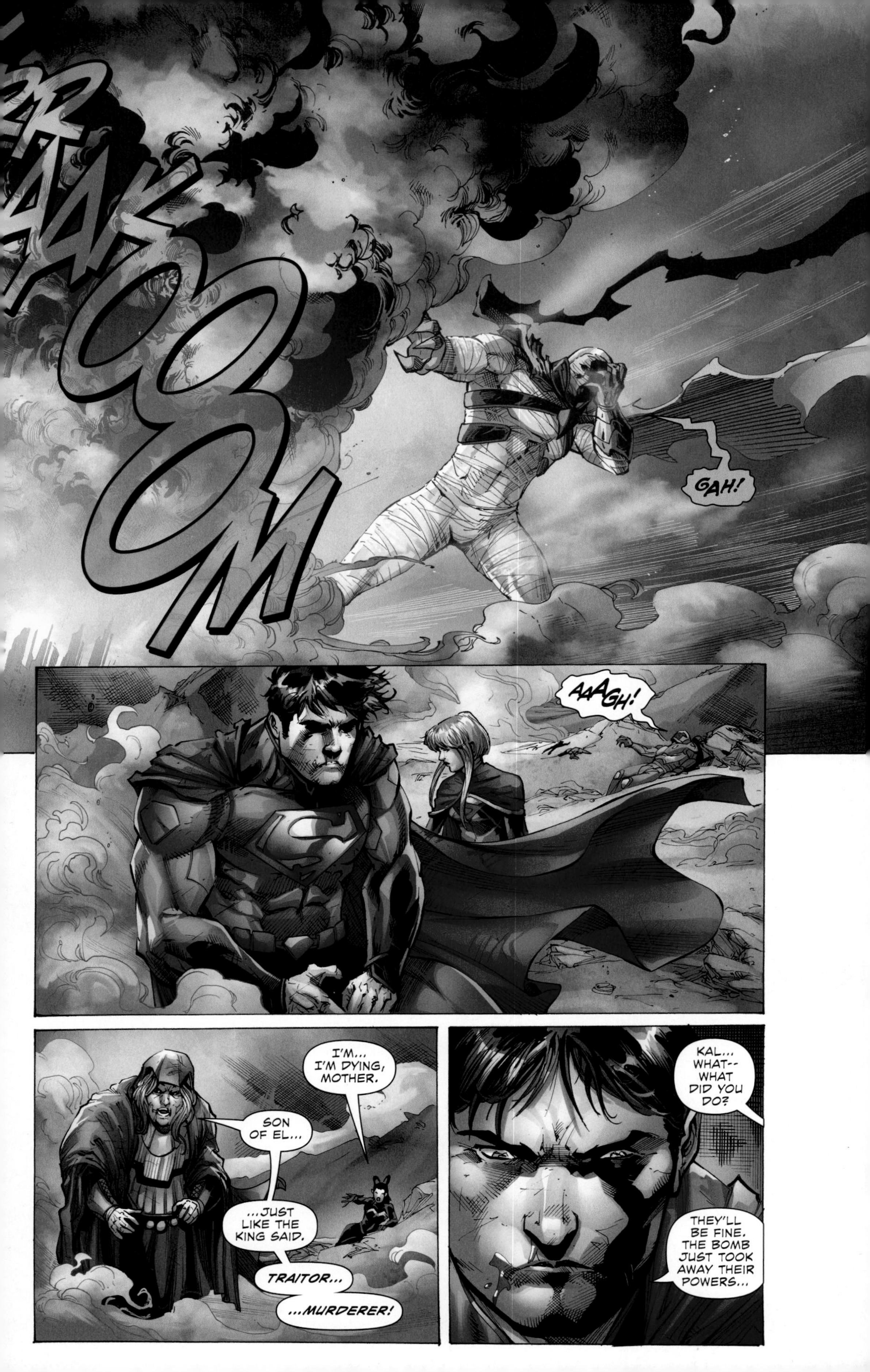
KRAKOOOM
GAH!
AAAGH!
I'M... I'M DYING, MOTHER.
SON OF EL...
...JUST LIKE THE KING SAID.
TRAITOR...
...MURDERER!
KAL... WHAT-- WHAT DID YOU DO?
THEY'LL BE FINE. THE BOMB JUST TOOK AWAY THEIR POWERS...

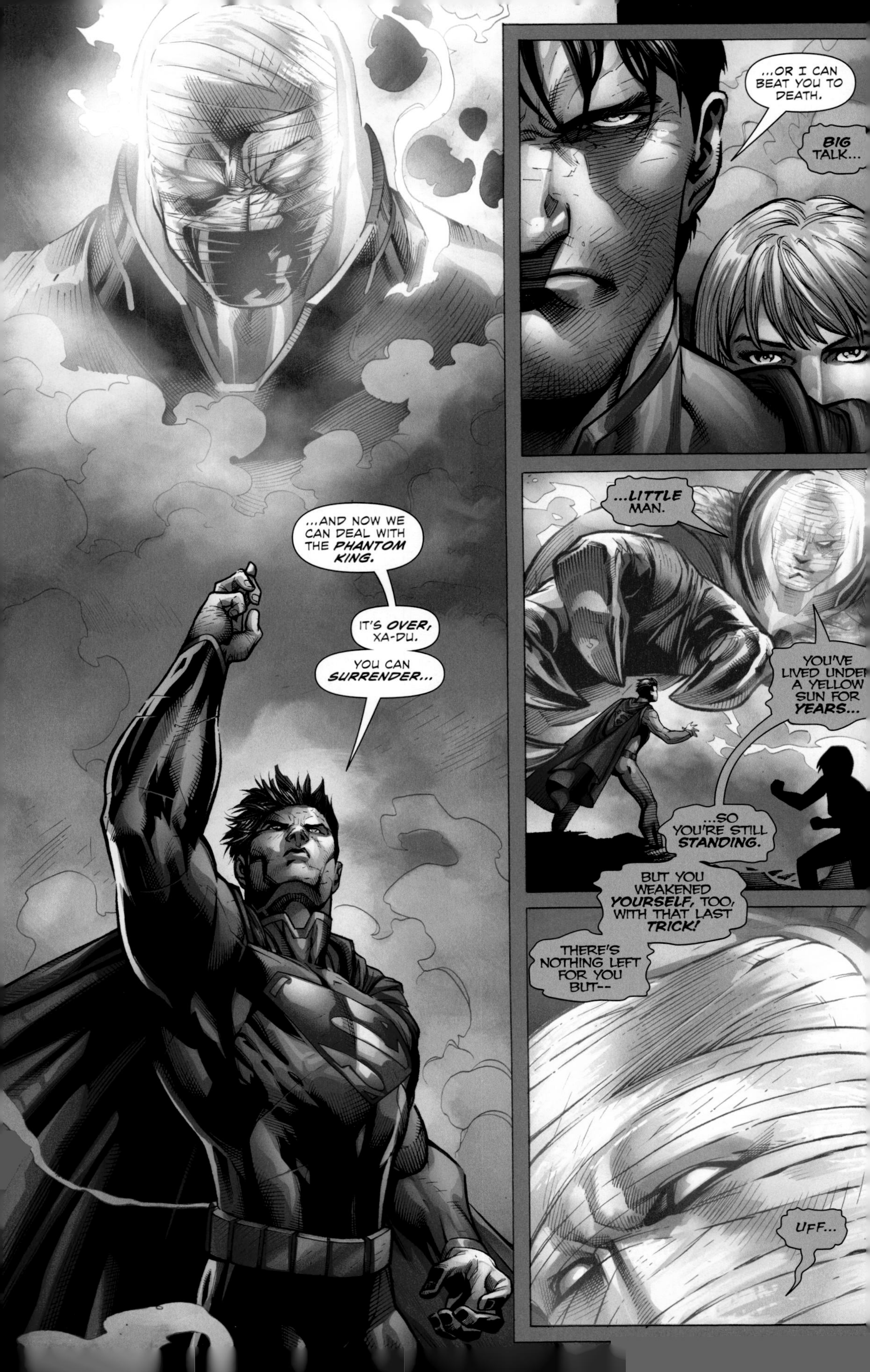
...AND NOW WE CAN DEAL WITH THE PHANTOM KING.
IT'S OVER, XA-DU.
YOU CAN SURRENDER...
...OR I CAN BEAT YOU TO DEATH.
BIG TALK...
...LITTLE MAN.
YOU'VE LIVED UNDE A YELLOW SUN FOR YEARS...
...SO YOU'RE STILL STANDING.
BUT YOU WEAKENED YOURSELF, TOO, WITH THAT LAST TRICK!
THERE'S NOTHING LEFT FOR YOU BUT--
UFF...

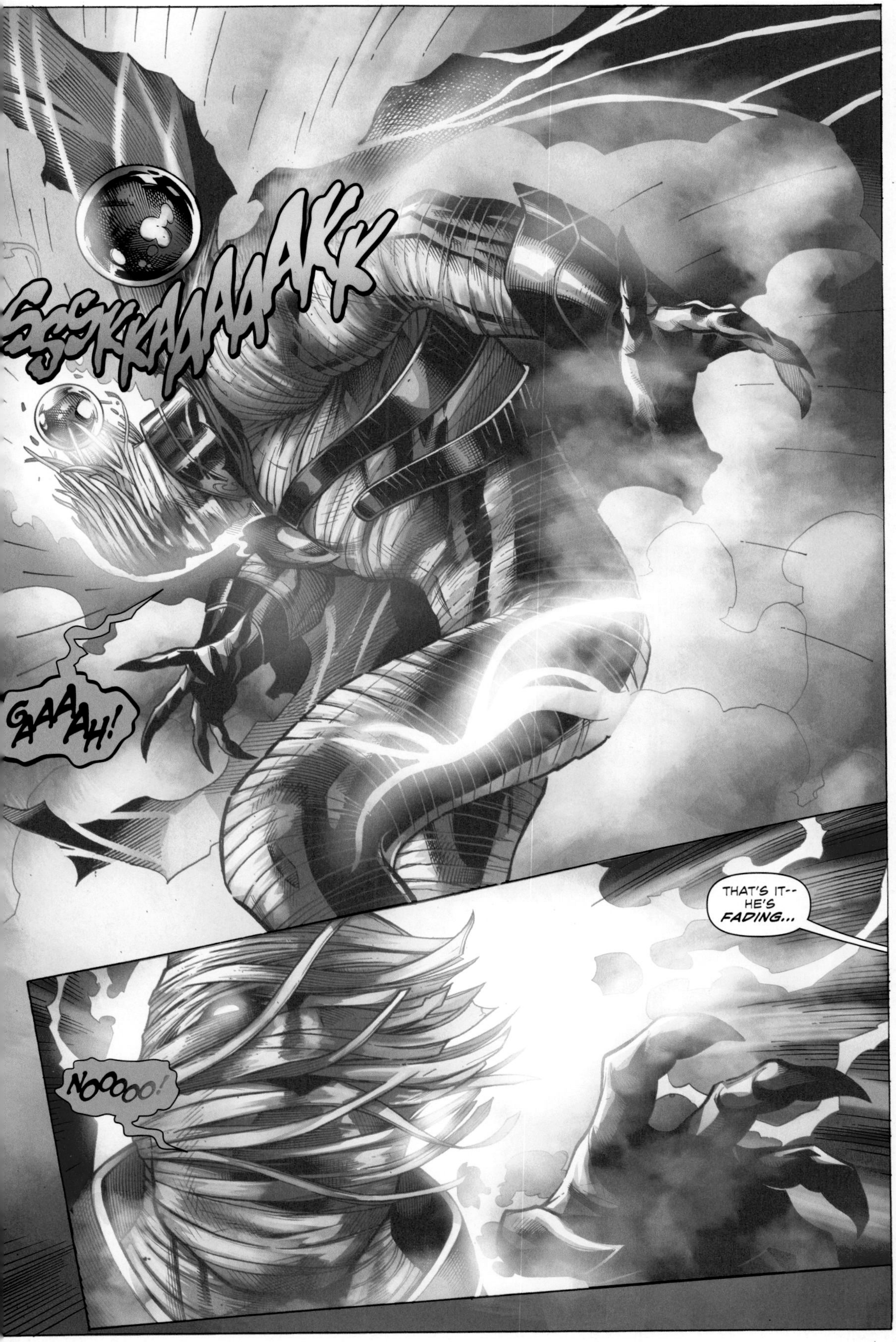
SSSKKAAAAAKK
GAAAAH!
THAT'S IT-- HE'S FADING...
NOOOOO!

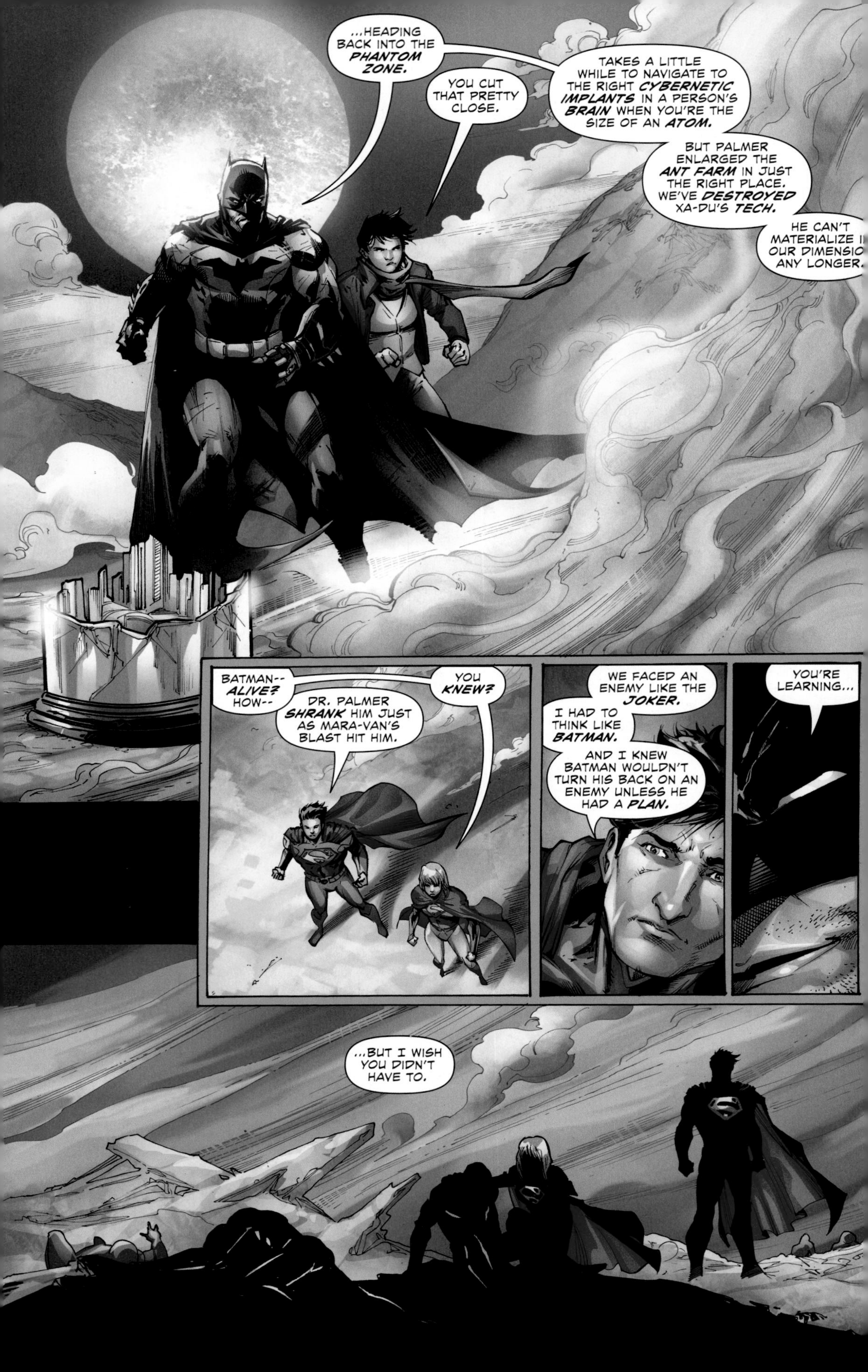
...HEADING BACK INTO THE PHANTOM ZONE.
YOU CUT THAT PRETTY CLOSE.
TAKES A LITTLE WHILE TO NAVIGATE TO THE RIGHT CYBERNETIC IMPLANTS IN A PERSON'S BRAIN WHEN YOU'RE THE SIZE OF AN ATOM.
BUT PALMER ENLARGED THE ANT FARM IN JUST THE RIGHT PLACE. WE'VE DESTROYED XA-DU'S TECH.
HE CAN'T MATERIALIZE I OUR DIMENSIO ANY LONGER.
BATMAN-- ALIVE? HOW--
DR. PALMER SHRANK HIM JUST AS MARA-VAN'S BLAST HIT HIM.
YOU KNEW?
WE FACED AN ENEMY LIKE THE JOKER.
I HAD TO THINK LIKE BATMAN.
AND I KNEW BATMAN WOULDN'T TURN HIS BACK ON AN ENEMY UNLESS HE HAD A PLAN.
YOU'RE LEARNING...
...BUT I WISH YOU DIDN'T HAVE TO.

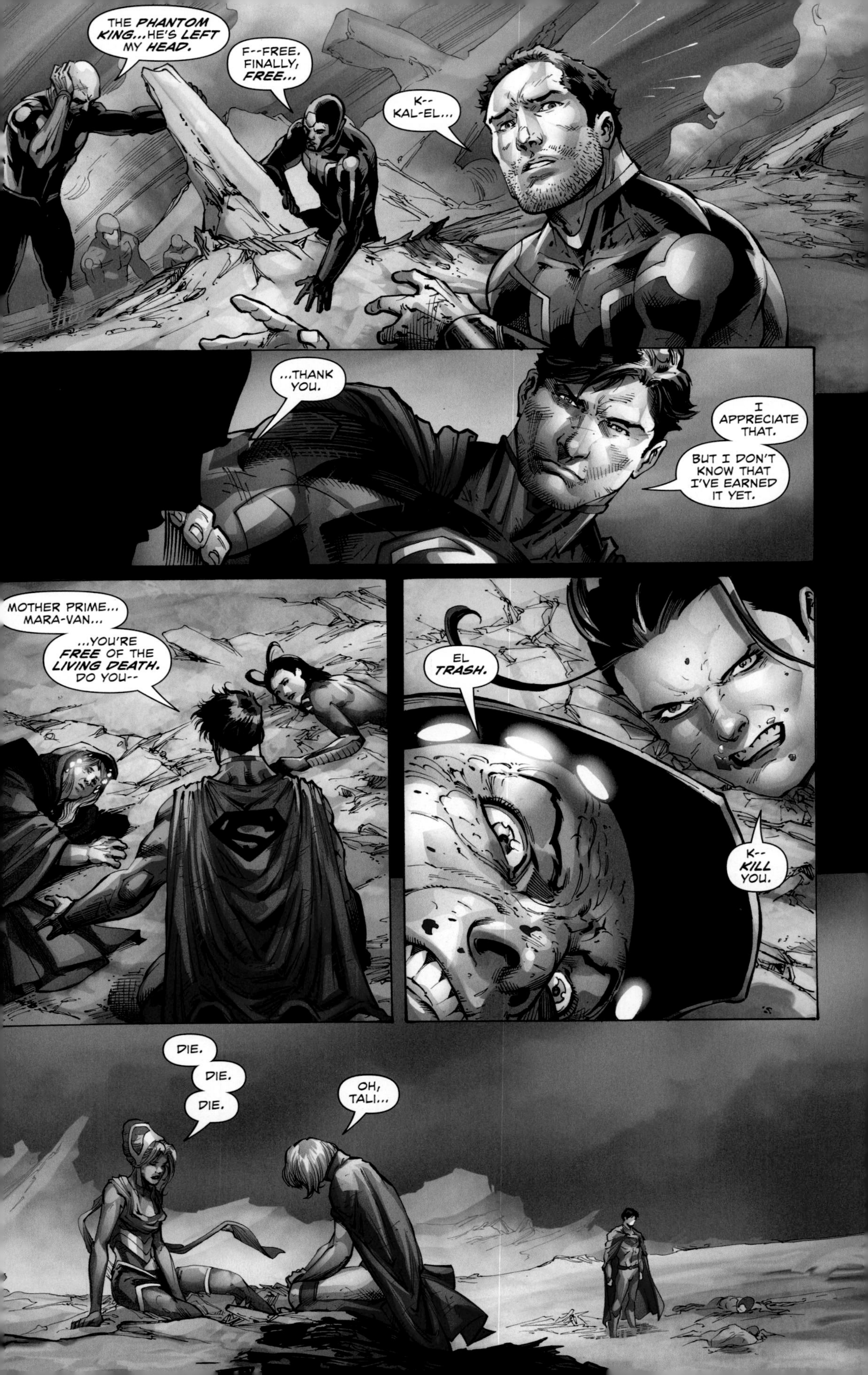
THE PHANTOM KING...HE'S LEFT MY HEAD.
F--FREE. FINALLY, FREE...
K-- KAL-EL...
...THANK YOU.
I APPRECIATE THAT.
BUT I DON'T KNOW THAT I'VE EARNED IT YET.
MOTHER PRIME... MARA-VAN...
...YOU'RE FREE OF THE LIVING DEATH. DO YOU--
EL TRASH.
K-- KILL YOU.
DIE.
DIE.
DIE.
OH, TALI...

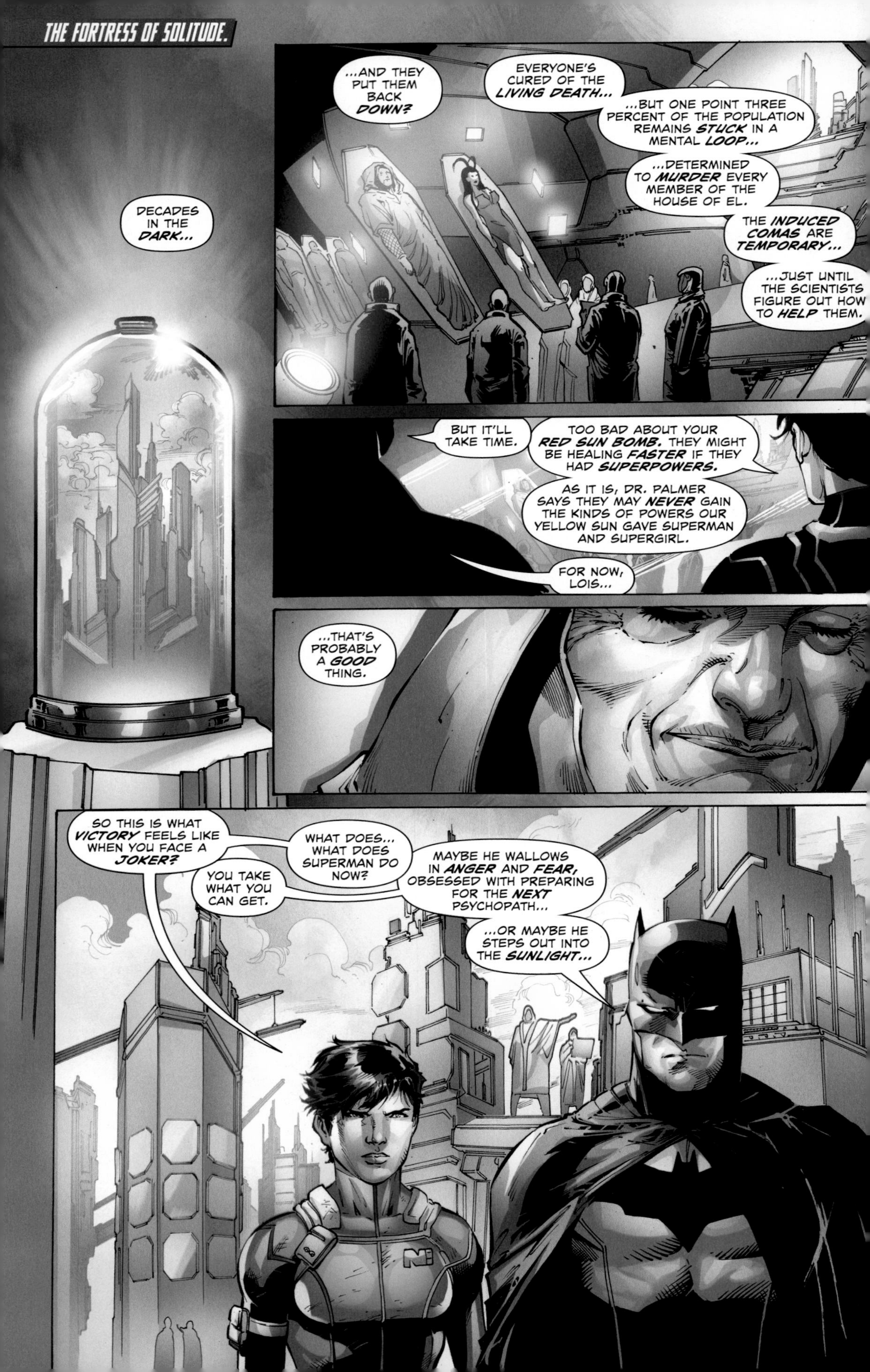
THE FORTRESS OF SOLITUDE.
DECADES IN THE DARK...
...AND THEY PUT THEM BACK DOWN?
EVERYONE'S CURED OF THE LIVING DEATH...
...BUT ONE POINT THREE PERCENT OF THE POPULATION REMAINS STUCK IN A MENTAL LOOP...
...DETERMINED TO MURDER EVERY MEMBER OF THE HOUSE OF EL.
THE INDUCED COMAS ARE TEMPORARY...
...JUST UNTIL THE SCIENTISTS FIGURE OUT HOW TO HELP THEM.
BUT IT'LL TAKE TIME.
TOO BAD ABOUT YOUR RED SUN BOMB. THEY MIGHT BE HEALING FASTER IF THEY HAD SUPERPOWERS.
AS IT IS, DR. PALMER SAYS THEY MAY NEVER GAIN THE KINDS OF POWERS OUR YELLOW SUN GAVE SUPERMAN AND SUPERGIRL.
FOR NOW, LOIS...
...THAT'S PROBABLY A GOOD THING.
SO THIS IS WHAT VICTORY FEELS LIKE WHEN YOU FACE A JOKER?
YOU TAKE WHAT YOU CAN GET.
WHAT DOES... WHAT DOES SUPERMAN DO NOW?
MAYBE HE WALLOWS IN ANGER AND FEAR, OBSESSED WITH PREPARING FOR THE NEXT PSYCHOPATH...
...OR MAYBE HE STEPS OUT INTO THE SUNLIGHT...

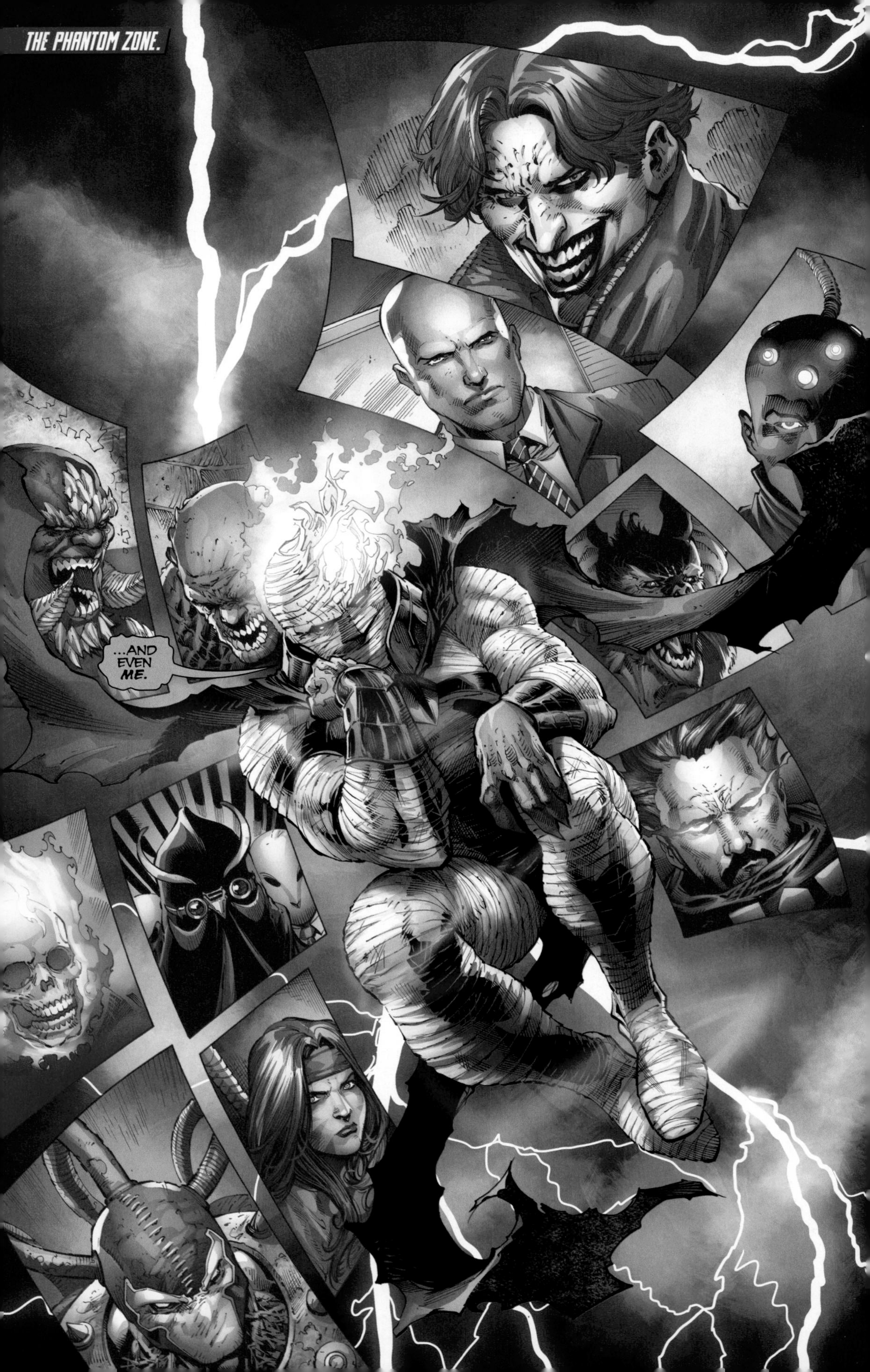
THE PHANTOM ZONE.
...AND EVEN ME.

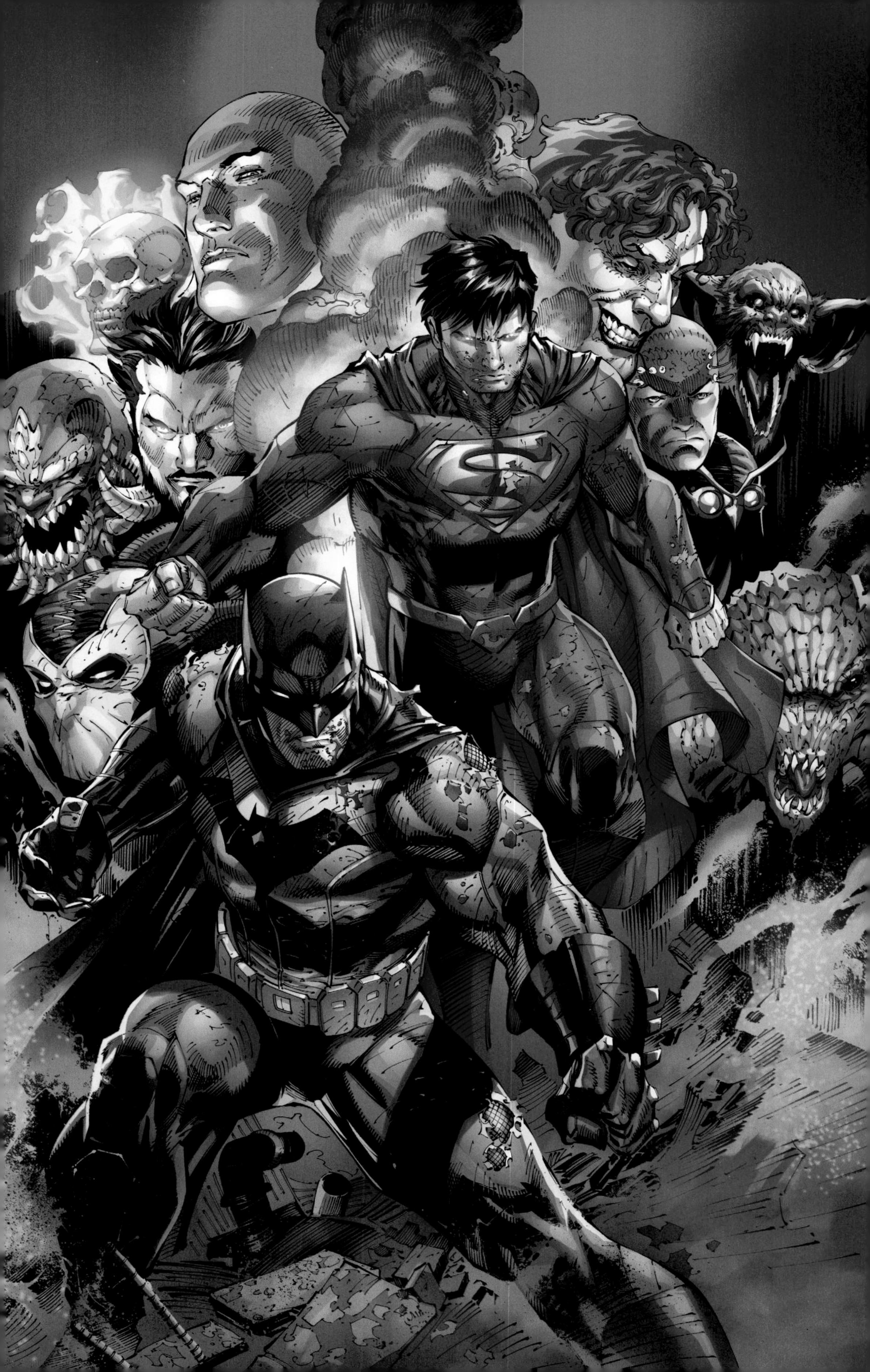

VICENTE CIFUENTES, TYLER KIRKHAM, MARK MORALES, JAIME MENDOZA, RAY MCCARTHY inkers ARIF PRIANTO, FAHRIZA KAMAPUTRA, JESSICA KHOLINNE, GLORIA CAELI colo
ROB LEIGH letterer cover by ARDIAN SYAF, JONATHAN GLAPION and ULISES ARREOLA

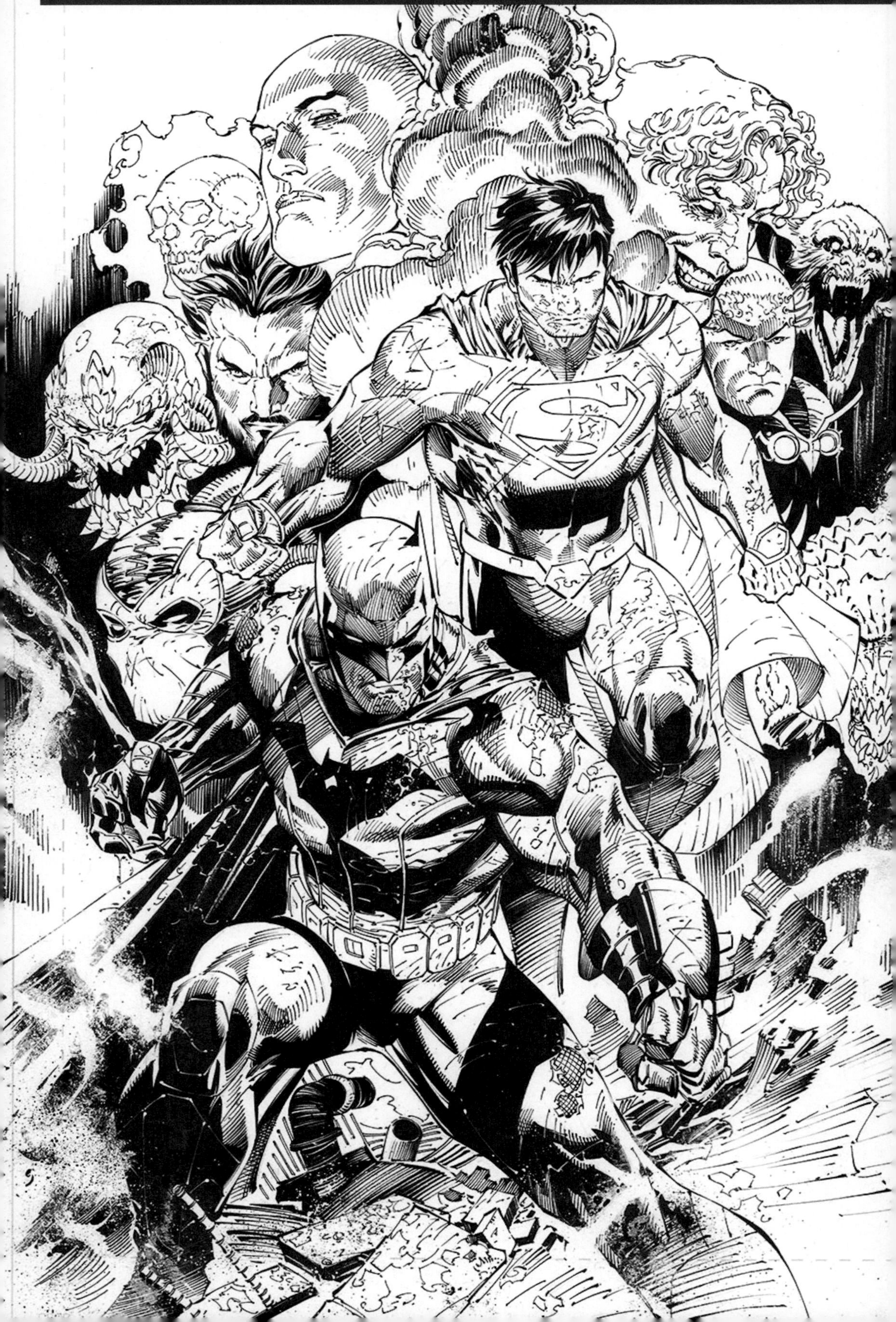

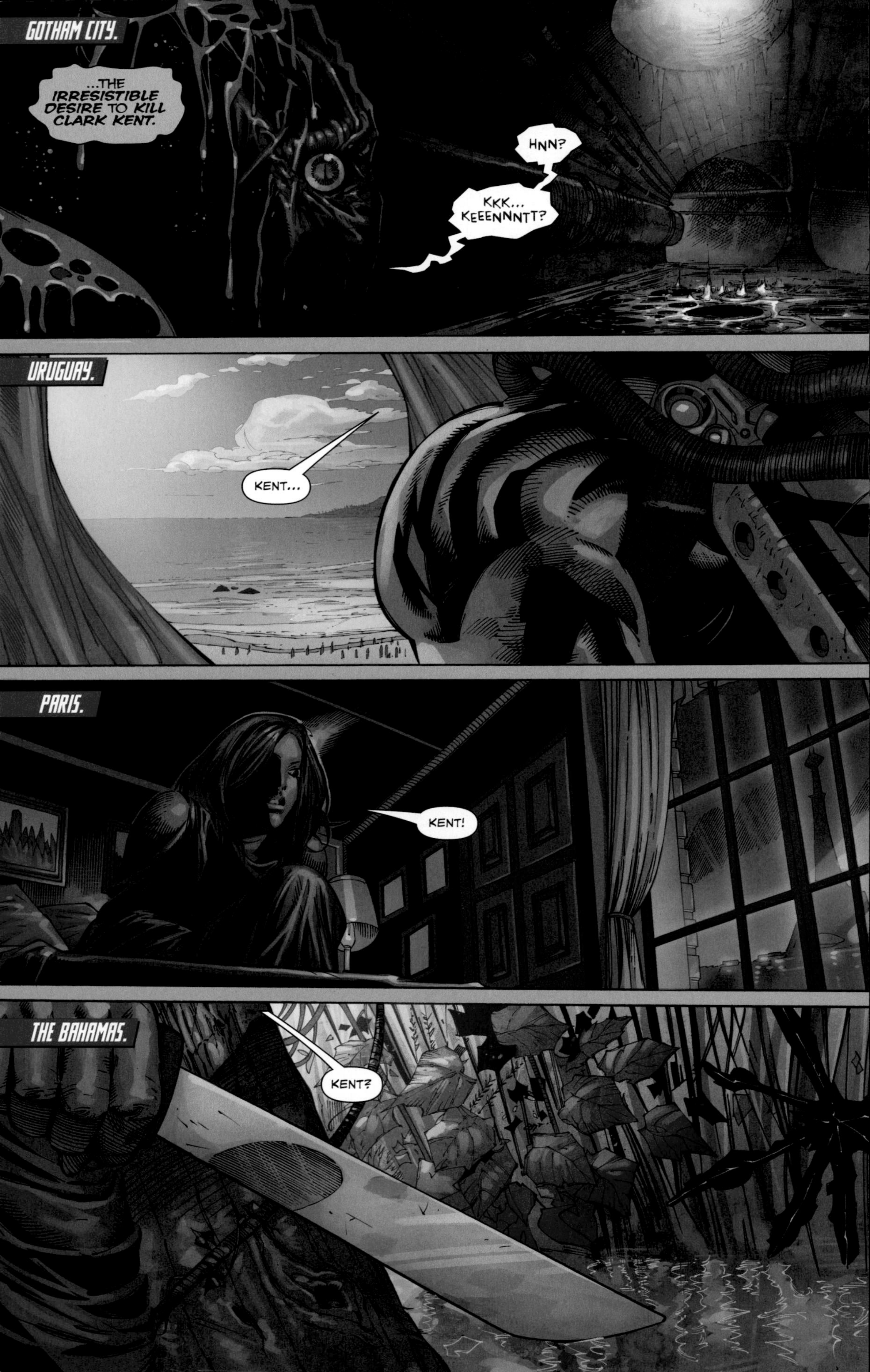
GOTHAM CITY.
...THE IRRESISTIBLE DESIRE TO KILL CLARK KENT.
HNN?
KKK... KEEENNNTT?
URUGUAY.
KENT...
PARIS.
KENT!
THE BAHAMAS.
KENT?

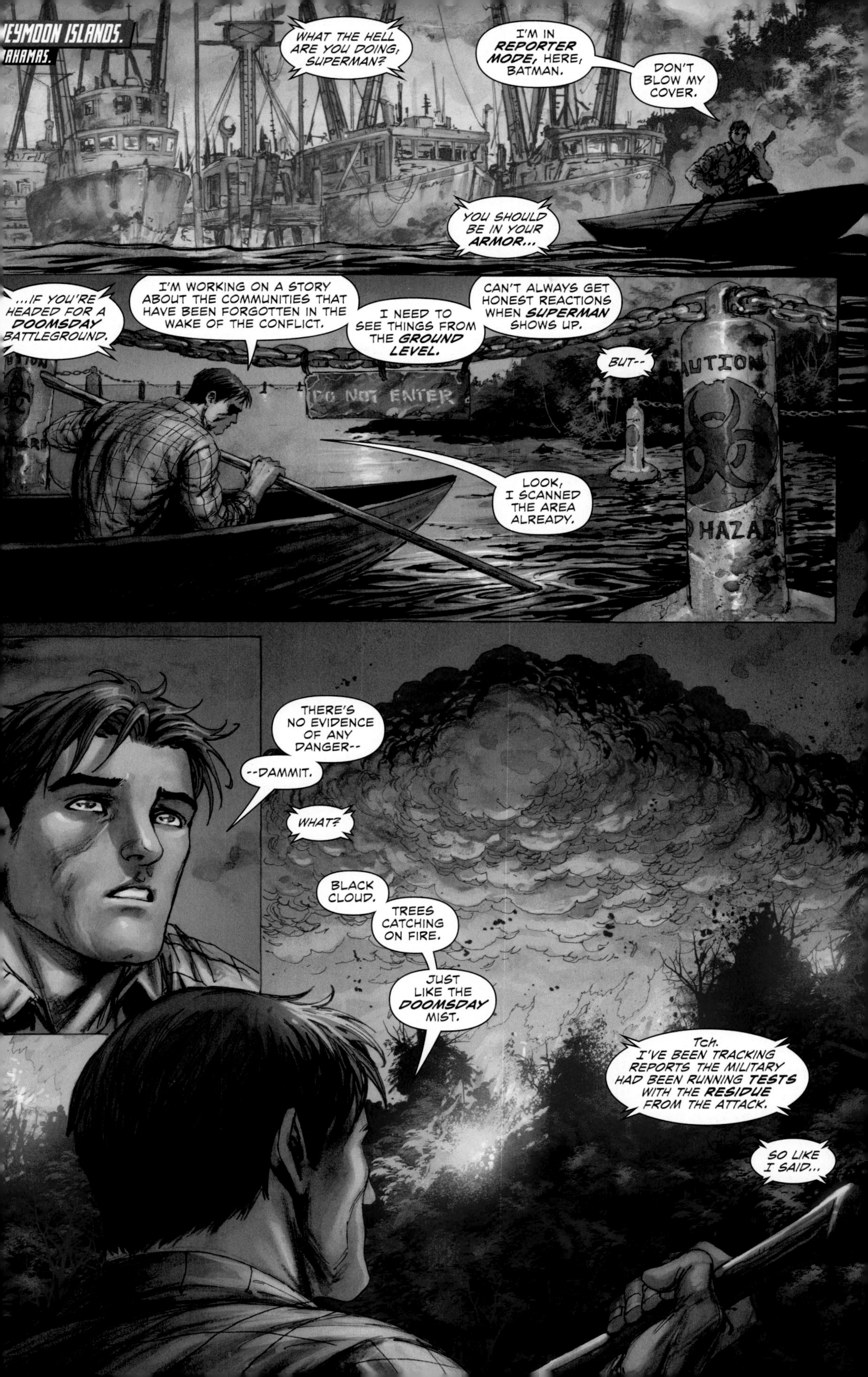

EYMOON ISLANDS.
AHAMAS.
WHAT THE HELL ARE YOU DOING, SUPERMAN?
I'M IN REPORTER MODE, HERE, BATMAN.
DON'T BLOW MY COVER.
YOU SHOULD BE IN YOUR ARMOR...
...IF YOU'RE HEADED FOR A DOOMSDAY BATTLEGROUND.
I'M WORKING ON A STORY ABOUT THE COMMUNITIES THAT HAVE BEEN FORGOTTEN IN THE WAKE OF THE CONFLICT.
I NEED TO SEE THINGS FROM THE GROUND LEVEL.
CAN'T ALWAYS GET HONEST REACTIONS WHEN SUPERMAN SHOWS UP.
BUT--
DO NOT ENTER
AUTION
HAZAR
LOOK, I SCANNED THE AREA ALREADY.
THERE'S NO EVIDENCE OF ANY DANGER--
--DAMMIT.
WHAT?
BLACK CLOUD.
TREES CATCHING ON FIRE.
JUST LIKE THE DOOMSDAY MIST.
Tch. I'VE BEEN TRACKING REPORTS THE MILITARY HAD BEEN RUNNING TESTS WITH THE RESIDUE FROM THE ATTACK.
SO LIKE I SAID...

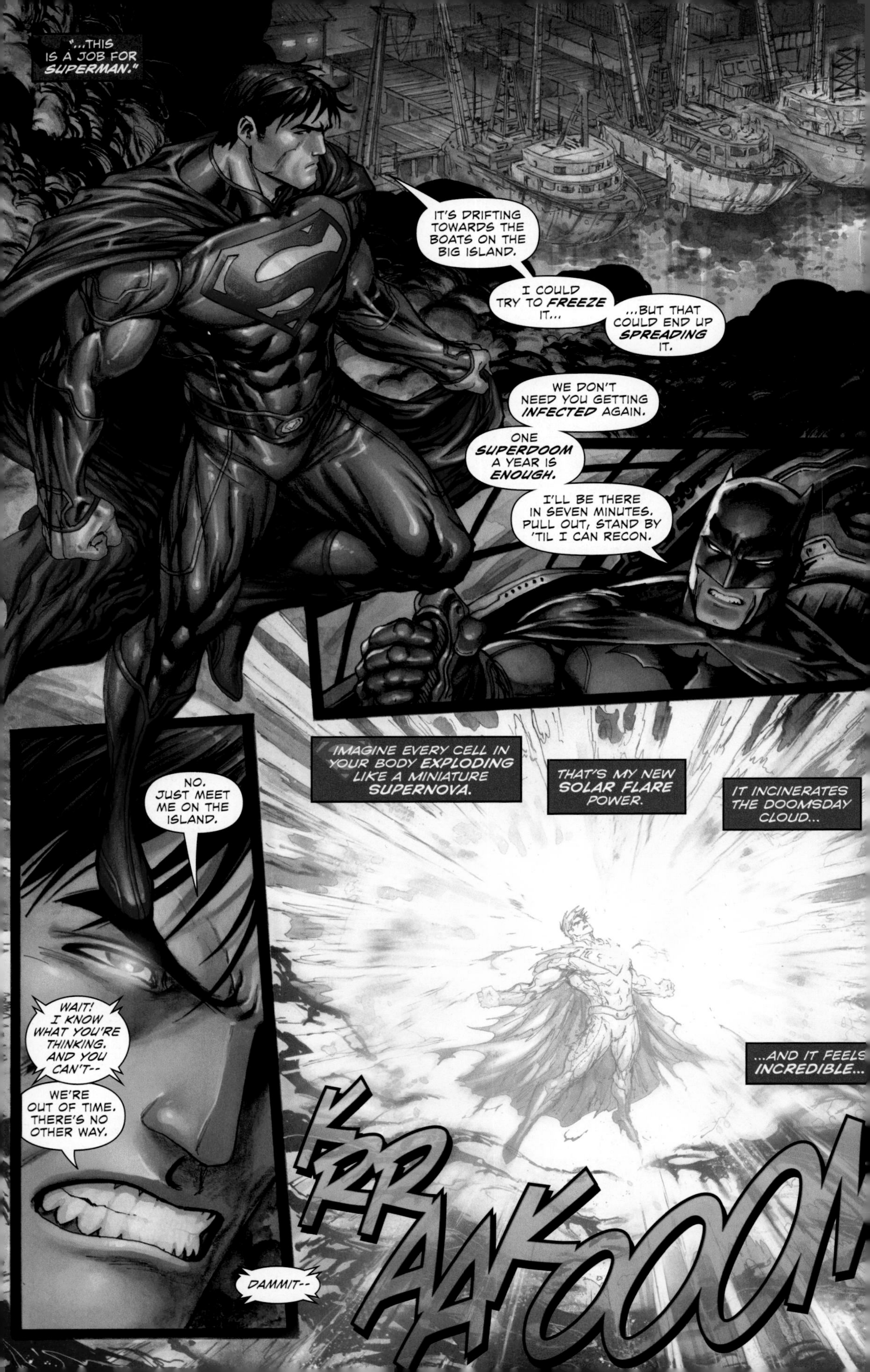
"...THIS IS A JOB FOR *SUPERMAN.*"
IT'S DRIFTING TOWARDS THE BOATS ON THE BIG ISLAND.
I COULD TRY TO *FREEZE* IT...
...BUT THAT COULD END UP *SPREADING* IT.
WE DON'T NEED YOU GETTING *INFECTED* AGAIN.
ONE *SUPERDOOM* A YEAR IS *ENOUGH.*
I'LL BE THERE IN SEVEN MINUTES. PULL OUT, STAND BY 'TIL I CAN RECON.
NO. JUST MEET ME ON THE ISLAND.
WAIT! I KNOW WHAT YOU'RE THINKING. AND YOU CAN'T--
WE'RE OUT OF TIME. THERE'S NO OTHER WAY.
DAMMIT--
IMAGINE EVERY CELL IN YOUR BODY **EXPLODING** LIKE A MINIATURE **SUPERNOVA.**
THAT'S MY NEW **SOLAR FLARE** POWER.
IT INCINERATES THE DOOMSDAY CLOUD...
...AND IT FEELS **INCREDIBLE...**
KRR AAKOOOM

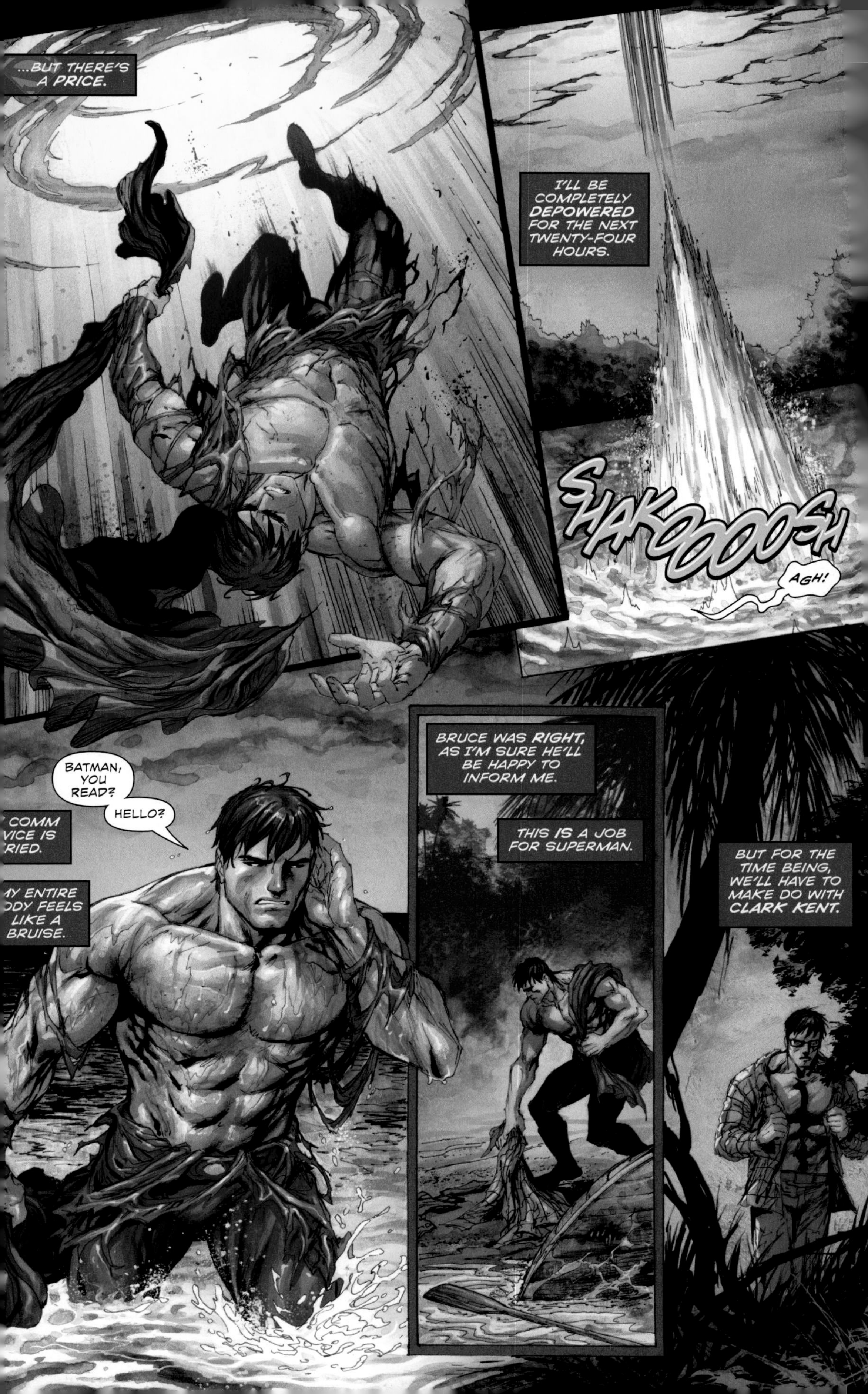
...BUT THERE'S A PRICE.
I'LL BE COMPLETELY DEPOWERED FOR THE NEXT TWENTY-FOUR HOURS.
SHAKOOOOSH
AGH!
BATMAN, YOU READ?
HELLO?
COMM VICE IS RIED.
MY ENTIRE ODY FEELS LIKE A BRUISE.
BRUCE WAS RIGHT, AS I'M SURE HE'LL BE HAPPY TO INFORM ME.
THIS IS A JOB FOR SUPERMAN.
BUT FOR THE TIME BEING, WE'LL HAVE TO MAKE DO WITH CLARK KENT.

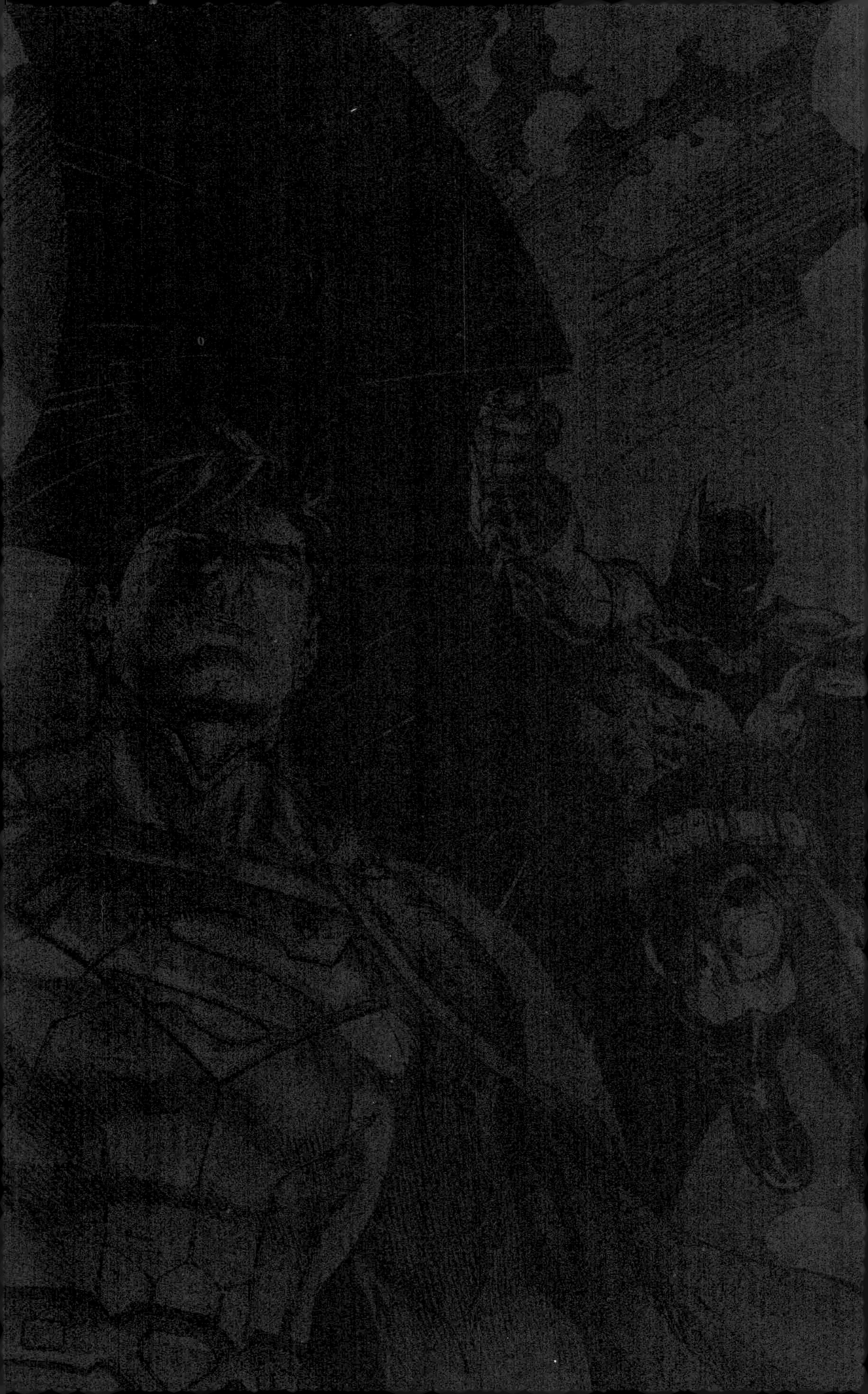

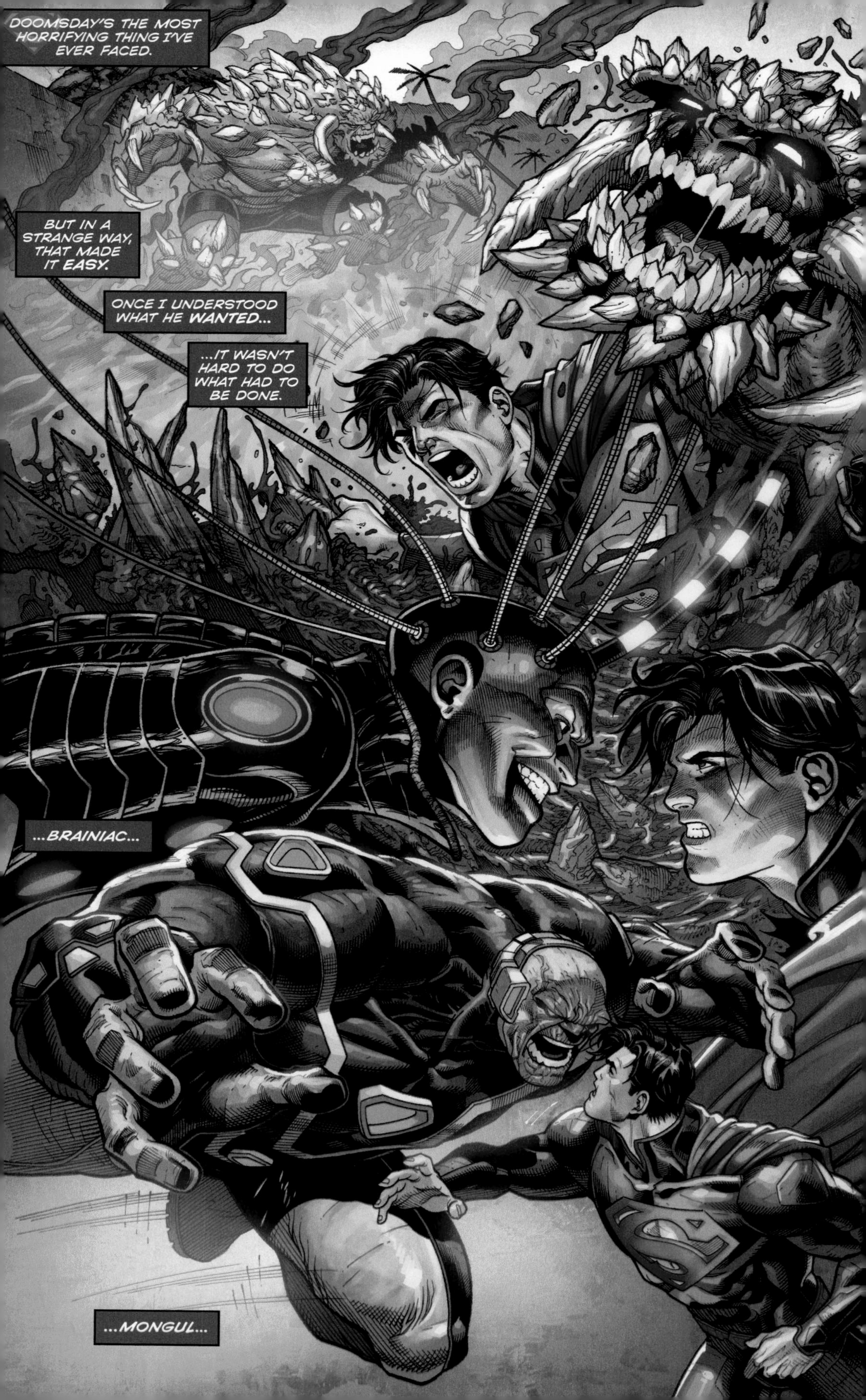
DOOMSDAY'S THE MOST HORRIFYING THING I'VE EVER FACED.
BUT IN A STRANGE WAY, THAT MADE IT **EASY**.
ONCE I UNDERSTOOD WHAT HE **WANTED**...
...IT WASN'T HARD TO DO WHAT HAD TO BE DONE.
...**BRAINIAC**...
...**MONGUL**...

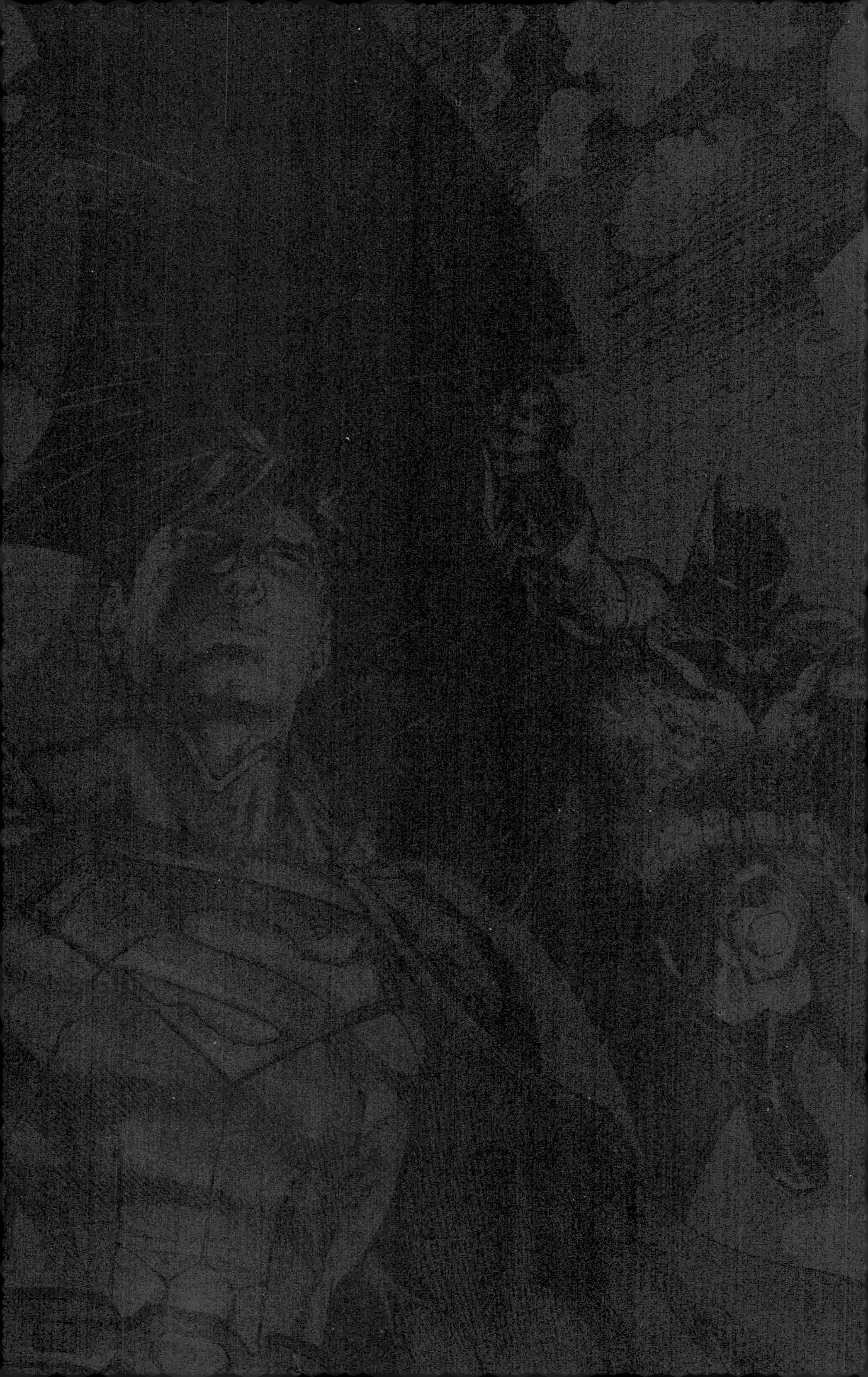

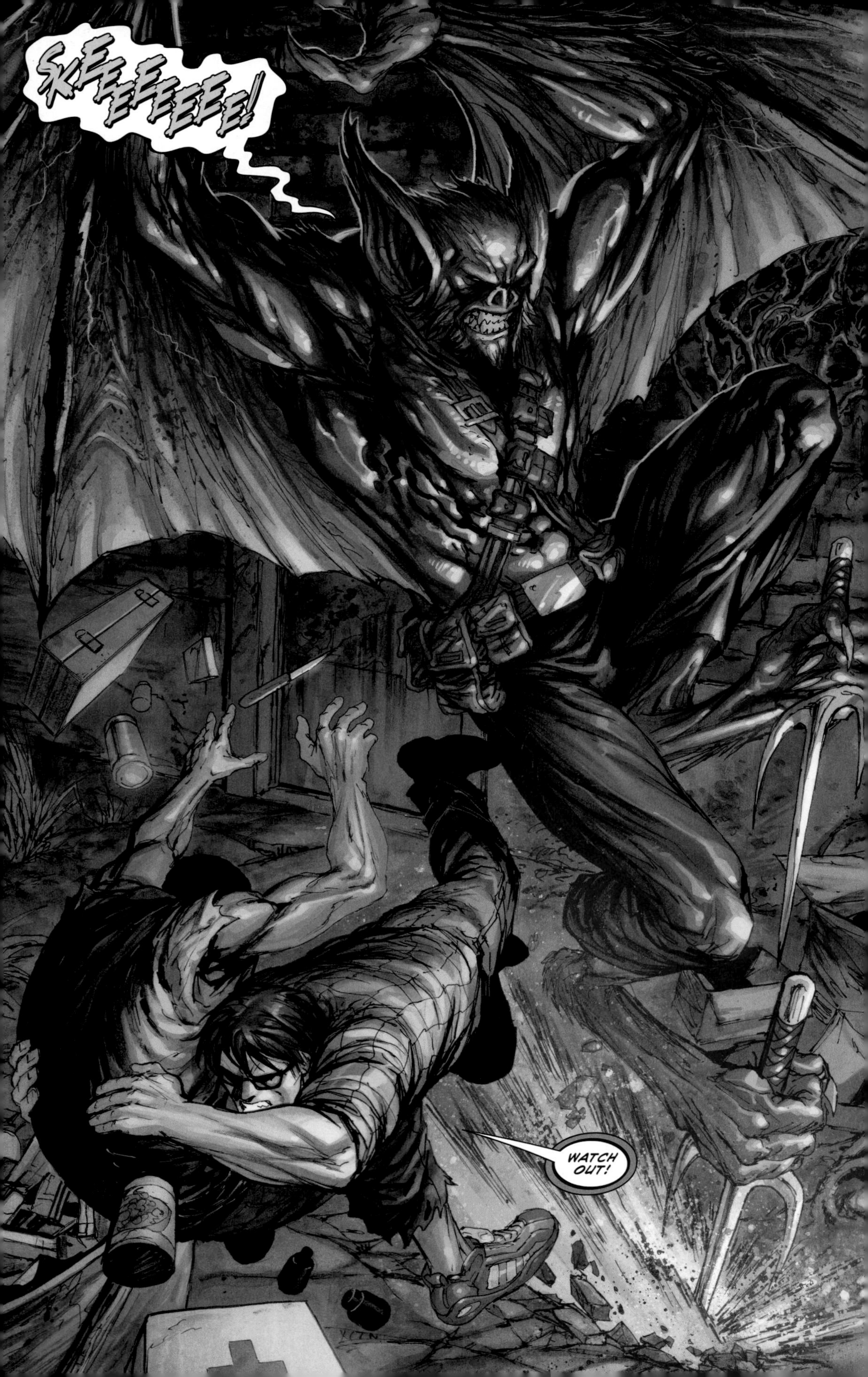
SKEEEEEEEEEE!
WATCH OUT!

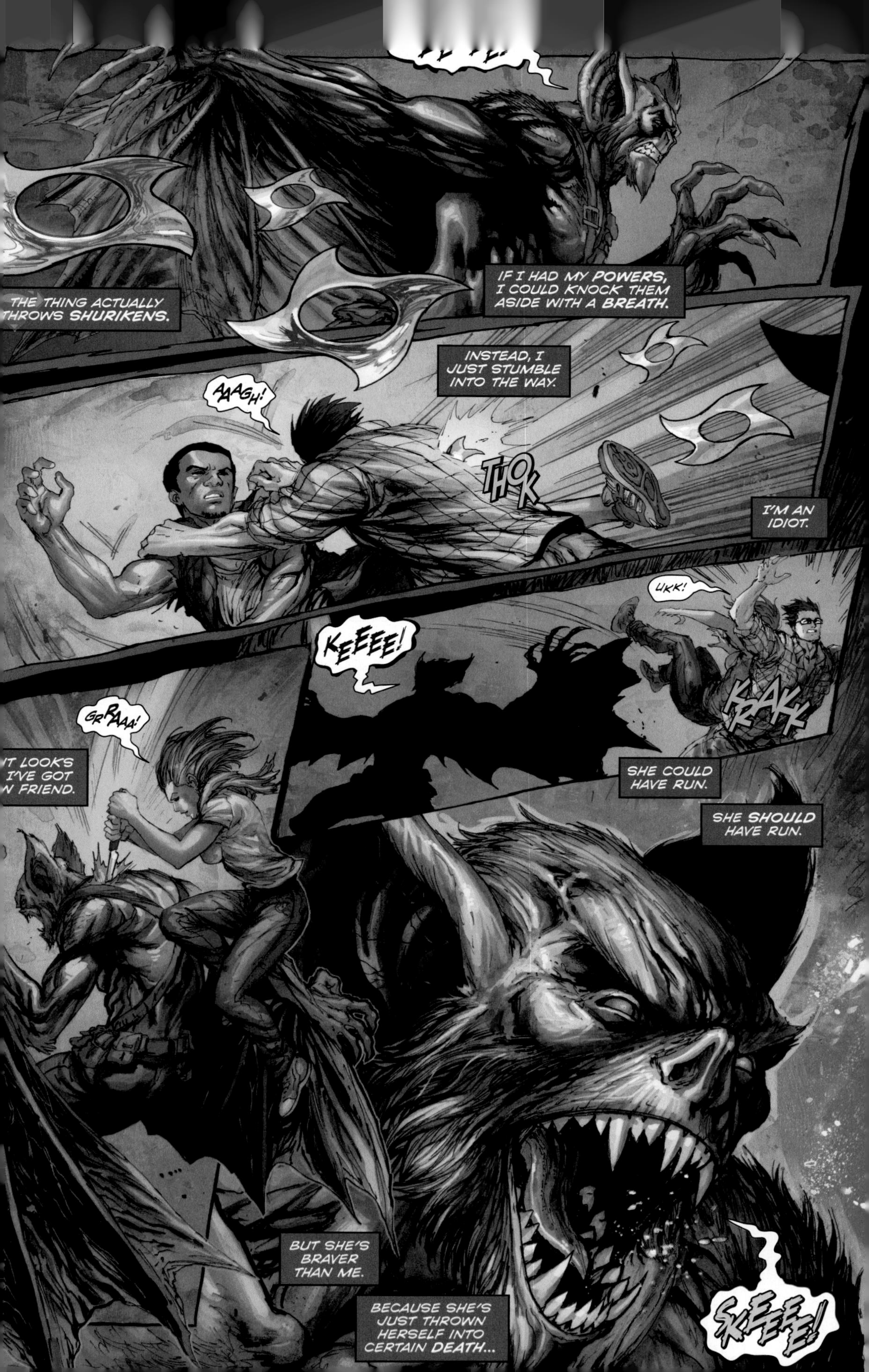

THE THING ACTUALLY THROWS **SHURIKENS.**
IF I HAD MY **POWERS,** I COULD KNOCK THEM ASIDE WITH A **BREATH.**
INSTEAD, I JUST STUMBLE INTO THE WAY.
AAAGH!
THOK
I'M AN IDIOT.
KEEEE!
UKK!
KRAKK
GRRAAA!
LOOKS I'VE GOT FRIEND.
SHE COULD HAVE RUN.
SHE **SHOULD** HAVE RUN.
....
BUT SHE'S BRAVER THAN ME.
BECAUSE SHE'S JUST THROWN HERSELF INTO CERTAIN **DEATH...**
SKEEEE!

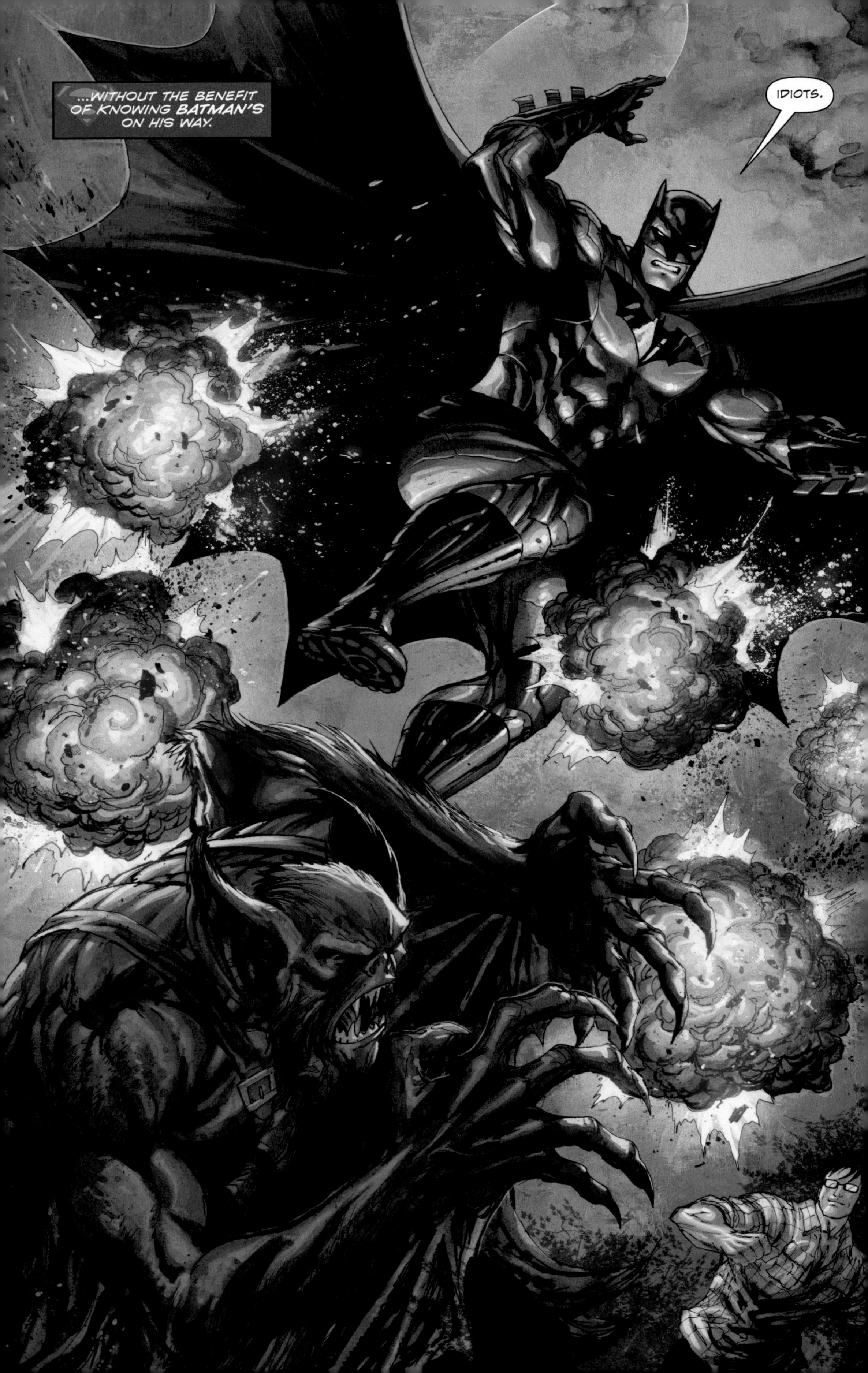
...WITHOUT THE BENEFIT OF KNOWING BATMAN'S ON HIS WAY.
IDIOTS.

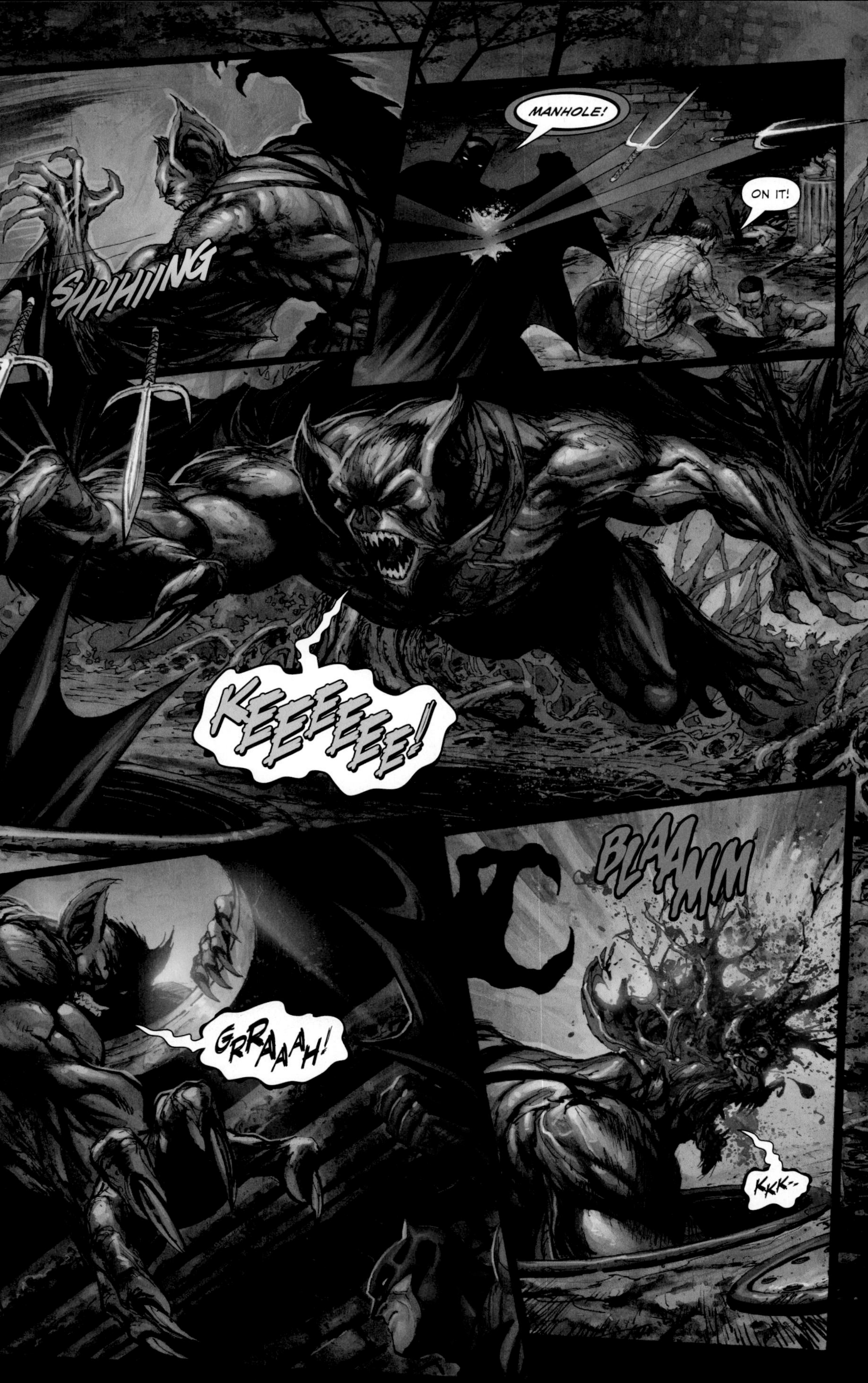
SHHHIING
MANHOLE!
ON IT!
KEEEEEEE!
GRRAAAH!
BLAAMM
KKK-

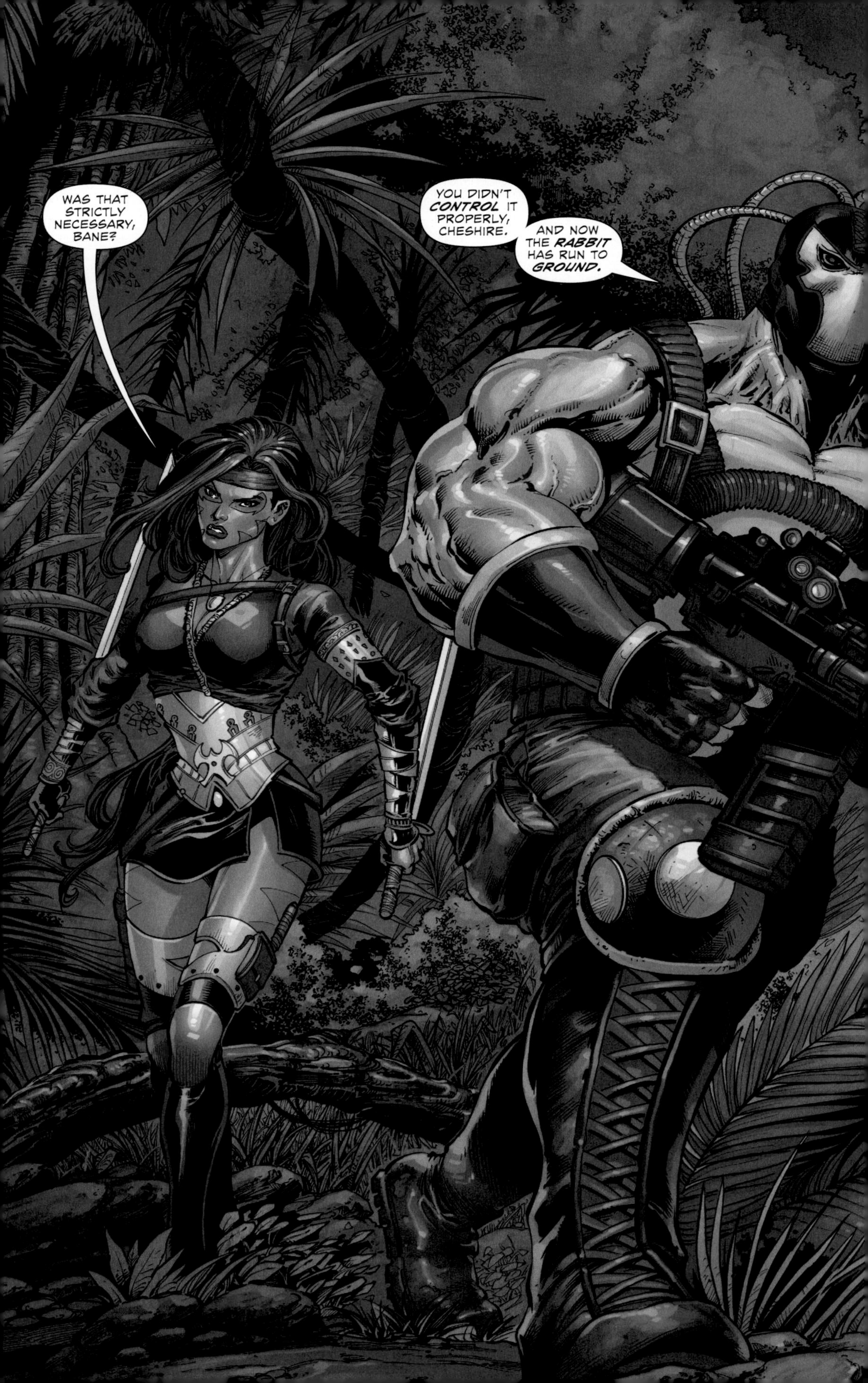
WAS THAT STRICTLY NECESSARY, BANE?
YOU DIDN'T *CONTROL* IT PROPERLY, CHESHIRE.
AND NOW THE *RABBIT* HAS RUN TO *GROUND.*

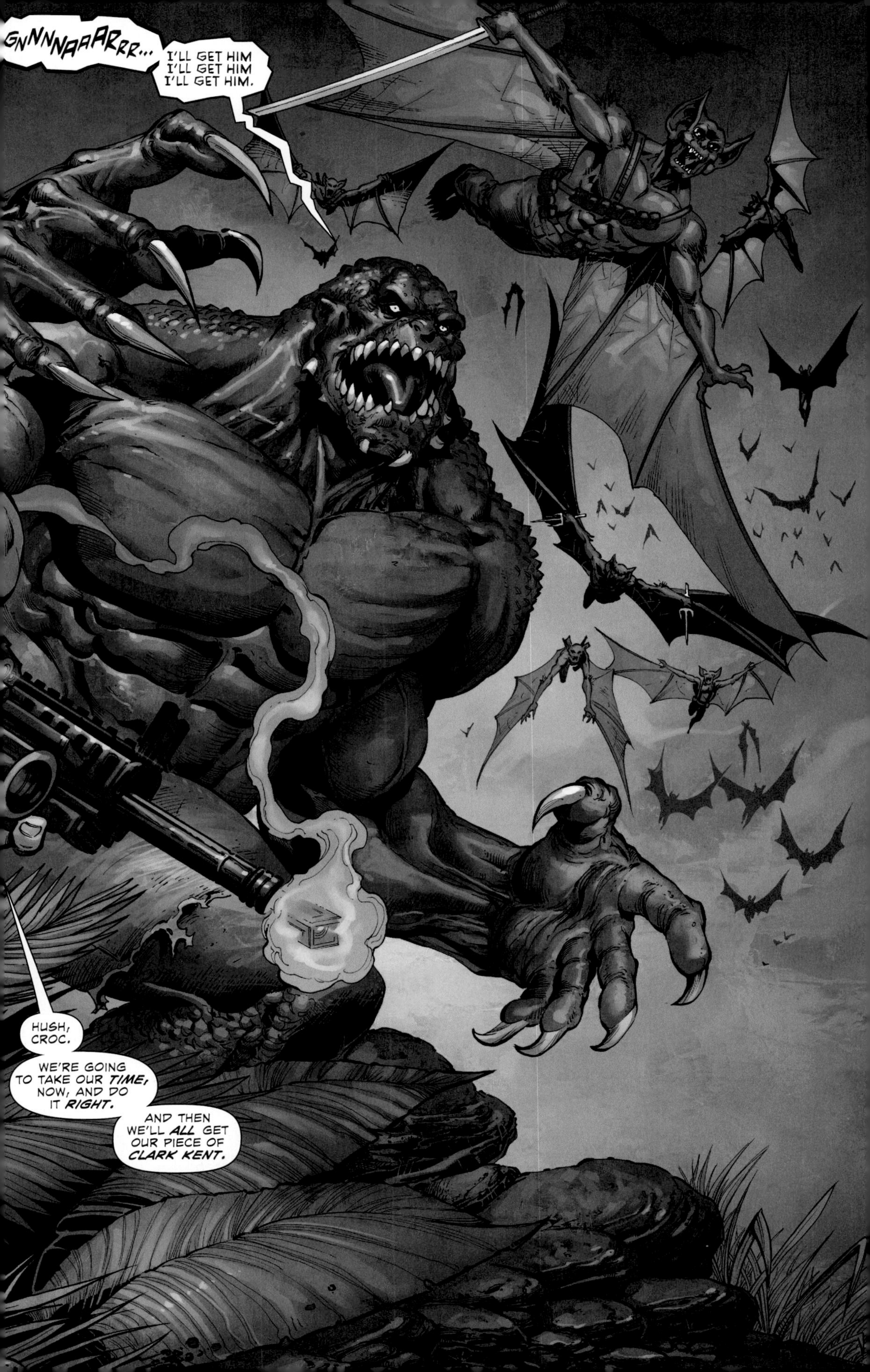
GNNNNAAARRR...
I'LL GET HIM
I'LL GET HIM
I'LL GET HIM.
HUSH, CROC.
WE'RE GOING TO TAKE OUR *TIME*, NOW, AND DO IT *RIGHT*.
AND THEN WE'LL *ALL* GET OUR PIECE OF *CLARK KENT*.

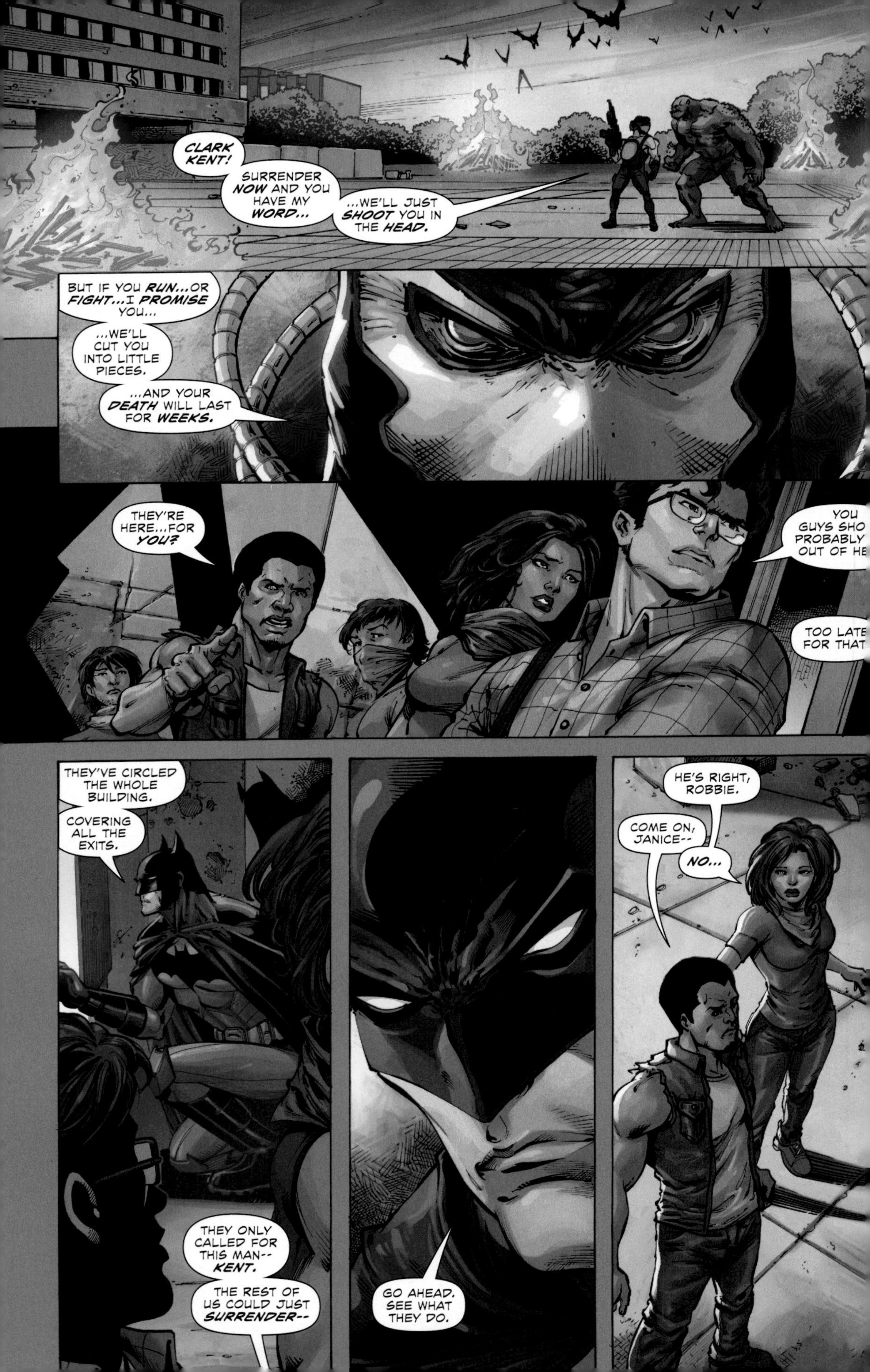
CLARK KENT!
SURRENDER NOW AND YOU HAVE MY WORD...
...WE'LL JUST SHOOT YOU IN THE HEAD.
BUT IF YOU RUN...OR FIGHT...I PROMISE YOU...
...WE'LL CUT YOU INTO LITTLE PIECES.
...AND YOUR DEATH WILL LAST FOR WEEKS.
THEY'RE HERE...FOR YOU?
YOU GUYS SHO PROBABLY OUT OF HE
TOO LATE FOR THAT
THEY'VE CIRCLED THE WHOLE BUILDING.
COVERING ALL THE EXITS.
THEY ONLY CALLED FOR THIS MAN-- KENT.
THE REST OF US COULD JUST SURRENDER--
GO AHEAD. SEE WHAT THEY DO.
HE'S RIGHT, ROBBIE.
COME ON, JANICE--
NO...

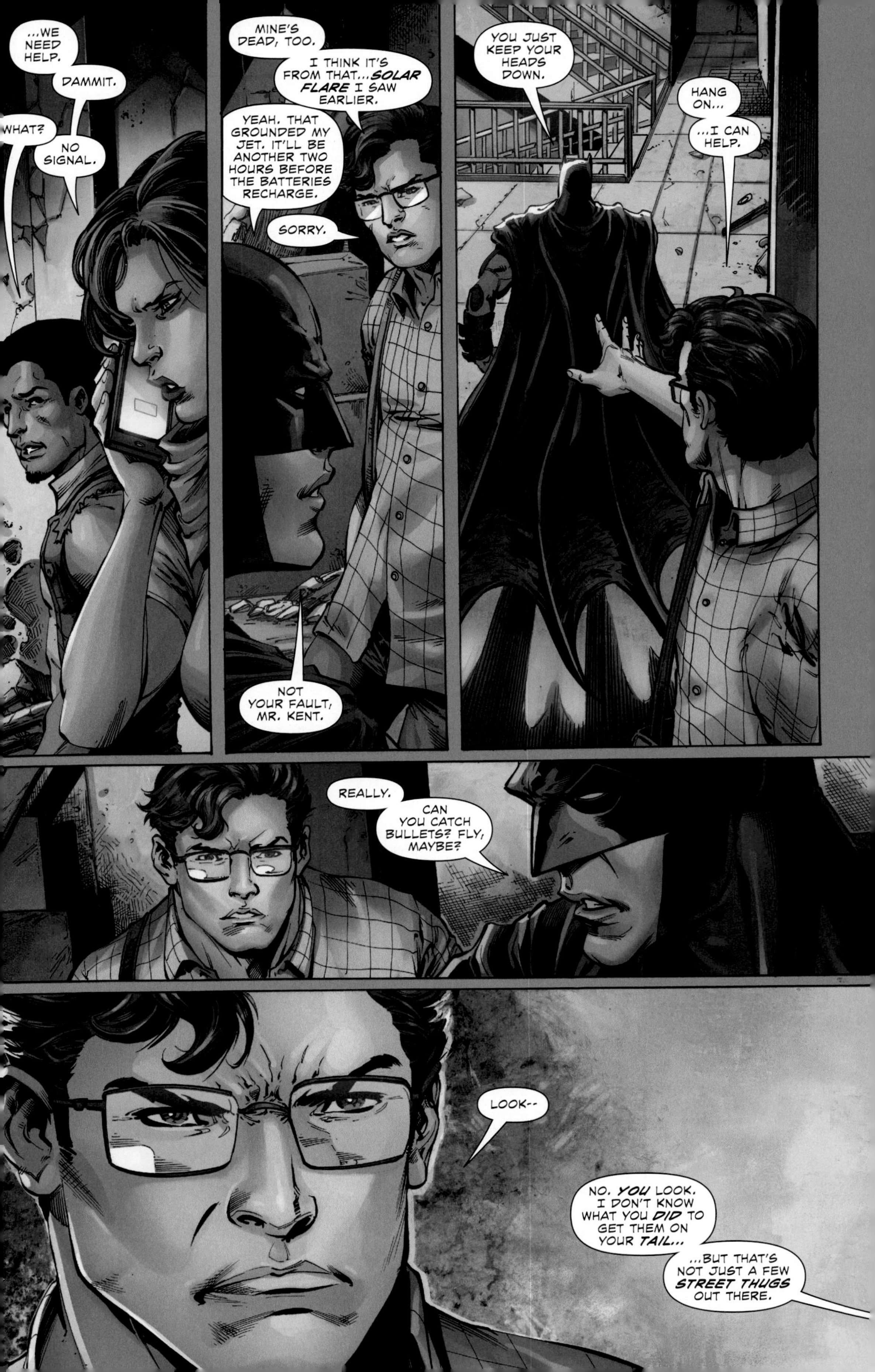
...WE NEED HELP.
DAMMIT.
WHAT?
NO SIGNAL.
MINE'S DEAD, TOO.
I THINK IT'S FROM THAT...SOLAR FLARE I SAW EARLIER.
YEAH. THAT GROUNDED MY JET. IT'LL BE ANOTHER TWO HOURS BEFORE THE BATTERIES RECHARGE.
SORRY.
NOT YOUR FAULT, MR. KENT.
YOU JUST KEEP YOUR HEADS DOWN.
HANG ON...
...I CAN HELP.
REALLY.
CAN YOU CATCH BULLETS? FLY, MAYBE?
LOOK--
NO. YOU LOOK. I DON'T KNOW WHAT YOU DID TO GET THEM ON YOUR TAIL...
...BUT THAT'S NOT JUST A FEW STREET THUGS OUT THERE.

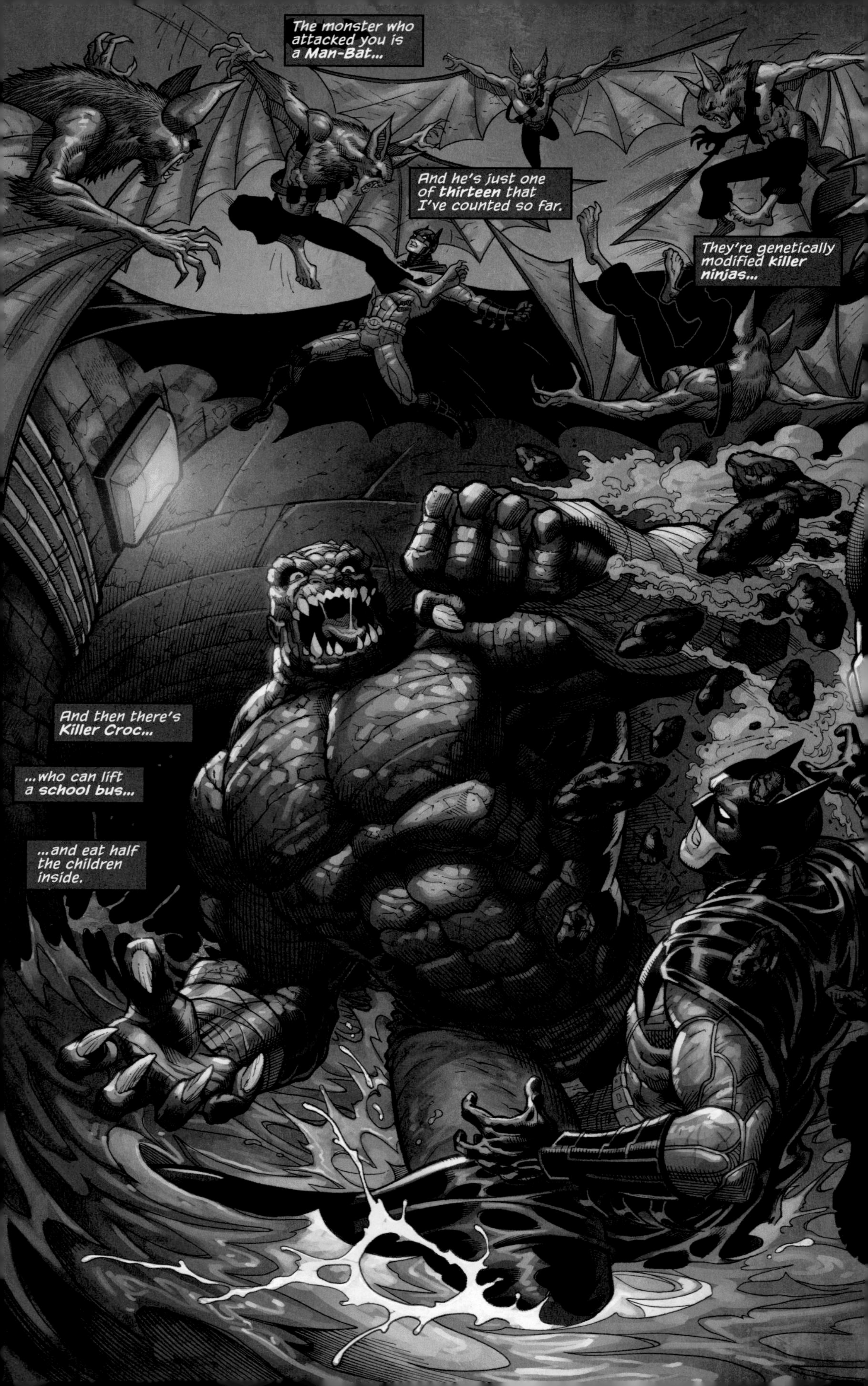

The monster who attacked you is a Man-Bat...
And he's just one of thirteen that I've counted so far.
They're genetically modified killer ninjas...
And then there's Killer Croc...
...who can lift a school bus...
...and eat half the children inside.

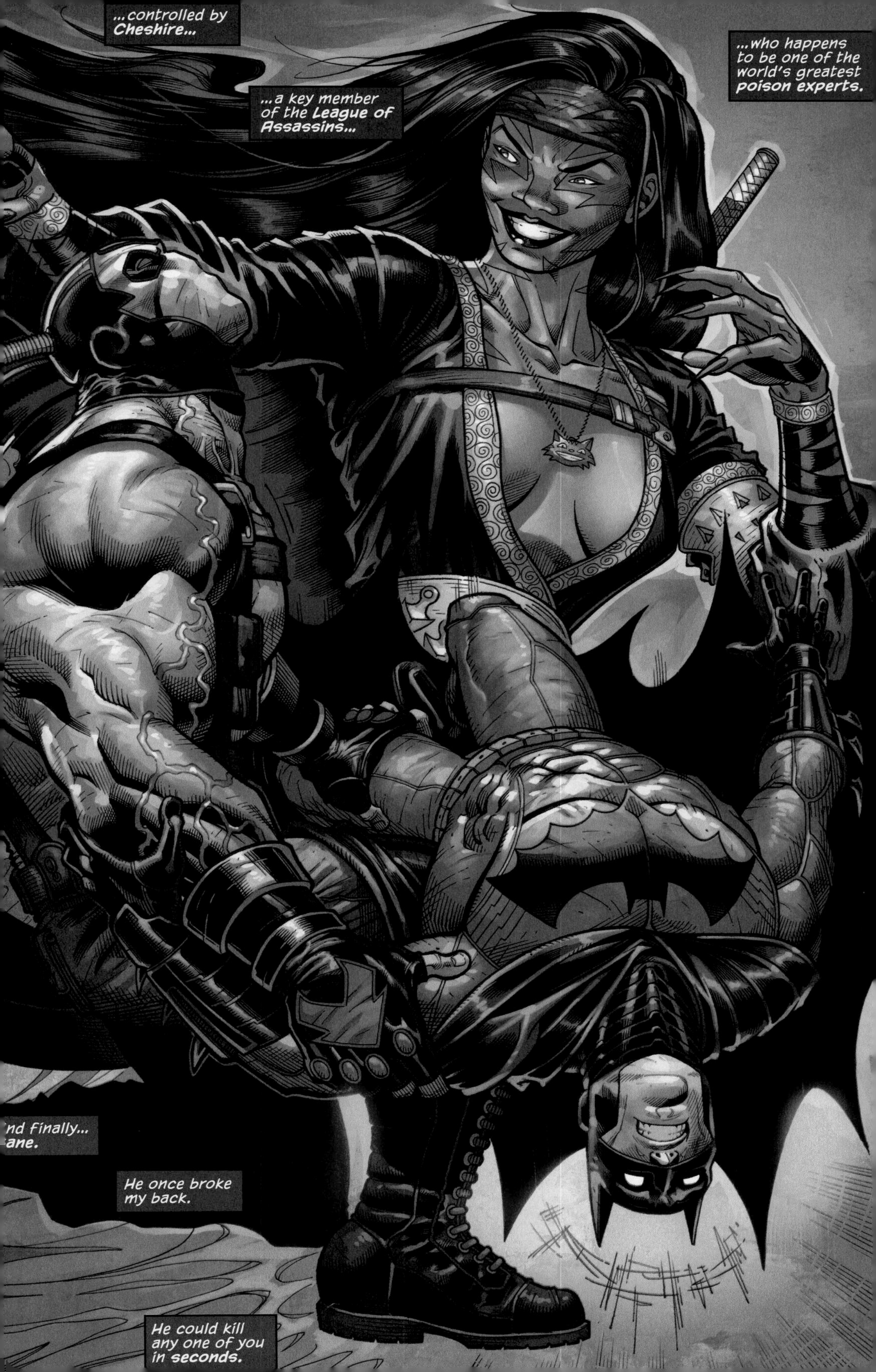
...controlled by Cheshire...
...a key member of the League of Assassins...
...who happens to be one of the world's greatest poison experts.
nd finally... ane.
He once broke my back.
He could kill any one of you in seconds.

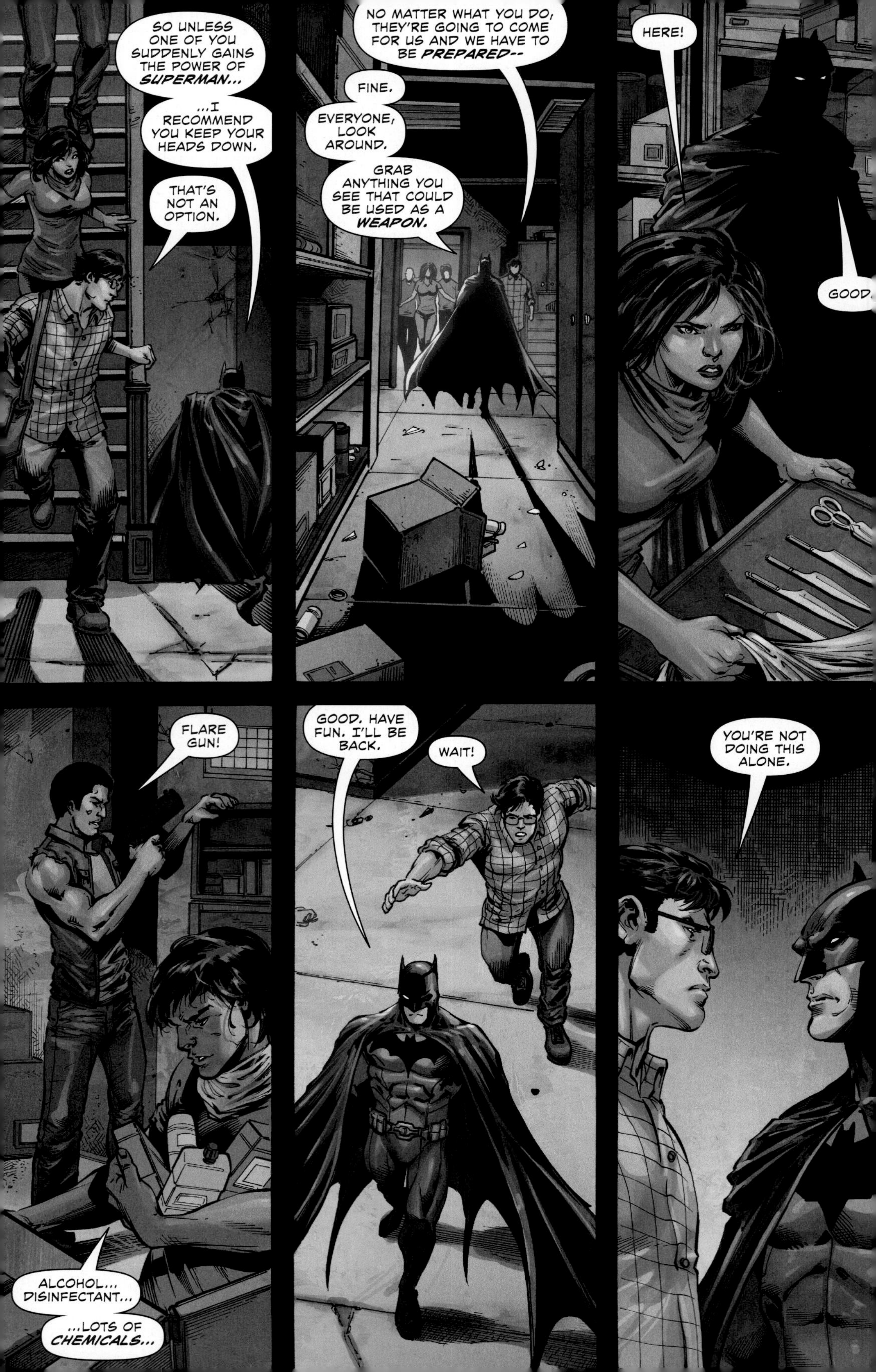
SO UNLESS ONE OF YOU SUDDENLY GAINS THE POWER OF SUPERMAN...
...I RECOMMEND YOU KEEP YOUR HEADS DOWN.
THAT'S NOT AN OPTION.
NO MATTER WHAT YOU DO, THEY'RE GOING TO COME FOR US AND WE HAVE TO BE PREPARED--
FINE.
EVERYONE, LOOK AROUND.
GRAB ANYTHING YOU SEE THAT COULD BE USED AS A WEAPON.
HERE!
GOOD.
FLARE GUN!
ALCOHOL... DISINFECTANT...
...LOTS OF CHEMICALS...
GOOD. HAVE FUN. I'LL BE BACK.
WAIT!
YOU'RE NOT DOING THIS ALONE.

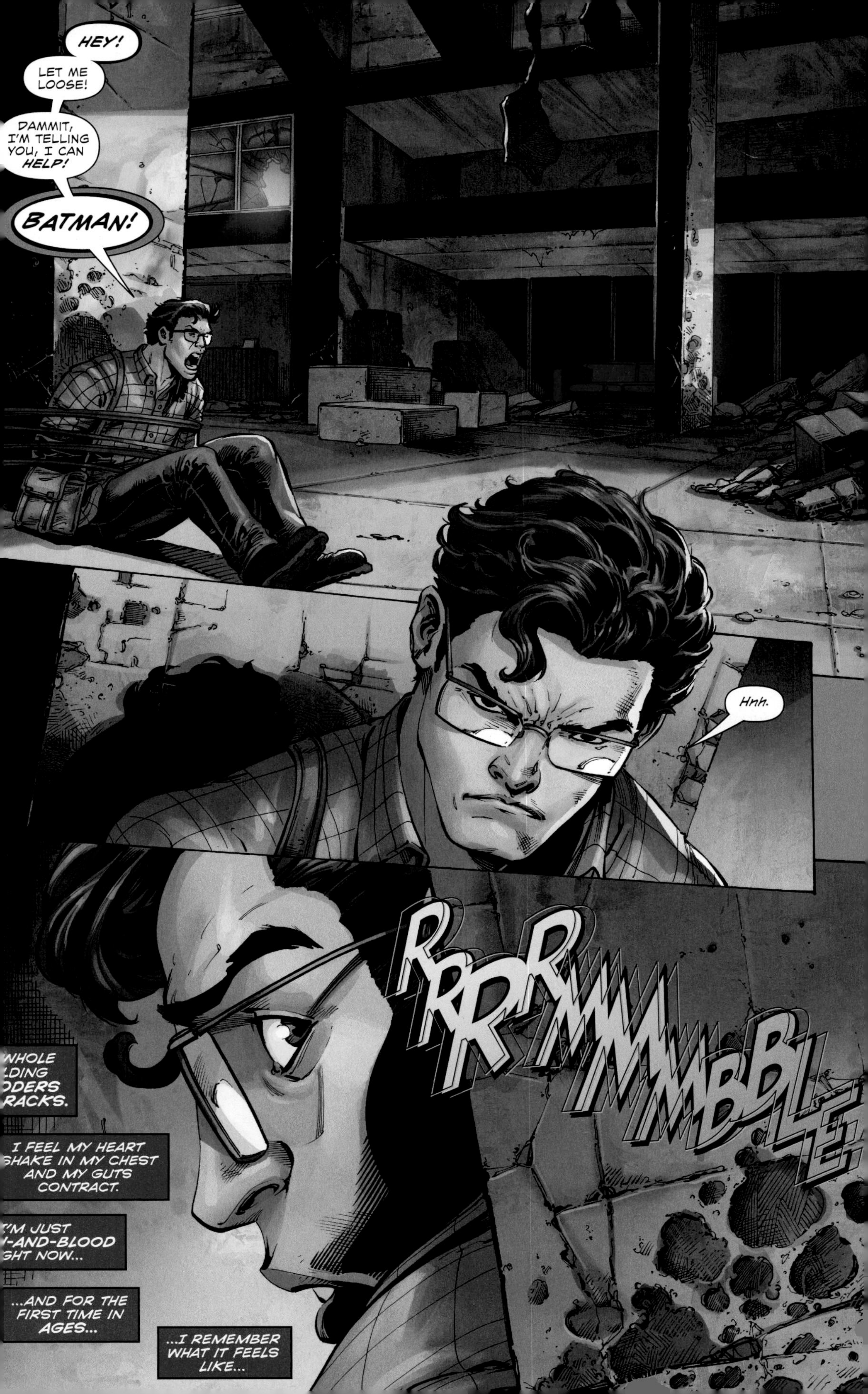
HEY!
LET ME LOOSE!
DAMMIT, I'M TELLING YOU, I CAN HELP!
BATMAN!
Hnh.
RRRRMMMBBLE
HOLE
LDING
ODERS
RACKS.
I FEEL MY HEART SHAKE IN MY CHEST AND MY GUTS CONTRACT.
'M JUST
-AND-BLOOD
GHT NOW...
...AND FOR THE FIRST TIME IN AGES...
...I REMEMBER WHAT IT FEELS LIKE...

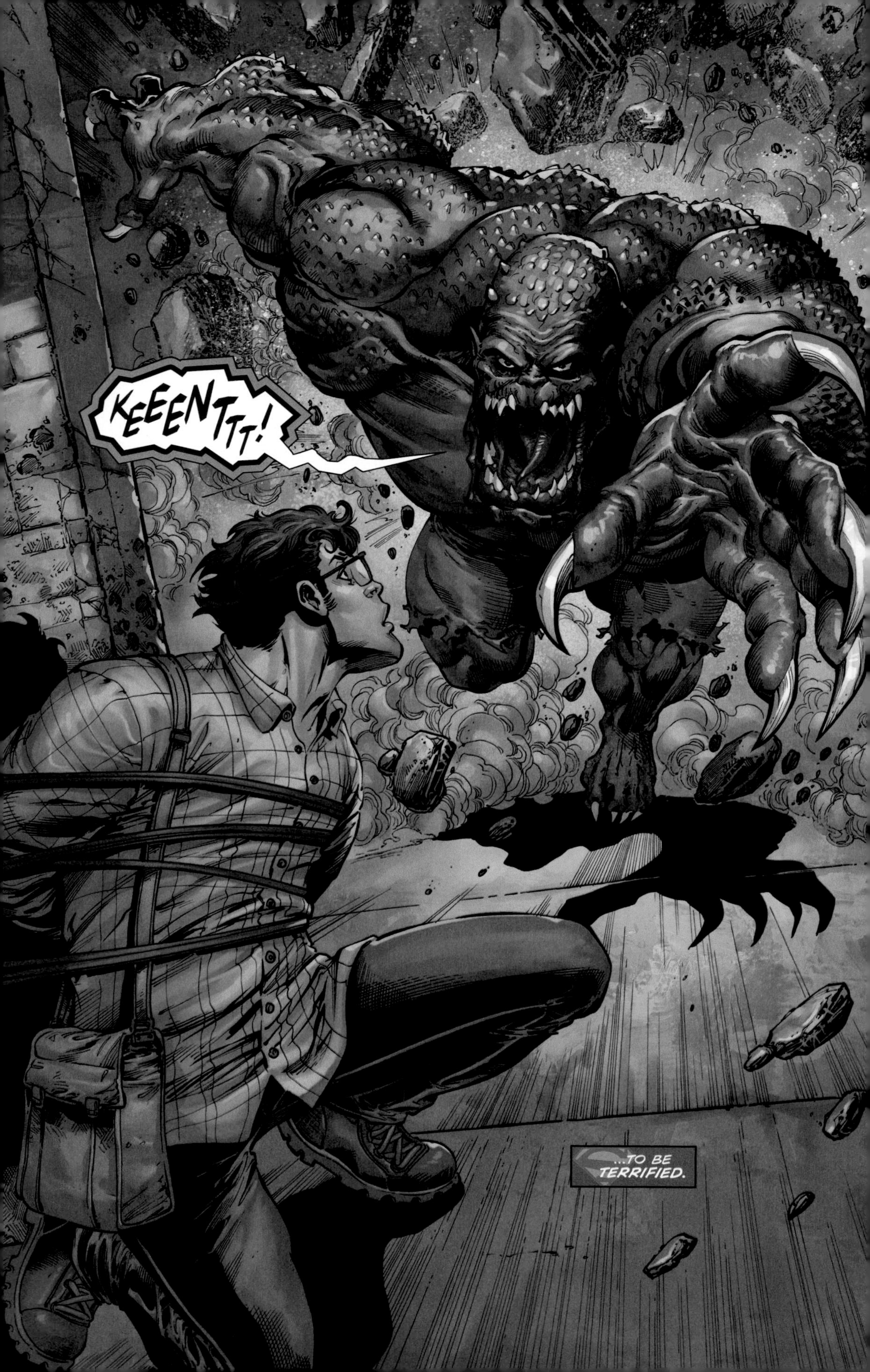
KEEENTTT!
...TO BE TERRIFIED.

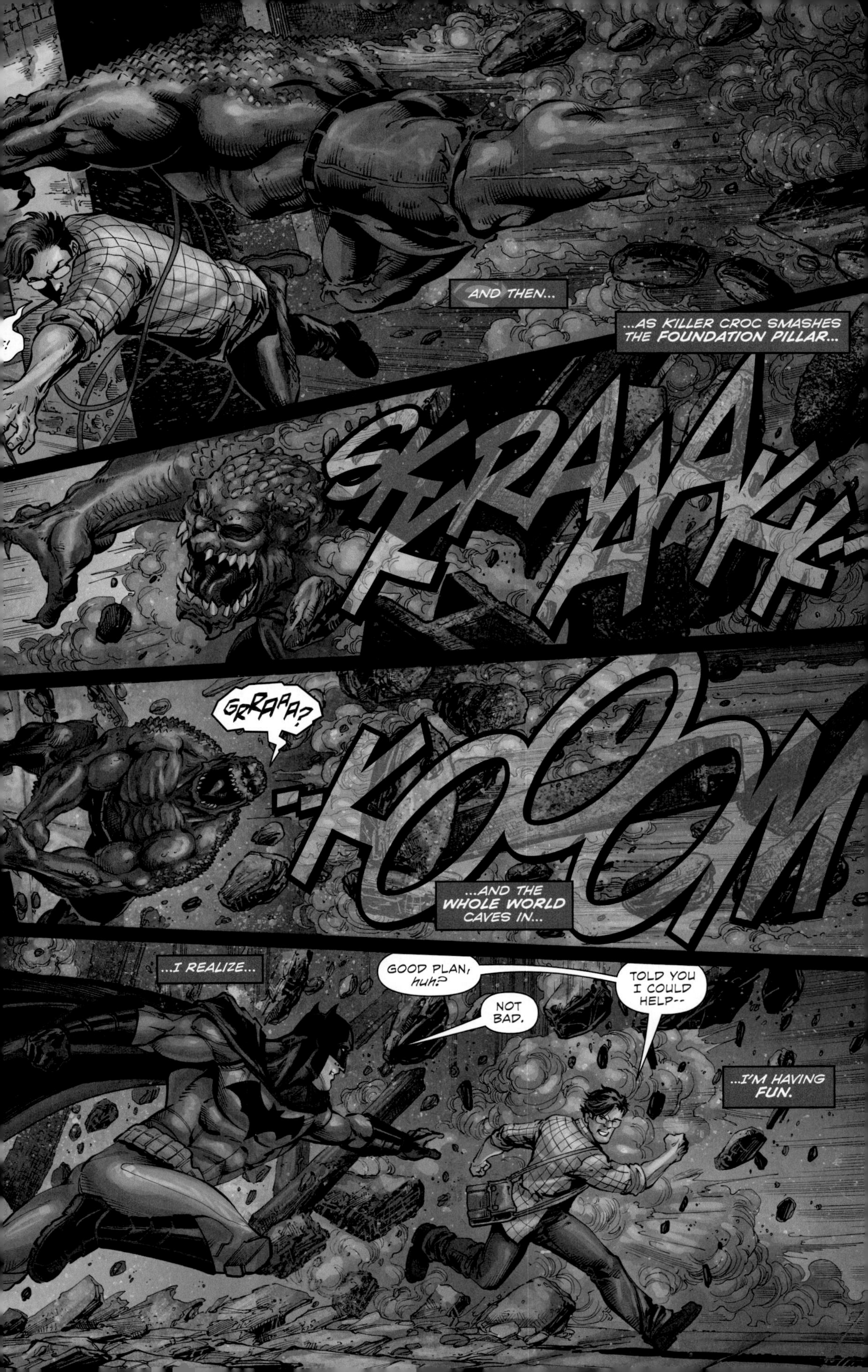
AND THEN...
...AS KILLER CROC SMASHES THE FOUNDATION PILLAR...
SKRAAAAKK
GRRAAA?
KROOOM
...AND THE WHOLE WORLD CAVES IN...
...I REALIZE...
GOOD PLAN, huh?
NOT BAD.
TOLD YOU I COULD HELP--
...I'M HAVING FUN.

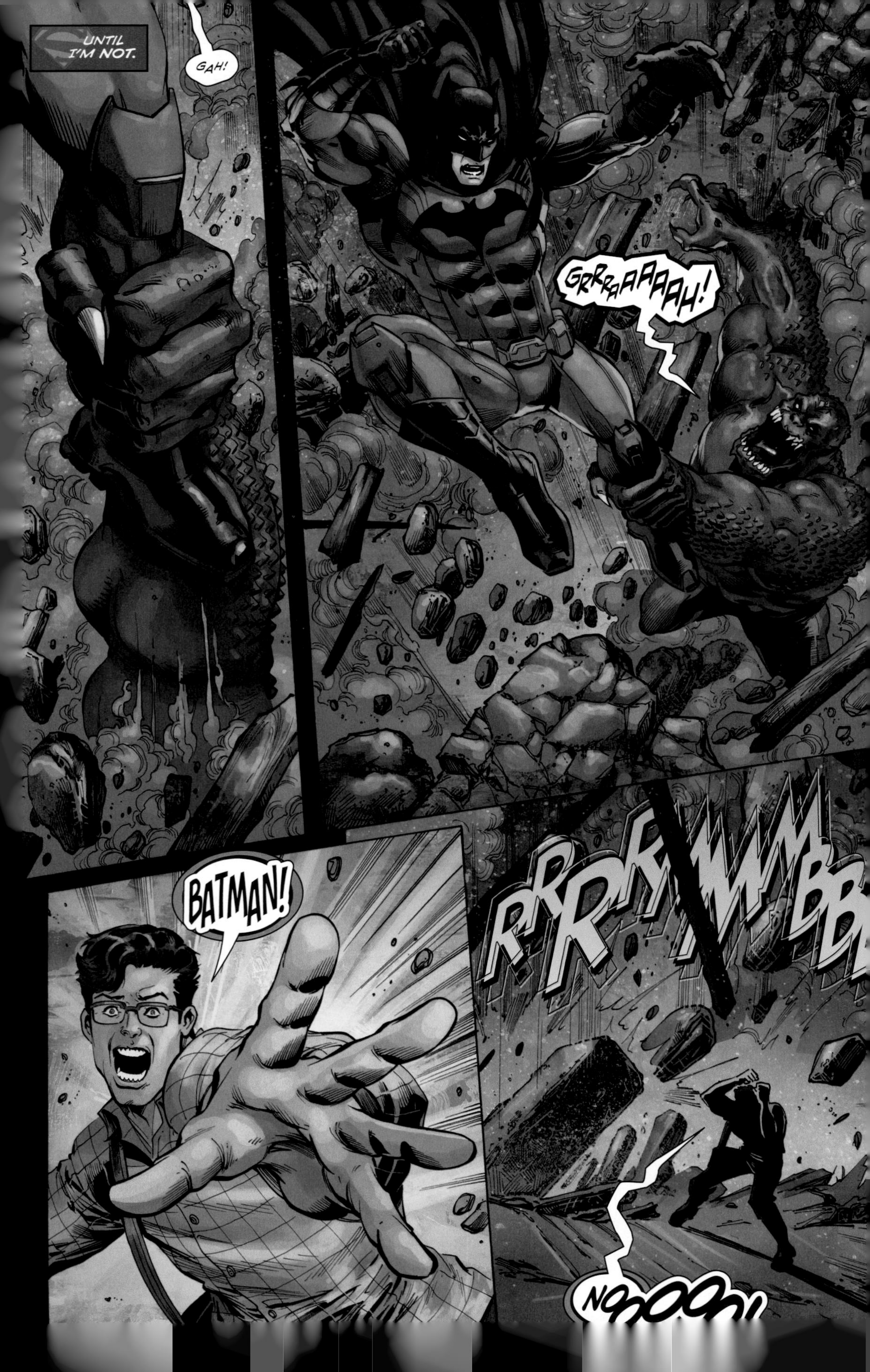
UNTIL I'M NOT.
GAH!
GRRRAAAAAAH!
BATMAN!
RRRRMMMBB
NOOOOO!

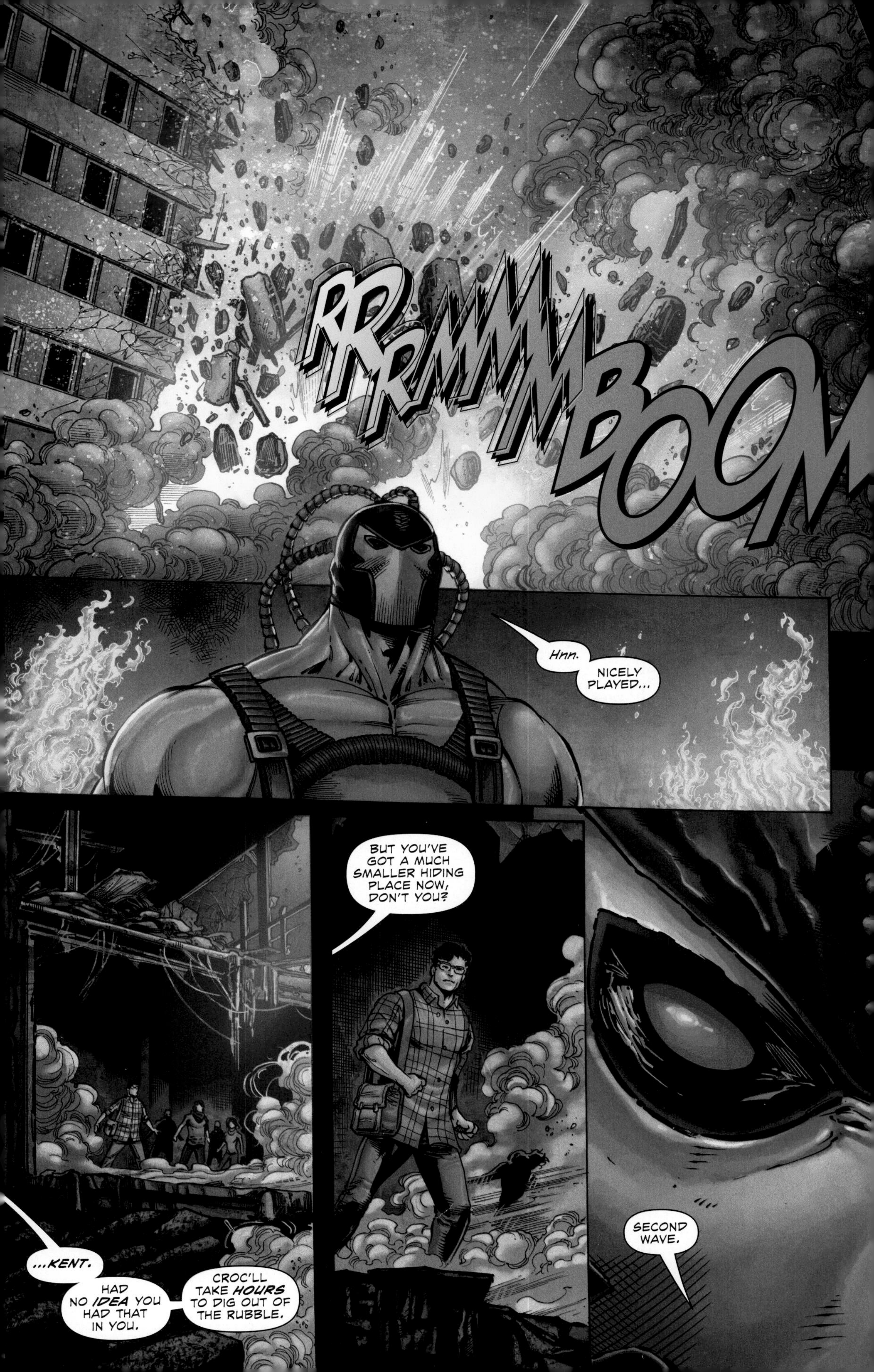
RRRMMMMBOOM
Hnn.
NICELY PLAYED...
...KENT.
HAD NO IDEA YOU HAD THAT IN YOU.
CROC'LL TAKE HOURS TO DIG OUT OF THE RUBBLE.
BUT YOU'VE GOT A MUCH SMALLER HIDING PLACE NOW, DON'T YOU?
SECOND WAVE.

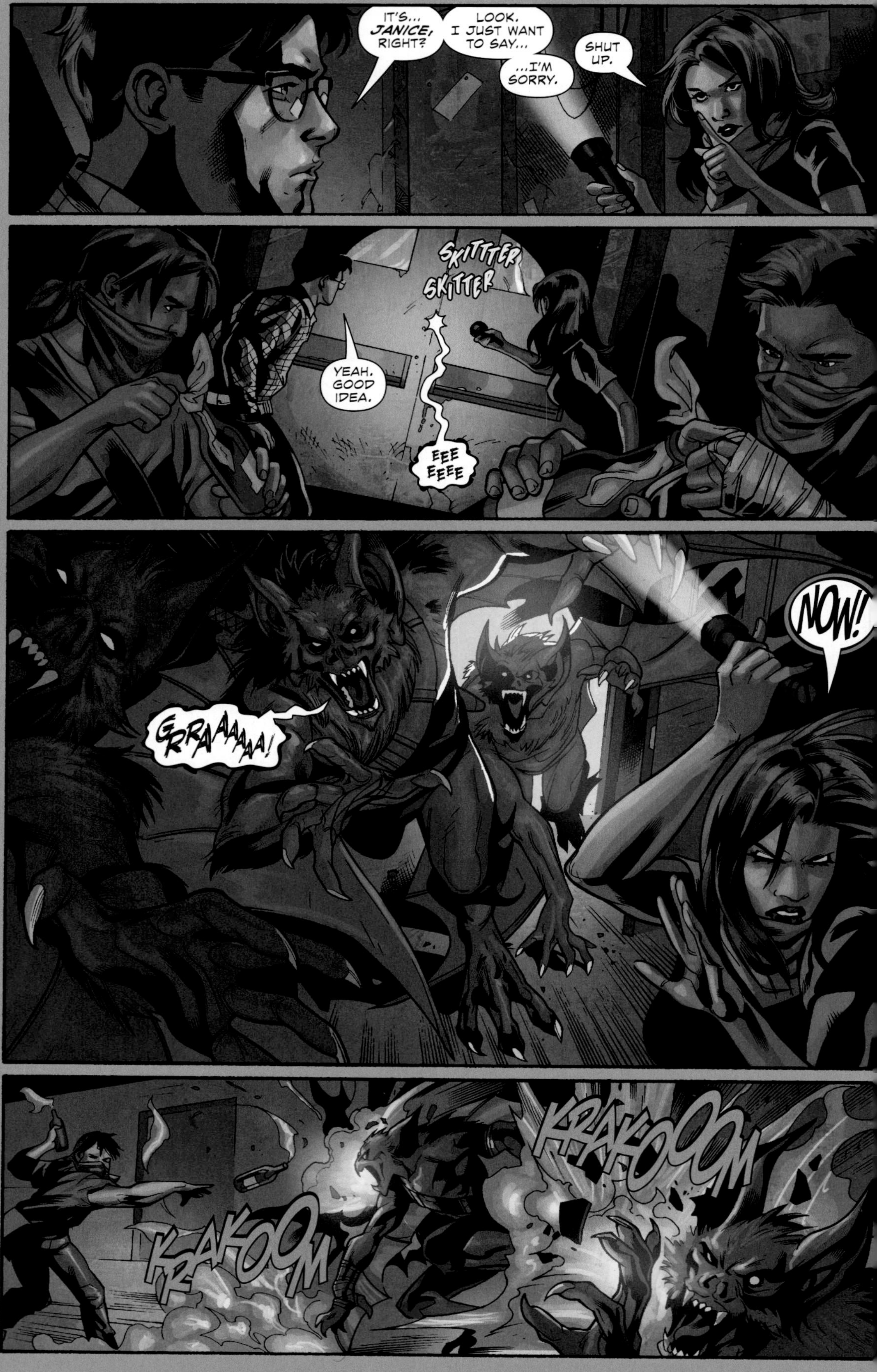
IT'S... JANICE, RIGHT?
LOOK. I JUST WANT TO SAY...
...I'M SORRY.
SHUT UP.
SKITTTER
SKITTER
YEAH. GOOD IDEA.
EEE EEEE
GRRAAAAAAA!
NOW!
KRAKOOOM
KRAKOOM

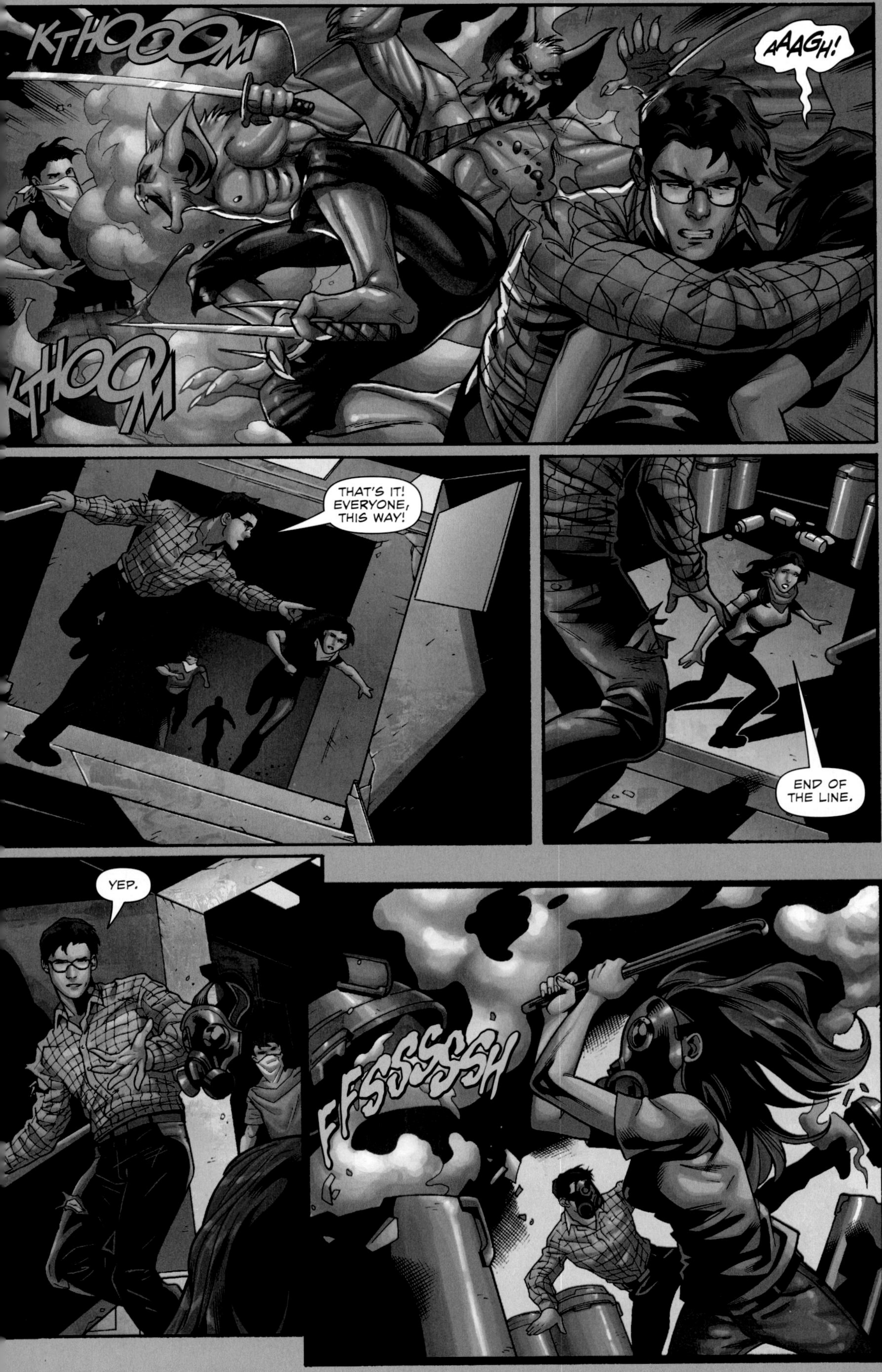
KTHOOOM
AAAGH!
KTHOOM
THAT'S IT! EVERYONE, THIS WAY!
END OF THE LINE.
YEP.
FFSSSSSH

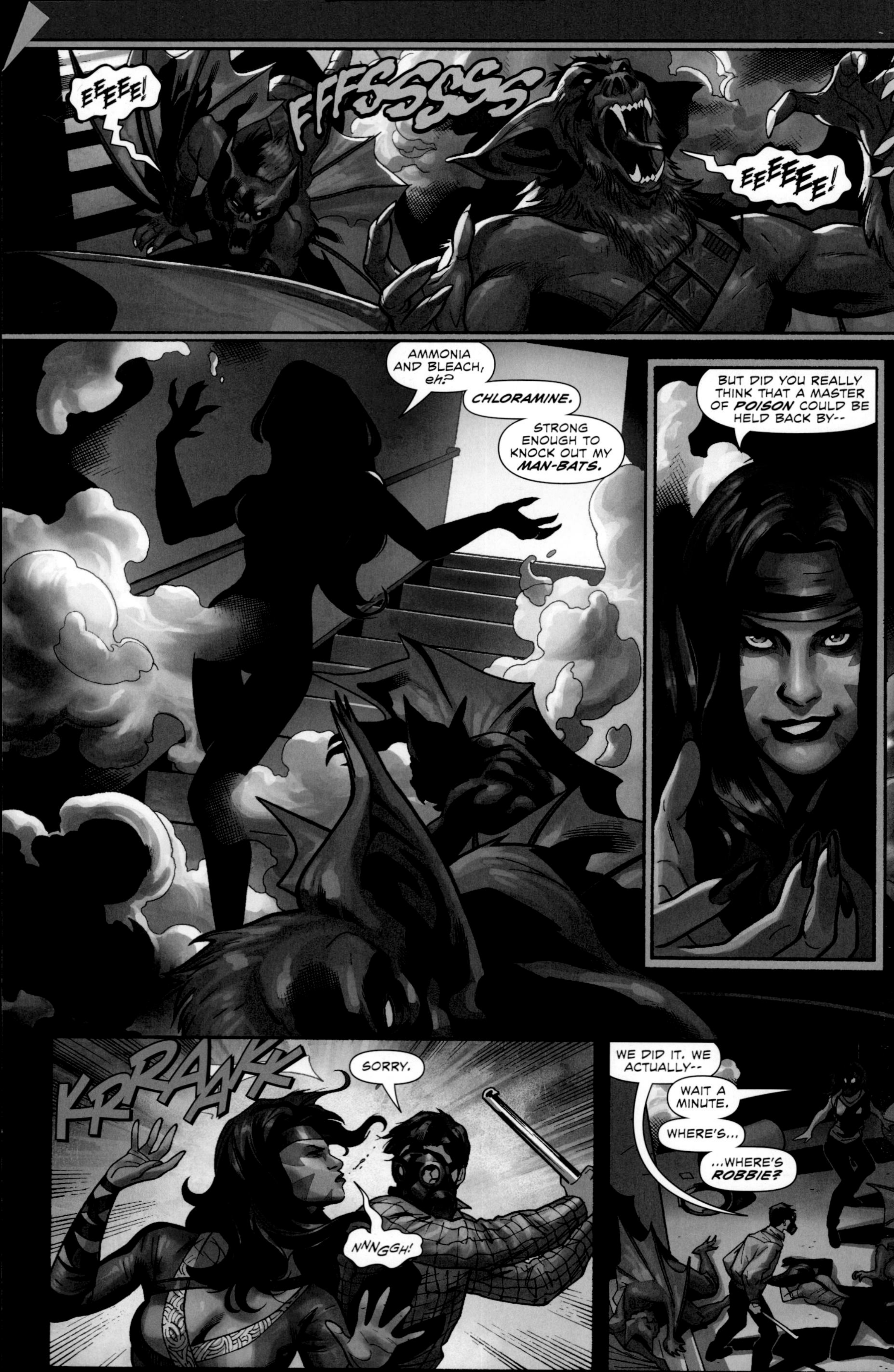
EEEEE!
FFFSSSSS
EEEEEE!
AMMONIA AND BLEACH, eh?
CHLORAMINE.
STRONG ENOUGH TO KNOCK OUT MY MAN-BATS.
BUT DID YOU REALLY THINK THAT A MASTER OF POISON COULD BE HELD BACK BY--
KRRAAKK
SORRY.
NNNGGH!
WE DID IT. WE ACTUALLY--
WAIT A MINUTE.
WHERE'S...
...WHERE'S ROBBIE?

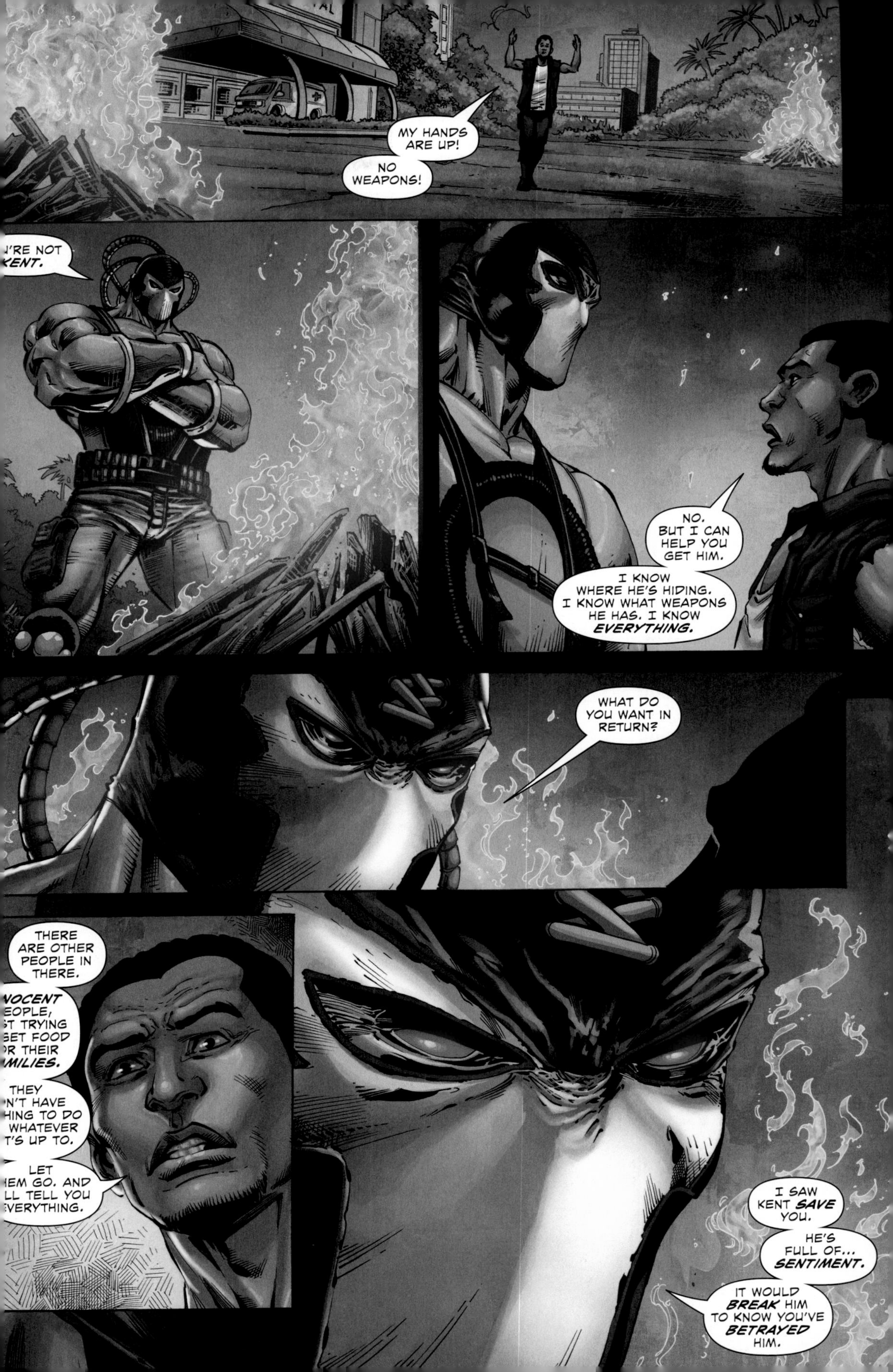

MY HANDS ARE UP!
NO WEAPONS!
'RE NOT KENT.
NO. BUT I CAN HELP YOU GET HIM.
I KNOW WHERE HE'S HIDING. I KNOW WHAT WEAPONS HE HAS. I KNOW EVERYTHING.
WHAT DO YOU WANT IN RETURN?
THERE ARE OTHER PEOPLE IN THERE.
NOCENT EOPLE, T TRYING GET FOOD R THEIR MILIES.
THEY N'T HAVE HING TO DO WHATEVER T'S UP TO.
LET HEM GO. AND LL TELL YOU EVERYTHING.
I SAW KENT SAVE YOU.
HE'S FULL OF... SENTIMENT.
IT WOULD BREAK HIM TO KNOW YOU'VE BETRAYED HIM.

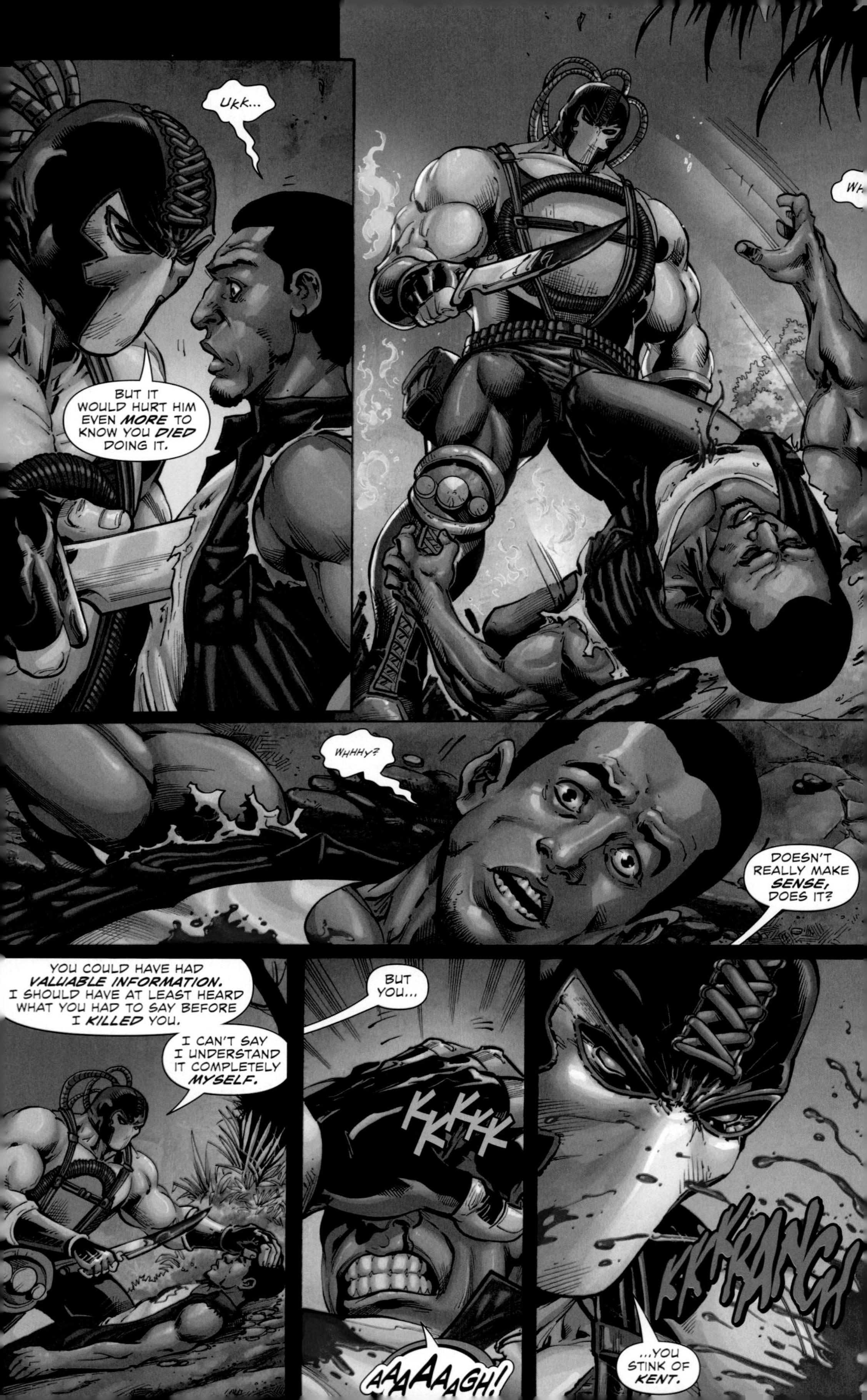
UKK...
BUT IT WOULD HURT HIM EVEN MORE TO KNOW YOU DIED DOING IT.
WHHHY?
DOESN'T REALLY MAKE SENSE, DOES IT?
YOU COULD HAVE HAD VALUABLE INFORMATION. I SHOULD HAVE AT LEAST HEARD WHAT YOU HAD TO SAY BEFORE I KILLED YOU.
I CAN'T SAY I UNDERSTAND IT COMPLETELY MYSELF.
BUT YOU...
KKKKKK
AAAAAAAGH!
KKKRANCH
...YOU STINK OF KENT.

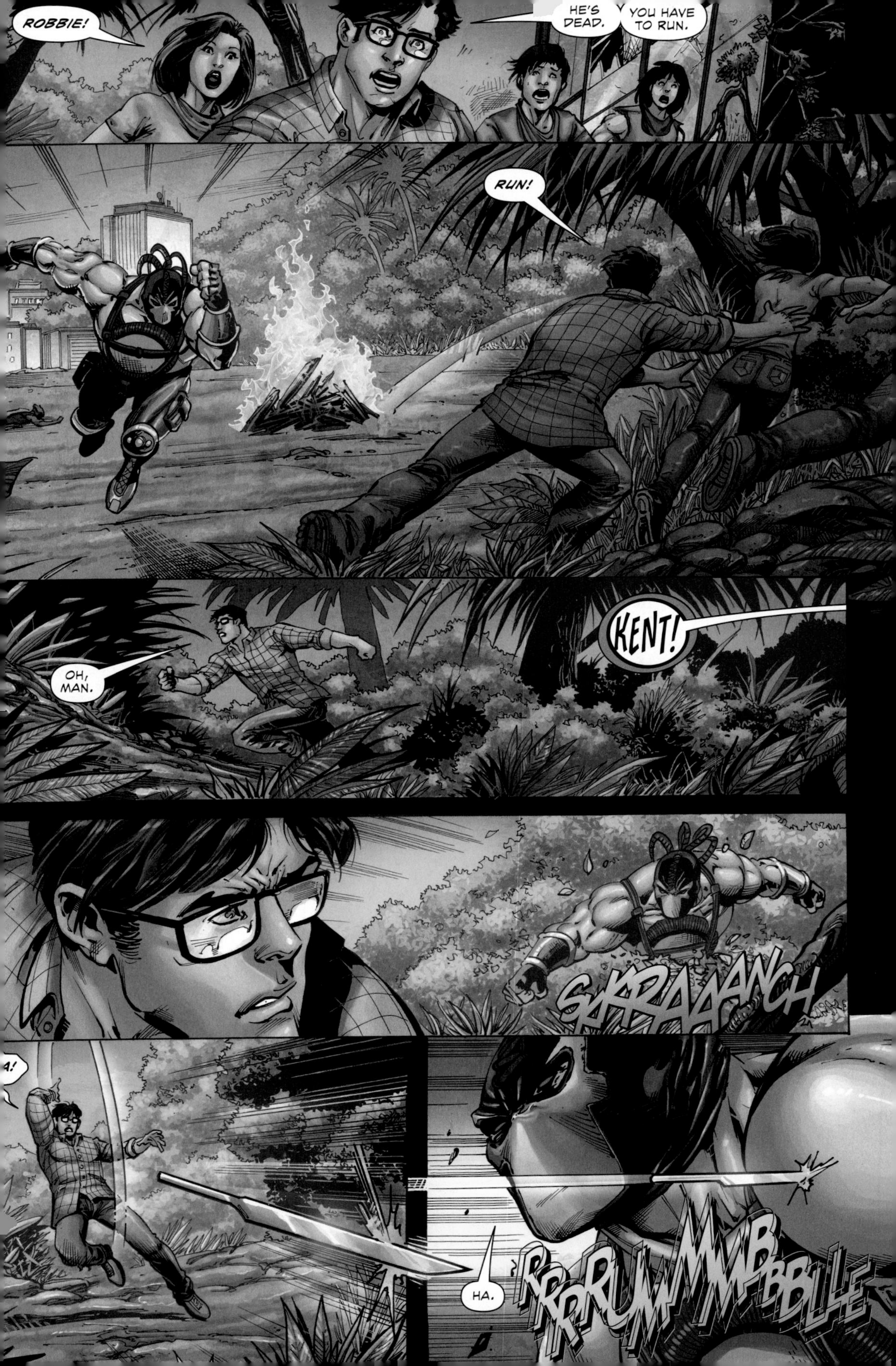
ROBBIE!
HE'S DEAD.
YOU HAVE TO RUN.
RUN!
OH, MAN.
KENT!
SKRAAAANCH
A!
HA.
RRRRUMMMBBLLE

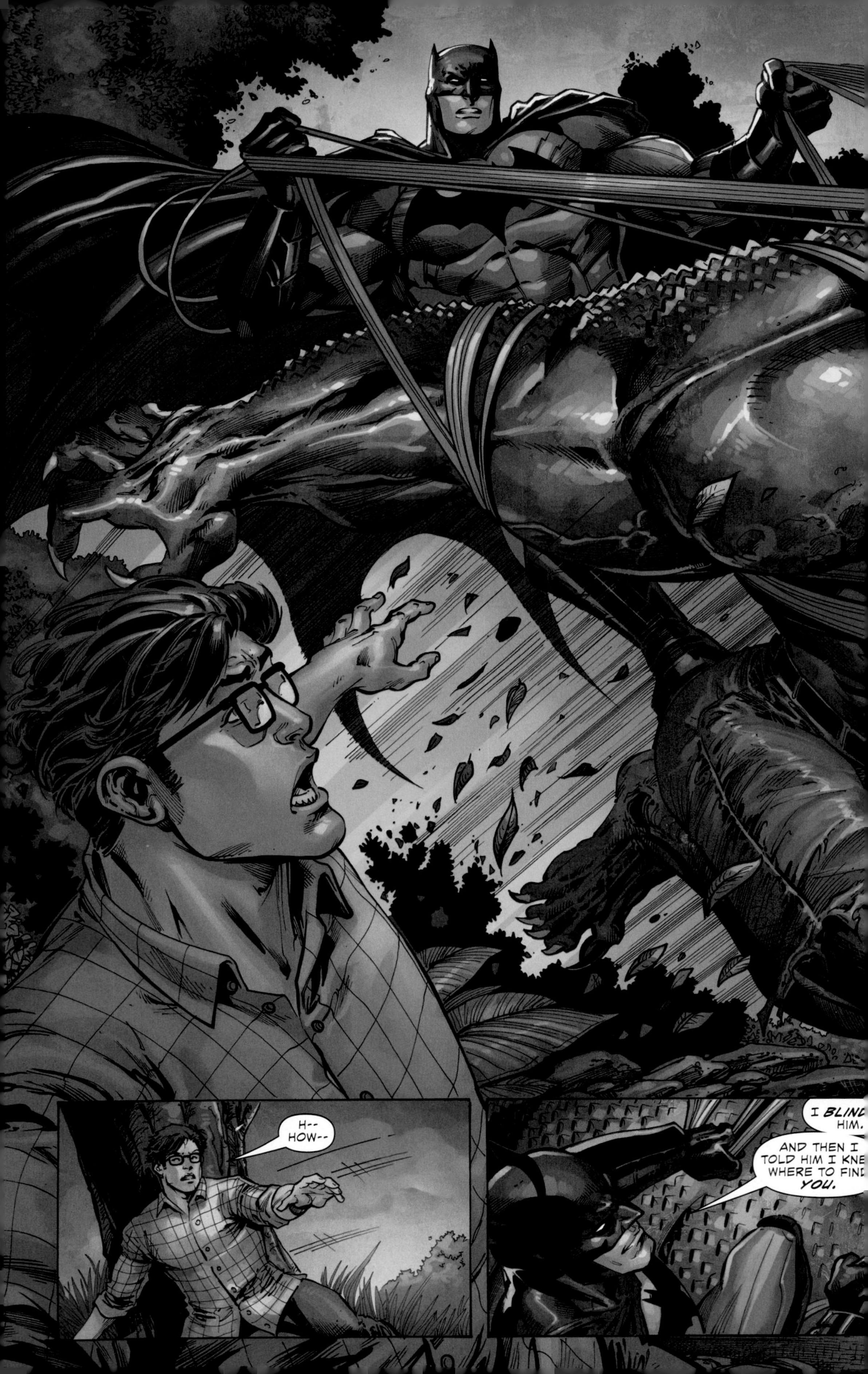
H-- HOW--
I BLIND HIM.
AND THEN I TOLD HIM I KNE WHERE TO FIND YOU.

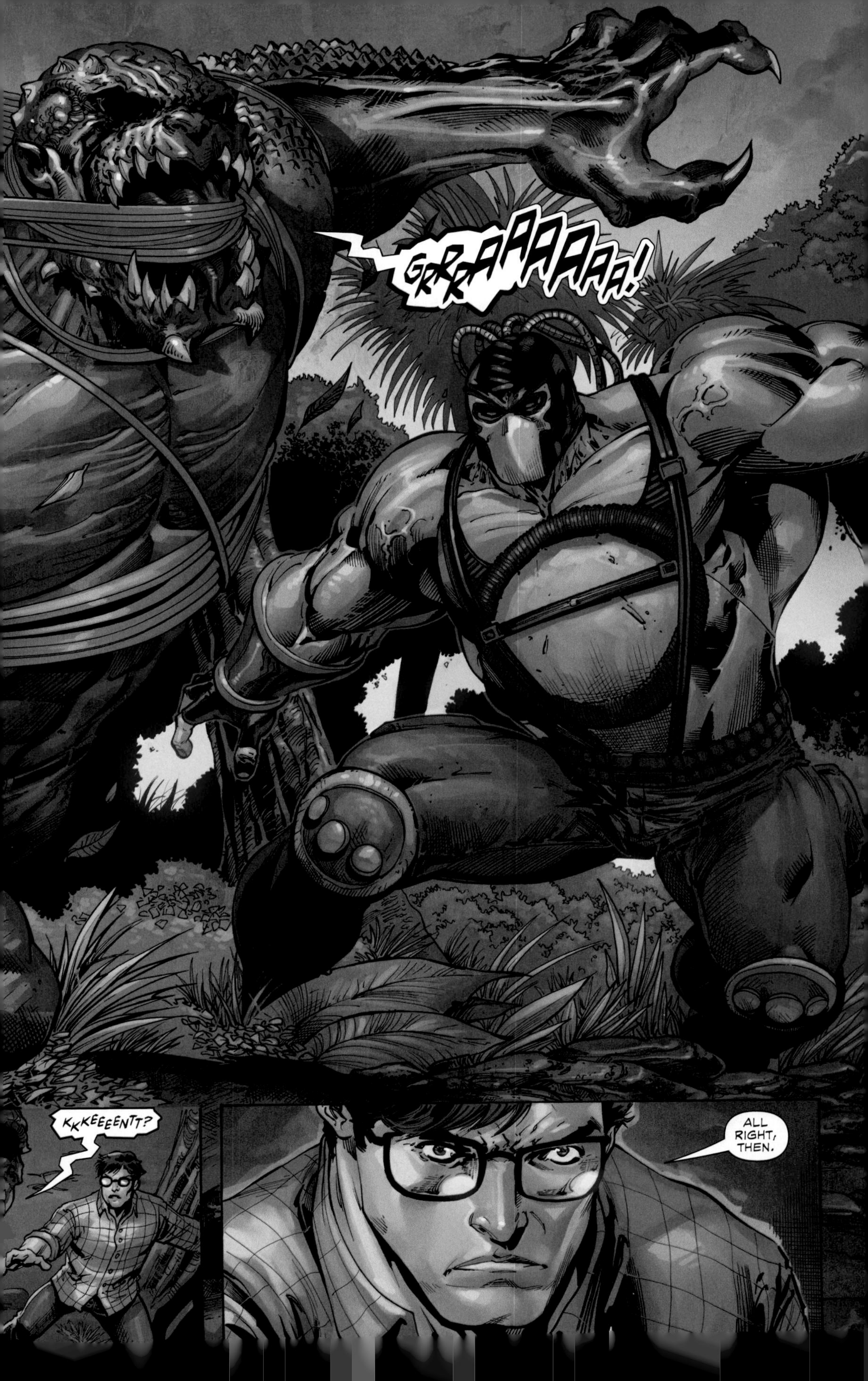
GRRRAAAAAAA!
KKKEEEENTT?
ALL RIGHT, THEN.

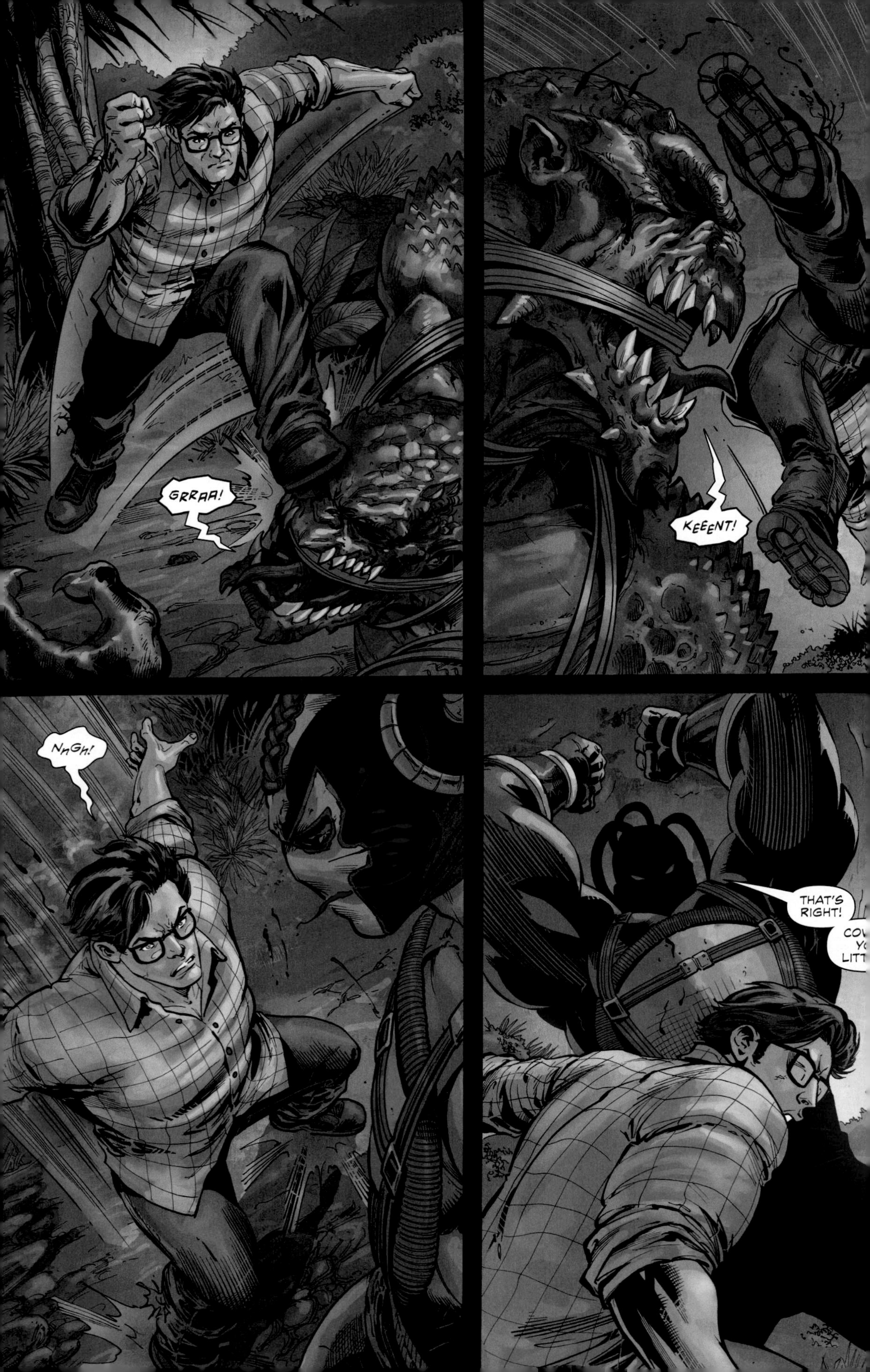
GRRAA!
KEEENT!
NnGh!
THAT'S RIGHT!

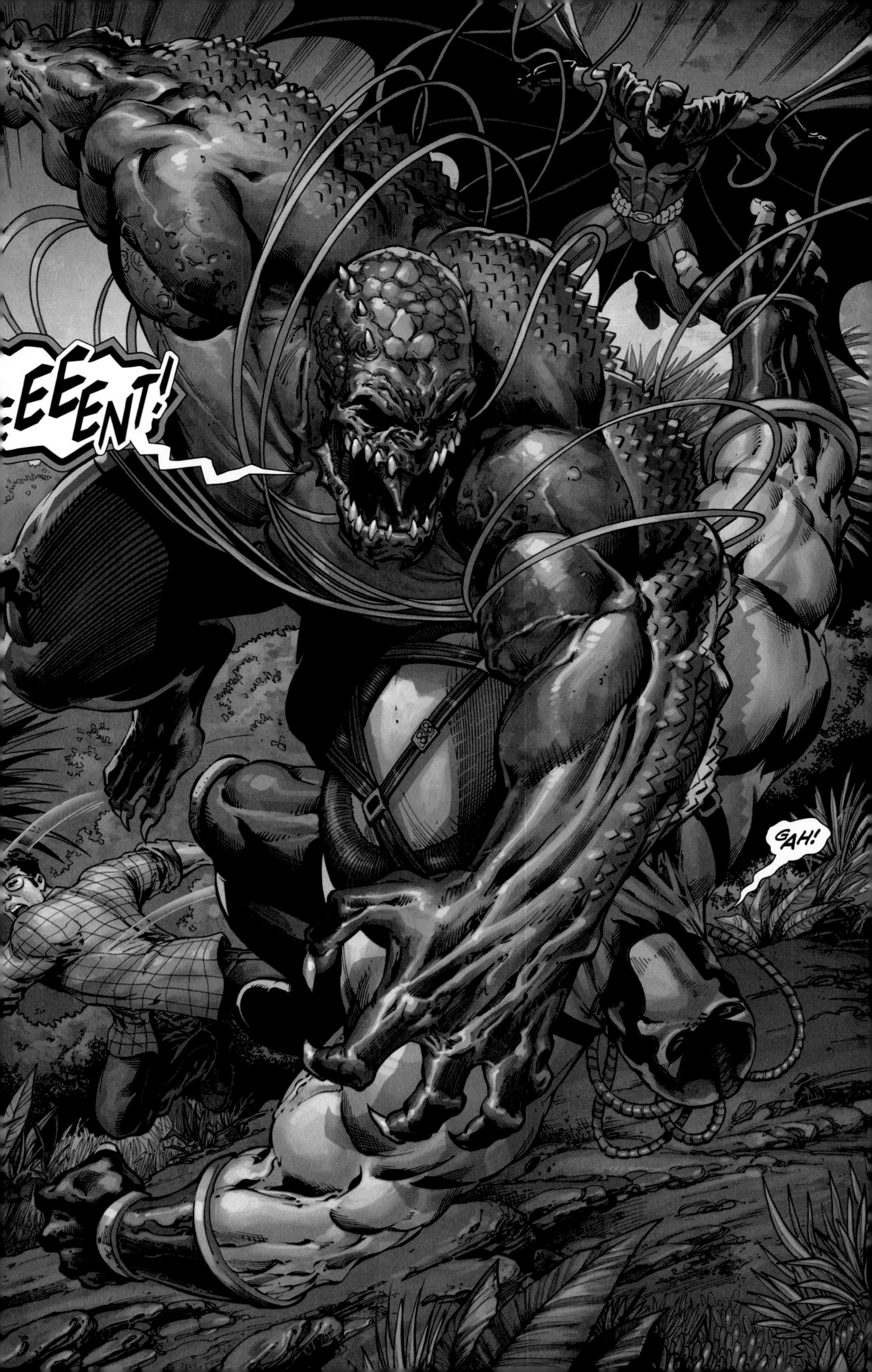

-EEENT!
GAH!

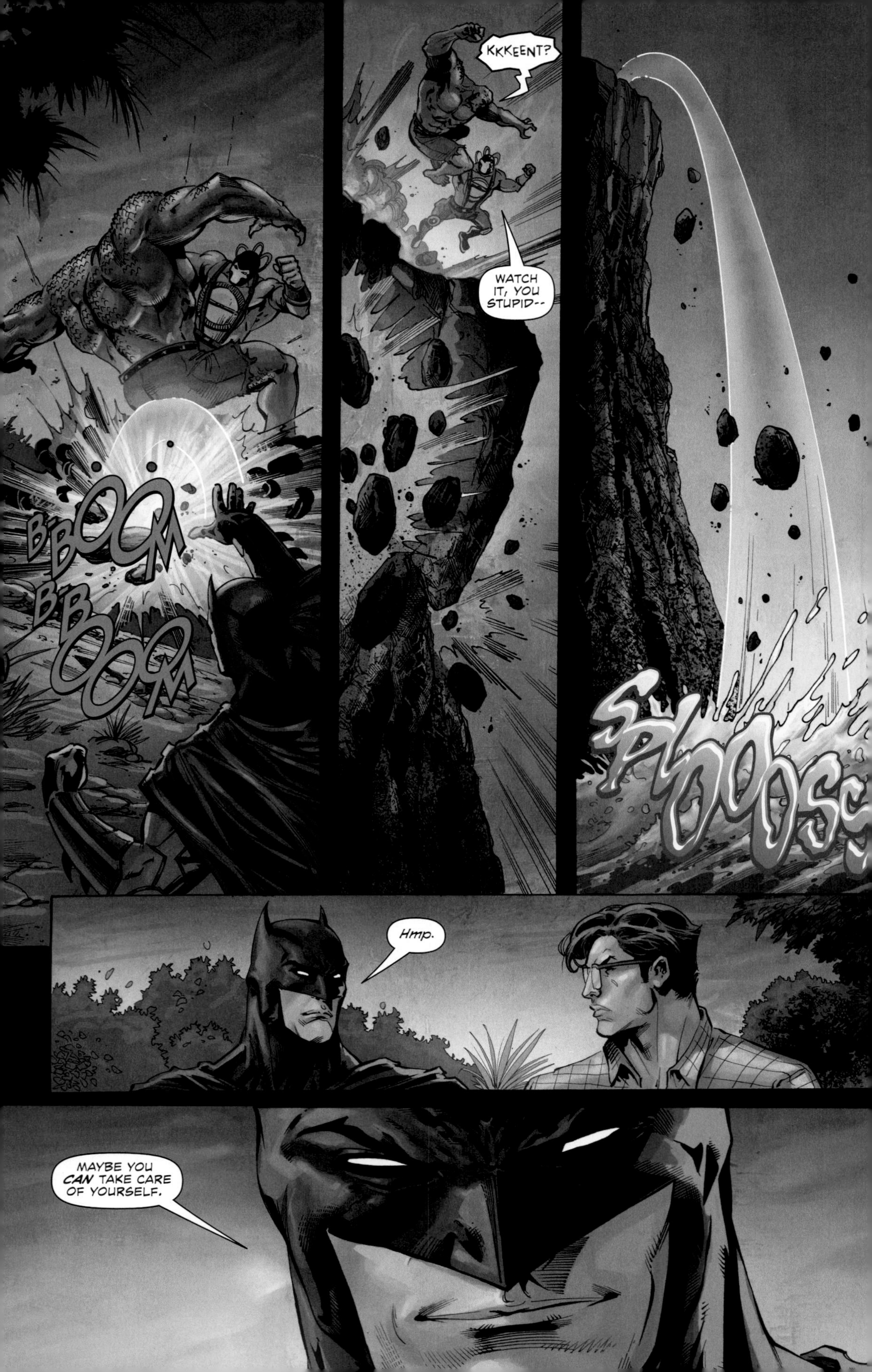
B-BOOM
B-BOOM
KKKEENT?
WATCH IT, YOU STUPID--
SPLOOSH
Hmp.
MAYBE YOU *CAN* TAKE CARE OF YOURSELF.

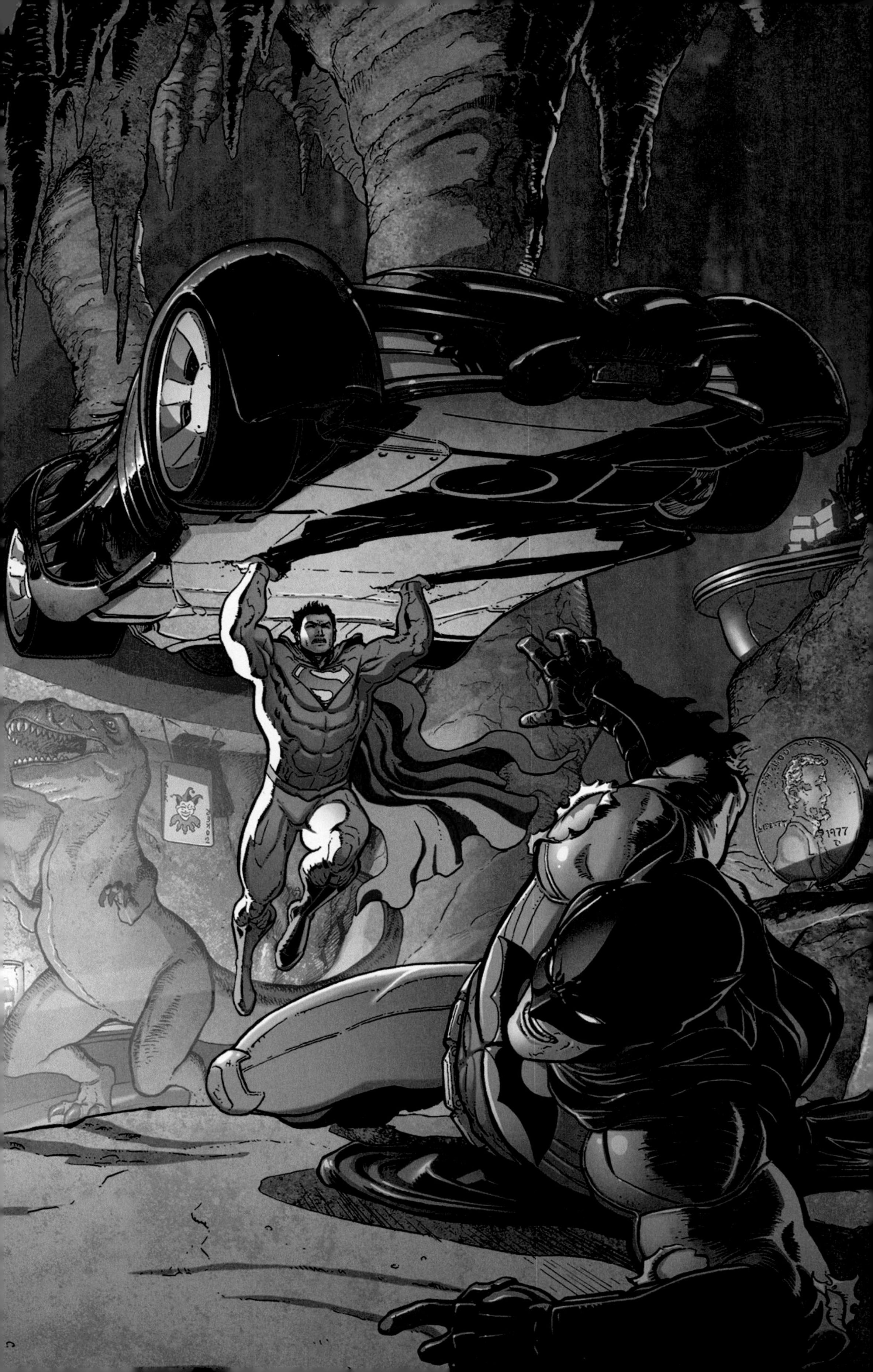
1977

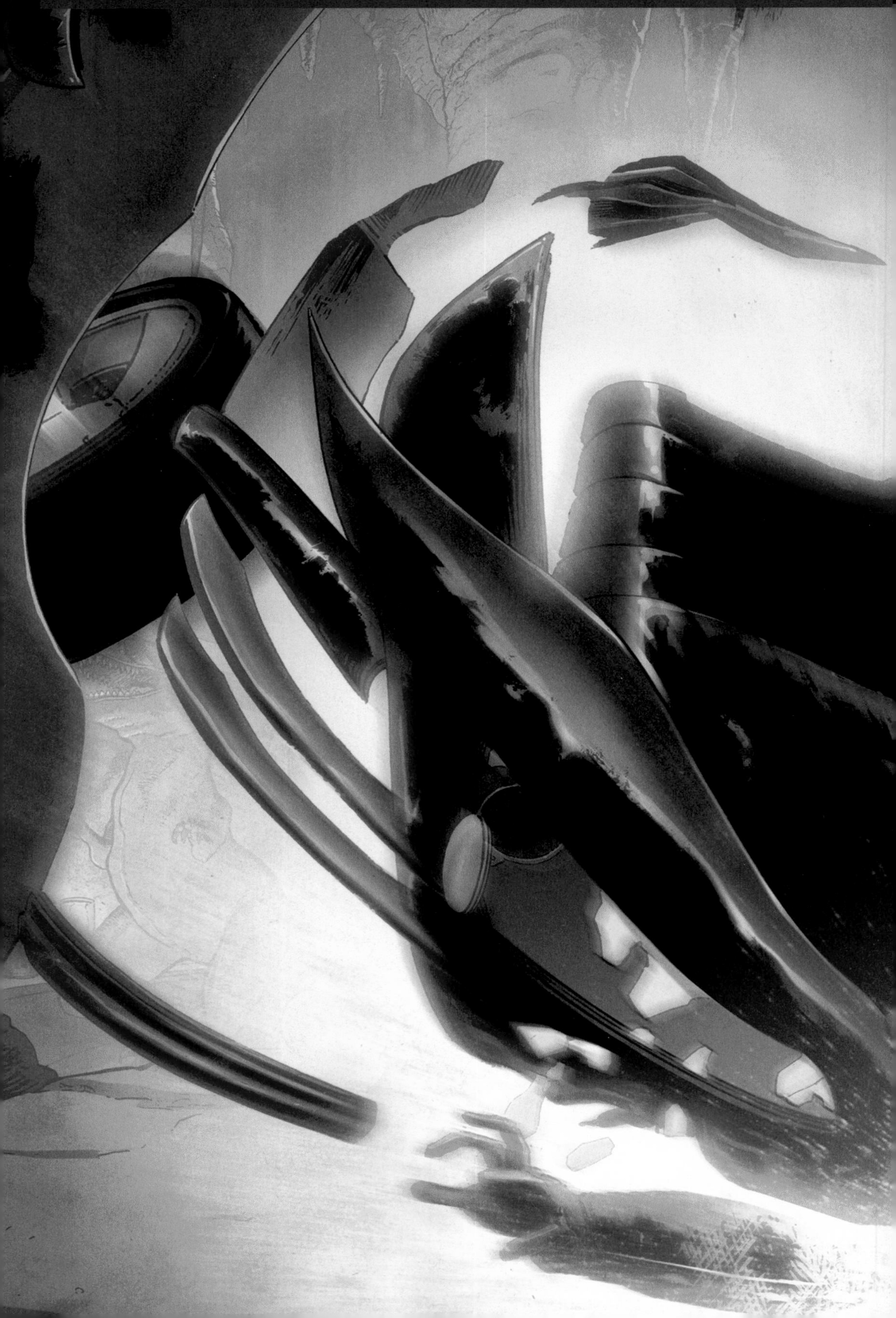

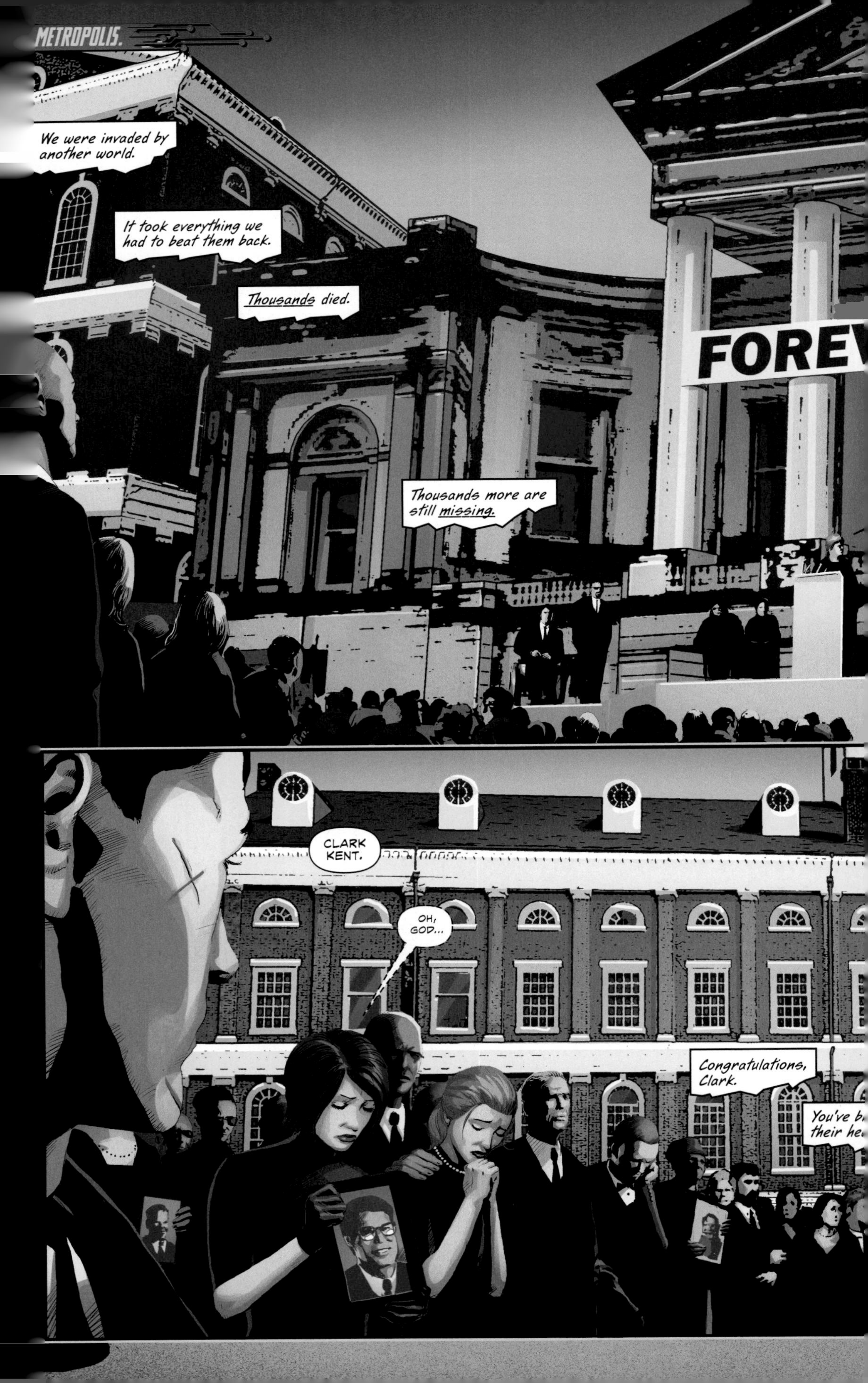
METROPOLIS.
We were invaded by another world.
It took everything we had to beat them back.
Thousands died.
Thousands more are still missing.
FOREV
CLARK KENT.
OH, GOD...
Congratulations, Clark.
You've
their

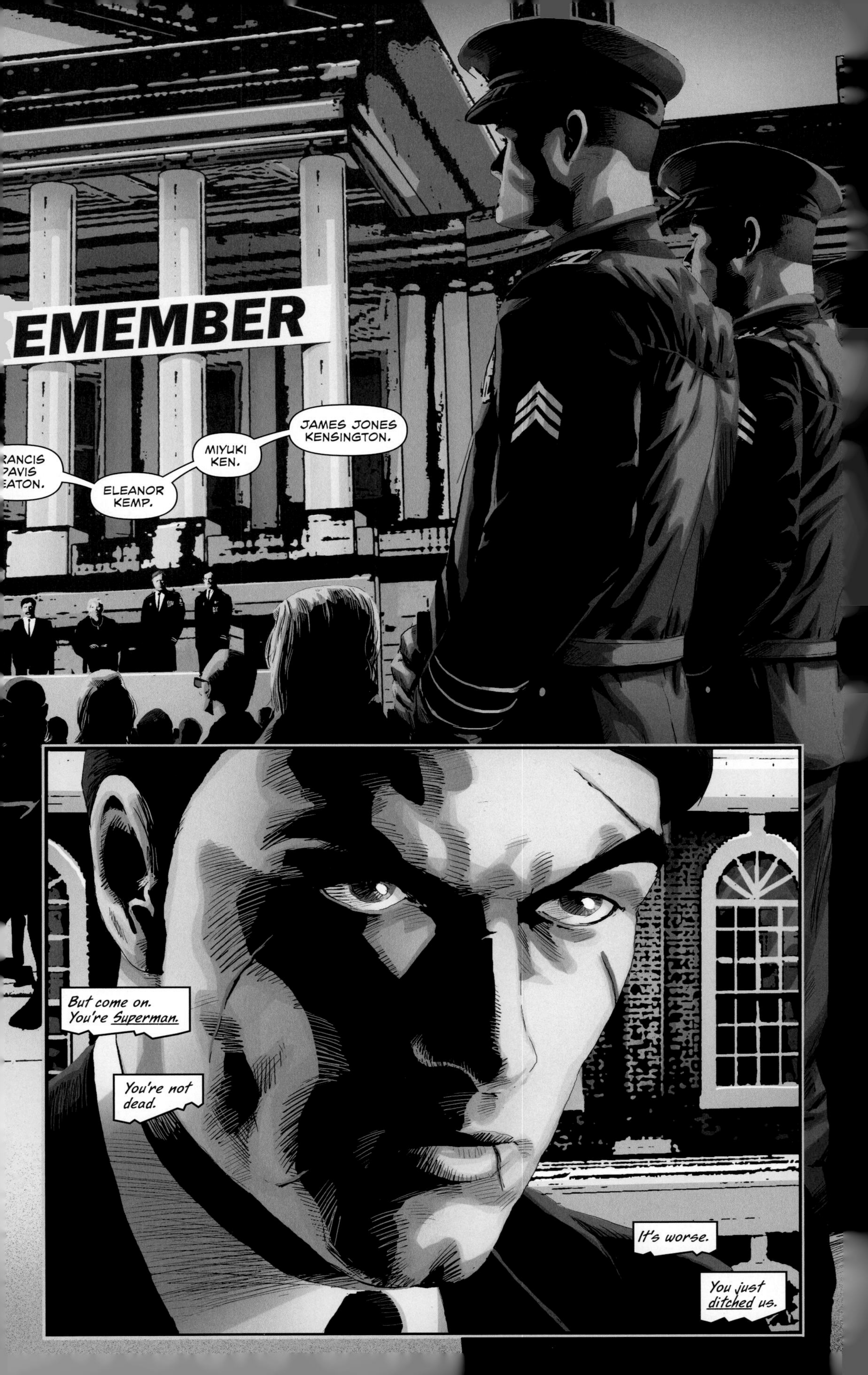
EMEMBER
RANCIS
PAVIS
EATON.
ELEANOR KEMP.
MIYUKI KEN.
JAMES JONES KENSINGTON.
But come on. You're Superman.
You're not dead.
It's worse.
You just ditched us.

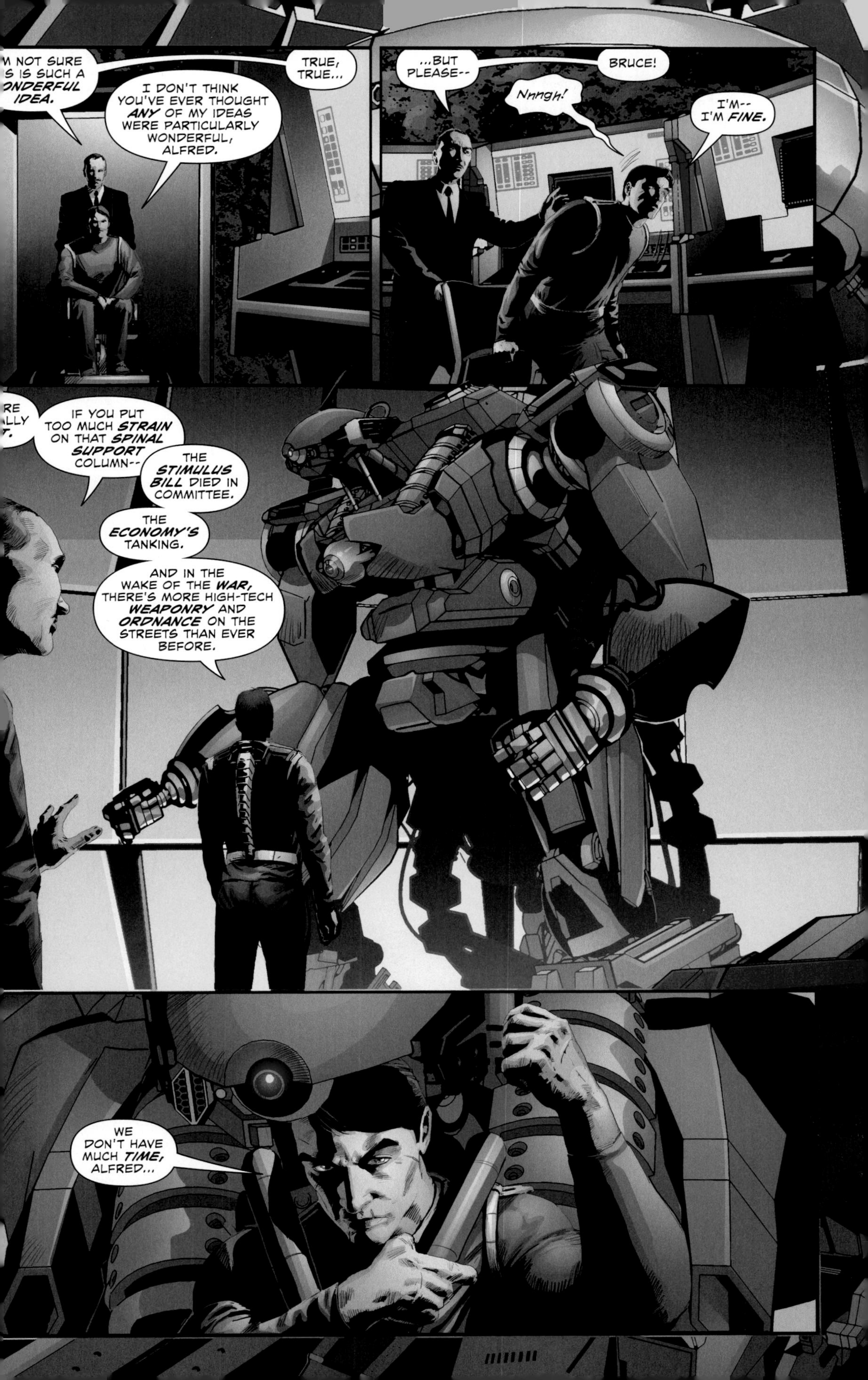
M NOT SURE
S IS SUCH A
ONDERFUL
IDEA.
TRUE, TRUE...
I DON'T THINK YOU'VE EVER THOUGHT ANY OF MY IDEAS WERE PARTICULARLY WONDERFUL, ALFRED.
...BUT PLEASE--
BRUCE!
Nnngh!
I'M-- I'M FINE.
RE
LLY
IF YOU PUT TOO MUCH STRAIN ON THAT SPINAL SUPPORT COLUMN--
THE STIMULUS BILL DIED IN COMMITTEE.
THE ECONOMY'S TANKING.
AND IN THE WAKE OF THE WAR, THERE'S MORE HIGH-TECH WEAPONRY AND ORDNANCE ON THE STREETS THAN EVER BEFORE.
WE DON'T HAVE MUCH TIME, ALFRED...

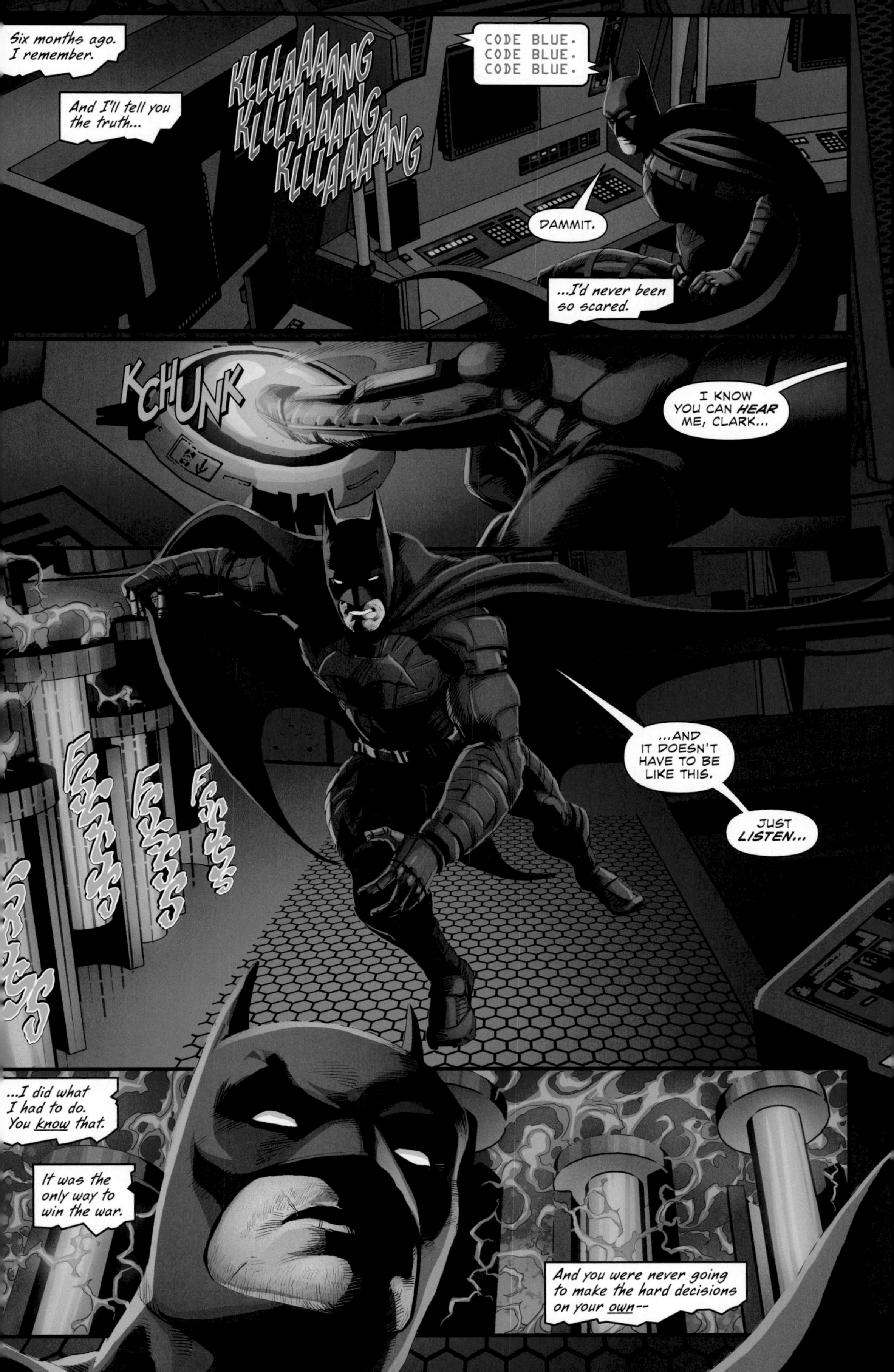
Six months ago. I remember.
KLLLAAAANG KLLLAAAANG KLLLAAAANG
CODE BLUE. CODE BLUE. CODE BLUE.
And I'll tell you the truth...
DAMMIT.
...I'd never been so scared.
KCHUNK
I KNOW YOU CAN HEAR ME, CLARK...
...AND IT DOESN'T HAVE TO BE LIKE THIS.
JUST LISTEN...
FSSSSS
FSSSSS
FSSSSS
FSSSSS
...I did what I had to do. You know that.
It was the only way to win the war.
And you were never going to make the hard decisions on your own--

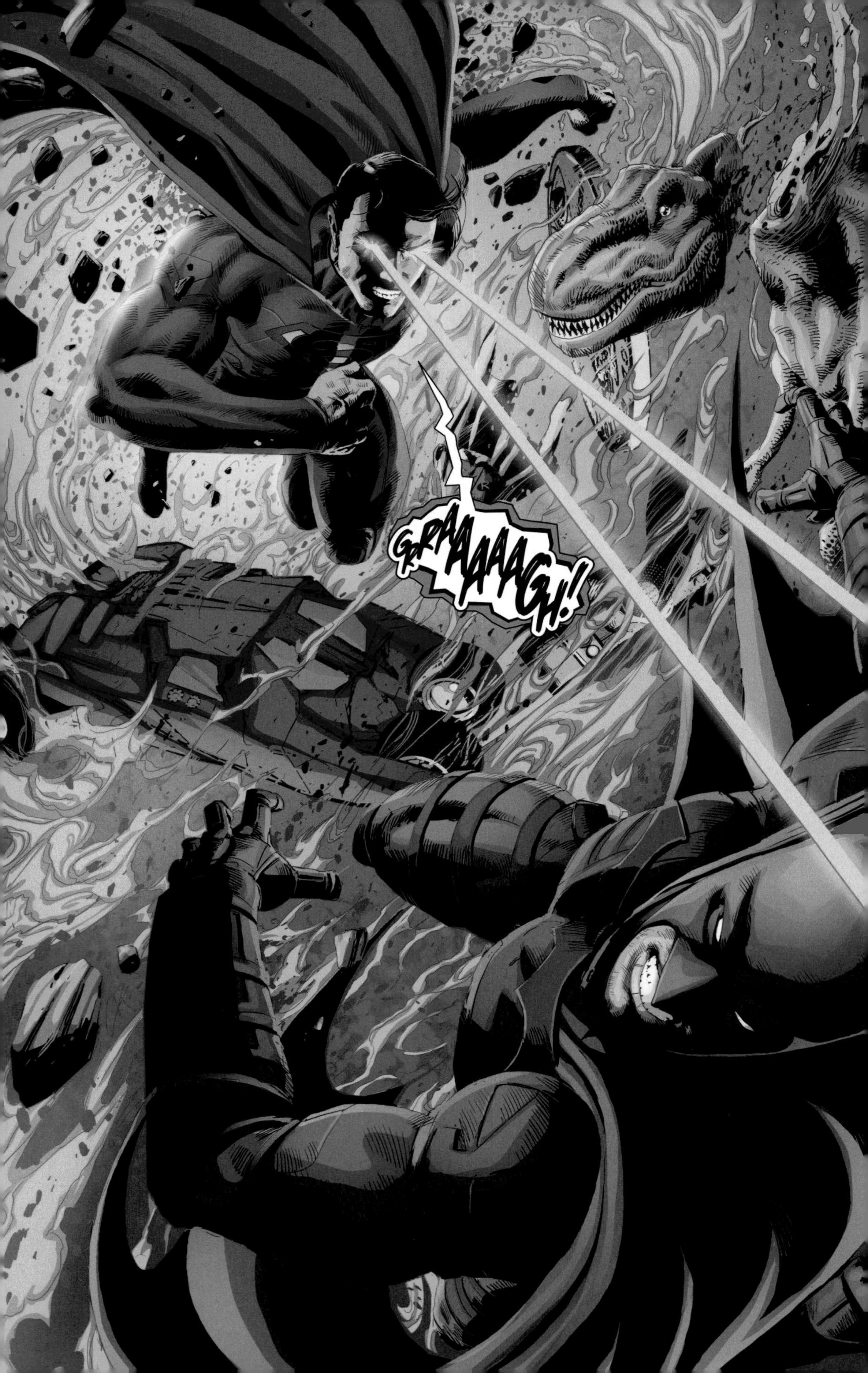
GRRAAAAAAAGH!

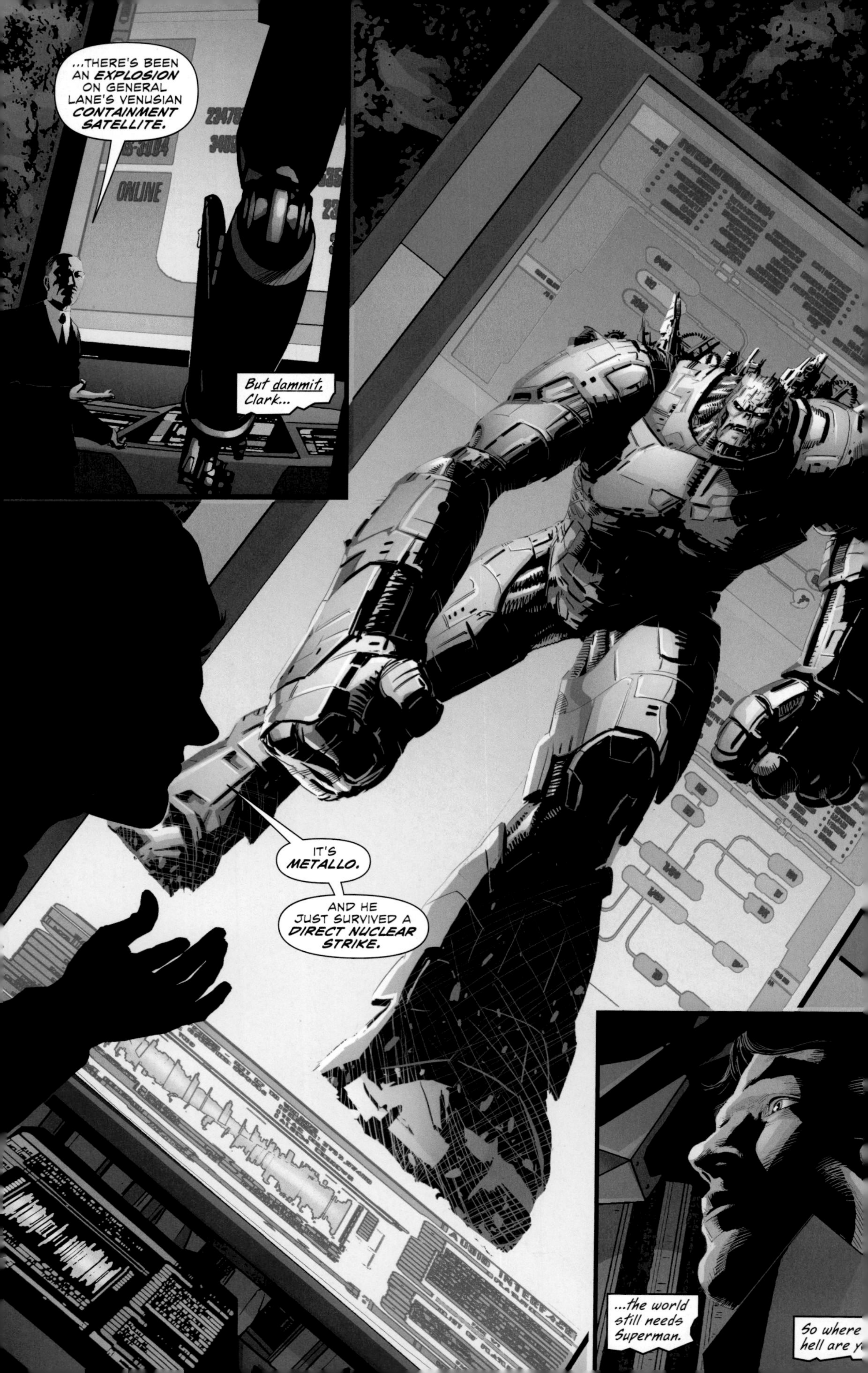
...THERE'S BEEN AN *EXPLOSION* ON GENERAL LANE'S VENUSIAN *CONTAINMENT SATELLITE.*
ONLINE
But dammit, Clark...
IT'S *METALLO.*
AND HE JUST SURVIVED A *DIRECT NUCLEAR STRIKE.*
...the world still needs Superman.
So where hell are y

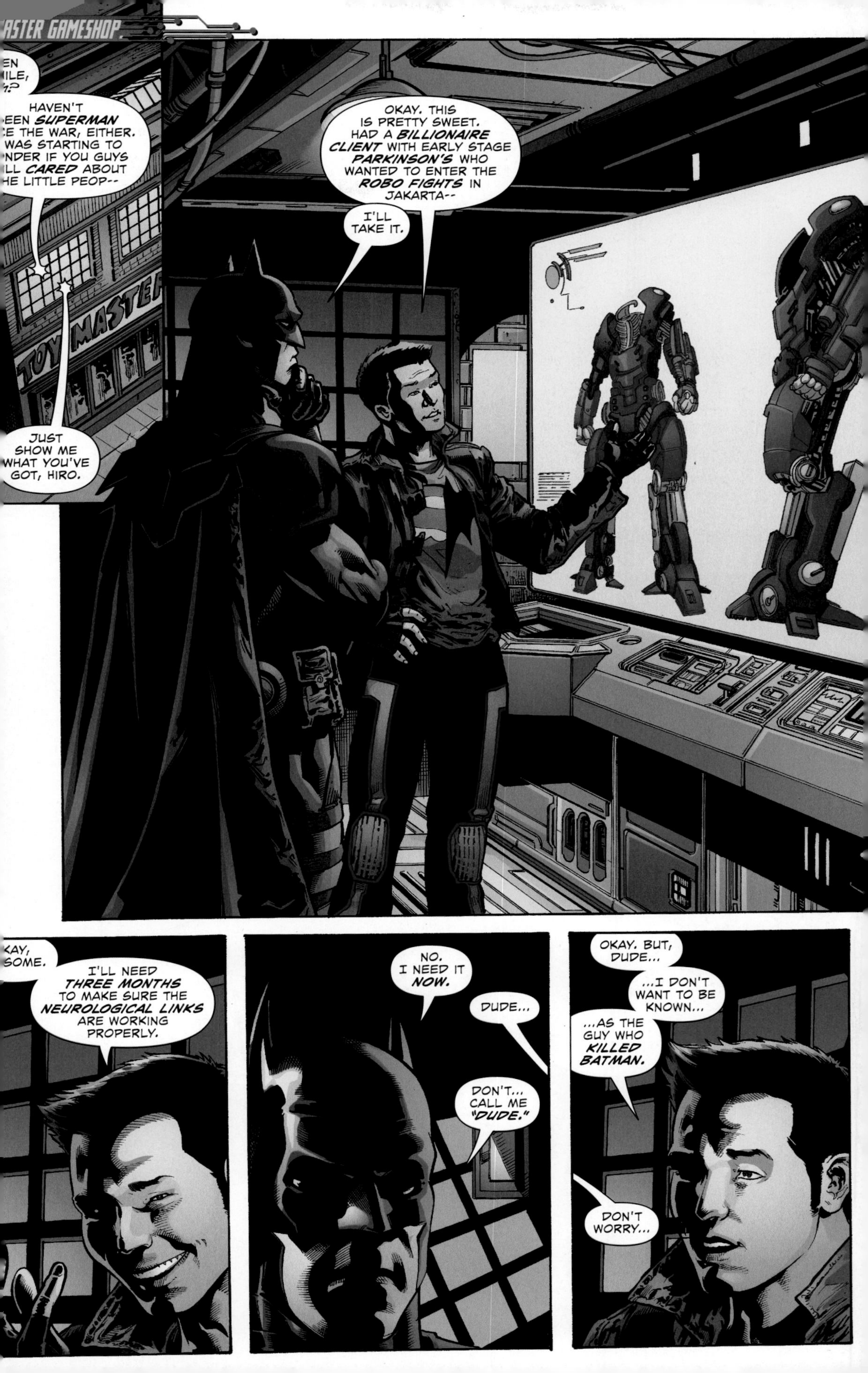

ASTER GAMESHOP
EN ILE,
HAVEN'T EEN SUPERMAN CE THE WAR, EITHER. WAS STARTING TO NDER IF YOU GUYS LL CARED ABOUT HE LITTLE PEOP--
JUST SHOW ME WHAT YOU'VE GOT, HIRO.
TOY MASTER
OKAY. THIS IS PRETTY SWEET. HAD A BILLIONAIRE CLIENT WITH EARLY STAGE PARKINSON'S WHO WANTED TO ENTER THE ROBO FIGHTS IN JAKARTA--
I'LL TAKE IT.
KAY, SOME.
I'LL NEED THREE MONTHS TO MAKE SURE THE NEUROLOGICAL LINKS ARE WORKING PROPERLY.
NO. I NEED IT NOW.
DUDE...
DON'T... CALL ME "DUDE."
OKAY. BUT, DUDE...
...I DON'T WANT TO BE KNOWN...
...AS THE GUY WHO KILLED BATMAN.
DON'T WORRY...

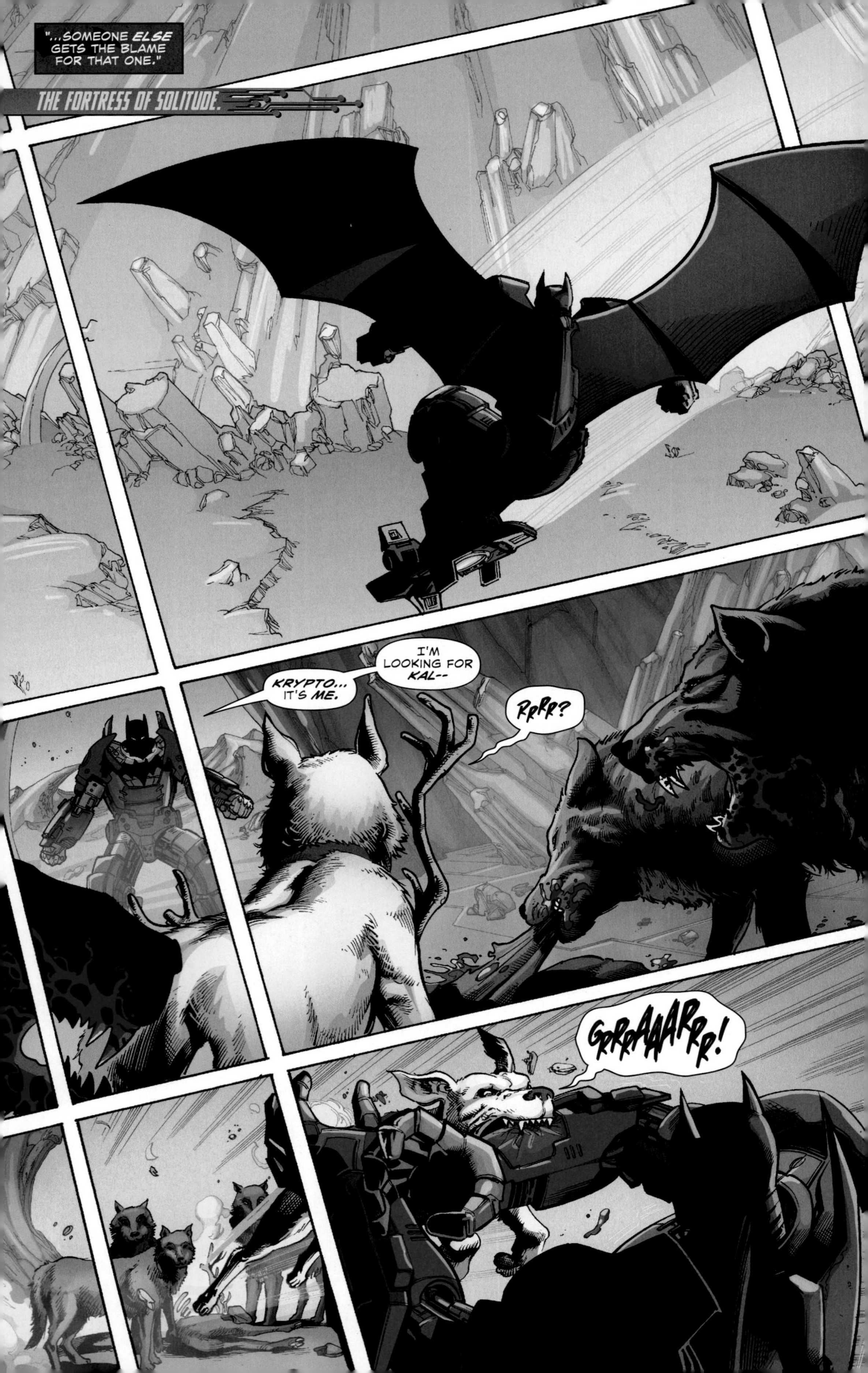
"...SOMEONE ELSE GETS THE BLAME FOR THAT ONE."
THE FORTRESS OF SOLITUDE.
KRYPTO... IT'S ME.
I'M LOOKING FOR KAL--
RRRR?
GRRRAAAARRR!

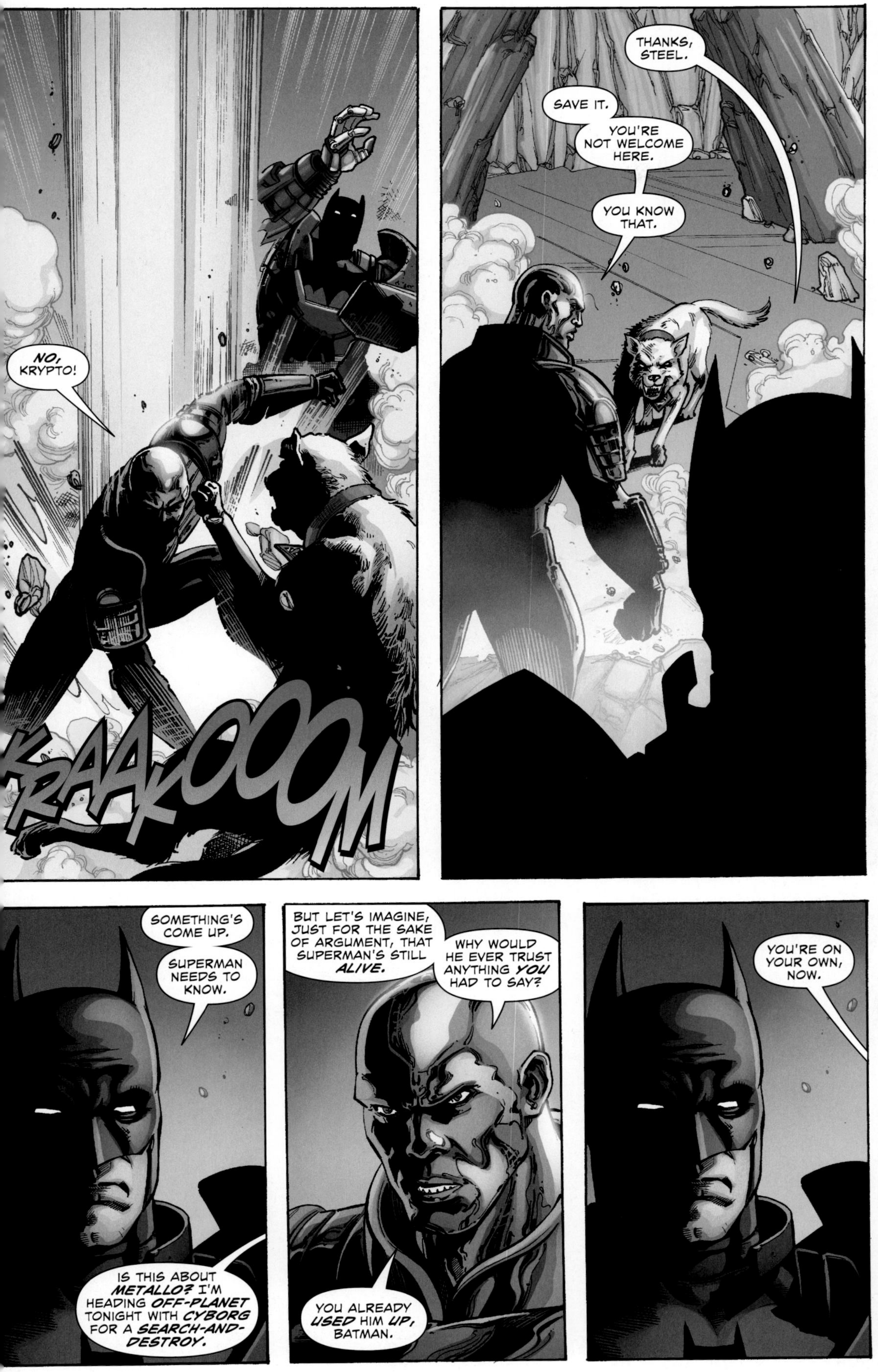

NO, KRYPTO!
KRAAKOOOM
THANKS, STEEL.
SAVE IT.
YOU'RE NOT WELCOME HERE.
YOU KNOW THAT.
SOMETHING'S COME UP.
SUPERMAN NEEDS TO KNOW.
IS THIS ABOUT METALLO? I'M HEADING OFF-PLANET TONIGHT WITH CYBORG FOR A SEARCH-AND-DESTROY.
BUT LET'S IMAGINE, JUST FOR THE SAKE OF ARGUMENT, THAT SUPERMAN'S STILL ALIVE.
WHY WOULD HE EVER TRUST ANYTHING YOU HAD TO SAY?
YOU ALREADY USED HIM UP, BATMAN.
YOU'RE ON YOUR OWN, NOW.

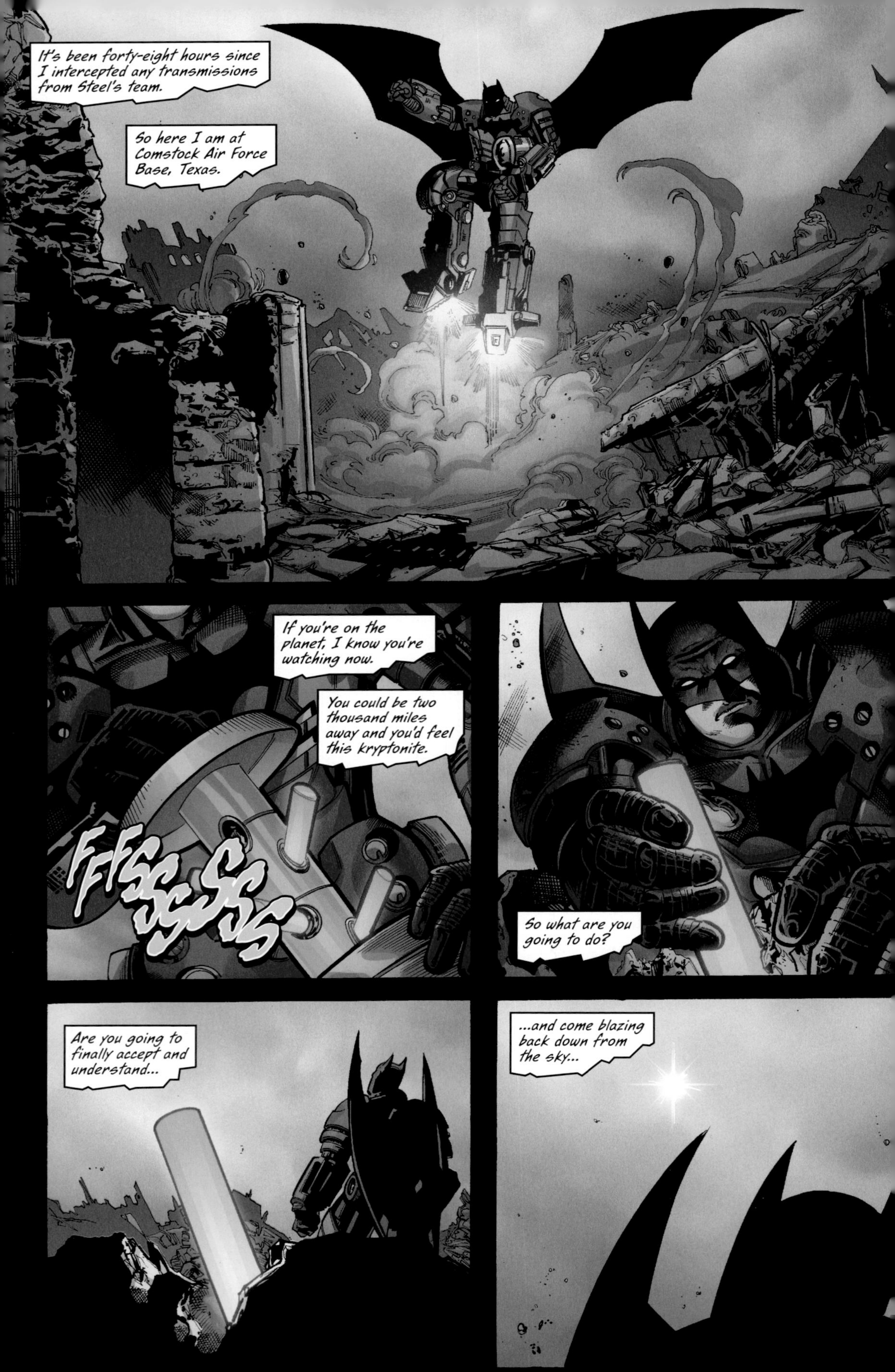
It's been forty-eight hours since I intercepted any transmissions from Steel's team.
So here I am at Comstock Air Force Base, Texas.
If you're on the planet, I know you're watching now.
You could be two thousand miles away and you'd feel this kryptonite.
FFSSSSSSS
So what are you going to do?
Are you going to finally accept and understand...
...and come blazing back down from the sky...

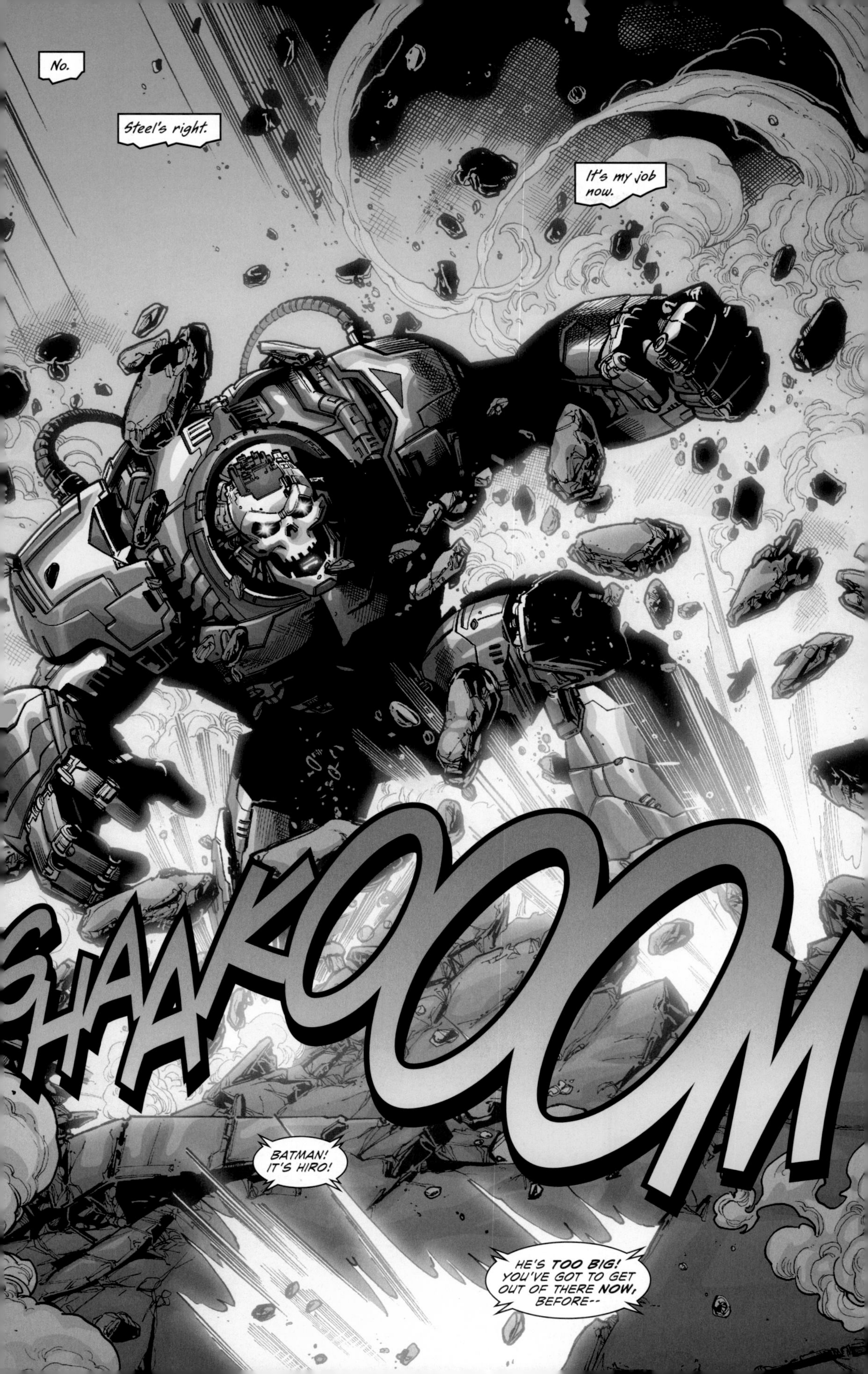
No.
Steel's right.
It's my job now.
SHAKOOOM
BATMAN! IT'S HIRO!
HE'S TOO BIG! YOU'VE GOT TO GET OUT OF THERE NOW, BEFORE--

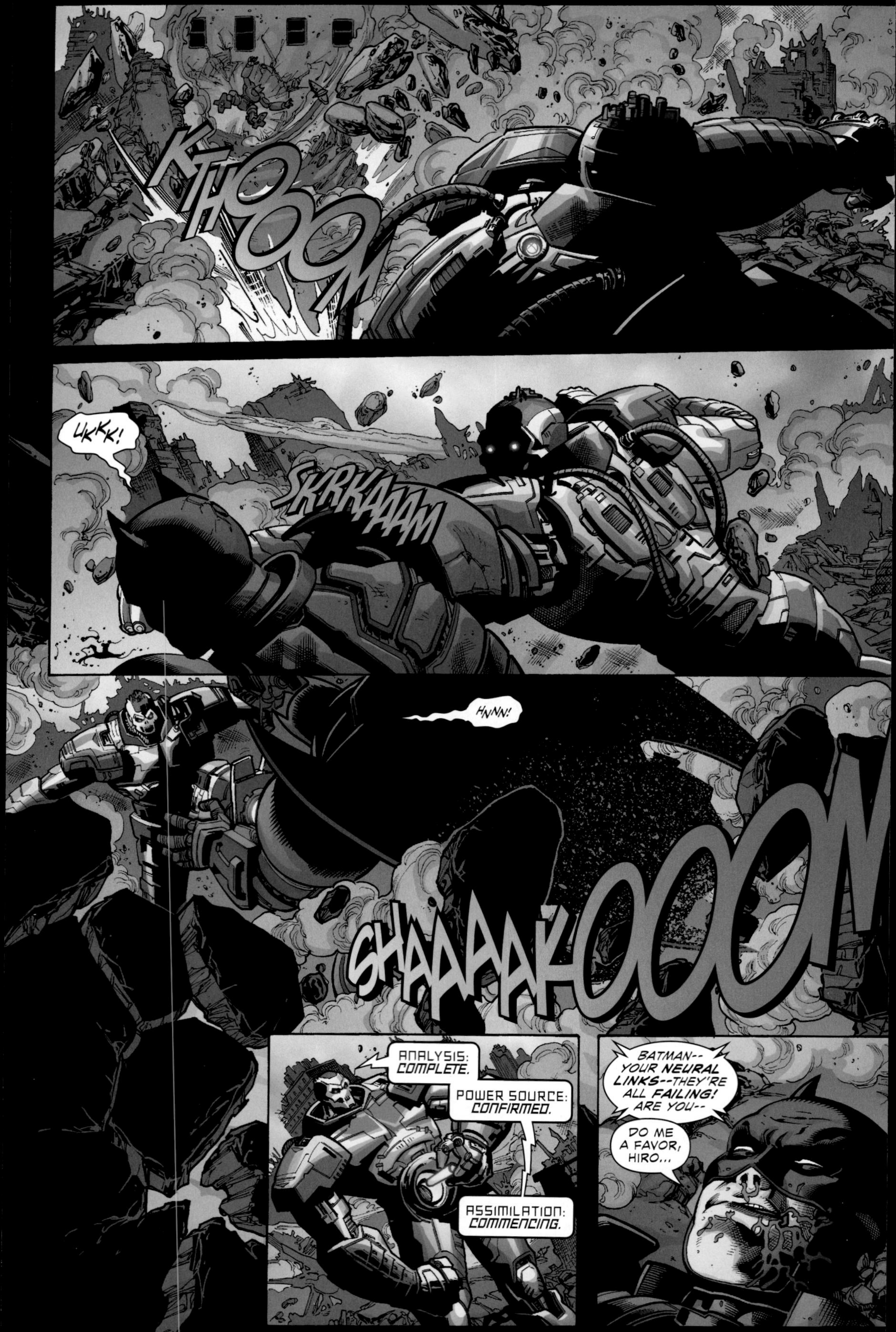
KTHOOM
UKKK!
SKRKAAAM
HNNN!
SHAAAAKOOOOM
ANALYSIS: COMPLETE.
POWER SOURCE: CONFIRMED.
ASSIMILATION: COMMENCING.
BATMAN-- YOUR NEURAL LINKS--THEY'RE ALL FAILING! ARE YOU--
DO ME A FAVOR, HIRO...

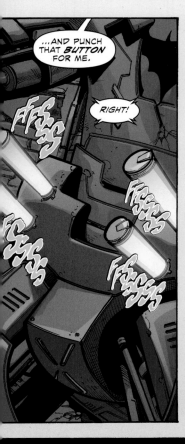

...AND PUNCH THAT *BUTTON* FOR ME.

RIGHT!

FFFSSS

FFFSSS

FFFSSS

KRYPTONITE LEVELS: *INCREASING!*

SYSTEM-- OVERLOAD!

SYSTEM-- OVERLOAD!

SYSTEM--

KTHOOM

HA HA!

THAT'S IT, BATMAN!

JUST LIKE WE PLANNED IT!

HEY, WE MAKE A PRETTY GOOD TEAM, HUH?

BATMAN?

BATMAN!

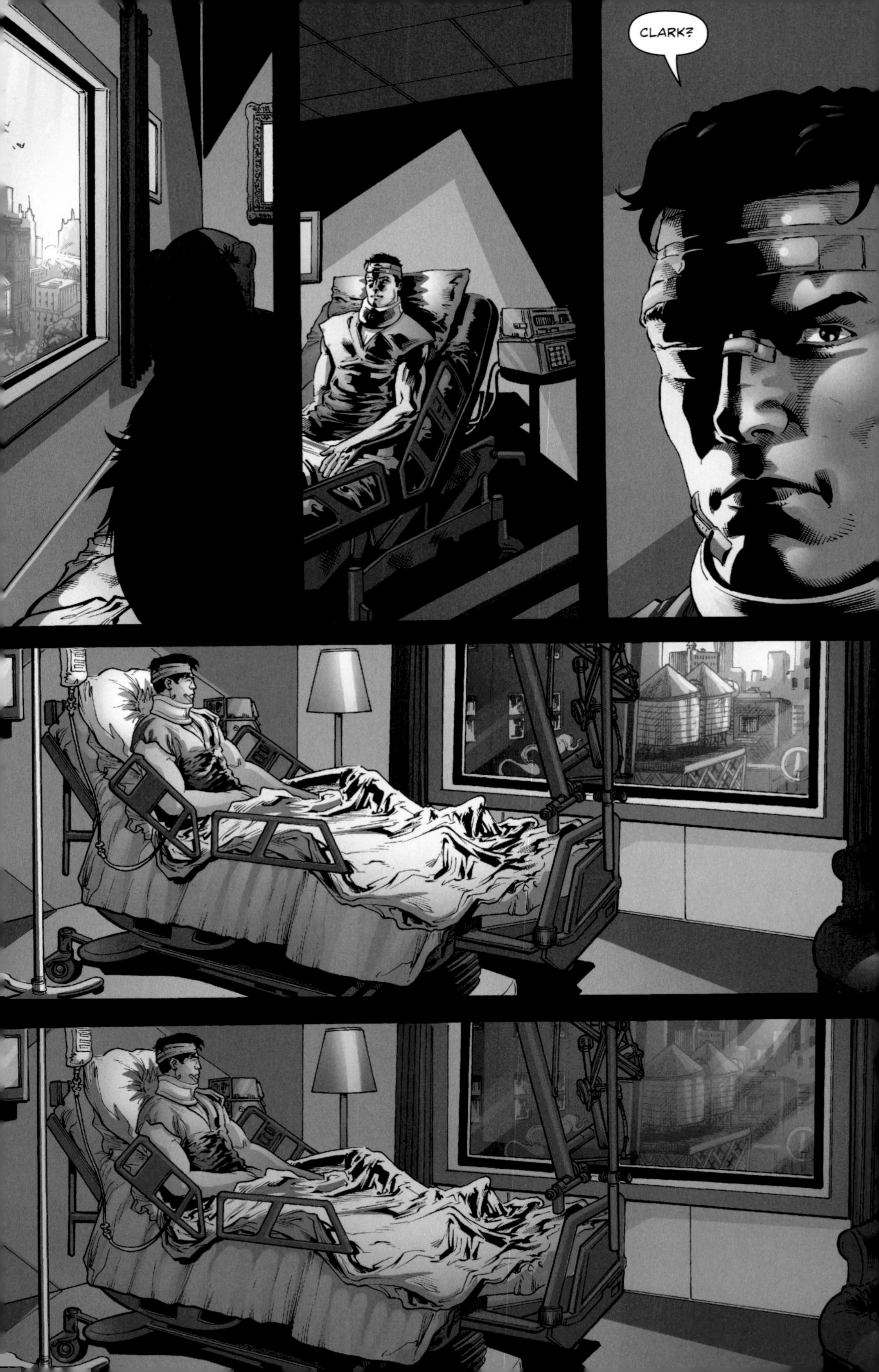
CLARK?

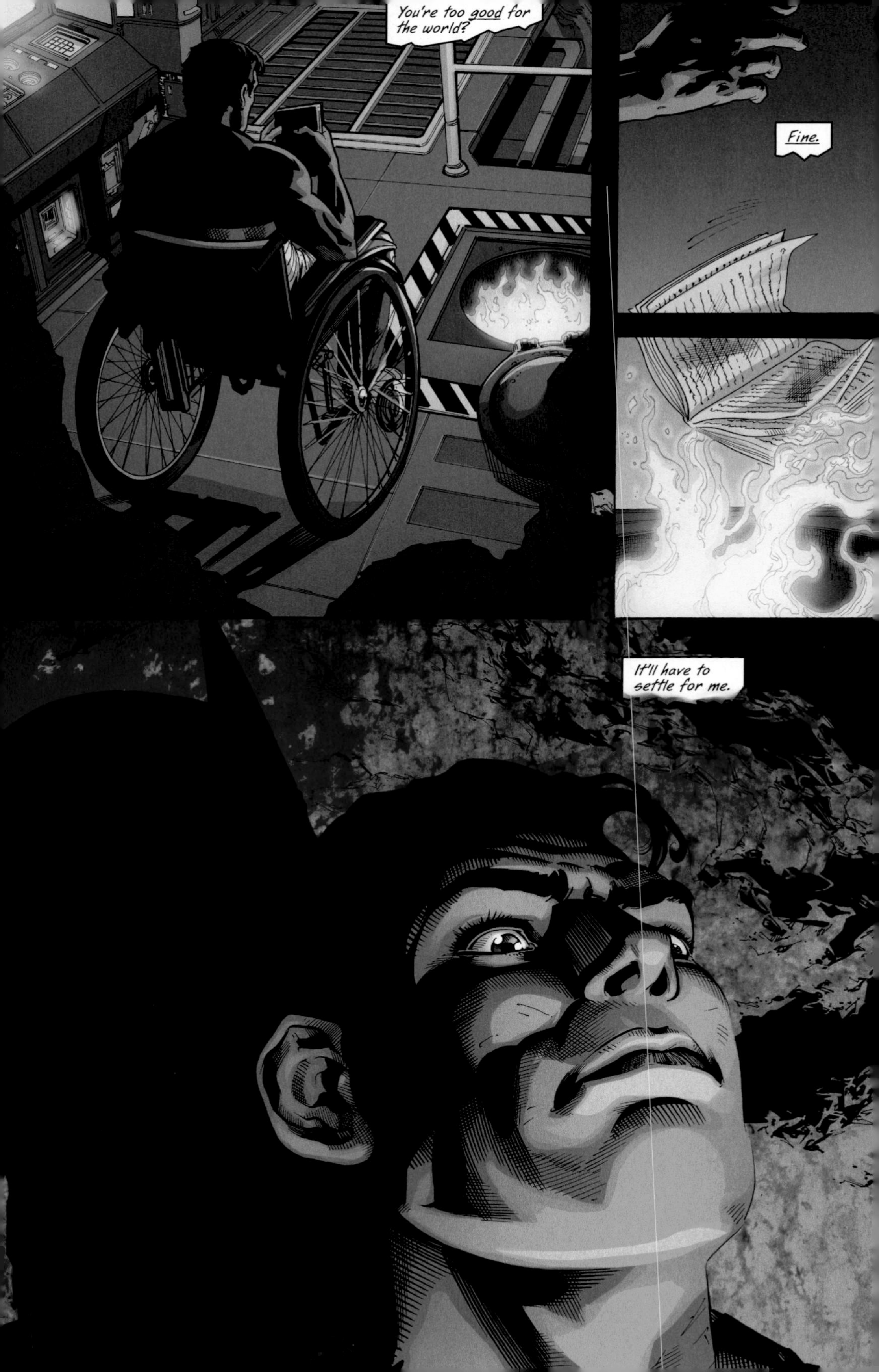
You're too good for the world?
Fine.
It'll have to settle for me.

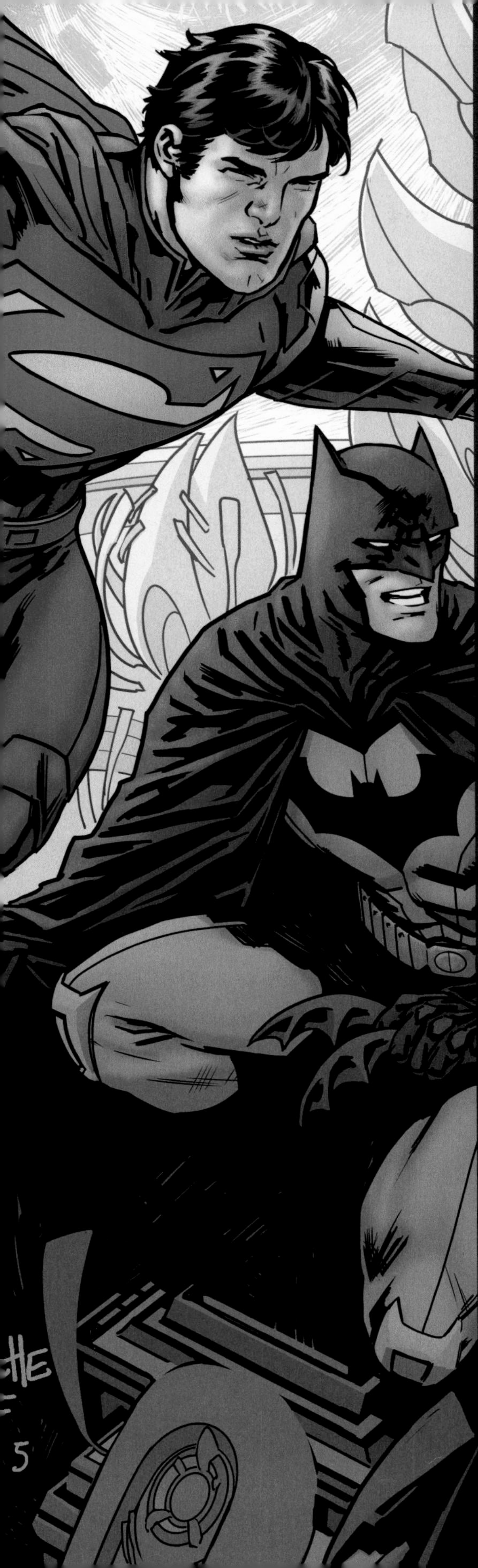

VARIANT COVER GALLERY

BATMAN/SUPERMAN #16
LEGO VARIANT COVER

BATMAN/SUPERMAN #16
VARIANT BY KEVIN WADA

BATMAN/SUPERMAN #17
VARIANT COVER BY DARWYN COOKE

BATMAN/SUPERMAN #17
VARIANT COVER BY LEANDRO FERNÁNDEZ AND ANDREW DALHOUSE

BATMAN/SUPERMAN #18
VARIANT COVER BY JUANJO AND TOMEU MOREY

BATMAN/SUPERMAN #18
FLASH 75TH ANNIVERSARY COVER BY JIM LEE, SCOTT WILLIAMS AND ALEX SINCLAIR

BATMAN/SUPERMAN #19
VARIANT COVER BY JOE QUINONES

BATMAN/SUPERMAN #19
HARLEY QUINN VARIANT COVER BY J.G. JONES AND ALEX SINCLAIR

BATMAN/SUPERMAN #20
VARIANT COVER BY YANICK PAQUETTE AND NATHAN FAIRBAIRN

BATMAN/SUPERMAN #20
MOVIE VARIANT COVER BY TONY HARRIS

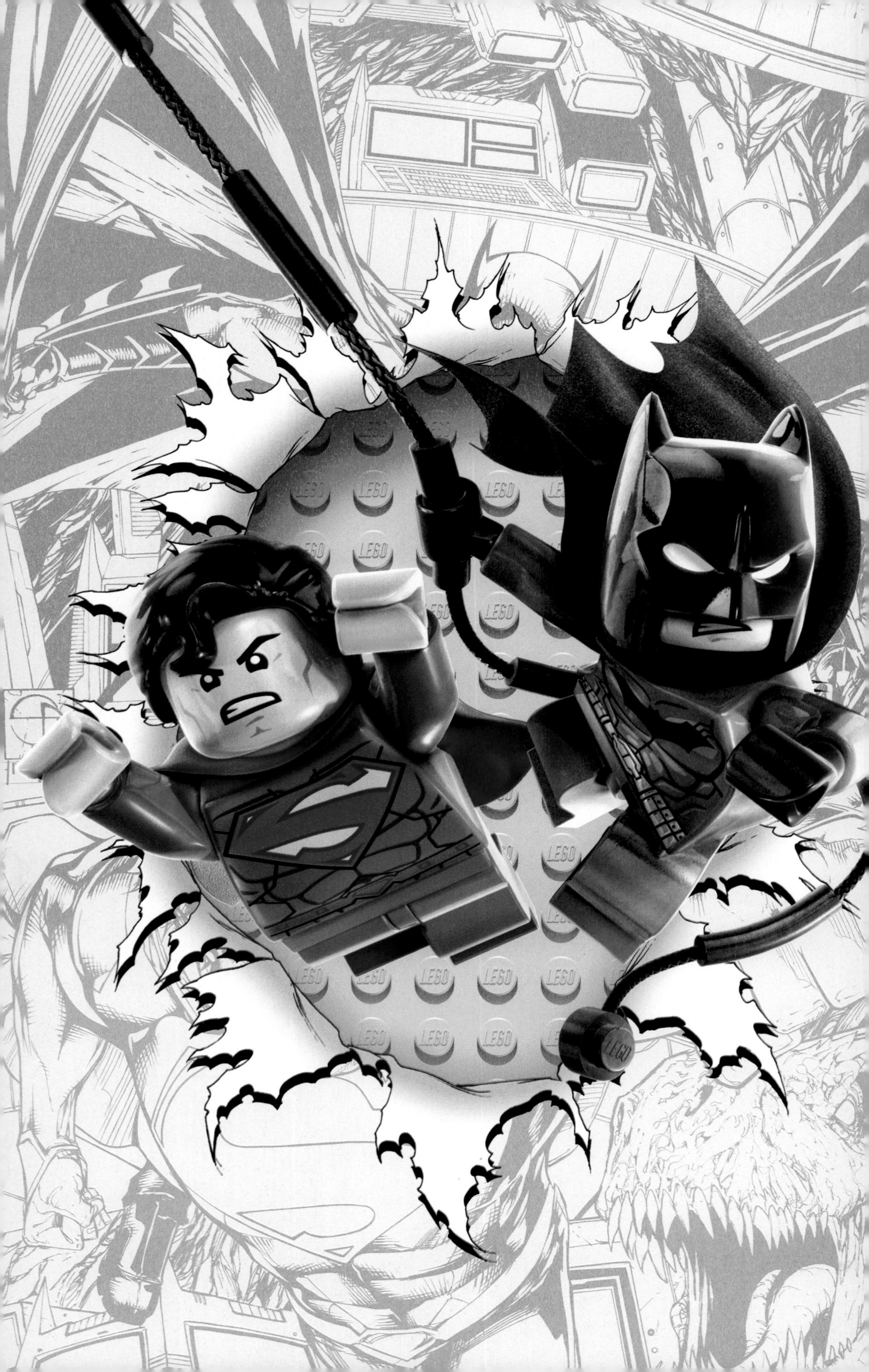

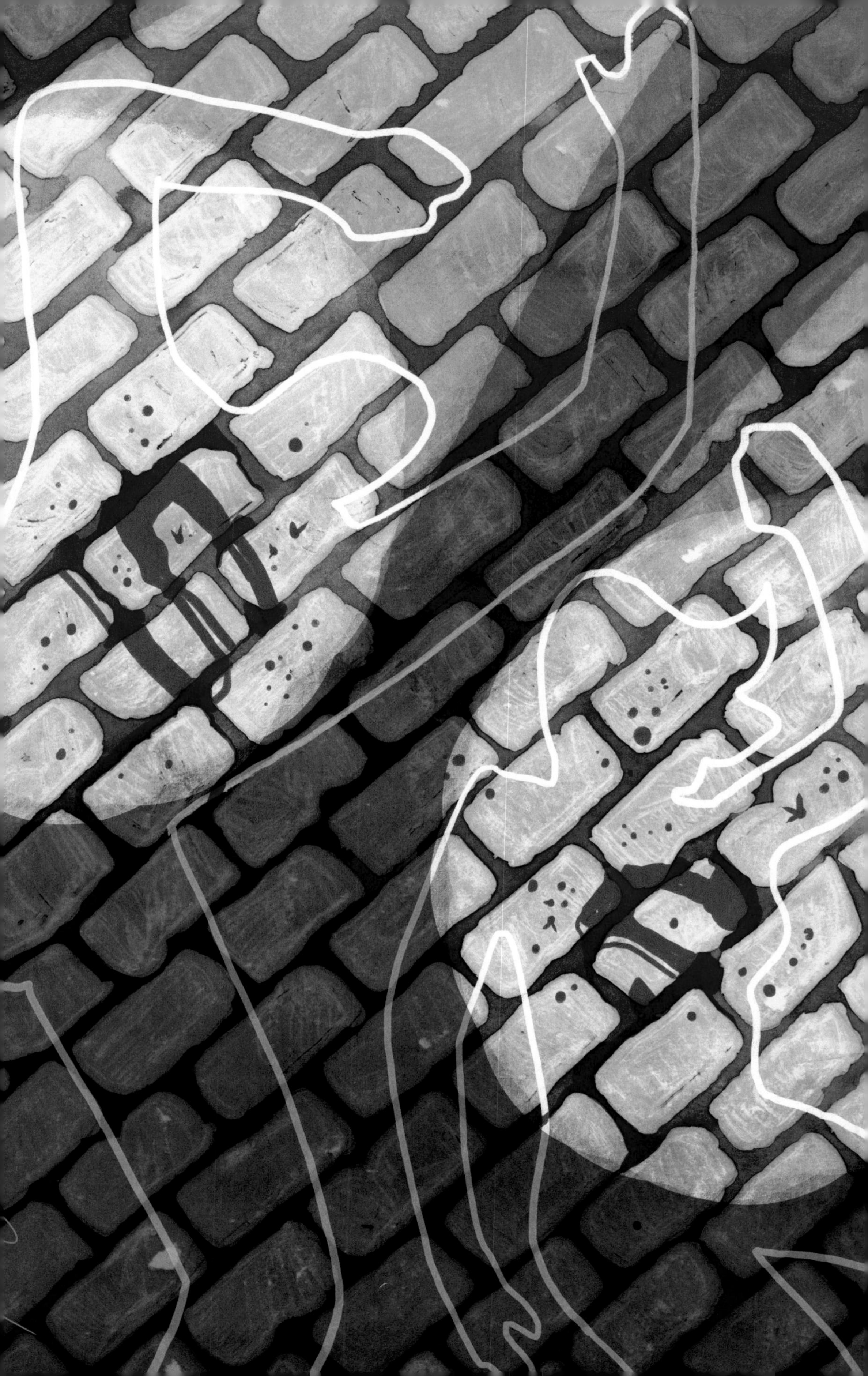

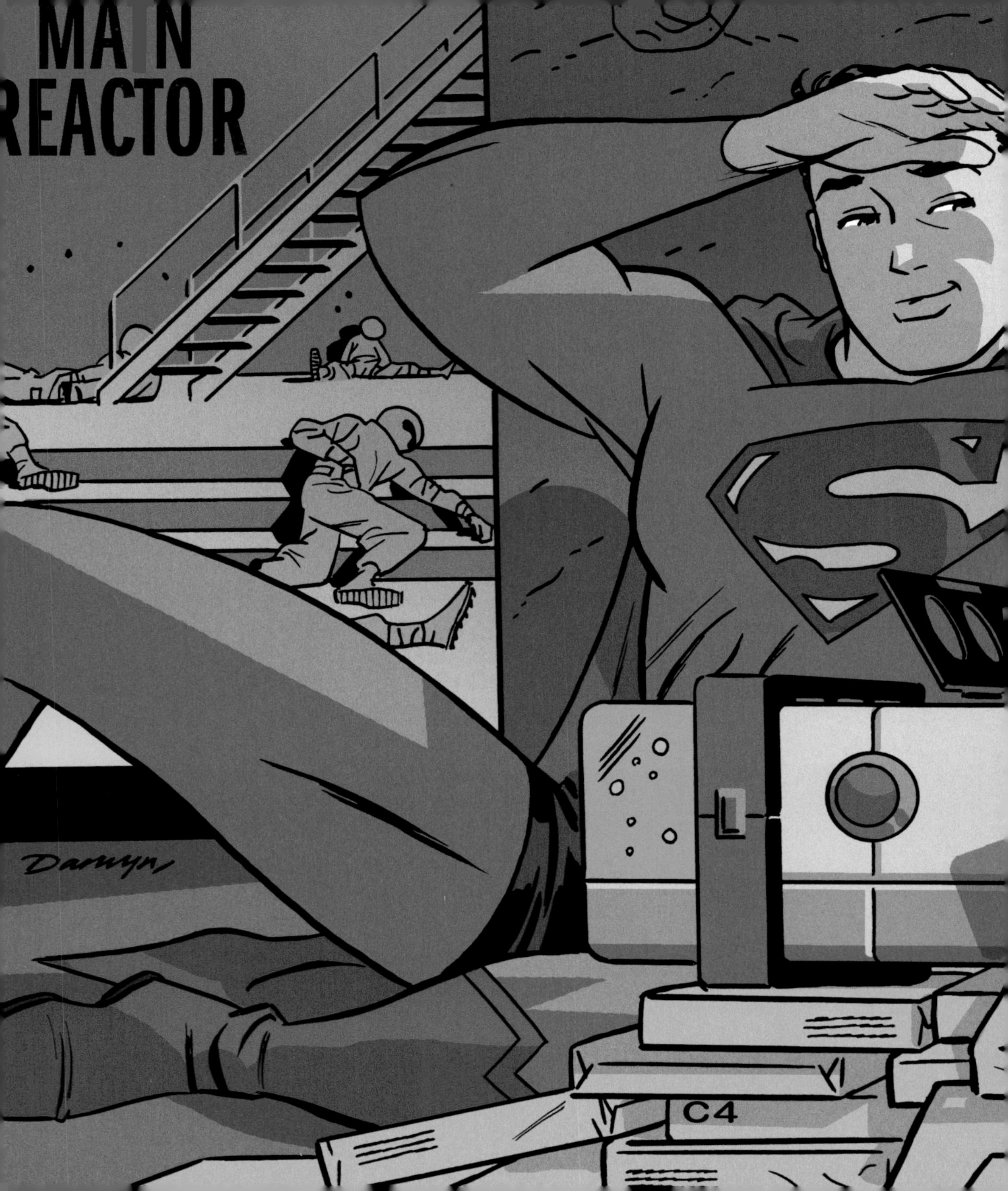
MAIN REACTOR
Darwyn
C4

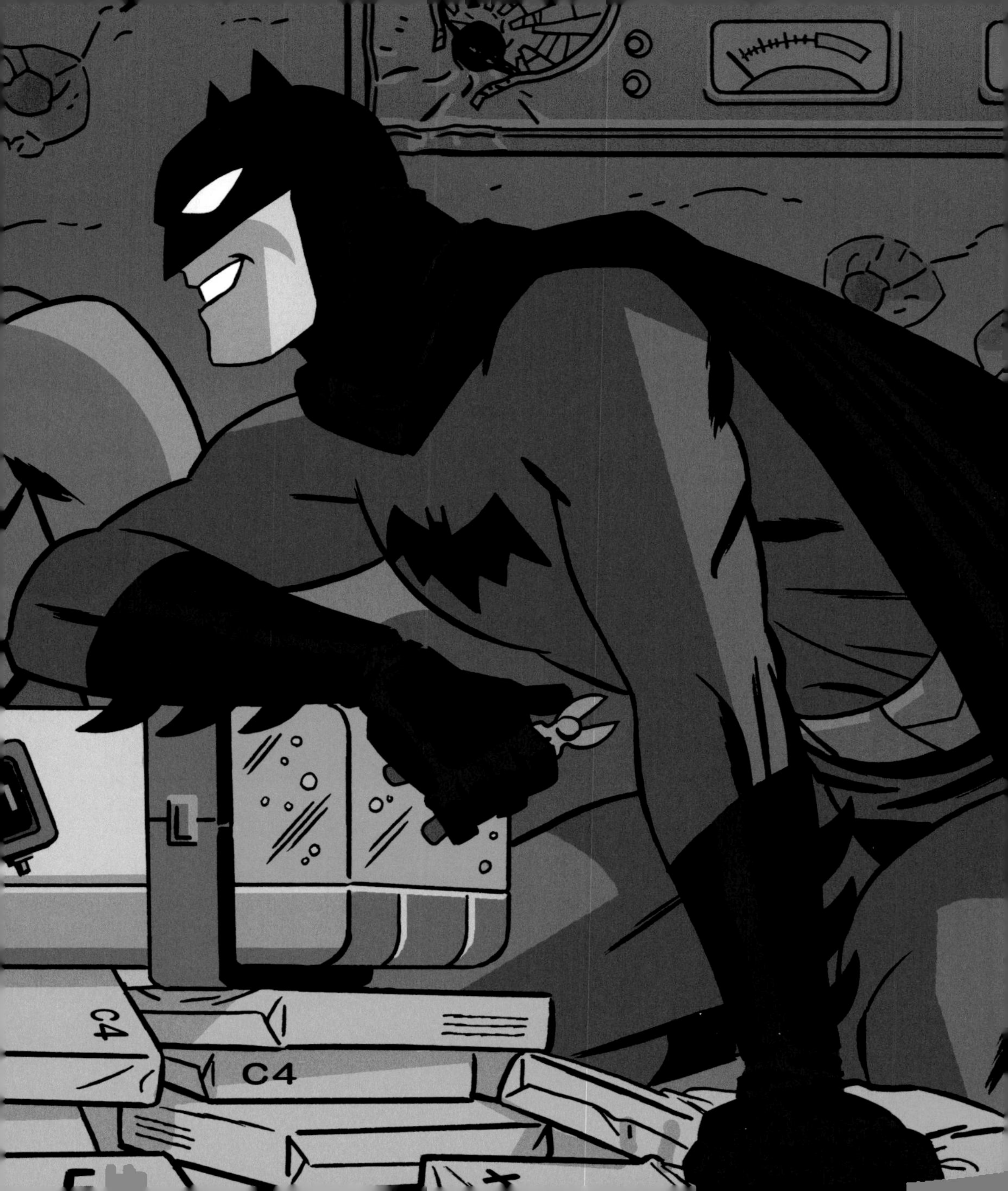
C4
C4

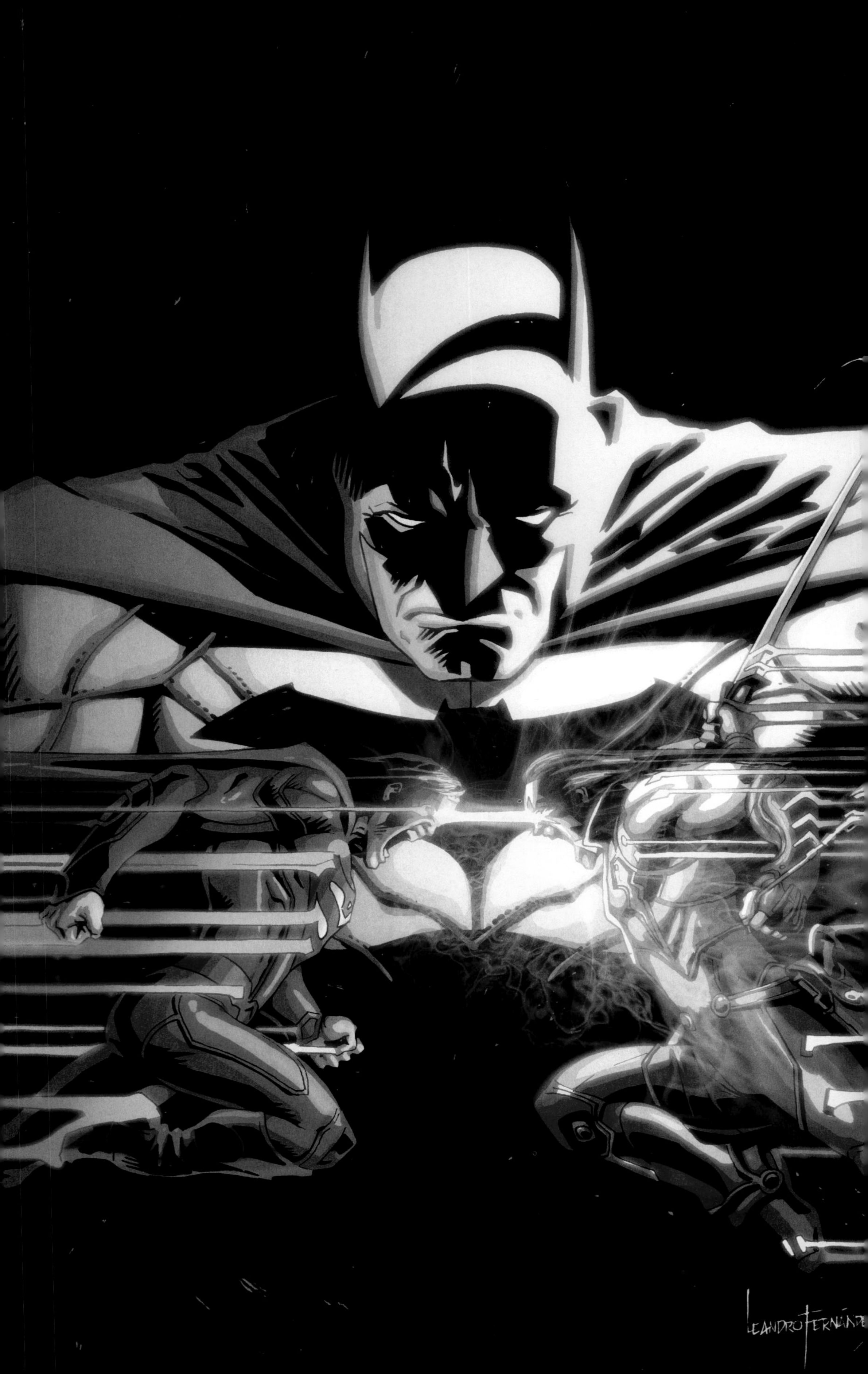

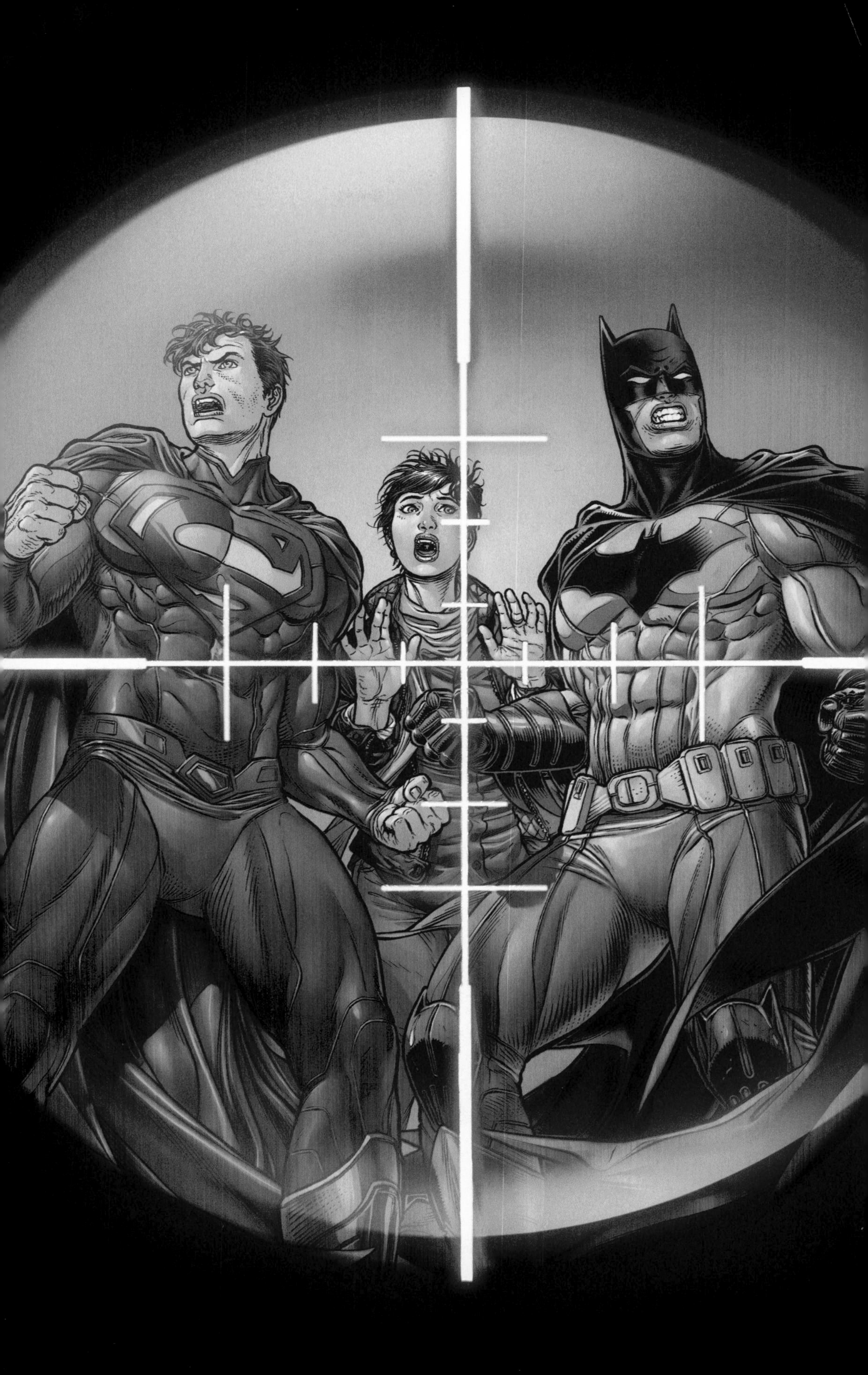

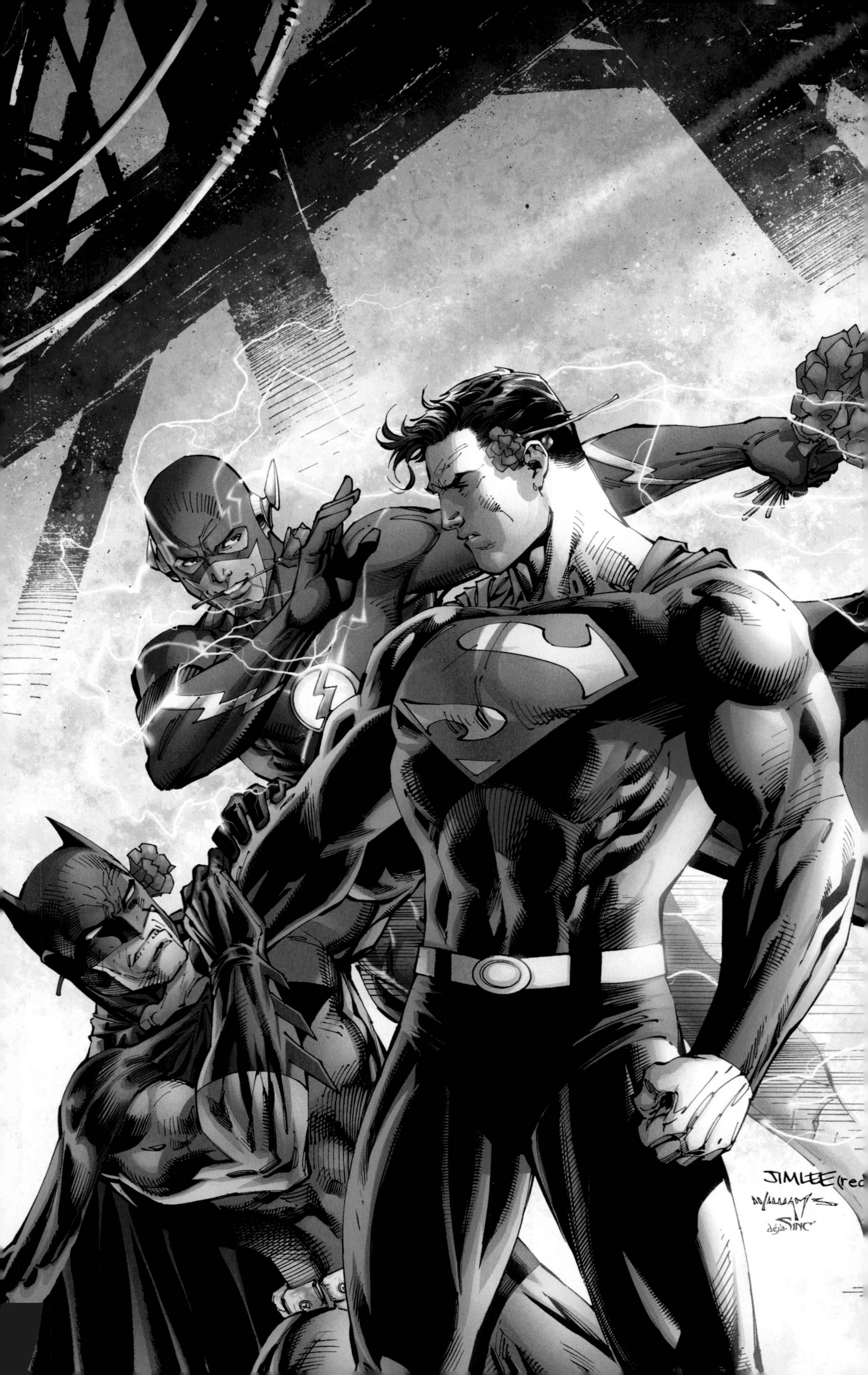

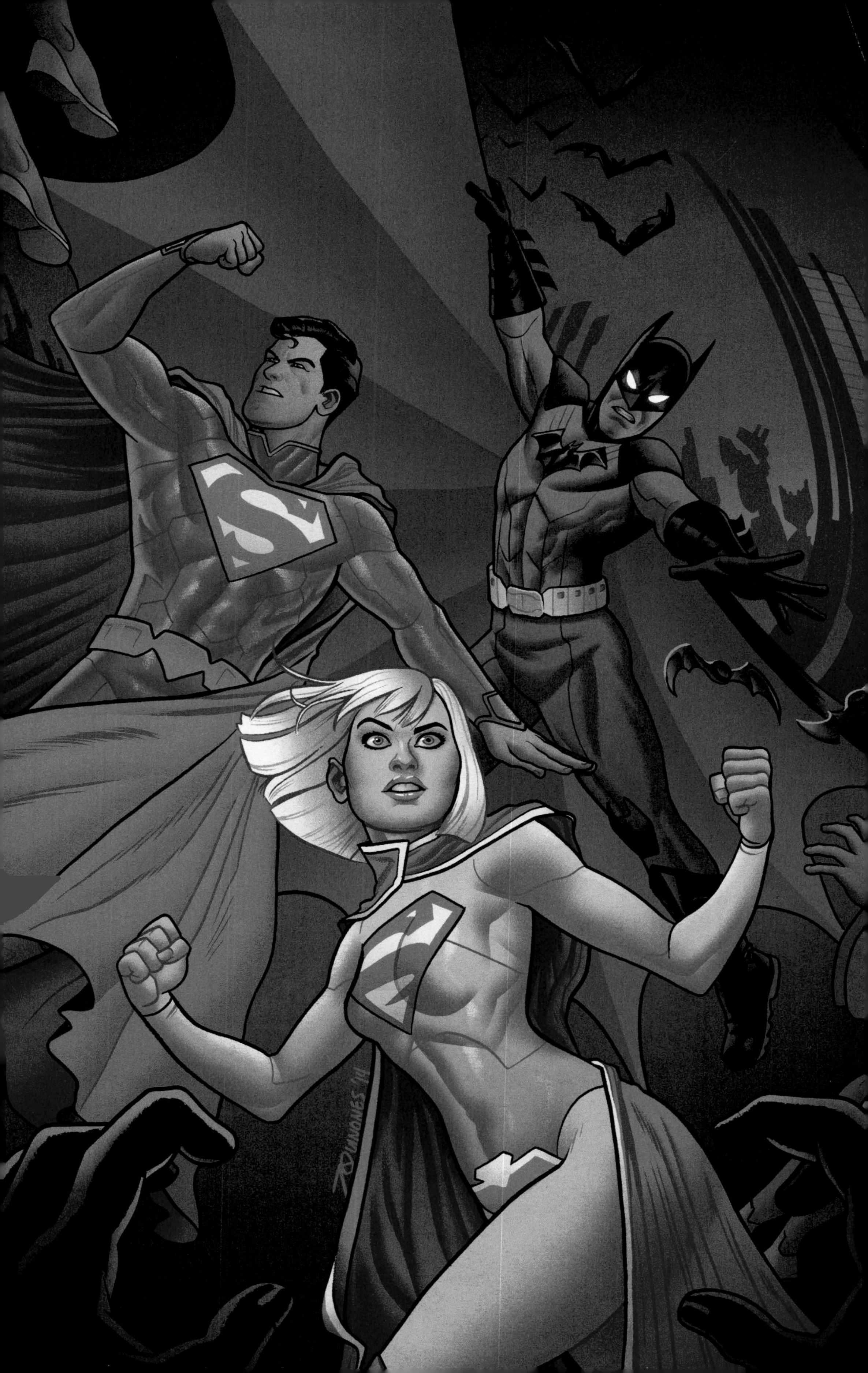

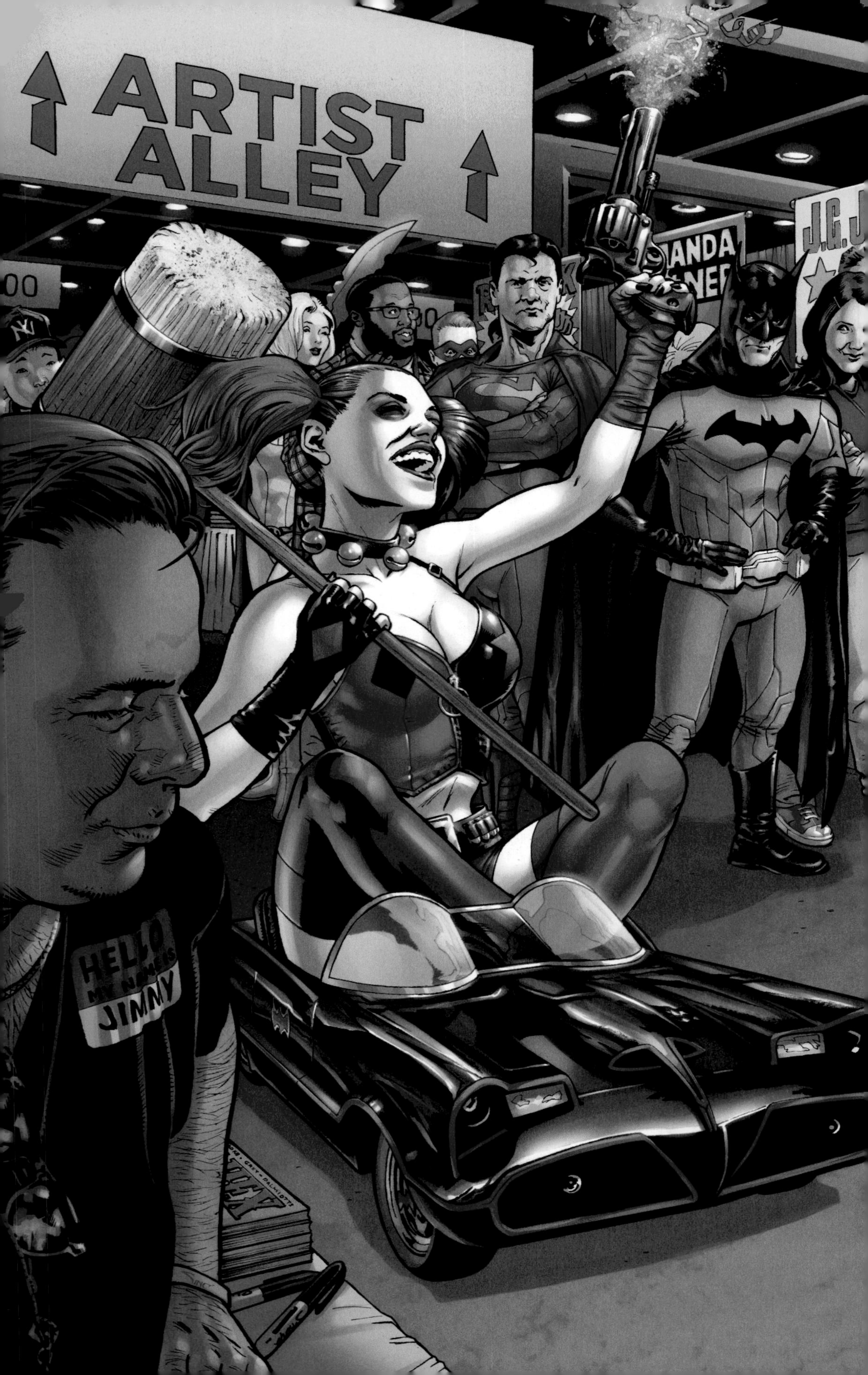
ARTIST
ALLEY
HELLO
MY NAME IS
JIMMY

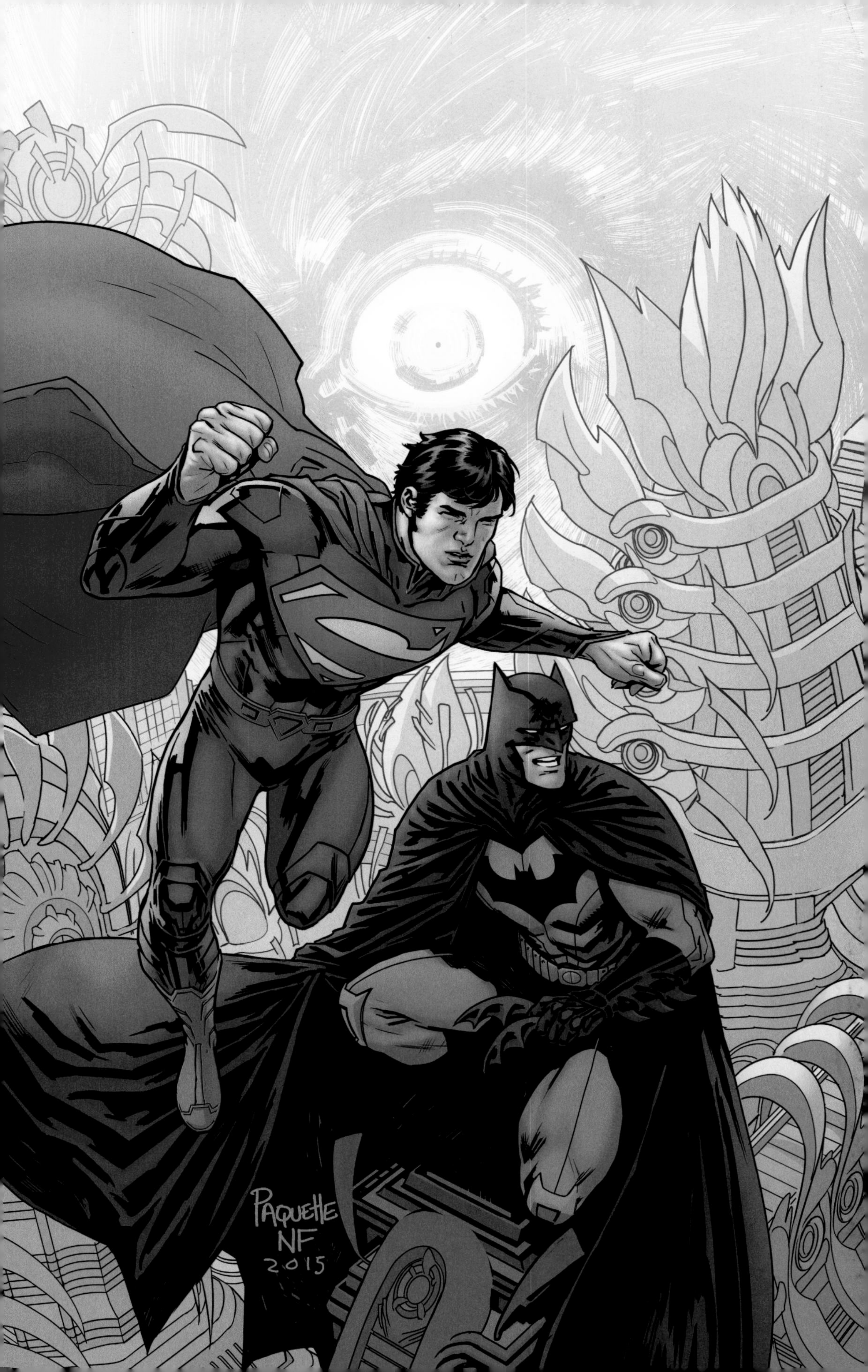
PAQUETTE
NF
2015

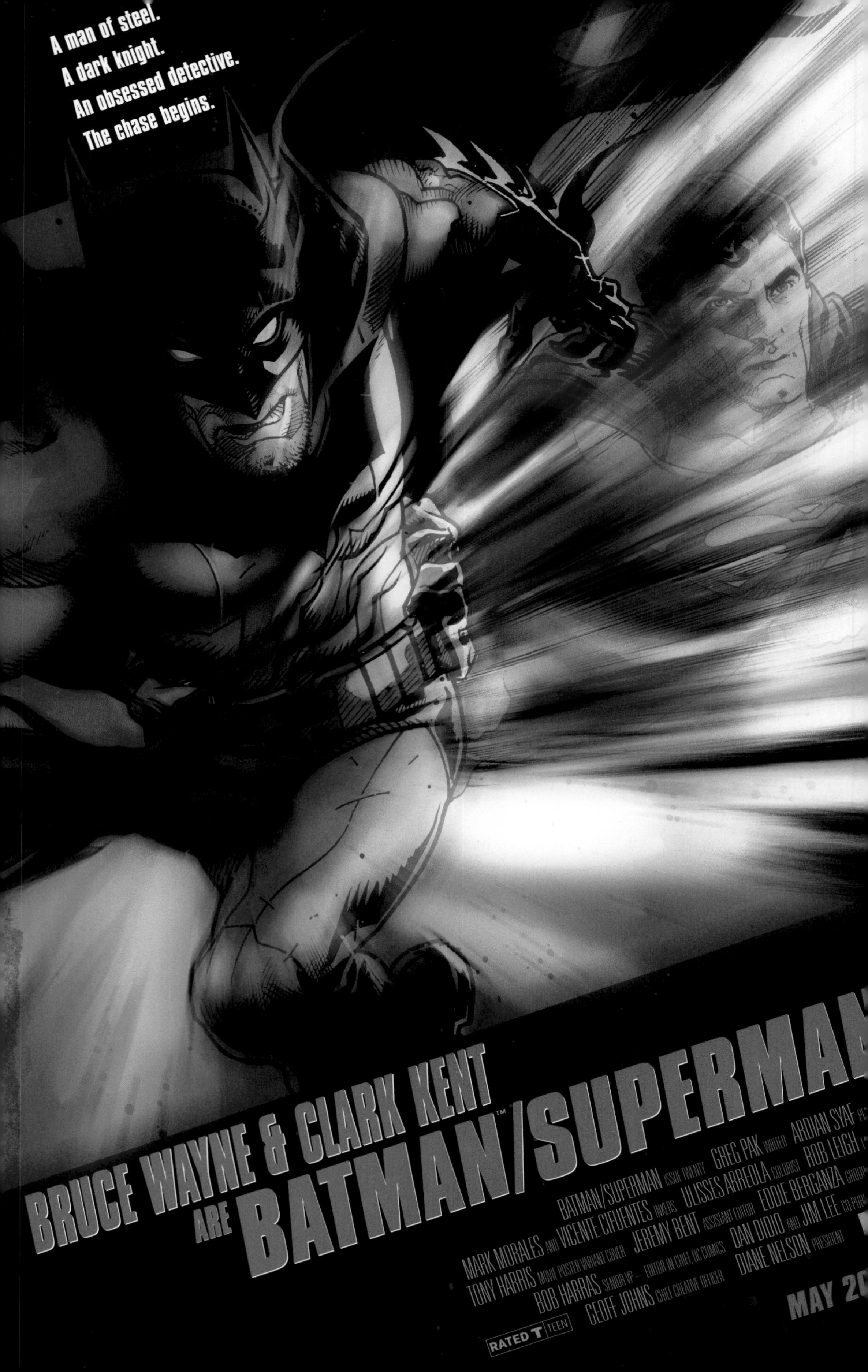
A man of steel.
A dark knight.
An obsessed detective.
The chase begins.
BRUCE WAYNE & CLARK KENT
ARE
BATMAN™/SUPERMA
BATMAN/SUPERMAN ISSUE TWENTY GREG PAK WRITER ARDIAN SYAF
MARK MORALES AND VICENTE CIFUENTES INKERS ULISSES ARREOLA COLORIST ROB LEIGH
TONY HARRIS MOVIE POSTER VARIANT COVER JEREMY BENT ASSISTANT EDITOR EDDIE BERGANZA
BOB HARRAS SENIOR VP — EDITOR-IN-CHIEF, DC COMICS DAN DIDIO AND JIM LEE
GEOFF JOHNS CHIEF CREATIVE OFFICER DIANE NELSON PRESIDENT
MAY 20
RATED T TEEN

GRAPHIC NOVEL BATMAN

Pak, Greg.

Batman/Superman. Volume 4,
 Siege

FEB **1 1** 2016